SOVIET ECONOMIC DEVELOPMENT

To Karen

SOVIET ECONOMIC DEVELOPMENT

RAYMOND HUTCHINGS

Second Edition

New York University Press
New York *and* London

© Basil Blackwell 1971, Raymond Hutchings 1982

First published in 1971
Second edition published 1982
New York University Press
Washington Square
New York, NY 10003

Library of Congress Cataloging in Publication Data

Hutchings, Raymond.
    Soviet economic development.

    Includes indexes.
    1. Soviety Union – Economic conditions – 1918-
I. Title.
HC335.H9   1982   330.947′08   82-14311
ISBN 0-8147-3419-7
ISBN 0-8147-3420-0 (pbk.)

Printed in Great Britain

CONTENTS

LIST OF TABLES

LIST OF DIAGRAMS

PREFACE TO THE SECOND EDITION

I should like to express my gratitude to reviewers of the first edition; I have taken their comments into consideration, and in many cases modified the text in response. The book retains its emphasis on facts, and perhaps even increases it, since there are now more facts to report. But there seems no reason to apologize. For one thing, the great majority of undergraduates in English-speaking countries have no knowledge of Russian and so cannot refer to original Soviet sources. For another, some students may later go on to factual analysis of the Soviet system. The book also contains certain generalizations – for example, relating to fluctuations in growth – that are not found in other books on the subject, regrettably, in my view.

In his joint review of the first edition, and of *The Soviet Economy* by David Dyker, Michael Kaser observed that in both books 'invention and innovation' were 'barely touched upon' (*Slavonic and East European Review*, July 1979, p. 469). While any comprehensive treatment of these topics would belong in a book with a different title, the new chapter 18 is intended to fill the gap so far as it is appropriate here. Chapter 19 has been extended by a section on the statistical handbooks. Most of the revision is aimed at bringing the book up to date.

PREFACE TO THE FIRST EDITION

The aim of this book is to give an account within a brief compass of the circumstances, sequence of events, origins and characteristic features of Soviet economic development. It is *not* a balanced economic history of the Soviet Union: for example, agriculture receives only summary mention because it shared less in development than other sectors of the economy. Economic thought is almost entirely ignored.

One can hardly doubt the importance of the subject. The USSR is the world's best-endowed country in mineral wealth. Its population is one-fourteenth of the world's, it has much the largest industrial labour force, its territory is more than twice as large as that of Canada — the next largest country. Soviet industrial growth has been rapid, and in volume of industrial output the USSR now stands second only to the United States.

This economy is also important as a type which has had a good deal of influence on others, and still has although to a waning degree. Long-term economic plans, which are one of its characteristics, are now quite common. State planning has become respectable, while almost every country now makes a feature, and many make a fetish, of achieving a high growth rate of the national income or of industrial output. Other aspects of Soviet economic development such as forced collectivization and forced labour have gained notoriety, rather than fame.

The Soviet economy faces now substantial problems, and the nature of its response to these problems is important not only for the USSR itself but for other countries.

One problem in writing about Soviet economic development is that much the largest growth has taken place since 1945, but many of the most dramatic events occurred, and policy decisions were taken, before 1932. For this reason, and also because one naturally writes first the history of the earlier period while to some extent the documentary sources are more abundant then and the controversies more interesting, the first 15 years since the Revolution have been written about at much greater length than the next 37 years. This problem has not been overcome here, but a compromise has been attempted: while Part II concentrates on the earlier period, Parts III, IV and V concentrate on the later one.

Although the book may be suitable as an undergraduate text, it does not claim to present a consensus of current opinion about the subject. My interpretation is, I believe, new in a number of respects. For this reason a rather full array of sources is provided.

The book grew out of lectures delivered between 1961 and 1967 at the University of Maryland, the University of Southern California and the Australian National University, to students most of whom were also pursuing more general economic history courses. Comparisons are accordingly made where possible with more familiar economies such as the United States, Britain (where the book was completed) or Australia. It was found to be desirable to include surveys (which are inevitably brief and impressionistic) of general Russian history or geography, and to minimize the use of Russian words. I want to take this opportunity of paying tribute to the students, whose probing questions prompted many changes and additions to my lecture notes.

I have drawn upon certain material which was included in my Ph.D. thesis 'Studies in Soviet Industrial Development' (University of London, 1958), in respect of which I would like to thank my supervisors at that time, Professor (now Lord) Robbins and Dr. G. H. Bolsover. I am also grateful to Basil Blackwell and Mott Limited and to the University of Glasgow for permission to reproduce material previously published in *Soviet Studies*, the Australian Institute of International Affairs for permission to reproduce part of an article published in *Australian Outlook*, and to the University of Western Australia for permission to draw on the text of a lecture given at their 1968 Summer School and published by them under the title *50 Years of Russian Socialism*, and to the Association for the Study of Soviet-type Economies for permission to draw on my article published in the Fall, 1962, issue of *The ASTE Bulletin*.

I have owed a great deal over the years to advice and help from academic and professional colleagues. I would especially like to mention in this connection the stimulating series of seminars at the London School of Economics 'Economic Problems of the Communist World'. Naturally, only myself can justly be blamed for the book's deficiencies.

I am grateful to the Royal Institute of International Affairs (Chatham House) for allowing me to complete the book while in their employment although this was not part of my regular programme of work.

Many thanks to several family members, including my sister Alice and daughter Theresa, for reading through various parts of the text. My greatest debt is, of course, to my wife Karen, who over a long period consistently encouraged me and effectively commented on many passages in the book; and who typed preliminary drafts and the whole of the final manuscript.

PART I

THE SETTING

1
GEOGRAPHY AND NATURAL RESOURCES

A. Geography

The subject of this book is Soviet economic development; and it is supposed that the reader already has some acquaintance with economics and economic history generally. It might seem possible to leave it at that, and to dryly pigeonhole Soviet experience among other categories in economic history. So one might, for whoever already knows like the back of his hand Russia's history, geography, and all her other characteristics. However, as it is possible that the reader does not belong to such a well-informed group, it will perhaps be desirable to make some preliminary traverses by space and time across the broad background to the subject.

The geographic aspect of Soviet economic development is extremely important. The subject must be seen in a geographic as well as in a historical context, and it is convenient to present the physical setting first.

Russians call their country 'the land you cannot encompass' and they scarcely exaggerate: its perimeter is nearly 60,000 kilometres. With an area of 22·4 million square kilometres (over 8·6 million square miles) this is the world's largest country: it is 2·4 times as large as the whole United States, for instance, or 91 times as large as the United Kingdom. Its widest east to west span is 8,000 kilometres, and from north to south about half as much. In the extreme east the day dawns eleven hours earlier than in the extreme west, so for almost half the year the sun never sets on the USSR. Sovereignty is asserted over the White Sea and Azov Sea. Per head of population, the Soviet Union boasts about twice as much land as the United States, although by comparison with Australia—which stands at a lucky extreme in this matter—only one-seventh as much.

Everyone knows that this territorial giant sprawls mainly across rather high northerly latitudes; but it is perhaps not so generally realized that Volgograd (formerly Stalingrad, formerly Tsaritsyn), although in the southern half of European Russia, nevertheless is virtually on the 49th parallel; or if translated to the corresponding southerly latitude, would be the south of New Zealand. Most of the Soviet Union is in fact situated in the latitude of Canada. Moscow, in latitude 56°N., is about level with Copenhagen or Edinburgh.

Three-quarters of the land area of the USSR is in Asia, one-quarter in Europe. But nearly three-quarters of the population live in Europe, so the average density of population is nearly nine times greater in the European part of the USSR than in the rest. Not that the Asian/European border has any other relevance: it is not marked in recent Soviet atlases, perhaps deliberately to efface its significance.

Most of Soviet territory necessarily lies at great distances from the sea, and so from the moderating effects of the ocean on temperatures. This is a continental type of climate: its continentality is intensified as one moves from west to east.

In winter the isotherms curve round north to south and then west to east: there is no very great difference between winter temperatures in north and south European Russia, but eastwards the temperature declines. In summer the isotherms run more nearly west to east. Naturally, it is warmest in the south, but Moscow and even Leningrad can be uncomfortably warm in summer. Murmansk, within the Arctic Circle, has occasionally recorded temperatures as high as 100°F. (38°C.) In Ukraine, Transcauscasia and Central Asia the summers are hot; the heat is much drier than in Western Europe or in eastern regions of the United States. It is considered to be a relatively healthy climate.

In European parts of the Soviet Union the winters are not extremely cold by Russian standards, which are not those of Western Europe (and by no means those of Australia): the thermometer rarely falls below $-30°C.$, i.e. $54°$ of frost F. However, the winter is very prolonged. Snow lies on the ground in Moscow between approximately end-November and mid-April. In Siberia the winter is longer still, and much colder: at Verkhoyansk (north-east Siberia) colder even than at the North Pole. Where the winter is so long and cold the short summer cannot unfreeze the subsoil. About two-fifths (42 per cent)[1] of the area of the Soviet Union consequently experiences permafrost: frozen hard in winter (in north-east Siberia the depth of permanently frozen ground reaches 400 metres), the terrain is nearly impassable in summer owing to the many lakes and swamps, which become breeding-grounds for myriads of mosquitoes.

Permafrost presents difficult obstacles to any kind of economic activity. The ground will only with difficulty support a railway or highway. Ground installations may be deformed because the snow cannot drain away when it melts. A large fraction of the land area of the Soviet Union is consequently land only by courtesy. It may be of strategic importance; at least it obstructs movement. Against this, ice of a sufficient thickness can be crossed by people or even vehicles. In 1941, when Leningrad was under seige, both railway tracks and roads were laid across Lake Ladoga. Even moderate degrees of cold cause inconvenience and raise costs. At temperatures below about $-25°$C. many kinds of mechanisms work more sluggishly or not at all. Try to start your car when the outside temperature is $-30°$C! Effective home heating and complete warm clothing become really necessary at these times of year. When the temperature gets down to $-40°$C. all outside work must legally cease. The contrast of $60°$C. or more between winter and summer temperatures powerfully influences the economy.

As one would expect, such a large country contains both high- and low-lying areas. The mountainous areas are chiefly (in terms of expanse) in east Siberia, i.e. farthest from the main centres of population in European Russia which on the whole is low-lying, although mountain-rimmed to the south-east and south-west. The Caucasus are genuine high mountains, and there are real mountains on the south coast of the Crimea, and on the western borders of the Soviet Union fronting onto Czechoslovakia (the Carpathians). The Urals, on the other hand, offer no barrier to transport. A map of European Russia shows ranges of hills, which are readily crossed. Russia-in-Europe is mainly flat. Unlike Western Europe, the Russian landscape changes little, sometimes not at all, over hundreds of miles.[2]

Because of the extent of the land mass, the distance between mountain ranges, and the generally low elevation, there are rivers of great length. The Soviet Union has the world's greatest river *system*. Though not equal individually to the Mississippi-Missouri, the Nile or certain others, the Ob', Yenisey, Lena, Amur and Volga are among the world's greatest rivers. Especially the Siberian rivers are distinguished by their volumes of water and have a gigantic hydro-electric potential. One which has recently been harnessed, the Angara, is the only river flowing *out* of the extremely deep Lake Baykal, which receives the water of 300 rivers. When the snow melts, floods reach extraordinary dimensions. But even the normal widths of the rivers are large: for instance, the Dnieper at Dnepropetrovsk, 320 km. from its mouth, is about 1½ km. wide. Such water volumes confer important irrigation possibilities, some of which have been exploited.

Most rivers, including the longest ones, flow roughly north or south, especially north, which makes them less useful for transportation as their terminus is the usually icebound Arctic. The largest *European* rivers flow into the Black and Caspian Seas and are consequently more useful. These rivers historically have been highways through which foreign trade penetrated into Russia. The southern regions

need water which the north has in excess, a discrepancy which has
suggested schemes of diverting one or more of the Siberian rivers
into the Caspian Sea whose level has been falling. Such a project may
be carried out within the next 10–20 years. The Siberian rivers carry
heat northwards; the European rivers cool *their* banks, though to a
smaller degree.

The extent and distribution of precipitation are more complicated
to describe than the temperatures. Broadly speaking, European Russia
has a fairly good precipitation (400–600 mm. or more a year) which
diminishes as one travels north, east or south from White Russia.
There is a subsidiary centre of high precipitation on the Black Sea
coast. Most of Siberia has less precipitation than Europe. The driest
areas are Kazakhstan and adjacent areas, and extreme north-east
Siberia. In the southern part of Ukraine the precipitation is small.
'Shelter belts' have not yet appreciably modified the climate of the
Volga regions (as we shall see, Stalin's 'Plan for the Transformation of
Nature' failed in this respect), though long-term plans will undoubtedly
aim at so doing.

An important share of precipitation is provided by the melting
of the winter snows (a depth of one metre of snow provides about
300 tons of water per hectare).[3] The depth of snow-cover, which
varies appreciably from year to year, also governs the protection
afforded by the snow against sharp frosts.

B. Natural Resources

Although the huge size of the country suggests immense resources
for agriculture, these seem smaller in relation to the population or
to the total land area. A broad strip of proverbially rich black earth
includes about half (the northern half) of the Ukraine and extends
east-north-east into Siberia to the north of the 50th parallel. But
over part of this area precipitation is inadequate, while the soil has
been overworked for long periods, with consequent damage to its
fertility and widespread erosion and formation of ravines – which
run, for example, through the city of Odessa. In eastern regions of
Ukraine and in Siberia and Kazakhstan the rainfall is uncertain, and
so harvests vary immensely. An eastwards extension of the sown area
since 1954 has enlarged the total grain crop but has also made it more
vulnerable to weather caprices, as was demonstrated in 1963.

The only important tracts which are more valuable for agricultural
purposes than the black earth are irrigated land (especially in Central
Asia), which produces nearly all the cotton crop; 5·5 per cent of
Soviet cultivated land is irrigated, which by an international measure

is a low proportion.[3] Some lands used for agricultural purposes are clearly sub-marginal by U.S. or Western European standards. Very much of the Soviet Union is too cold, too wet or too dry for productive agriculture. In general, the hotter regions are too dry for agriculture, the wetter regions too cold.[4]

The continental climate is a serious handicap. The severe winters restrict the growing of winter wheat (which is more productive than spring wheat) to the western part of European Russia. In Siberia and Kazakhstan the winters are particularly long, so that the growing season is very short. This sets problems in the timing of agricultural operations.

Climate, precipitation and soils govern the vegetation and crops. Only about 24 per cent of the whole area of the Soviet Union is used for any agricultural purpose (including cultivation and live-stock-rearing). About 55 per cent is totally unfitted for agriculture owing to soil or climate. Cultivated land comprised about 7·1 per cent of the land area in 1953, 8·75 per cent in 1959, 9·28 per cent in 1970, 9·76 per cent in 1979. Most cultivated land lies within a 'fertile triangle' which is bounded roughly by Leningrad, Odessa and Irkutsk (and particularly within the more southerly half of this triangle: towards the north for instance between Moscow and Leningrad, cultivation is only intermittent). Indeed, the triangle includes large tracts of little value. There is practically no cultivation to the north of Leningrad.

Mainly to the north of this triangle, a very large region is timber-covered. Forest extends over about a quarter of the total area of the USSR. (This equals three times the forested area of the United States.) The commonest trees are larch, pine and fir. The forest zone (*tayga* or coniferous forest) extends chiefly between latitudes 60° and 70°. Towards the east the southern limit of this zone trends southwards; in east Siberia roughly along the frontier with China.

In European Russia, therefore, the forest zone lies within the northern half. Moscow lies within this zone, but hereabouts is by no means continuous forest. Overflying from Kiev to Moscow, one sees at first little forest; this then becomes more and more connected. There are still extensive forests in Karelia, and further east around Archangel. However, owing to excessive cutting of timber, logging has largely migrated to the Asian side of the continental border. In fact, the distribution of timber reserves is now the direct opposite of that of population (this is, of course, no accident − the nearest trees were felled first) and most of European Russia is short of timber. The southern regions of Ukraine are treeless. Further south in sheltered spots on the Black Sea riviera one finds evergreens, palms and other sub-tropical vegetation.

Currently, timber consumption is much below natural growth,

but consumption will rise. Afforestation has been carried out to break the force of the hot, dry winds from the desert regions of Kazakhstan and Turkmenia, to arrest the north-west march of the desert sands, and to trap precipitation.

The total mineral resources of the Soviet Union are also huge. The USSR has claimed 41 per cent of the world's iron ore, 88 per cent of the surveyed manganese, 54 per cent of potassium, almost one-third of phosphorite and apatite, 60 per cent of peat, 57 per cent of coal deposits. (These proportions vary according to the date of the estimate and the exact category understood.) New reserves are discovered every year. The USSR is claimed first in the world among discovered deposits of the ores of iron, manganese, copper, lead, zinc, nickel, and asbestos, second as regards natural gas and coal, and 'in one of the first places' as regards oil.[5] There are adequate deposits of vanadium and titanium, but cobalt, molybdenum and tungsten seem scarce. Tin is mined in northeast Siberia. There appear to be difficulties with copper, for which aluminium is often substituted. Gold is mined, though probably on a much smaller scale than by South Africa; platinum and various semiprecious stones are found. Diamond pipes have been discovered in Central Siberia, near the Vilyuy river (in 1954). In total the Soviet Union has the world's largest mineral reserves, although the United States leads in particular respects.

Soviet minerals are less conveniently situated than those of the United States, so that as a rule longer hauls are required while climatic and soil obstacles are more formidable. Particular areas although rich in minerals generally may lack important requirements.[6] Many of the largest deposits have been found in the most remote areas (for example, huge coal deposits in Central Siberia). Yet, some reserves nearer to hand are not lacking, such as an iron ore base deep underground being developed 480 km. south of Moscow (the 'Kursk Magnetic Anomaly' which is described as surpassing the entire iron ore deposits of the USA[7]). Discoveries of natural resources are still being made even in European Russia. In the 1930s very large deposits of apatites, mined in the Kola peninsula, began to be exploited. More recently, natural gas has been discovered in the Ukraine, and oil in Belorussia.

Resources are scattered. For instance, the south is rich in grain but lacks timber, while the north abounds in forests but has little grain. The Urals and the Kuznetsk basin exchange iron ore and coal over a distance of more than 2,000 km.

C. Transport

In view of the low density of population, the wide expanses, uneven settlement, and still continuing development which entails migration and the founding of new inhabited places, transport is exceptionally important.

In old Russia, transport was primarily by water. The cost of carrying 1 ton of goods over 1 km. of unpaved roads was reckoned the same as carrying it 60 km. by rail, 120 km. by river or 960 km. by sea. So the earliest freight railways in Russia were built to link river routes. The location of the rivers encouraged canal building, the great era of which in the USSR has been the twentieth century. River traffic is still cheaper than rail despite the long winter intervals in navigation. Timber, grain, salt and oil make up 90 per cent of total river freight turnover. Over half is timber and firewood. Almost a half of river transport moves along the Volga and its tributaries; oil especially. By a sequence of construction which was concluded in 1952, when the Volga-Don canal was opened, Moscow has been linked by canal with five seas: the White, Black, Caspian, Baltic and Azov. The most important canals are the Baltic-White Sea (built in the 1930s with forced labour) and the Volga-Don. The erection of huge dams, such as at Kuybyshev and Volgograd, in the midst of broad plains has created sizeable inland lakes.

Sea routes cross the Black and Caspian Seas. In the north, Murmansk never freezes, but an east—west sea-route in the Arctic Ocean can function only in midsummer.

Now, the USSR is predominantly a railway country. Already in Tsarist times 60,000 km. of railways were built (corresponding to 71,700 km. within the present borders of the Soviet Union). The 1979 network amounted to 141,100 km., not quite twice as much as in 1913. In the Soviet period lines have been added such as the Turk-Sib (Semipalatinsk to Lugovaya, 1930) and the South Siberian line (traversing Kazakhstan), completed in 1953 with forced labour,[8] while the BAM (Baykal-Amur-Mainline) heading eastwards to the Pacific coast, should be completed by 1982–84, by Military Construction Troops.[9] The goods turnover (weight times distance) of the whole rail network within present borders rose by 47·5 times between 1913 and 1979. Out of the total turnover of freight in 1979 of 5984·6 milliard[10] ton-kilometres, 56·0 per cent went by rail, 14·2 per cent by sea, 3·9 per cent by river, 19·1 per cent by pipeline, and 8·8 per cent by truck. In the last twenty years there has been a large proportionate increase in sea transport (1960 – 7·0 per cent), though most recently this has declined slightly (1970 – 17·1 per cent). One may correctly deduce from this increase that Russia has advanced on the international scene, has become a maritime power, both merchant and naval. The percentage going by rail has declined since 1960 (then 79·8), while that going by pipeline or by road has increased, particularly the former: in 1960 only 2·7 per cent of the freight turnover had gone by pipeline.

The average length of railway haul (798 km. in 1960, 861 km. in 1970) is now far longer than it was in 1913 (496 km.), which reflects the geographically far-flung development combined with the centralized ministerial system. The average distance travelled by a passenger, 90 km., has not changed in recent years.

The rail network, which focuses on Moscow and Leningrad, is concentrated in Europe, yet even here is by no means dense by Western European standards. In Siberia it is very much sparser: only one (double-tracked) line runs all the way to Vladivostok. This section is burdened by extremely heavy traffic (on the main sections, trains run every 5–7 minutes). The density of traffic per 1 km. of track has risen over twenty times since 1913; it has even doubled since 1960. This is putting a growing strain on the rail system.[11]

Air transport for passengers has expanded. The fares used to be quite competitive with rail transport, but were raised on 1 April 1977.[12] Air freight is vital in communication with posts in the Far North and Far East. The average flight length is about 1,000 km.

The highway network, which can be optimistically depicted in road atlases,[13] has according to official statistics expanded from 155,300 km. in 1945 to 713,100 km. in 1977 (all hard-surfaced roads). Since the war, among republics, Kazakhstan has been the most conspicuous beneficiary, evidently in connection with the ploughing-up of virgin lands in that area.

Means of transport are State-owned except for personal bicycles and motor cycles (which are fairly numerous), private cars (still relatively few), collective farm trucks, and in the countryside horses, carts and sleighs (plus some boats, skis, skates, etc.). The transport network is rather inflexible and impersonal; this is partly a response to distance and climate but also suggests that individual mobility is not greatly encouraged. Some two-fifths of Soviet territory is barred to foreigners — an immense area, equal to four-fifths of all Europe!

Notes

1 V. Soldatenkov, *Gudok*, 9 February 1968, p. 3.
2 The great plains of Eastern Europe resemble topographically those of the United States (*USA: Its Geography and Growth*, Third Edition, 1960, p. 12).
3 I. A. Sharov, *Polya utolyayut zhazhdu (V seriya Sel'skoye khozy- aystvo 1963)*, pp. 3 and 5.
4 The more favourable combination for maize growing of rainfall and warmth in the United States than in the USSR is depicted in H. Raupach, *System der Sowjetwirtschaft, Theorie und Praxis* (1968), p. 195.

5 A. N. Kosygin, *Vestnik akademii nauk*, no. 7, 1961, p. 93.

6 For example, 'Eastern Siberia may be called a region of unlimited natural resources in general, but this can hardly be said to apply to cement materials'. (V. P. Gukov, *Soviet Geography*, May 1964, p. 68).

7 V. D. Kamayev *et al., Nauchno-tekhnicheskiy progress v SSSR* (1962), pp. 140–1.

8 V. Conolly, *Siberia* (1975), p. 158.

9 *The Cambridge Encyclopedia of Russia and the Soviet Union* (1982), p. 443.

10 1 milliard = 10^9. Metric tons are used throughout this book.

11 Particularly on its track. I have heard a Soviet railwayman remark that the special strength of Soviet railways was in their rolling stock, of British railways in their track.

12 M. C. Kaser in Kaser and Brown (eds.), *The Soviet Union Since the Fall of Khrushchev* (Second Edition, 1978), p. 293.

13 In 1959 I travelled along a road, well-marked on the map, which was barely passable even for a Land Rover.

2
RUSSIAN ECONOMIC HISTORY UNTIL 1913

The preceding chapter should have left an impression of Russia's vastness and – by comparison with Western Europe – emptiness. We must now briefly see how, during a relatively short historical period, this great area was welded into a unified state.

One of the principle themes of Russian history is expansion: in population, territory, international influence; and in economic history– of labour force, resources and production, first agricultural and then industrial. Our theme of economic development, in other words, is embedded in a more general progress of development of the Russian state: it must not be understood as an accidental or extraneous phenomenon. Indeed, economic development came to Russia much later than these other attributes of a super-power.

Physically, the Russian state spread outwards from a heartland around Moscow, in all directions – but because of the stronger resistance offered by more densely populated and advanced nations of Western and Northern Europe, or around the Black Sea littoral, especially eastwards. One thinks of a spring which gradually uncoils after having been compressed. The chief city of old Russia, Kiev, which had defended itself successfully against picturesquely named barbaric tribes, succumbed in 1240 to the Tatars, who occupied the whole region on the Asiatic side of a line running to the east of Moscow and in the general direction south-west to north-east. For two centuries the Tatars acted as suzerain of Russia: they levied tribute and demanded military contingents. Otherwise, however, they left the Russian princes in control. Although Alexander of Novgorod ('Nevsky') beat the Teutonic knights on Lake Peipus (also 1240), his policy towards the Tatars was based on conciliation and submission. There is a striking parallel here with present-day attitudes in the governing circles of certain East European countries *vis-a-vis* the Soviet Union and the West. History's tide eventually turned, and left the Tatars marooned among a sea of other minor nationalities. The two-centuries-borne Tatar yoke is blamed for some negative features in Russian history, such as that Russia was untouched by the Renaissance. For protection against the Tatars, economic life retreated northwards, into the forest belt where pursuit was more difficult.

The principality of Moscow was established at the end of the thirteenth century. Having thrown off the Tatar yoke (1480) Moscow in 1523 united all Russian territories, putting itself at their head. Thereafter, for nearly four centuries, this nucleus went on growing. Under Ivan the Terrible (ruled 1547–84) the Tatar states of Kazan and Astrakhan were conquered, which brought Russian borders to the Urals and the Caspian Sea. The more fertile Ukraine ('borderland') became a kind of no-man's-land, which harboured semi-autonomous armies of freebooters and fighters (the Cossacks).

In the seventeenth century there was a constant push eastwards. A fortified post was set up at Yakutsk in 1632. In 1647 a party of Cossacks reached the Pacific; the next year another group sailed through the Bering Straits. This was as far eastwards on land as one could travel. In the next century Russia strengthened her hold on this huge territory. Alaska and the Aleutian islands were acquired and some Russians infiltrated southwards on the North American continent. Towards the west Tsar Peter the Great secured his 'window onto Europe' where he founded a new capital (St. Petersburg, 1703). Subsequent wars extended Russian dominion across the Baltic states and into Poland. The Ukraine was absorbed (1654) and subsequently Turkish territories north of the Black Sea. In the nineteenth century Russian rule spread across what is now the Kazakh republic and the central Asian republics of the USSR, and across the Caucasus. Only from America did Russia recoil, selling Alaska to the United States (1867) and evacuating California; while in Asia, the rising sun of Japan eventually admistered a rebuff.

Russian dominion penetrated into ever-wilder regions and so could be represented as a civilizing mission, so far as the east was concerned. This was not so in the west, but not much ground could be gained in this direction as strong resistance was soon encountered; however, Sweden was' eventually defeated, and Russia has taken part in four partitions of Poland.

The expansion can be divided into two sectors with sharply differing characteristics. The advance into the Ukraine engulfed more fertile and climatically favourable areas than the northern forests, whereas the eastwards advance was into harsher and remote areas. Correspondingly, the first encountered stiff resistance, the second only token resistance.

The eastwards expansion is obviously comparable with the westwards colonization by several nations of Western Europe. Its timing – the first half of the seventeenth century – is also much the same. Each half of Europe expanded in the direction where it met least resistance.

Geography decided that Western Europe should expand across the oceans, Russia eastwards across the Euro-Asian continent. Unlike most of the other European empires, that of Russia still stands, and is defended with much show of self-righteousness.

The extension of Russian role into the Ukraine is a remarkable occurrence from a viewpoint of universal history. As Ellsworth Huntington has pointed out, movement had usually been 'polewards and stormwards'. In contrast, the Ukraine was a less rigorous region, and its absorption was made possible only by military prowess.[1] One may find in this fact the genesis of the Russian preoccupation with military power as the precursor and basis of economic strength. It was a little as if the Northern English had eventually won back Southern England from the Danes — extending their dominion finally to the Isle of Wight whose shape so strikingly resembles that of the Crimea, although the Crimea is 67 times larger. Whence came the military and political strengths which made this expansion possible?

They were derived from centralization of power in Moscow. One aspect of this was the mutual support of government and church. The overthrow of the Tatars by the Muscovites (1480), following the capture of Constantinople by the Turks in 1453, made it seem that Moscow was the true successor to Constantinople and the 'Third Rome'. Political centralism was abetted by ecclesiastical centralism. The crowning of the grand prince or Tsar (i.e. Caesar) followed the establishment in 1589 of the Russian patriarchate. Continuous struggle against adherents of other faiths enhanced Russian religious consciousness. A kind of religious patriotism emerged, resembling the scientific and economic patriotism that one sees in the Soviet Union today.

The economy was based almost wholly on agriculture, livestock, and the forest. Like Australia in her early days,[2] Russia could enter international trade only by offering products which were worth long-distance transport. Russia's offering in medieval times was honey. Trade was waterborne: in the early days it had been controlled by the Norsemen. Its importance increased as the forests began to be cleared. The towns, like Novgorod, contained merchants, craftsmen and ecclesiastics. Recent excavations have revealed an almost immobile economic history of Novgorod over several centuries, except that far-off political events left such traces as a greater or lesser abundance of discarded walnut shells—the routes from the south being eventually cut by the Mongol invasions.[3] Two centuries later Novgorod was crushed by Ivan the Great, heading Muscovite imperialism.

Within Muscovy, centralization and admistrative complexity demanded the formation of hierarchical layers. At the summit the Tsar, an absolute ruler, ruled through a bureaucracy and *ad hoc* commissions.

The peasantry had been for the most part free, although of lowly estate. Increase of population led to repeated scarcities of food, while the State demanded money, and the army soldiers; the natural *dénouement* under conditions of static productivity was a feudal relationship, and so in 1597 villeinage, or serfdom, became formally established as a legal institution in Russia, 100–200 years after it had disappeared in Britain or France.[4] Its introduction had been a gradual process, but it stuck deep roots.

Serfdom gave economic and legal expression to the fact that Muscovy had become a settled population. Local village administration passed into the hands of the mir, a communal institution. A new pattern of territorial units, which endured until the nineteen-twenties, was established. The State administration was fiscal, and the towns were exempt from serfdom as such. Muscovy was organized in separate estates: nobility, church, burghers, peasants. The natural economy was gradually replaced by a monetary one, although substantial traces of payment in kind, or through labour services, remained and some indeed have survived to this day.

Russia was backward by comparison with the advanced states of Western Europe with which, despite the addition of big tracts of Asia and a time-slip in sequences of development, she often compared herself. This backwardness applied to all aspects of life. It was due basically to isolation from the main European centres, which in turn was due to distance, to long dominion under the Tatars, and to differences of religion, language and alphabet. Not only bringing civilization to Moscow, but disseminating it over such a broad territory, presented problems. However, a beginning towards overcoming this isolation was now being made. A mercantile class grew up (a subdivision of the burghers) and trade was begun with certain Western European powers (with England already in the sixteenth century). Nevertheless, contacts with abroad were few. The chief agent in multiplying them was Tsar Peter the Great (early eighteenth century) who visited and studied in Western Europe. Russia sought assistance from western experts (Italian architects in Moscow and St. Petersburg; Scotsmen; Germans; French). But she was still conscious of past battles, and that her broad expanses were a conspicuous temptation. Thus was born the dual attitude to foreigners, at once deferential and suspicious, which still persists. Despatches written by the English ambassador to Russia in the sixteenth century would require technical amendment if written today, but otherwise the attitudes of Russians to foreigners have not greatly changed.

And thus was born from centralization, from backwardness, from an awareness of the dangers of outside attack which contact with the outside world now stimulated, a long-standing tradition in Russia of State intervention and control in economic affairs.

Peter the Great was prominent in founding this tradition too. He set up new industries such as weaving of silks and woollens, protected them by tariffs, imported skilled workers for them, determined what they should produce. Entrepreneurship was encouraged by the grant of substantial privileges. Convicts and vagabonds were assigned industrial work, as were some serfs. Different kind of serfs were distinguished. About a third were 'manorial serfs'. About half were 'free serfs' who had commuted their services in exchange for a payment (*obrok*); these are said to have worked better than the rest. In addition, many peasants worked at handicrafts, these being of indigenous origin whereas factory industries came from outside, and had to be artificially stimulated.

Russian progress in the eighteenth century in machine industry was considerable. Manufacturers were built up primarily to satisfy government demand, especially for iron and steel, and by the end of the century Russia was producing more pig iron than Britain. But thereafter Russia fell behind Western Europe, where progress was faster.

Russia had certain strengths in manufacturing, but these were wholly of an extensive nature. Transport, crediting and selling arrangements were undeveloped. Both raw material and labour were abundant. Likewise the market was large in numbers of people. But there was a general lack of technical knowledge and organizing ability, further hampered by the sharp class divisions – hence productivity was low and costs inversely high (despite long working hours), and as wages were no more than proportionate the purchasing power of the internal market was relatively small.

A shortage of capital was accentuated by the fact that the factory often had to provide some social infrastructure, such as rudimentary barracks to house its workers. The Russian factory worker remained, as a rule, a peasant. Even in the Moscow area, most workers belonged to a village community in which they paid taxes and from which they needed to have leave of absence. They would usually lend a hand with getting in the harvest, and many factories shut down in this season. Manufacturers could not count on a regular or permanent work force, while workers had less incentive to improve their skills because they did not wholly depend on their wages.

There was a constant townwards migration, and as building did not keep pace with the growth of the urban population, overcrowding resulted, while for those housed in hostels, leisure as well as working hours were subject to regulation. Protests in the form of strikes against these conditions became more frequent. In 1905 – a unique year – strikers numbered several million. Trade unions had not been allowed; the government attempted to establish innocuous substitutes, but without lasting success.

Serfdom, which had lasted in Russia for about three centuries, was abolished formally in 1861, which is not so long ago. Thereafter, the majority of Russians still faced back-breaking toil in the fields in the summertime, which alternated with prolonged periods of winter idleness. (This refers at least to the men: the peasant women worked all the year round.) Judging by contemporary accounts Russian workers were (and mostly are) very hardy and uncomplaining, endured extremes of temperature, rough and airless living quarters, monotonous and poor quality food; they showed unlimited patience; but suffered from the defects of these virtues, being slow in reaction, reluctant to take any initiative.

Despite these weaknesses, which have not been peculiar to Russia, industry made substantial progress. The first joint-stock company had been founded in 1799; by 1853 there were twenty-six.[5] About 1850, the value of manufactured product per head of the population was about one-third of that of France (a moderately developed country of Western Europe), but most of this was contributed by handicraft industry. However, the number of factory workers grew three- or fourfold between 1860 and 1900. Whereas by 1850 the agricultural output was more than five times as valuable as the industrial, by 1900 (according to an estimate for European Russia only) industry (manufacture and mining) was contributing 24 per cent of the total national income (as compared with 45 per cent from agriculture and 5 per cent from forestry and fishing).[6] Rather more than one-third of the industrial component was contributed by *factory* industry. Between 1870 and 1914 output grew eightfold, about as fast as United States industrial output over the same period, and thus faster than output in Western Europe. Among manufacturing industries, textiles (nearly a third of total output), metal-working (a sixth) and food (over a third) were the largest branches. The oil industry (centred on Baku) was important: if one neglects the much larger share of firewood at the earlier date, the percentage share of oil in the national fuel balance reached in 1913 what it was planned to reach again in 1965. The distribution of industry was very uneven. Factories were located almost exclusively in European Russia, and especially in the St. Petersburg, Moscow and Ivanovo areas (textiles), the Ukraine (coal-mining), and Baku.

A beginning was made with factory legislation. Laws of 1 June 1882, 12 June 1884, and 3 June 1885, *inter alia* limited the hours of work of children, and to some extent of women.[7] Adult working hours *per diem* were limited to 11½.[8]

Techinically, in productivity of labour, or in social background, Russian industry lagged behind the most advanced countries of Western Europe or America. Yet, in the second half of the nineteenth century organizational forms in the more developed branches of Russian industry were adopted which had been reached in other capitalist countries only after much longer periods.[9] Russian industry was much more 'concentrated' than industry in Western Europe, i.e. very large factories were relatively numerous. As the revolutionary leaders expected, this concentration favoured dissemination of their doctrines among the 'working masses'.

Since 1843, when the first main line (joining Moscow and St. Petersburg in a straight path, therefore by-passing Novgorod, and said to have been traced by the Tsar with a ruler) was begun, a network of railways – its pattern dictated by military as well as economic desiderata, in which the Crimean War (*vide infra*) was influential – spread across the land. The Trans-Siberian Railway, begun in 1891, was completed by stages, the Middle Siberian line being opened in 1899.[10] By 1914 there were nearly 80,000 km. of track (nearly one-fifth of the US figure at that date) in a more spacious gauge (5′) than the standard 4′ 8½″. Railway construction in Russia is associated with the name of Sergius Witte, the Minister of Communications and later Minister of Finance (1892–1903). The road network remained very undeveloped (Russia in 1928 contained a smaller mileage of metalled roads than Britain, a country with one-ninetieth the area, had had of turnpike roads more than a century earlier), while for Russia the great age of canal building has been the twentieth century (not, as in Western Europe, the eighteenth or nineteenth). Russia owned very few seagoing ships. The railways – and rivers – accordingly had to bear an unusually heavy traffic. However, as rail links, converging on St. Petersburg and Moscow, were built, a measure of adaptation to distance was gradually achieved.

The Russian terrain is generally easy to move across. High mountains are mostly round the rim or in uninhabited areas. The long cold winter climate did not offer much of a barrier to hardy people who often travelled long distances by sleigh. Thick forest sometimes hindered movement, as did many rivers, but these were temporary obstacles. Distances certainly were great, and before the Trans-Siberian was opened, voluntary movement towards the east was not on a large scale. The population was accordingly scant and so could not, even had it wanted, oppose any permanently effective resistance to orders from Moscow. Because migrants arrived by land, they did not congregate in a few large ports, which tended to be the case in North America and Australia. Probably for this reason, and because their opportunities for trading were more limited, settlements did not evolve towards independence.

Financial practices were improved. Annual budgets began to be published only after 1861, following disclosures by émigrés of the unpublished figures. A democratic assembly, the Duma, set up after the revolution of 1905, did useful work in improving administration, such as publishing accounts and statistics and fostering schools. But one must return to the subject of agriculture, which until 1861 was based on serf labour. Serfs were literally their owners' property. Down to 1833, a serfowner could at any time break up a family by selling one member of it apart from the others. The serf was treated as a factor of production rather than as a human being; he was in effect money, a part of the natural economy, as T. G. Masaryk observed.[11]

The *Sobornoye Ulozheniye* (Assembly Code) of 1649 had codified existing legislation and custom. The obligation of the peasant became hereditary; flight from the place where he was held in bondage was made a criminal offence. Peter the Great further extended serfdom by permitting the purchase of serfs for industrial employment, but since his reign witnessed a systematic enforcing of obligations on *all* classes, the relative burden upon the serfs then appeared less. The special viciousness of the system was revealed when the obligation of service of the nobility was revoked (1762). During the reign of Catherine II serfdom was extended to the Ukraine, and then to the Crimea and the Caucasus (1773–75). The sale of serfs by public auction was prohibited; but this was merely window-dressing. During the eighteenth century the system became more oppressive, while the extent to which it favoured one class to the disfavour of the rest became obvious.

After the French Revolution, apologists for serfdom found themselves on the defensive: the contrast with Western Europe became increasingly glaring. Slavery still continued in America, and the eventual emancipation of the serfs and freeing of the slaves took place within five years of each other. Although certain other parallels can be drawn,[12] one must remember that the origins of the two systems were entirely different. Catherine's successor Paul took two important steps to prepare the way for the eventual emancipation. A regulation of 1798 applying to Ukraine prohibited the sales of serfs apart from their land. In 1797 an imperial 'recommendation' was issued that a serf's working days for his lord should be three days a week. The separate sale of members of a peasant's family was forbidden by laws of 1833 and 1847.

Complete emancipation was considered, but the Tsars drew back from reform because concessions appeared to threaten their absolute power. Alexander I at first had been the centre of liberal hopes, but these hopes were disappointed and Alexander was succeeded by the reactionary Nicholas I. The system remained extremely severe: a serfowner could sentence one of his serfs to exile in Siberia or to long service in the army (at first this was for 25 years, later the term was reduced). In 1773–74 there had been a regular popular revolt, the Pugachevshchina. Now, there were periodic rebellions, incendiarism, murder and terrorism. All outbreaks were repressed, but they seemed to be becoming more frequent. Abroad, Russia supported the aspirations of the Greeks towards national independence; at home, her own people had no rights.

Leading opponents of serfdom were Russian authors. Radishchev's *A Journey from St. Petersburg to Moscow*, written already before the French Revolution, made a violent assault on the system. Tsar Alexander II declared that reading *A Sportsman's Diary* (Turgenev) had convinced him that serfdom must be abolished.

The unsuccessful Crimean War also played its part. In British history this is highlighted by the charge of the Light Brigade, and by Florence Nightingale. In Russian history its associations are quite different. Although they had a large numerical superiority, and were fighting to defend their homeland, the Russians failed to defeat the British and French. Apparently there was something seriously amiss in Russia, and the obvious culprit was serfdom.

The new Tsar, Alexander II, had decided on reform. Increasing pressure was put on serfowners to produce workable recommendations. Although in the mass reluctant and unwilling, the serfowners were not of one mind: the more liberal groups accepted and cooperated with the proposal. An Imperial Rescript of 1857 to the nobles of certain Lithuanian provinces, who had requested permission to free their peasants *without* land, became a point of departure for working out the mechanics of emancipation.

The emancipation law was signed on 19 February 1861, the sixth anniversary of the Tsar's accession, but was not published until 5 March, the eve of Lent, in order to discourage popular outbreaks. (Reckoning by another calendar, it happened to be on the same date, 92 years later, that Stalin died.)

The law was enormously long and detailed. Complicated arrangements were laid down for various transition periods. Four major special statutes were issued, one for each of the major geographical divisions (Great Russia, a part of Ukraine, Western Ukraine, and Lithuania and White Russia). Two methods of granting land to the peasants were formulated: free grants of one-quarter of the maximum size fixed by law for holdings in that locality, or redemption. The 1861 law permitted the latter only if the landowner agreed, but it was made compulsory in 1881.

The law of 1861 gave the serfs their freedom: they could work at what job they pleased, and change their residence as long as they paid their taxes. In contrast to the Polish emancipation, or to the enclosure movement in Western Europe, which had that result for some, Russian peasants were not to be landless. They were given full power to settle their affairs in the village community. This settlement is the best example of a gigantic reorganization, commanded from above, of which there are other examples in Russian and particularly Soviet economic history. Some 47 million serfs, comprising about three-quarters of the population, were freed: besides agriculturists these included factory workers, miners, and servants in the often grossly over-staffed noble households.

The land assigned to the liberated serfs was over 350 million acres (1,400,000 square km.), which equals nearly four times the area of California or Japan. It comprised half the land used for agricultural purposes.

The favourable results of the emancipation were not fully apparent at once. Obviously time was required for readjustment. The plan was designed to leave serfs and lords about the proportions of the land which they had under the old system. This happened in some places. Big variation in land fertility led to considerable differences in the areas assigned to serfs in different regions, but at least half the people (70 per cent, according to a more extensive investigation made in 1897) did not get enough land to feed a family and occupy its labour. As earlier with the English enclosures, a disproportionate share of meadow, pasture and forest remained in the hands of the lords. On the whole, the land farmed by the peasants was less by a fifth after the emancipation. For land which they received the peasants had to make redemption payments to the state, which had bought out the landowners. In 1881 the payments were reduced, and later on further reductions were made. The arrears were cancelled during the revolutionary period of 1904–6.

The emancipation was on the whole a compromise, which as the population continued to grow quite rapidly bequeathed to the peasants a growing land hunger. Moreover, as land was held by a peasant not individually but as a member of the mir, the emancipation augmented the power of the latter.

The mir periodically redistributed land, and as in Western Europe in the Middle Ages, it decided the crops to be grown and the sowing and harvesting times, and preserved the ancient system of cultivation in scattered strips. The mir conferred a measure of equality and protected against destitution. Against this, individual initiative was curbed, and improvement retarded.

To overcome this obstacle Prime Minister Stolypin (1906–11) introduced laws which enabled an individual peasant to claim his share of the land, and so assemble his strips into a compact holding. If one-fifth of the householders in a village demanded consolidation, it had to take place. By 1914 nearly a quarter of the peasants had grasped this opportunity and had secured small compact farms of their own. Yet this large-scale movement was not really popular. Inevitably, the beneficiaries were chiefly the more enterprising peasants; though certain restrictions, which precluded the buying-out of poor, peasants by rich ones, were retained. The reform led to some gain in agricultural performance: imports of agricultural machinery and fertilizers increased, as did the area tilled and the average yield. However, the wooden plough or *sokha* continued to be typical of Russian agriculture. Whatever improvement was effected in productivity was — if related to the more advanced farming of Western Europe — from a medieval level. Cultivation on the large estates was much more efficient than on the peasants' holdings, and the former supplied the bulk of Russian agricultural exports.

Although backward, agriculture remained long after the Revolution the dominating force in the economy. In the last century, upon it and particularly on the grain harvest — the principal crop — almost everything depended: how much people could eat; largely, what was available for export and thus, fairly directly, how much could be imported, which in turn would influence industrial development and in the short run, industrial performance itself.

Several links connected the harvest with the level of industrial activity. If the harvest were bad, food prices would rise, and buyers of food would then have less to spend on industrial goods. The supply of raw materials for processing might be affected — either foodstuffs or textiles (the latter if one has in mind cotton, wool or flax). The supply of labour to man the factories would be impaired. In time of famine factory workers, who still kept one foot in the countryside, would head back to their villages. Those who remained would now be ill fed, and so would be less able to work effectively. Finally, at the last stage, famine could kill. The year 1891 was such a year of famine, which had other consequences too, such as that a graph of birth-rates makes a dip in 1892.

I compared changes in the size of the harvest and changes in industrial production over the period 1885–1913, for which we have information. Over the period considered as a whole, the two quantities are not significantly related. But if we break up this period into two, an interesting difference emerges. In the first half, the size of the harvest is clearly correlated with the volume of industrial production in the following year. In the second half, it is not: something else now is beginning to dominate the rhythm of industrial activity. This other force can only be the general level of business activity in the world as a whole. In short, during the last quarter of the nineteenth century and the first decade and a half of the twentieth, industrial performance in Russia began to be influenced by trade fluctuations in the world outside. Russia was beginning to be included within the world economy.[13]

The year of famine, 1891, marks a turning-point in Russian history, including economic history. The same year a secret treaty was concluded with France; and thereafter French capital flooded in. Belgian and English capital were prominent. A coalmining town in the Donbass, the chief coalmining basin, was named after an English capitalist, Hughes – Russianized as Yuzovka. Agricultural exports were enabling industrial equipment to be improved. They also permitted Russia to pay interest on the foreign loans which were needed not only to finance development but to balance a budget that was burdened with heavy war debts, further augmented after Russia's humiliating defeat by Japan in 1904. But within Russia living standards remained rather exiguous. There was no decisive upward trend in food production relative to population and the larger part of exports consisted of foodstuffs, even though a large proportion of the population was going hungry for part of the year.

The population had nevertheless grown, and was still growing fast. No census was taken until 1897, but the bureaucratic organization and class structure required that estimates of population should be available. The Tsarist Empire at the time of the death of Peter the Great (1725) is estimated to have contained only about 20 million people, less than that of contemporary France. At the present time, the Soviet population is very nearly five times as big as the French. Especially in the nineteenth century, the population of the Empire grew rapidly. Curiously, in the second half of the century the *Russian* population was roughly keeping pace with the last two digits of the year *Anno Domini*: thus, in 1859 the population was estimated at 58·6 million, and in 1897, according to the census, 94·3 million. To find the total population of the Empire we must add in the non-Russian element, which was swollen during this period by territorial annexations: it increased from 6·4 million in 1859 to 31·3 million in 1897, making a grand total then of 125·6 million. By 1914 this grand total is reckoned to have grown to about 142·4 million[14] within the present frontiers of the USSR or to 159·2 million within the contemporary frontiers.[15] Although a good many people emigrated, the proportion was much smaller than from some countries in Western Europe; while *immigration* has been negligible throughout modern Russian history.

Russian economy and society were now, in the first decade and a half of the present century, evolving more quickly than before. This economy was still predominantly rural, with the vast mass of the people living in villages – and indeed many towns were not unlike villages (Moscow's nickname was 'the gigantic village'). Meanwhile industrial production, although still contributing only a minor part of national income and occupying a still smaller fraction of the working population, was growing quite rapidly. While the gap between town and country life was widening, within the towns the sharp social divisions persisted and were seized on by an increasingly effective revolutionary movement, which had already tried out its strength in 1905.

On the whole, one has an impression of a country living on an average not much above subsistence level, albeit fast developing, with a great potential, but which now faced serious problems. And the greatest question was, would economic progress win or lose the race against revolutionary agitation?

Notes

1 Cf. in this connection my 'Geographic Influences on Centralization in the Soviet Economy', *Soviet Studies*, January 1966 (vol. XVII. no. 3).

2 See Geoffrey Blainey, *The Tyranny of Distance* (1968).

3 M. W. Thompson, *Novgorod the Great* (1967), especially pp. 7–8 and 13–14. This is a compressed version of Russian accounts describing the excavations. Certain streets were relaid identically 28 times between A.D. 953 and 1462.

4 Note that in Prussia, too, serfdom was introduced much later than in Western Europe.

5 Clive Day, *Economic Development in Europe* (1942), p. 548.

6 Ibid., p. 563.

7 M. Tugan-Baranovskiy, *Russkaya fabrika v proshlom i v nastoyashchem* (1898), pp. 308–12.

8 M. S. Miller, *The Economic Development of Russia, 1905–1914*, Second Edition (1967), p. 231.

9 N. Pertsovich, *Sovetskiye tresty i sindikaty* (1925), p. 3.

10 P. Lyashchenko, *Istoriya narodnogo khozyaystva SSSR, tom II* (1956), p. 693.

11 T. G. Masaryk, *The Spirit of Russia*, vol 1 (1919), p. 134.

12 See G. P. G. Sinzheimer, 'The Economics of Russian Serfdom and the Economics of American Slavery—a Historical Comparison', *Jahrbücher für Geschichte Osteuropas*, Neue Folge, Band 14, Jahrgang 1966, Heft 4, December 1966, pp. 513–28.

13 Thus, Lyashchenko notes the accentuating effect upon irregularity of development of the important participation of foreign capital (op. cit, *tom* II, pp. 226–8).

14 F. Lorimer, *The Population of the Soviet Union* (1946), p. 30. This is Volkov's estimate; Lorimer estimated 140·4 millions (ibid., p. 36).

15 *Narodnoye khozyaystvo SSSR v 1967 g.* (1968), p. 7.

3
MARXISM AS A BACKGROUND TO SOVIET ECONOMIC HISTORY

At this point one must digress briefly into the nature of this agitation. The first volume of Karl Marx's *Das Kapital* was translated into Russian and appeared in 1872, only five years after the German version. Marx's labour theory of value came to be accepted in Russia at an early date; and the Communist Manifesto and 'historical materialism' were also disseminated there.

The reasons why Marxism found a ready acceptance in Russia, at least among the intellectual groups who still found themselves divorced from power, were various. Any complete exposition would take us too far afield, but the following elements would certainly need to be included:

(1) The normal tendency for opponents of an oppressive, authoritarian regime to seize on a dynamic and extreme theory to further their cause, that is to say, extremes provoke extremes;

(2) The strong and still much-alive traditions and forms of communal economic organization in Russia, such as the mir and various co-types of co-operative bodies (e.g. artels);

(3) The unimpressive performance in Russia of capitalism where this represented a native growth, in contrast to experience in the West and in contrast to the more effective role of the State in Russian economic development;

(4) Russia's relatively simple and very sharply delineated class structure.

There were doctrinal divergences, however, of many different sorts. For instance, the inevitability of history was the general interpretation of Marxism in Germany and passed over into the *Menshevik* doctrine. The *Bolsheviks* on the other hand placed the emphasis on conscious action, as a party that sought political power was bound to do. (True, Communists are nowadays not consistent in this, but according to circumstances emphasize determinism or conscious action.) Russian

Communism also emphasised maximizing production rather than redistribution of wealth according to some just principle. In this form, too, Marxism became a dynamic doctrine, evidently more inspiring to many than egalitarianism which the Bolsheviks later sacrificed for the sake of stepping up output.

At the time when Marx wrote no socialist system had existed apart from small, idealistic and often unsuccessful communities. Marx wrote primarily as a critic of capitalism and prophet of its overthrow. What he said about a future socialist system is vague, but one can infer something about it from what Marx criticized in capitalist systems.

(1) This would be a 'planned economy' (this follows from Marx's analysis of the evils of unplanned 'bourgeois' economies, which permit booms and slumps).

(2) Means of production would be commonly owned. 'Surplus value' (deriving from private ownership of means of production) would therefore be eliminated, and so wages would rise. This would become possible also owing to the striking off of monopoly 'fetters' on production.

(3) The price system would obviously have to be changed if value measured in labour time were to be the guiding principle.

(4) Wages, too, would be proportionate to labour time, presumably taking account of differences in skill.

One can infer something more from the situation which Marx envisaged on the eve of the revolution, if the correct revolutionary tactics had been followed.

This would be one in which all or most of the sequences of capitalist development that Marx foresaw had actually occurred. The capitalists would be comparatively few, the proletarians very many. The bankrupting of small firms and consequent growth of large ones would have proceeded to the point that firms were very large. Total production would be on a fairly large scale though, due to monopoly restrictions, not as large as it could be if known technologies were fully exploited. Manufacturing industry must consequently be fairly highly developed relatively to agriculture, which implies a fairly advanced stage of development.

Techniques would also be comparatively highly developed as what Marx called the 'organic composition' of capital would be high (i.e. large volumes of capital would be employed per unit of labour). Differences in incomes would be wide. A big proportion of total production would be of luxury goods. We nowadays would say there would be a serious and growing problem of technological unemployment (though Marx's capitalists would welcome the existence of a growing reserve army of unemployed which would help to keep wages down). Exports to underdeveloped countries would be large (because of marketing difficulties at home), while finance capital would have assumed an international character. The country would be rent by irreconcilable social and political divisions, and would nourish an increasingly effective revolutionary movement.

This picture would by no means apply altogether to Russia, in the stage that she had reached before 1917. Certain features would apply: for instance, industry actually reached a high degree of concentration. There were also sharp social divisions and an increasingly effective revolutionary movement. On the other hand, despite important progress, industry was not yet highly developed: The vast mass of the population were still living in the countryside. The volume of industrial exports of finished products was negligible.

However, the features which Russia had in common with Marx's vision proved to be the determining ones. Those which Russia did not share turned out to be less important than Marx had supposed. He correctly predicted the ending, though his arguments did not all apply. A particular element in Marx's strength lay in his attention to the interaction of different forms of economic organization and institutions.

Marx's picture contains two elements: the impersonal ones of concentration, rate of exploitation, income differentials, unemployment etc.; and people's reaction to those conditions, culminating in the revolutionary movement. He envisaged that both would march in unison: the more concentration proceeded the more unemployment there would be, and so the nearer the revolutionary movement would come to explosion.

However, economic factors are not the only ones to determine whether a revolutionary movement begins and how it goes. Such a movement, especially in the nineteenth century, would also have political aims. In Britain, for example, such aims were being gradually realized through the extension of the franchise. The character of such a movement depends also on how effectively the opposition can organize itself, and on whether there are traditions of violent action. Such traditions in Britain mainly belonged to a rather distant past. In France there were such traditions in more modern times, and in fact in March 1871, the Paris 'Commune' was proclaimed (though it was soon crushed). Above all there was a tradition in Russia, both of violent action and of extremist thinking, which was nourished by the exile of would-be revolutionaries and reformers in Siberia, or abroad.

A revolutionary response can, of course, be generated by more than one set of circumstances. For instance, as technology progresses different nations starting along the road of industrialization will begin to apply different actual technologies. One might then, for example, find a relatively high 'organic composition of capital' in a particular branch of industry within an otherwise backward economy. Similarly with the concentration of capital. These are aspects of what we would now call the 'dual economy' that is characteristic of present-day underdeveloped countries.[1] In a huge country, there might be considerable industries and yet the proletariat might still comprise a minority. If in such a mainly agricultural country there were an acute land hunger which could not be satisfied, this would create an 'industrial reserve army' whether or not there were also technological unemployment in industry.

In Russia, not only were there wide gulfs between the incomes of workers and peasants, on the one hand, and capitalists on the other hand, but both workers and peasants still earned very little in absolute terms. Intellectuals were opposed to a system of government which allowed them little say and restricted intellectual freedom. The peasants had gained their freedom from serfdom within the living memory of some, but its results had been disappointing. Because of rural overpopulation, industrial wages were kept low (among other things, an effect of 'the reserve army'). Industry had been expanding rapidly, especially after 1890, but this expansion was largely financed by foreign capital (French, Belgian, English)[2] which reinforced nationalistic feelings; the degree of concentration was high, so that, as Marx had predicted, indoctrination of the workers in revolutionary themes went on despite all the secret police could do. Russia became involved in wars; the first with Japan for the sake of colonial ambitions, and under the mistaken expectation that victory would be gained and would divert popular attention from domestic troubles, the second for the complex of reasons which led to the Great War.

The Soviet economy does conform in a certain degree to Marx's implied specification. This is a 'planned economy'; means of production are State-owned; prices are managed. On the other hand, it is not clear that labour-time offers much clue to relative prices or wages, although the 'labour day' was prescribed as a conventional measure of work by collective farmers.

Marx also bequeathed a preoccupation with economic growth; an emphasis on the importance of economic institutions; a concern with technical progress; an emphasis on the distinction between the output of capital goods (Group A in Soviet terminology) and that of consumption goods (Group B); a belief in economic determinism; and, of course, an antagonism towards capitalism and capitalists. In all these respects too the Soviet system reflects Marx's approach.

Yet one should resist any temptation to think of the Soviet system of economy as Marxist first of all. It is Soviet first of all. It has to be approached mainly through itself — through a specifically Russian, and then Soviet, background. The Soviet system is influenced by Marxism, *because* Marxism found a sympathetic chord in Russian experience: it was this resonance that did so much to shake to pieces the old order. We might say that Russian ideology had older roots than Marxism. Against this, Campbell argues that it is important to reject the idea that the Soviet economy is applied to Marxism.[3] Certainly it is a far cry from Marx's generalities to the immense, complex, bureaucratic Soviet system of the 1970s, but Marxism now joined with Leninism supplies a rather imprecise ideal that can bolster up opposition to some innovation or may, on the contrary, promote it. In the USSR, the only social thinking which may be expounded publicly is Marxism-Leninism. Ideological conservatives have often opposed innovations — for example, Khrushchev's proposal to sell agricultural machinery to the collective farms — on ideological grounds. If a proposed reform demonstrably fits in with Marxist or Marxist-Leninist principles, it has a better chance of being adopted, and it is adopted sooner. Moreover decisions have a cumulative effect: a decision which has been taken at time 1 limits the choices which are possible at time 2, and so on, so that it is of particular importance which decisions are taken first. Now, the influence of ideology upon Soviet economic development was manifested as soon as the Bolsheviks seized power, and decisions taken at that time concerning fundamental questions of management and ownership have remained for the most part in force. Where, as in agriculture, a final solution was not reached immediately, an ideological approach greatly influenced the final outcome.[4]

The attention paid to ideology when decisions were taken in connection with economic developent was decided by the contemporary leader of the Party.[5] The influence of ideology therefore shaded into the influence upon economic life of a highly centralized system of government. The goal of full Communism ('from each according to his ability, to each according to his needs'), the vague ideal to which lip-service is still paid, is of course ideological in character.

Notes

1 See H. Myint, *The Economics of the Developing Countries* (1967), pp. 65–6, 71–2, 83–4.
2 Foreign capital comprised in 1890 more than a third of all share capital invested in Russia, in 1900 almost a half (P. Lyashchenko, *Istoriya narodnogo khozyaystva SSSR, tom II, p. 154*).
3 R. W. Campbell, *Soviet Economic Power* (1960), pp. 7–10.
4 A case study of comparative ideological and economic influences upon agricultural policy is presented in Chapter 10.
5 Cf. Alan Bullock, *Hitler, A Study in Tyranny* (1962), p. 157.

PART II

ECONOMIC DEVELOPMENT SINCE 1913

4

WAR, REVOLUTION AND WAR COMMUNISM

To return to the question: would Russian economic progress win or lose the race against revolutionary agitation? History has not settled this question, because a successful revolution broke out only after three years of demoralizing and eventually disastrous war. The harm done by the war, yet for several years borne by the economy, shows that the latter by 1913 had accumulated a certain reserve. By 1917, as compared with 1913 — the last full year of peace — the cultivated area was down by a sixth, owing to the call-up of peasants (15 million men were mobilized) and horses; the grain harvest was down by 14 per cent. Exports of grain almost ceased. Industry suffered from the occupation of the Russian part of Poland by the Central Powers, but elsewhere industrial employment increased. Output sagged but did not fall catastrophically: neglecting the loss of Poland, by 1916 the output of pig iron was 10 per cent below 1913, but total industrial output was 22 per cent above 1913. The economy was under strain but not beaten down.

In 1917 the situation worsened sharply: the output of pig iron, for example, declined by more than a sixth. By comparison with 1913, total industrial production was now down by a quarter. A serious shortage of fuel was felt. Because of transport bottlenecks (by the end of 1917 one-third of the locomotives were out of action) vital supplies often could not be moved; the volume of money in circulation increased twelvefold as compared with July 1914. Prices of consumer necessities rose threefold between 1914 and January 1917, but then sixfold between January and December 1917.[1]

The difficulty of transporting goods, combined with the shrinkage in agricultural output, must in any event have caused serious shortages of food in the towns. Against this, the almost complete cessation by 1916 of grain exports would have brought some relief to the home market. But industry had been diverted to producing war supplies and munitions, so that little was left with which to supply the country-side in return for the food which the towns could not do without. The farmers in consequence ceased to trouble to sell food for which they would be paid in rapidly depreciating paper money, or even to sow crops except to feed themselves. At this point the dissolution of the economy, which depended on exchange between countryside and town, was at hand. Yet things were to get much worse still before they got better. Agriculture recovered faster, but not until 1926 was the pre-war level of industrial output regained. Soviet economic statistics for a long while harked back to 1913 (although sometimes because this showed Soviet achievements in a more favourable light than a later base-date would have done); and we shall do the same, at the end of each chapter in Part II.

There were two revolutions in 1917: that of February deposed the Tsar, that of October installed the Bolsheviks in his place. The interim period, during which industrial anarchy, fomented by the Bolsheviks, increased, set the economy firmly on a downward path but otherwise left no distinctive trace on Soviet economic development.

The second and more famous revolution (on 25 October 1917, by the old-style calendar: hence, the 'October Revolution') affected all aspects of society. It took place under war conditions, with all that these implied – at a time when Russia was headed inevitably towards defeat. The war was followed by losses of territory (the Baltic States and other areas, temporary German occupation of Ukraine), Civil War, Allied intervention and blockade, harvest failure and famine. An estimated two million people, comprising a large fraction of the upper and intellectual class, emigrated between 1913 and 1923.[2] During the period, economic *policy* fluctuated sharply in response either to events or to changes of mind of the leadership.

Conditions were abnormal in the fullest sense then imaginable. Economic historians usually prefer to skim over abnormal periods, when the ordinary rules of economic behaviour cease, or partly cease, to apply. But since the economy from now on is abnormal by all previous standards, one must not pass cursorily over the immediate post-Revolution period merely because of its abnormality. Economic policy had already impinged heavily on the development of the economy of pre-Revolutionary Russia. In 1917 the reins of power were seized by a group whose interest in economic affairs and determination to control them were far stronger than the Tsars'. Certainly, even the Bolsheviks' control turned out to be not unlimited; as experience teaches, while a number of economic laws continue to operate in the USSR, some in full force and some in a modified way, others cease to apply. In general, in dealing with Soviet economic history one must attend closely to economic policy. The early period must therefore be studied because it leaves its mark on all that follows.

The most important of the measures adopted, in most cases, almost immediately by the Bolshevik government were:

(1) Nationalization of the land, announced on the day after the revolution (26 October 1917).
(2) Establishment of a Supreme Council of National Economy, or VSNKh (2 December 1917).
(3) Nationalization of all industrial enterprises employing more than five workers (three years later, on 29 November 1920).
(4) An eight-hour working day (29 October 1917).
(5) The Council of People's Commissars became the supreme governmental body (26 October 1917).
(6) Nationalization of foreign trade (22 April 1918).
(7) Nationalization of banks (December 1917).

There were numerous other measures involving regulation, requisition, confiscation, organization and reorganization.

The Bolshevik government repudiated the debts of Tsarism. But it did not repudiate in practice the vast inheritance of territory from the Empire, although it was compelled to fight to maintain or regain this inheritance.

In practice, events often marched ahead of the Bolsheviks and sometimes even in contrary directions. When the Revolution took place, the peasants took from the landlords the land which they had so long coveted. For the time being the Bolsheviks were more than happy that they did so, although their ultimate intention was not to leave the land in private hands and indeed the decree of 26 October 1917 had specifically abolished private ownership of land. The peasants were of course, capable of tilling the soil, so their taking it over did not threaten any catastrophe, although the resulting fragmentation later became − or came to be regarded as − incompatible with continued growth of the economy along the lines enforced by the leadership.

The workers, in many instances, seized the factories where they worked. The Bolsheviks were also happy to see the factory owners expropriated, but Lenin insisted that this kind of chaotic nationalization was a step backwards from the ultimate aim of setting up a planned economy. Workers had to spend part of their time foraging for food: sometimes they were paid in what the factory itself produced (nails, for example) which they themselves would try to barter for other necessities. Obviously this was no way to run an economy. *Organized* nationalization of enterprises proceeded more slowly: universal nationalization of large-scale industry was decreed on 28 June 1918, and complete nationalization was hardly achieved (in November 1920) before policy in this field was abruptly reversed.

The generic term for the system of economy between December

1917 and August 1921 is 'War Communism'. Russia remained at war with Germany until the signature of the Treaty of Brest-Litovsk (March 1918); thereafter (with only a few months' interval) Civil War between Reds and Whites raged until 1920. 'Communism' became the norm. (In the countryside, after the flight of the landlords, farming was fragmented into innumerable peasant holdings, but the ancient village community continued to be important.) During this period ordinary accounting ceased to be practiced. Enterprises indented for supplies. Conscious attempts were made to eliminate the use of money, perhaps not surprisingly considering that there was so little to spend it on! (Malafeyev pointedly notes that theories of abolition of money gain ground at times of sharp deficit of consumption goods.[3]) In 1919–21 workers were being paid mainly, and increasingly, in kind: from the end of 1920 workers in the chief industrial centres were being supplied with rations free of charge.[4] The average supply of rationed goods in relation to total consumption by the urban population up to 1 July 1921 was 25 per cent to 28 per cent.[5]

Within the State sector of the economy everything happened by command. War Communism signified extreme centralization. The Supreme Council of National Economy (VSNKh) was at first entrusted with general direction of the economy, but soon its dominion was more realistically contracted to industry only. Under VSNKh, industrial management was assigned to chief adminstrations or chief committees (*glavnyy komitet* or *glavk* – plural *glavki* – for short). These were successors to committees which had been set up during the War by the former government. The fact that centralization was most extreme in branches where already before the War larger undertakings had ousted smaller, also shows a degree of continuity: Russian industry was already then highly concentrated. The system of economic organization was apparently also much influenced by the German example during the war, which had been studied by Larin, a very early representative of the Council of People's Commissars on VSNKh.[6]

After 1918, economic activity declined a long way further. Military operations, and shortages of fuel and other necessities, disrupted communications. By 1921, total industrial output had declined to less than one-third of 1913,[7] while that of 'large-scale industry' was down to little more than one-eighth.[8] The harvest of chief grain crops fell by 36 per cent between 1917 and 1920 while total agricultural output in 1920 was only half the prewar quantity. Foreign trade virtually disappeared. These catastrophic falls were due to the conjoined effects of economic degeneration, blockade and military campaigns (the Red Army grew from let us say: 1 million in 1918 to 5 million in 1920), to a disastrous harvest in 1920, but also to the disadvantages of the system of extreme centralization of economic administration and to the effects of workers' control and chaotic nationalization.

The outputs of most items produced by large-scale industry were derisorily small in 1921: for instance, steel was only 5 per cent of 1913, cement 4 per cent, granulated sugar 4 per cent. Only oil (41 per cent of 1913) and coal (33 per cent) maintained any at all reasonable level of performance.

Notes

1 A. N. Malafeyev, *Istoriya tsenoobrazovaniya v SSSR (1917–1963)* (1964), p. 18. Alec Nove's review of this most useful book in *Soviet Studies*, January 1965 (vol. XVI, no. 3), brought it to my attention.
2 F. Lorimer, *The Population of the Soviet Union* (1946), p. 39.
3 A. N. Malafeyev, op. cit., p. 149.
4 Ibid., p. 24.
5 S. A. Pervushin, *Vol'nyye tseny i pokupatel'naya sila russkogo rublya 1917–1921 gg.* (1921), p. 3.
6 E. H. Carr, *The Bolshevik Revolution* (1952), vol. II, pp. 73, 86 and 361–2, and S. N. Prokopovicz, *Histoire Economique de l'URSS* (1952), pp. 335–7.
7 Thus we have the following series:

Year	Total Industrial Output
1913	100
1917	75
1921	33

8 From 10,251 million roubles in 1913 to 1,410 million roubles in 1920.

5
NEP AND POST-WAR RESTORATION

Victory in the Civil War was achieved finally by the Bolsheviks in 1920. In an attempt to rebuild the shattered economy the government decreed retreat from War Communism. A New Economic Policy (NEP) was proclaimed in August 1921, only nine months after the sweeping nationalization decree of November 1920.

A decree of private enterprise was now legalized in agriculture and trade, and foreign 'concessions' in industry (and in other sectors) were invited. By a law of 1921, industrial plants which remained under State ownership were to be organized into *trusts*, to which was assigned a degree of autonomy; these began to be formed. The authority of VSNKh was contracted to include only the most important industrial enterprises. Enterprises which although already legally nationalized had not in fact been taken over, or which employed fewer than 20 workers, were restored to their previous owners or were leased to new ones (often, to industrial co-operatives).

Against this, the government kept its grip on what it called the 'commanding heights' of the economy. Foreign trade remained a State monopoly; the land was still nationalized; main industries were still under central control; and the government kept the power to make, if it chose, further fundamental changes.

In the same year, 1921, the first long-term plan of electrification (GOELRO) was projected and a State Planning Commission (Gosplan) was set up (February 1921) to implement it. These innovations were meant to counterbalance the anticipated 'petty bourgeois anarchy'.

The new policy favoured trade and monetary relations generally. For example, consumers' co-operatives ceased to be governmentally supplied and had to manage their own accounts. Free distribution of foodstuffs and free communal services were terminated.

Two keys at least are necessary for understanding the evolution of the Russian economy in the few years after 1920 and in certain other periods.

(1) One is the impact of war on an economy. As is natural, economic

history is concerned mainly with economic development and construction: but in real life regression and destruction also occur. The following simple propositions can perhaps assist in generalizing the effects of war on an economy:

(a) The more advanced the economy, the more readily it can be damaged by a given degree of wartime destruction; as a sub-proposition of this, this applies particularly to the more advanced sectors of an economy (account being taken of the physical vulnerability of installations, for instance, a hydro-electric plant is vulnerable to a single explosive charge, while mines are often subject to flooding); and vice versa in each case;

(b) Military operations harm an economy mainly because of their dislocating effects, only subsidiarily because of direct destruction (this is really the reason for (a)).

(c) In a postwar situation, once any necessary fundamental reorganization or readjustment (e.g. a currency reform) has been made, the highest rates of growth are achieved by economies which suffered the most from dislocation or destruction; similarly, as between sectors the highest rates are achieved by those *sectors* that have suffered most.

(d) A civil war has peculiarly dislocating effects, because the front line may run through or even bisect the most heavily populated areas, and because whereas a foreign war is not usually accompanied by civil war, a civil war nearly always provokes external intervention.

These propositions have commonly been valid in the recent past. They are generally true in Soviet history at this period. The Civil War affected different branches of the economy unequally.[1] Rail transport, coalmining and metallurgy suffered especially great destruction.[2]

The scale of population losses was almost comparable to what might be expected after a nuclear exchange. The population in 1914 has been estimated at 142·4 million. Had it continued to grow as between 1897 and 1914, at an annual rate of 1·41 per cent of the population, this total would have become 161·5 million by 1923. The 1923 population appears to have been in fact only 136·1 million, which implies a deficiency of 25·4 million or of 16 per cent. Such an estimate can only be very rough, but one may agree with Lorimer who remarks that during those years 'the Russian people underwent the most cataclysmic changes since the Mongol invasion in the early thirteenth century'.[3] Yet, as even after the Second World War, the impact of human losses on economic development by reducing the workforce generally is not very conspicuous.[4] The more easily traceable phenomena relate to dislocation, in accordance with our principle (b).

(2) Secondly, there is the peculiar importance of the industrial-agricultural goods exchange ratio in a country which, like the USSR, is mainly self-sufficient, relying little on foreign trade – particularly at

the period we are now considering, when trade had dwindled to a volume far smaller than before World War I – and where agriculture is technically much inferior to industry.[5]

It was pointed out earlier that, before the war, Russia was being drawn into the world economy.[6] From 1917 or 1918 onwards, following the establishment of a State monopoly of foreign trade and much later the promulgation of increasingly detailed and large-scale plans, the link with the world economy was cut while the intimate link between domestic agriculture and industry was re-established.

The famine of 1920 was followed by pronounced fluctuations of the relative prices of agricultural and industrial products. The most advanced sectors of the economy (industry and transport) had suffered relatively most from the war and Civil War, agriculture relatively the least. After peace returned, industrial output for several years remained lower, relative to agricultural, than it had been before the war. (Industrial output declined by two-thirds, or by more in the case of large-scale industry; whereas agricultural output declined by not more than 40 per cent.)

However, the rate of exchange of agricultural for industrial products would be influenced not only by relative changes in their output proportions, but by the relative elasticities of demand. The elasticity of demand for agricultural products was much smaller than that for industrial products, because the towns could not do without the food that the countryside supplied whereas the countryside could at a pinch do without what the towns supplied (for the countryside could itself make simple tools and household objects, as had been done for centuries: these craft industries were always stimulated when exchange difficulties between town and country became acute).[7] For this reason an attempt under War Communism to organize direct exchange of industrial for agricultural products, despite the despatch of armed detachments to seize agricultural surpluses, had not worked. The legalization of private trade in August 1921 had an immediately favourable effect on supplies.

Entry into the period of NEP and the legalization of private trade substantially altered the character of price-formation, as the law of value began to operate in other conditions.

In a relatively short time the sharp deficit of consumption goods, explicable owing to the decline of production to far below the volumes which corresponded historically to the level of living standards of the urban and rural population, was outlived....

All this led to...an alteration in relative prices of industrial and agricultural goods in the direction of bringing this relationship closer to the prewar one.[8]

In other words, agricultural prices were enabled to rise. This is the basic reason for the rise in agricultural prices relative to industrial during 1922, although industrial output remained far below its 1913 level.

The following year, 1923, the situation was reversed. The area sown to grain, and the grain crops, expanded, and by 1923 reached 70 per cent of the 1916 figure. The quantity of agricultural produce placed on the market (the surplus over peasant home consumption) remained below this level, first because it was a surplus, and so would naturally decline proportionately more than the total, and secondly because fragmentation of holdings as compared with pre-1917 had resulted in a higher consumption on the farms. Against this, there were not quite so many mouths to feed. Prewar, the marketable surplus had amounted to just over 30 per cent of the total crop, whereas in 1923 it amounted to less than 25 per cent. Still, this represented an improvement over immediately preceding years, so that, other things being equal, one would expect industrial prices to have risen relative to agricultural prices. But what in fact happened in 1923 was a much larger rise in this ratio than the supply situation by itself justified.

Essentially, this ratio rose because the improvement in food supplies permitted the underlying disproportion in proportionate outputs to express itself in their relative prices. However, this was not the only reason for what came to be known as the price 'scissors' in 1923. Another was that the government was pursuing a policy of high prices for industrial goods (produced by *State* industry) in order to extract funds from the peasants (belonging to the *private* sector of the economy), in order to finance investment in industry. State industry was trying to exert a monopoly leverage with the aim of making super-high profits. (Note that this was happening in the land which applauded Marx's strictures on the evils of 'surplus value' resulting from private ownership of the means of production, and on the noxious consequences of capitalist 'monopolies'.) A third reason is found in the contemporary organizational forms of State industry.

The trusts set up in 1921–22 were not well acquainted with the state of the market. They were staffed with people who had little understanding of supply-and-demand relationships (not a strong point in Marxist economics at any time), and who, from the viewpoint of the Party Left Wing, were only too ready to heed the government's exhortations to make profits (now clearly set out in a decree of 10 April 1923 and on ordinance of 16 July 1923). Syndicates (commercial organizations which the trusts banded together to form, in the initial stages voluntarily but later compulsorily) were also favouring high prices, though less emphatically than the trusts did as their duties brought them more closely into touch with market conditions. A policy of cheap money adopted by the (nationalized) banking system sustained the illusion that industrial prices could be screwed up to any desired height. The State monopoly of foreign trade, being applied to keep out industrial goods (moreover, Russian exports had not recovered to the prewar level and could not pay for any important influx of imports), sheltered Russian industry from foreign competition, which had it been allowed a free hand must have immediately punctured the inflated price level.

In addition, by comparison with 1913 industrial costs had risen owing to higher wages, fixed costs, and amortization and fuel expenditures.

Malafeyev argues, further, that agricultural costs had been reduced due to the change in rent relations: abolition of payment of rent for land to landlords, and diversion of a portion of differential land rent to the 'working peasantry'. Previous indebtedness to banks was also annulled. He calculates that agricultural prices might have been reduced in consequence by about 20 per cent.[9]

The consequence of this price divergence was that exchange between the countryside and the towns again broke down. The supply of foodstuffs to the towns was choked off.

The prices themselves had long passed into the realm of astronomical. Currency emission had increased as follows: second half of 1918 17·6 milliard roubles, 1919 163·7 milliard, 1920 943·6 milliard, first quarter of 1921 518·1 milliard.[10] Prices naturally rose correspondingly; indeed, as the value of money declined even more rapidly, a shortage of money developed and substitutes emerged such as bread, salt or cheap cloth. By the end of 1922, which was a year of runaway inflation, the total of rouble notes in circulation had risen to just short of 2^{15}. From the government's point of view one gain was recorded: inflation had wiped out the savings of the bourgeoisie. But in addition calculations of money costs had become impracticable. No recovery could be achieved until the monetary value of the rouble could be stabilized. In 1923 a new stabilized *chervonets*, backed by gold and foreign exchange, was introduced and for a while circulated side by side with the old currency (*sovznaki*). In March 1924 the monetary reform was completed,[11] which at last made cost definitely calculable.

Considerable progress had already been made in overcoming the industrial-agricultural price discrepancy. Various measures were employed to bring industrial prices down. Credit restrictions, and subsequently a policy of making government aid dependent on prior reductions in prices, proved to be effective measures. Administrative pressure was also applied: a Commission for Internal Trade, as well as VSNKh, began to exercise in earnest price-fixing powers which they already possessed. It also became apparent that price controls would have to be reinforced by controls over stocks.

The policy of high industrial prices with the aim of generating large profits, so that industrialization could be financed at the expense of the peasantry, was thus — for the time being — abandoned. Supply and demand had won.[12] The attempt to pit the State monopoly of industry against the decentralized responses of the peasants had failed. The government held the 'commanding heights', but it could not at present use them to achieve the breakthrough towards industrialization which the Bolsheviks wanted. Further progress would have to wait on organizational developments, on clearing up economic dislocation and on some gain in general prosperity.

In these circumstances, trusts were forced to concentrate on building up their working capital, especially their liquid assets. The quickest way to do this was to sell off their 'basic', or fixed capital. The consequence was a 'sell off' (razbazarivaniye), in the course of which private individuals came to own capital valued at 300 million roubles.[13] This may not all have been 'basic'; it was, in any event, equivalent to some 6 per cent of the basic capital belonging to industry controlled by VSNKh.

This potential threat to the existence of State industry and therefore to Socialism touched on a sensitive chord and gave rise to the decree of 10 April 1923. In order, 'first, not to permit trusts to sell off property entrusted to them', the decree abolished their right to dispose of certain types of capital. Trusts' property was divided into categories according to whether, and if so in what circumstances, it might be alienated. These categories were: (a) land (which was not subject to alienation); (b) basic capital not subject to alienation; (c) basic capital subject to alienation only on permission from VSNKh; and (d) working capital, which was made subject to alienation in precisely the same degree as capital of all kinds which belonged to private industry.[14]

The clear statement of the extent to which trusts might be held liable improved their financial standing.[15] Above all, henceforward a special kind of invulnerability surrounded State undertakings. There could be no question from now on of any contest on equal terms between the private and public sectors. Since basic capital, unlike circulating capital, was not subject to seizure in case of default, trusts now had an incentive to invest in basic capital rather than in material and monetary funds. A parallel — which must not, of course, be pressed very far — can be drawn with the British Limited Liability Act of 1855, which by limiting the risk of loss stimulated business activity and investment.[16]

The price scissors of 1923 can be regarded as only the most extreme example of a more persistent tendency in the 1920s for industrial prices to rise relative to agricultural, and then to return to approximately the

1913 relationship.[17] By comparison with prices in other major industrial countries, the industrial price level in Russia was high, just as it had been in 1913. Indeed the difference had increased.

Besides the year-to-year movements in relative prices, variations occurred *during* a year, due to the much higher levels of agricultural prices in spring than in autumn. Between 1923/24 and 1926/27 this seasonal difference was sharply reduced.[18]

Under NEP, signs of prosperity began to appear. Private enterprise flourished, especially in retail trade which in 1923 was almost 80 per cent in private hands.[19] The area sown to crops reached 104 m. hectares in 1925 as compared with 105 m. hectares in 1913, while the head of livestock, except horses, surpassed the 1916 totals. Both agricultural and industrial production expanded, including output by privately owned industry (by 53 per cent between 1923/24 and 1926/27).[20] In 1923, 1925 and 1926, especially, industrial output increased markedly (see Diagram III) and by 1926 the 1913 level of output had been regained.

During the middle-1920s the Party began to shift its attention from agriculture and trade towards industry. Let us look in more detail at the factors affecting industrial development under NEP. Output increased primarily due to the bringing back into operation of already existing but idle plants.[21] (See Table 1 and Diagram I.) Assuming that a market exists for a product, that transport and finance are in order, and that enough fuel and other needed supplies are available, bringing back into operation would involve clearing up, repairs, accumulation of stock, and recruitment of management and labour. Many plants retained their prewar technology and regained many of their workpeople who had long been absent on other missions. As such plants were in essentials already in being, output could rise quickly in response to a relatively small expenditure. Once the necessary stocks of raw materials, semi-finished goods etc., had been amassed, an increasing

Table 1[22]

De-Conserved Property in All-Union and Republic Industry

Year	Million Roubles	% to Capital Total at Start of Year ((a) in Diagram I)
1924/25	256·1	9·9
25/26	125·7	4·3
26/27	64·8	2·0
27/28	25·0	0·7
28/29	25·9	0·6

share of further gross investment could comprise investment in basic capital.

Technical depreciation, i.e. the percentage difference between the full restoration cost of capital in industry and its current estimated value, would increase (other things being equal) the more time had elapsed since the first installation; or decrease, the more work had been done in restoration and repair. A rise in this ratio ((c) in Diagram I) would signify that obsolescence was winning the race against restoration whereas a fall would signify that restoration was triumphing over obsolescence.

There had been *some* investment even in 1920/21, but up to 1924/25 it did not compensate for the amount of wearing out.[23] Obsolescence at last ceased to encroach further and began to be rolled back. Between 1924/25 and 1926/27 substantial investments were made, but in working or 'circulating' capital – raw materials, fuel, stocks of finished products, ready funds – rather than in basic (fixed) capital.[24] The priority had to be given to investment in working capital because this was the more depleted.[25] The share of investments in basic capital rose at first steeply but then very gradually: from 57·8 per cent in 1925/26 to 75·8 per cent in 1928/29 ((b) in Diagram I). This rise in the ratio

$$\frac{\text{gross investment in basic capital}}{\text{gross investment in basic and circulating capital}}$$

was important in the contemporary process of industrialization. Simultaneously the proportion of 'productive construction' devoted to housing declined (from 16·1 per cent in 1924/25 to 8·0 per cent in 1927/28).[26]

Investment in industry had increased almost fivefold between 1923/24 and 1926/27, but not until 1926/27 did it surpass the volume of investment in the best prewar year (1912/13).[27] Costs had been falling, but in 1925/26 they rose slightly as worse equipment was now being brought into operation, while the wages bill increased. More money had to be printed (1925). The question arose what course should now be followed, as the prewar pattern of organization at plant level, and prewar technology and comparative output proportions which so far had essentially held sway, were on the point of being outgrown, and would need to be if progress were to continue.[28]

The sharpest and most momentous shift in the direction of investment after 1928 as compared with the NEP period was the shift *away* from investment in housing *towards* investment in productive objects, and particularly industry. (See Chapter 15). Thus housebuilding was the main emphasis in construction during NEP. In 1928 the output of

DIAGRAM I

Capital and Investment Trends in the 1920s

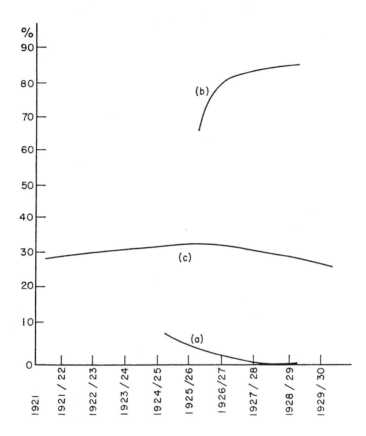

The diagram shows:

(a) De-conserved capital in All-Union and Republic industry as a percentage of capital existing at the start of each year;

(b) The percentage of gross investments in basic capital only to gross investments in both basic and circulating capital in industry planned by VSNKh;

(c) The percentage difference between the full restoration cost of capital and its current estimated value.

Table 2

Industrial Output, 1913–28

		1913	1916	1921	1925	1928
Pig Iron	(thousand tons)	4216	3804	117	1309	3282
Steel	(thousand tons)	4231	4276	220	1868	4251
Oil	(thousand tons)	9234	9970	3781	7061	11625
Coal	(thousand tons)	29117	34482	9531	16520	35510
Electric Power	(million kilowatt hours)	1945	2575	520	2925	5007
Paper	(thousand tons)	197·0	—	–	211·0	284·5
Cement	(thousand tons)	1520	—	64	872	1850
Granulated Sugar (*sakhar-pesok*)	(thousand tons)	1347	1186	51	1064	1283
Peat	(million tons)	1·7	1·6	2·0	2·7	5·3

producer goods was slightly larger than in 1913; for instance, of steel by 0·5 per cent, of coal by 22 per cent, of cement by 22 per cent. The output of consumer goods was about equal to 1913. The growth of output of some principal items of large-scale industry between 1913 and 1928 is shown in Table 2.

Notes

1 A. Erlich, *The Soviet Industrialization Debate, 1924–1928* (1960), p. 75.
2 S. G. Strumilin, *Chernaya metallurgiya v Rossii i v SSSR* (1935), p. 283.
3 F. Lorimer, op. cit., p. 42.
4 Malafeyev notes that there was an increase in agricultural costs, following from the loss of adult males, but says that this loss was partly compensated by movement of urban population into rural areas (op. cit., p. 43).
5 Approximately the same set of circumstances would apply to the world as a whole, but fluctuations should be less marked in the larger unit. See M. K. Atallah, *The Long-Term Movement of the Terms of Trade between Agricultural and Industrial Products* (1958).
6 Cf. M. S. Miller, *The Economic Development of Russia 1905–1914*, Second Edition (1967), p. 256.
7 E.g. in late 1923 (A. N. Malafeyev, op. cit., pp. 54–5).
8 Ibid., p. 30.
9 Op. cit., pp. 43–4. According to economic theory, 'economic rent' does not enter into production costs. However, payment of actual rent does of course diminish profits (in the short period, by its own magnitude).
10 Ibid., p. 26.
11 The old money was repurchased, at a rate of 50,000 *sovznaki* = 1 new rouble. (M. Dobb, *Soviet Economic Development Since 1917* (1948), p. 175).
12 E.g. Malafeyev, op. cit., p. 65.
13 A. A. Arutinyan and B. L. Markus, *Razvitiye sovetskoy ekonomiki* (1940), p. 190.
14 A. V. Venediktov, *Gosudarstvennaya sotsialisticheskaya sobstvennost'* (1948), p. 385.
15 Ya. S. Rozenfel'd, *Promyshlennaya politika SSSR* (1926), p. 256.
16 Shannon, 'Coming of General Limited Liability', *Economic Journal History Supplement*, 1931.
17 See for example Malafeyev, pp. 35 and 104–5.
18 A. N. Malafeyev, op. cit., pp. 115–16. At this time the business year ran from 1 October to 30 September of the following calendar year.
19 Sh. Ya. Turetskiy, *Sebsetoimost' i voprosy tsenoobrazovaniya* (1940), p. 176.
20 A. N. Malafeyev, op. cit., p. 83.

21 This is a theme of important novels of the period, such as Gladkov's *Tsement* (Cement).
22 S. V. Minayev (ed.), *Osnovnyye momenty rekonstrukstii promyshlennosti SSSR* (1931), p. 75.
23 M. A. Barun, *Osnovnoy kapital promyshlennosti SSSR* (1930), pp. 223–6.
24 S. Rozentul, *Planovoye khozyaystvo*, no. 1, 1929, p. 301.
25 A. Baykov, *The Development of the Soviet Economic System* (1947), p. 117.
26 M. A. Barun, op. cit., p. 262.
27 Ibid., pp. 238 and 241.
28 During the restoration period, prewar levels were attained successively in (a) labour productivity, (b) volume of output, (c) basic capital and (d) numbers of workers (Sh. Ya. Turetskiy, *Sebestoimost' i voprosy tsenoobrazovaniya* (1940), p. 56). The attainment of (c) was therefore a relatively late warning-bell. The slow reattainment of the labour force total can be remembered when it is time to account for the disappearance of unemployment (see below).

6
THE FIVE-YEAR PLAN

Lenin, who had determined the changes of course of War Communism and of the transition to NEP, died on 21 January 1924 and was succeeded by a triumvirate, among whom Stalin gradually emerged as the chief, and finally as the absolute dictator. Against the doctrine of 'permanent revolution', expounded by the brilliant Commissar of War Leon Trotsky, Stalin expounded his doctrine of 'Socialism in One Country', a trite but relevant formula which affirmed the possibility of 'building Socialism' in Russia whatever the Western Europeans might or might not decide to do. His doctrine gained the day; so that it was for the first time accepted in Russia that the centre of gravity of the world socialist movement had shifted from Western Europe to inside the Soviet Union. Trotsky was discredited. Acceptance of Stalin's doctrine was the ideological preliminary to the large-scale planning and construction during the Five-Year Plan that was to follow.

Another doctrinal preliminary was to clear the ground as regards what kind of State planning to adopt. Although the necessity of 'planning' under Soviet conditions was not questioned, a discussion arose as to whether this should be primarily passive, i.e. the compilation of forecasts of what could be expected to happen, or active, which would involve the issuing of instructions as regards what course to pursue. This was in a specific context the issue between the Bolsheviks and the Mensheviks mentioned earlier. At this time, the heads of Gosplan (Groman, Bazarov) were Mensheviks and favoured the more passive kind of planning. Stalin favoured the more active kind. The heads of Gosplan were brought to trial and imprisoned. (Ten years later they would have been shot.) The Party now took charge.

There was the question of what pace of industrialization to aim at. But perhaps one should ask first why industrialization should be pursued at all. In the present day a developing country, especially one so large and with such diverse resources as Russia, will invariably aim at industrialization. But in the nineteen-twenties this was not invariably taken for granted. An alternative for Russia would have been to give priority to agricultural development. This would have the advantage that the resource chiefly needed, land, was abundant, and as compared with industrial development, it would require smaller amounts of capital per head.

Among the Communists the matter was not discussed in those terms: the question was not whether to industrialize, but how fast. Still, it makes sense to ask what were their motives. There were several.

There was first the motivation of economic independence of the foreigner. One may look on this as economic, political, ideological, or military, or as all these things at once. Economically, there would be the rationale of liberating Russia from what could be seen as a thraldom of booms and slumps imposed from outside, although here Russia's political and economic institutions already interposed an important barrier. Ideologically, it was necessary to demonstrate that a socialist system would work not only in a relatively backward and mainly agrarian country (as Russia was), but in an advanced and industrialized one (as Russia hoped to be). Politically, there was the need to assert Soviet independence against an allegedly hostile international environment (the 'capitalist encirclement'). Militarily, there was the recollection of the overwhelming superiority in material in World War I of the Central Powers on the Eastern front.

It was argued too that industrialization offered the key to further development not only of industry itself but of other sectors of the economy, such as transport and agriculture. True, one might conceive that Russia could continue to import most of her requirements in capital goods, and pay for these by agricultural exports. This would involve marketing problems, and the world slump in prices of food-stuffs in the 1930s would not have blessed such a course. Such a programme would also have perpetuated the dependence of Russia on the foreigner which it had been one of the aims of the Revolution to abolish.

There was the aim of underpinning the regime by multiplying the industrial proletariat. In theory, the State was a 'dictatorship of the proletariat'. In reality, there was a dictatorship of the Party, or rather of the top Party leadership. Yet the base of allegiance to the Party was indeed to be found in the town proletariat, which drew its wages from State industry. Certainly the government acted as if it represented their interests against those of the peasantry. The peasantry was regarded ambiguously by the leadership, particularly at this time when it made up the largest part of the private sector — while the better-off peasants were soon to be treated as enemies. To concentrate on developing agriculture would strengthen the private sector, whereas to concentrate on developing industry would strengthen the public sector. In the nineteen-twenties, the proletariat were still only one-fifth as numerous as the peasantry. In the long run, if the former did not grow to comprise a substantially larger proportion of the population, the 'dictatorship of the proletatiat' could perhaps not be maintained.

This motive was clearly expressed by Stalin, when addressing in April 1929 a plenum of the Central Committee of the Party:

> As you know, we are not needing *any* growth of the productivity of the national labour. We are needing a *certain* growth of the productivity of the national labour, namely – that growth which secures a *systematic outweighing of the socialist sector of the economy over the capitalist sector.*[1]

It is clear from this formulation, as well as from the way the intention was carried out, that the political aspect of the Five-Year Plan weighed heavily in the choice of the direction of development. The political significance of 'construction' continued to be emphasized.[2] Stalin used a very similar formulation to justify the type of industrialization, which was chosen in order to ensure that socialistic forms predominated over capitalistic ones.[3]

Finally, if one concentrated on agriculture this would give priority to a sector of the economy which was, and was expected to remain, technically backward. Russia's huge and varied raw material resources would then continue to be under-used, or would be exploited only with the aid of foreigners who would remit their profits out of the country. The diverse skills of the population would continue to be incompletely used.

The combination of these arguments seemed at that time to be overwhelmingly in favour of industrialization, and it would be difficult to argue now from hindsight that such arguments were erroneous, whatever errors and excesses were indeed committed during industrialization. As to which motives weighed heaviest with the leadership, there is room for discussion. As the regime placed first its internal and external strength, and as each of these demanded industrialization, the decision was bound to go in its favour. Had these motives led to opposite conclusions, we could be more sure how heavily they weighed in relation to each other.

The Left and Right wings of the Party differed as regards the pace of industrialization. Trotsky had taken up an extreme Left position, which favoured maximum speed combined with maximum violence towards the peasantry. The Right view was that industrialization should go at a more measured pace, taking 10 or 15 years to achieve what the extreme Left wing wanted to achieve in five. Their argument was that very rapid growth would impose a huge strain on the country, and expecially on the peasantry. With Trotsky out of the way, Stalin repulsed this view and the more ambitious course was adopted!

However, even after the Five-Year Plan came into operation the view continued to be urged that Russia should go more slowly. Stalin rebutted these views in a forceful speech, delivered on 4 February 1931. He went on to say:

> We have lagged fifty to a hundred years behind the leading countries. We must cover this distance in ten years. Either we do that, or they crush us.[4]

Just ten years later Nazi Germany attacked Russia, and one can hardly doubt that if there had been a slower build-up of industry, the attack would have been successful and world history would have evolved quite differently. Although this has to be remembered even if one cannot excuse Stalin's other mistakes and crimes, Stalin may not at this time have envisaged *Germany* as aggressor; nor did he name any particular capitalist country as a probable enemy, and in the event certain of them became Russia's allies. None the less, his words are in retrospect a striking prophecy.

With the benefit of hindsight it is easy in regard to this period to visualize logical sequences which were not, in fact, present. To give one example, the Five-Year Plan which is always dated from 1 October 1928 was not launched at the time: the contemporary press does not mention it. This date was fixed only in retrospect.

However, one may still ask why this particular date could be named. In general terms, the Plan could begin in 1928 because industrial restoration had by then been completed so that any further expansion would require larger volumes of capital investment; because domestic opponents had been crushed and foreign intervention repulsed; and because techniques of planning were thought to be adequately advanced, or at any rate some experience in composing plans had been gained. Furthermore, during NEP experience had been gained in acquiring new techniques from abroad, these having been introduced by foreign concessionary firms.[5] As a large part of the equipment required for investment in the new industries had to be imported, this experience was important.

Since its formation in 1921 the Gosplan had been developing more detailed and comprehensive plans. 'Control Figures', referring to the immediately following year, were issued annually between 1925/26 and 1929/30, Whereas the Control Figures for 1925/26 declined to formulate any general tasks and even denied that this was possible, those for 1926/27 formulated a directive of maximum development of productive resources with a strengthening of the position of socialism; industry was recognized as the leading link. However, it was envisaged that both governmental and private sectors would continue to exist. The Control Figures for 1927/28 required more concrete and exact accounts and a detailing of separate plans. New elements were included, mainly concerning social-cultural work. Many elements were grouped in republic or district divisions. The Control Figures for 1928/29, which appeared in 1929, reflected the decisions of the XVIth Party Congress concerning the Five-Year Plan. Those for 1929/30 reflected the operation and tasks of the Five-Year Plan.[6]

The Gosplan was instructed to prepare a long-term plan to last for five years. This was prepared in two versions, a less optimistic one and a more optimistic. The two variants projected the same general programme, but rested on different assumptions; the less optimistic would accomplish as much as the more optimistic, but would take about a year longer.[7] The Party adopted the more optimistic version, which was entitled the Five-Year Plan (*Pyatiletka*) or now in retrospect the *First* Five-Year Plan. A period of *five* years was chosen because average agricultural results could then be expected; because such a period should be long enough to complete all but very large projects; and because it was long enough for contemplation of real shifts in resources and substantial output increases.[8]

To secure the country's defence, and as a basis for developing other branches of industry and of agriculture (really, for the quintessence of the reasons that shaped the decision in favour of industrialization), heavy industry was to be developed as a first priority; although the outputs of light industry and of agriculture were also intended to increase. Agriculture was to supply manpower to the factories, exports to pay for imports of foreign machinery, and greatly enlarged quantities of foodstuffs to feed the bigger industrial labour force. Labour productivity both in industry and in agriculture was supposed to rise sharply. There was little reason to expect these latter hopes to be fulfilled.

The main effort was expected to be in the field of capital investment. The paramount need for capital investment was considered so obvious that there was no need to demonstrate it.[9] As foreign loans on a large scale were not expected – this is before the era of international economic aid – and in accordance with the doctrine of 'Socialism within one Country', Russia was to provide from its own resources the capital required for development. However, no world economic crisis was foreseen, and the optimal variant presupposed a broad development of links with the outside world.[10]

In the anticipated relations between industry and agriculture a deadlock was encountered. Industry could not be developed without an increased supply of food, while agriculture could not be developed without a growth of industrial production to supply it with agricultural machinery.

The gravamen of the issue involving agriculture and industrialization was, however, more deep-rooted. We noted that after the Revolution the interrelations between the two main sectors of the economy had become still closer. In this context, the vital issue was whether agriculture could be relied on to deliver, and would in fact deliver, sufficient foodstuffs to the towns to satisfy the needs of what would necessarily be an expanding urban population.

It is not intended here to enter into the controversy over a comparison by Stalin of prewar and 1926/27 grain marketings.[11] These were lower at the later date, perhaps 25 or 40 per cent lower, even if not the more than 50 per cent lower that Stalin claimed. The reduction pointed in any case to a conclusion that adequate supplies would almost certainly not be available. If that were so, dare the government give the go-ahead signal? In such a situation, it would indeed by very understandable if the government exaggerated the quantitative gap, in order that the case for action should appear more overwhelming. In any event: Stalin claimed that the reduction in size in individual peasant properties was the reason for the decline in marketed produce, and deduced that they would have to be combined into larger collective units.[12] As long as agriculture was fragmented, the goverment would not control the terms or the extent to which the peasants were willing to exchange their products for what the towns had to offer. Because of the anticipated concentration on heavy industry, the towns would have little to offer the peasants. But to implement its programme the Party needed, by one means or another, to be able to ensure food supplies for the towns, whether the peasants were willing to provide them or not. When, in Soviet economic history, a vicious circle is encountered, recourse is had to the government's power to alter the forms of economic organization. The means selected to ensure these supplies was collectivization, by which was meant:

(1) The dispossession and deportation into the interior of the better-off groups of the peasants or 'kulaks' ('elimination of the kulaks as a class');
(2) The merging of land and other means of production;
(3) The creation of a relatively small number of large farms in place of the huge number of peasant holdings.

The organizations which extracted 'procurements' of grain and other produce from the peasants had already been streamlined and simplified. Whereas, when NEP was introduced, the peasants had been granted the right to dispose of their own grain, this right was now (March 1928) abrogated. Measures were taken to isolate the richer peasants who had

made good during NEP. The overcoming through government action of
seasonal difference in prices (see above, Chapter 5) had helped the
poorer peasants against the better-off ones. Other measures of inducement and pressure were employed. Goods funds were shifted about like
armies. Kulaks were prosecuted and their grain confiscated. Illegal
searches and other applications of force took place. The method of
contracting (*kontraktatsiya*) began to be widely applied from 1928/29
onwards (peasants and government accepted varied mutual obligations
to supply produce, seeds, etc.). This also served to emphasize the crops
particularly required as industrial materials or for workers' supply. It
acted as a 'bridge' leading towards collectivization.

Collectivization had begun earlier, but so far had been voluntary.
In 1930 the decisive step was taken to make joining collective farms
compulsory. In January 1930 the goals of complete collectivization
within three years and of the 'liquidation of the kulaks as a class' were
announced.

Forced collectivization was announced at a time of special stress in
the implementation of the Five-Year Plan. This had begun well – the
growth of industrial output was accelerating – but per head consumption had declined and the atmosphere of struggle, both of government against the peasants and in particular their better-off strata, and
of combating obstacles to industrialization generally, was intense. The
government had certain incentives to induce collectivization at its
disposal, notably a certain number of tractors, to be released only for
the use of collective farms (*kolkhozy*) and State[13] farms (*sovkhozy*). It
had stirred up animosity against the better-off peasants which had the
most to lose by any agricultural upset. The Party's theory was: ally
with the poorer peasants; neutralize the middle peasants; and eliminate
the richer peasants. The administrative and propaganda machines were
now turned against these latter. There ensued an ugly process of Party-
engineered invasion of the households of those labelled as kulaks
(who themselves were not well-off by any Western standard); the
stripping them of their belongings; their deportation eastwards. This
was in mid-winter, when the Russian countryside is bitterly cold. The
actual timing may have been decided because this would be a slack
period for fieldwork, but surely the contribution that would be made
by the climate to the discomfiture of what was seen as the class enemy
was not disliked.

On March 1930 (three months after the beginning of forced collec-
tivizations), Stalin issued a statement entitled 'Dizzy from Success'.[14]
He said that there had been excessive haste and laid the blame on
cadres (trained Communists) who had exceeded their orders – a dis-
tasteful subterfuge. Forced collectivization was halted. Peasants who
wished were permitted to leave the collective farms, and very many did

so. From 1930, collective farm markets (where prices were allowed to find their natural level through supply and demand) were permitted to function.

The course of collectivization was therefore erratic.[15] A steep rise in the percentage of peasant households collectivized begins in the last quarter of 1929; then after Stalin's statement 'Dizzy from Success' there is a steep fall; then after a pause the upward movement is resumed, this being achieved by less terroristic methods, for instance by penal taxation of would-be independents. By July 1932 60 per cent of peasant households were collectivized.

The economic effects of forced collectivization were far-reaching. Most visible now in statistics (data were not published at the time) is a catastrophic decline in numbers of livestock and horses. Everywhere the peasants killed their stock. This was probably due to a combination of sabotage; of a belief that the collective farm would not pay fair prices for livestock; a wish not to be classed as a kulak; and a naive belief that the farm would provide whatever was needed. The scale of the decline is astonishing – it actually exceeded the livestock losses suffered during World War II. Between 1928 and 1933 the head of horses and pigs declined by more than half; of sheep and goats by almost two-thirds; of cattle by almost half. Official statistics state that the total agricultural output declined by 23 per cent between 1928 and 1932. (According to the Five-Year Plan, it should have increased.) The output of livestock products took about ten years to recover even to the 1928 level.

A recent Soviet interpretation of the damage wrought by forced collectivization in as follows:

> The reduction in the gross output of agriculture, and particularly of livestock rearing, was connected with crude mistakes and sharp turns in the carrying out of the collectivization of agriculture, which were evoked by Stalin's artificial forcing from above of the tempos of collectivization, which led to the replacement of organizational-explanatory work among the peasants by crude administerizing.[16] Infringements of the Leninist principle of voluntariness in collective-farm construction evoked discontent among the peasants, especially among the middle peasants.[17]

At the time, collectivization was hailed as a great victory.

When the effects of collectivization are contrasted with the arguments which have often been cited in favour of it, it becomes clear that its protagonists completely failed to envisage the totality of the effect which such an extreme and hasty measure would produce. The assumption seems to have been that a class war would be won, procurements would be increased and the peasantry now and forever would be compelled to deliver what it was told – and there would be an end of the matter.

If we try to assess whether collectivization was justifiable, we must distinguish between the speed of collectivization as it was actually carried out and the desirability of promoting either collectivization or some other reorganization of agriculture. The haste, lack of preparation, the harshness of the treatment of the kulaks or of individuals supposed to be associated with them, certainly caused great misery which was not compensated by any gain in productivity or efficiency. However, one could probably agree that it was desirable to make some radical change in the agricultural system. As long as agriculture swallowed up most of the labour force, and yet was so unproductive that the meagre surplus would hardly feed even the diminutive urban population, any sizeable improvement in the economic situation could not be expected. Successive pre-Revolutionary governments had been far from indifferent towards the need for reorganization. As for the Bolsheviks, they might have argued that they had allowed the peasants to seize the land – and now they themselves had seized it back. What they had allowed to be taken they could take back. They did not in fact argue this way, because their propaganda did not refer truthfully to what was happening.

It is seldom that the possible courses in economics are so narrowly restricted, or their eventual full consequences so perfectly known, that a particular course of action can be positively identified as the single unique solution to a difficulty. Where such a course cannot fail to overturn the established economic structure of the largest sector of the economy, whatever else it may or may not accomplish, it is at the very least necessary to examine with great care whatever imaginable alternatives may exist and what would probably be the final results of one course or another. In the Soviet approach to collectivization these elementary requirements were far from fulfilled. The government decision to go for all-out collectivization was taken hurriedly, with an almost frivolous and certainly criminal disregard for the possible consequences.[18] The reason was, of course, that the decision was intended to serve a political as well as economic purpose: to crush the peasant private sector and so complete the political consolidation of the regime.

In staging a massive reorganization of agriculture, the Bolsheviks were following in the footsteps of Tsar Alexander II and of Prime Minister Stolypin. But collectivization differed in two fundamental respects from these earlier reforms. Whereas these were undertaken primarily for the sake of their beneficial effects on agriculture itself, collectivization in so far as it had an economic objective was undertaken for the sake of non-agricultural sectors – for the contribution which it was expected to make to industrial development. And whereas these earlier reforms rowed with the stream by creating more scope for individual initiative, by creating conditions in which the more ambitious and efficient could get ahead, collectivization, because it involved the uprooting and destruction of precisely the more successful farmers, had at least in its early stages a directly opposite and deleterious effect.

On many occasions then and subsequently collectivization has been presented – and less understandably and excusably, understood by many Western students – as if it were synonymous with mechanization. However, the equipping of farms with machinery proceeded much more slowly, and in principle the two processes are quite distinct.

Collectivization had profound effects other than the directly agricultural ones. One to which collectivization appears to have largely contributed was that urban unemployment disappeared.[19] During NEP, unemployed registered at labour exchanges (which latter were mainly in urban areas) were quite numerous (about 1½ million), and their numbers were not showing any tendency to decline. From about April 1929 the number of registered unemployed began to fall away sharply, and on 9 October 1930 the People's Commissar of Labour announced that unemployment had disappeared and that payment of unemployment relief was to cease forthwith. Soviet statistical handbooks report that unemployment disappeared in the forth quarter of 1930, and from that day onwards there has officially been no unemployment in the U.S.S.R.

The most commonly advanced explanation of this alleged disappearance (which, it is generally accepted, was not fictitious) is that the demand for labour expanded during industrialization. Certainly this was *one* important cause. However, probably a larger role was played by collectivization, as farmers who were working only temporarily in towns now returned to establish their status as members of the collective farm, to stake their claim to property looted from the kulaks, or to protect their families and secure their interests in a time of upheaval. Moreover, the farms themselves, since they were required to extend to dependents of collective farmers who were away working the same or better rights as those who remained behind, had an incentive to require working members of households to stay and work on the farm. Collective farms consequently discouraged their working members from going away to work. Acting in this way, the farms reassumed powers which the forerunner of the collective farm, the mir – itself now superseded – had possessed. At the same time, collectivization prevented any escape *back* to the land by the industrial worker.[20] It thus hindered labour mobility between agriculture and industry in

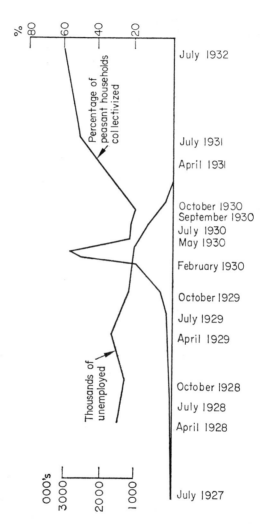

DIAGRAM II

Collectivization and the Decline of Unemployment

% 80 60 40 20

Percentage of
peasant households
collectivized

Thousands of
unemployed

000's 3000 2000 1000

July 1932

July 1931
April 1931

October 1930
September 1930
July 1930
May 1930

February 1930

October 1929

July 1929

April 1929

October 1928

July 1928

April 1928

July 1927

either direction.

Another consequence of collectivization was a large expansion of forced labour. Dispossession of probably about 1 million kulak families may have resulted in the deportation of some 5 million people (the average peasant family had about five members) to various forms of exile, in part to forced labour camps. This movement doubtless gave a fillip to the development of sectors where forced labour could be most usefully employed (such as mining, and construction especially involving earth-moving), and to development in the Far North and the Far East. Some at least of these schemes were flagrantly uneconomic, but owing to lack of data no complete history of forced labour can be written at this time.

No official mortality figures due to forced collectivization are available, but a Soviet demographer recently admitted that: 'at the start of the 1930s the radical breaking of the age-old order of peasant economy could not fail to react on demographic processes'.[21] This means that more people than usual died while fewer than usual were born. The census results of 1939 revealed a deficiency of about 10 million persons, a loss which is partly attributable to forced collectivization.

Because of the halving in the number of horses – the main motive power in agriculture – industrial plans had to be hastily revised to enable the production of more tractors,[22] while other changes had to be made in the direction of producing the equipment of larger dimensions required by collective farms rather than the smaller tools previously bought by small cultivators.[23] Stalin reported that other diversions had to be made to build up armaments to counter an external threat from Japan. Large numbers of workers were taken on in the factories, while average labour productivity dropped.

As the wage bill mounted, especially in heavy industry, retail prices rose. According to Malafeyev, all trade prices indices rose as follows: 1927/28, 100·0; 1928/29, 106·6; 1930, 132·0; 1931, 179·7; 1932 (first half), 251·8.[24] There were sharp rises in retail prices on 27 January 1932.[25] Prices of foodstuffs on the free market rose even more steeply – for the most important items, to 12–15 times the level of the fixed market price.[26] Rationing in towns was introduced (1929–34), a maximum of about 50 million people – nearly one-third of the population – being included in the bread-rationing scheme. Real wages declined, as expressed in index-numbers, from 100 in 1928 to 88·6 in 1932.[27] Owing to the derangement of agriculture in 1931 and 1932 the harvests in those years were bad, while in addition the grain collections were exorbitant; the consequence was famine conditions in some southern areas in the winter and spring of 1932–33 which doubtless contributed to the retardation of population growth. An area of the

Ukraine and North Caucasus was placed under a form of martial law.[28] Food shortages were further accentuated by increased exports, to pay for increased imports of industrial equipment necessitated by the investment programme.

While these damaging consequences were in preparation, during the first two full years of the Five-Year Plan, 1929 and 1930, industrial expansion had been accelerating. (See Diagram III.) This went to the heads of the Soviet leaders and they stepped up the targets. The statistics were constantly being revised upwards. Naum Jasny has called this the period of 'Bacchanalian planning'.[29] But the revised targets were not reached, and in 1932–33 owing to various reasons, including the famine, the momentum of growth fell off: gross industrial output rose by 22 per cent in 1930 but by only 5 per cent in 1933.

The Five-Year Plan was terminated prematurely at the end of 1932 — after only 4¼ years. It was claimed to have been fulfilled, as regards 'all industry', by 93·7 per cent.[30] In spite of this apparently rather satisfactory outcome the general results were quite out of balance. Consumption per head had been supposed to increase, but actually declined sharply. On the other hand, heavy industry had in certain respects, especially engineeering, developed faster than the Plan had expected. And this has turned out to be the usual pattern of Soviet plan results: heavy industry has received priority over the production of consumer goods. One's suspicions that plans are not by any means the only forces that govern the development of the Soviet economy are reinforced, and we shall revert to this problem.

The industrial results of the Plan were mixed. Coal, oil and iron and steel did not rise to the output levels planned for them. On the other hand, the outputs of machinery and of electrical equipment surpassed the Plan targets. According to official statistics, industrial gross output increased from 132 in 1928 to 267 in 1932 (1913=100), and thus approximately doubled. However, there are good grounds for supposing that the true increase in total industrial output is exaggerated. The probable sources of exaggeration are analysed in Part V, but we may note that local handicraft industry, which had been very important as late as the beginning of the century, went into a steep decline which in part offset the rise of large-scale industry.

During the Plan period six-sevenths of total investments in industry went into heavy industry. The orientation of investments was austere, the biggest share going into branches which would yield no immediate benefit. Producer goods were emphasized above all: for example, out of 24,065 motor vehicles produced in 1932, 23,845 were lorries.[31] Certain quite new industries were set up (such as tractors and synthetic rubber), and a 'metallurgical base' was established in Magnitogorsk in the Urals. In general, a foundation of heavy industry was laid which did prove to be indispensable later, in circumstances which were foreseen more accurately than is normal in international relations. However, this was secured at very heavy cost to many other areas of the economy, in disruption of social and economic patterns, of a slowdown in population growth, and generally in human hardship and suffering. This is a classic case of industrialization at artificially pricked-on tempos, under orders from the State. The problems of industrialization, involving the construction of enterprises in untrodden regions, recruitment of new and untrained workers on a massive scale, the supposed necessity to synchronize industrial and agricultural reorganizations, were more acute at this time than ever before or since.

Other organizational changes affected labour, trade and finance, while simultaneously there was an upsurge in foreign trade. All this contributed to organizational tenseness: the period was hard on the nerves, which perhaps helps to account for some aberrations in behaviour displayed later on, during the period of the purges. It was also an epoch which demanded − and evoked − heroic deeds and great sacrifices. In Soviet experience it is a unique period, and it cannot be paralleled in the experience of any other country. None have adopted the Soviet choice of priorites in economic development; Soviet circumstances were exceptional, but in view of the Soviet experience, none rationally will adopt it.

One should avoid concluding that growth rates rose during the Plan. Actually, they fell (see Diagram III). Although the industrial growth rate speeded up in 1929 and 1930, this was from a low starting-point. In percentage terms the NEP period recorded more impressive progress than the Five-Year Plan, but it had the easier and less complex task. One must also make the following qualification as regards the effort required by industry during those years, that many hands tended to make lighter work. The working day had been *reduced* in 1927 to seven hours, and was not increased again, and then only to eight hours, until June 1940. The 'shift coefficient' (the average number of shifts worked per 24-hour spell) in industry generally rose from 1·2 in 1927 to 1·6 in 1931.[32]

Throughout the NEP total imports of producer goods had been on a lower level than in 1910−13.[33] An important contribution to implementation of the Plan was made by imports of machinery and equipment.[34]

The Plan was accompanied by changes in industrial organization. In 1929 (by a decree of 5 December) more emphasis was put on the plant or enterprise, as distinct from the trust, as the basic unit of industrial administration. In 1930 the Supreme Economic Council (VSNKh) was reorganized. In 1932 it was dissolved. Its place was taken by three 'people's commissariats' of heavy industry, light industry and timber industry. From then on the number of people's commissariats grew. As a rule, each one was made responsible for a particular 'branch' of industry; there was no single formula for defining 'branch', but type of final product was the normal criterion. As long as VSNKh survived the Gosplan could concentrate on long-term planning. It had now in addition to hold the balance between newly created branches of industry, each of which was competing for available supplies and for more than its fair share of investment funds. (This aspect is considered in more detail in Part IV.) The Gosplan was expanded, and began to resort to a method of priorities. A system of materials allocation grew up. From 1927/28 onwards categories of consumers were gradually exempted from the common pool of the mass market, and goods funds were allocated to these categories. By 1933 the 'mass market' had shrunk to a single clause in a heterogeneous assembly on the same footing as the GULAG (Chief Administration of Camps – a forced labour organization – 21 May 1933), and the OGPU (secret police).[35] Allocation was necessitated by the shortage of materials. In engineering, for example, three main production sectors received priority supplies: equipment for ferrous metallurgy, for rail transport, and the established programme of mass consumption goods; some other branches such as agricultural machinery received supplies matching their programmes, while other branches shared what was left.[36]

In contrast, with earlier practice, the Five-Year Plan proposed building specialized factories which were to 'co-operate' with each other: for instance in engineering, automobiles, electrical equipment. One of the features of the period was the beginning of construction of large combined projects, which would involve the co-operation of major industrial branches. The Urals-Kuznetsk combine (the building of coalmines in the Kuznetsk basin and metallurgical works in the Urals) is the best example of this kind of combination, whose characteristics included: very large size signifying a more complete utilization of raw materials, the linking together of a number of productive stages, and the fact that such a combination might transform the whole life of a region, attract new industries.[37] However, extreme specialization in manufacturing proved to be difficult to attain. Never popular with industrial executives, who had actually to procure the supplies which the planners could assume would be available yet could not assure, the policy of specialization and co-operation found it hard to make headway against the long-standing tradition of maximizing self-sufficiency. In metallurgy, for instance, 1932 was the watershed: experience showed that factories which had not aimed in self-sufficiency paid for it with lower construction tempos,[38] and industrialists drew the conclusion which economists were reluctant to admit, until it was underlined by wartime experience.[39]

Many factories were built on a larger scale than the original plans had allowed for. Construction was sometimes begun in advance of detailed plans, as this helped to ensure that funds would be released. Many existing factories were greatly enlarged. The attempt to do everything at once could not succeed, and a substantial backlog of unfinished building,[40] and of other unfinished business, was left.

It is interesting to turn back to what Professor N. D. Kondrat'ev, an internationally-known economist, wrote about one version of the Plan in 1927. His main conclusions were that it suffered from too great attention to statistics, and too little to the methods of compostion; but considered in the light of its internal interrelations, there was a lack of correspondence between certain indices; it was especially serious that the rate of growth of agriculture and of other branches was too slow, which was due to an incorrect appraisal of the position of agriculture; the Plan would consequently not achieve its aims of deveopment without crisis, or the satisfaction of mass needs, and would lead to the growth of economic difficulties; its fundamental fault was that it attempted to pursue too many aims without realizing that in their extreme form they would come into collision with each other.[41] Even after fifty years and with all the advantage of hindsight it would be difficult to improve on these comments.

In 1932 the output of a number of producer goods was in the region of 50 per cent to 100 per cent larger than in 1913. For instance, the output of steel was 40 per cent larger, of coal 121 per cent larger. Items whose growth had been emphasized had, of course, expanded much more: thus the output of metal-cutting machine tools was 13 times larger, and of electric power 7 times. The output of textiles was about on the 1913 level, but of other consumer goods produced by large-scale industry was slightly higher.

Notes

1 I. Stalin, *Voprosy leninizma*, Eleventh Edition (1945), p. 253. The italicized words are in heavy print in the original. The point is further rammed home in the immediately following sentences.

2 E.g. by Molotov, in December 1935 (A. Zverev, *Gosudarstvennyye byudzhety soyuza SSSR 1938–1945 gg.* (1946), p. 16).

3 E. Lokshin, *Tyazhelaya industriya v 3 godu pyatiletki* (1932), pp. 16–17.

4 I. Stalin, op. cit., p. 329.

5 The evidence for such transfers is examined for the first time in detail in Antony Sutton, *Western Technology and Soviet Economic Development, 1917–30* (1968). See also Ch. 18 below.

6 Z. Mindlin, *Planovoye khozyaystvo*, nos. 11–12, 1930, pp. 192–8.

7 *Pyatiletnyy plan narodno-khozyaystvennogo stroitel'stva SSSR,* tom I, *Svodnyy obzor* (1929), pp. 11–12.

8 As the chairman of the State Economic Commission for Long-Term Planning (a successor to Gosplan) later pointed out, five years is 'that average period, which at the present level of development of science and technique is needed to build and put in operation powerful industrial undertakings, hydro-electric power stations, canals, railways, and other objects which demand large-scale capital investments' (N. Baybakov, *Kommunist,* no. 6, 1956). Cf. G. M. Krzhizhanovskiy, *Planovoye khozyaystvo,* no. 3, 1927, p. 7.

9 *Fabrichno-zavodskaya promyshlennost' SSSR, vypusk 5* (1929), p. 7.

10 Reference as footnote 7 (this chapter), p. 11.

11 See R. W. Davies, 'A Note on Grain Statistics', *Soviet Studies,* January 1970.

12 S. N. Prokopovicz, *Histoire économique de l' URSS* (1952), pp. 140–1.

13 State farms were analogous to State factories.

14 I. Stalin, op. cit., pp. 299–304.

15 See Diagram II.

16 A euphemism meaning the indiscriminate issuing of orders.

17 A. N. Malafeyev, op. cit., p. 126.

18 All this is thoroughly investigated by M. Lewin, *Russian Peasants and Soviet Power* (1968). See also J. Miller, *Anglo-Soviet Journal,* September 1969, p. 37.

19 See in this connection my 'The Ending of Unemployment in the USSR', *Soviet Studies,* July 1967 (vol. XIX, no. 1), and Diagram II above.

20 M. Dewar, *Soviet Studies,* October 1957 (vol. IX, no. 2), p. 179.

21 B. Ts. Urlanis, *Rozhdayemost' i prodol'zhitel'nost zhizni v SSSR* (1963), p. 131.

22 Horses eat substantial amounts of grain (cf. G. Blainey, op. cit., pp. 122–3), so their destruction was not an unmixed disaster. A reduction in the head of horses normally occurs as a side effect of agricultural mechanization, but not so precipitately as occurred in Russia.

23 N. S. Burmistrov, *Ocherki tekhniko-ekonomicheskogo planirovaniya promyshlennosti* (1936), p. 8.

24 Op. cit., p. 163.

25 Ibid., p. 166.

26 Sh. Ya. Turetskiy, *Sebestoimost' i voprosy tsenoobrazovaniya* (1940), p. 198.

27 A. N. Malafeyev, op. cit., p. 174.

28 See Dana G. Dalryimple, *Soviet Studies,* January 1964 (vol. XV, no. 3) and April 1965 (vol. XVI, no. 4), and L. E. Hubbard, *Soviet Trade and Distribution* (1938), p. 162.

29 Naum Jasny, *Soviet Industrialization 1928–1952* (1961), pp. 73–80.

30 A. Baykov, *The Development of the Soviet Economic System* (1946), p. 165 (quoting the official report).
31 K. A. Petrosyan, *Sovetskiy metod industrializatsii* (1951), p. 72.
32 A. S. Vaynshteyn (ed.), *Voprosy sebestoimosti promyshlennoy produktsii* (1935), p. 145.
33 A. Baykov, *Soviet Foreign Trade* (1946), p. 46.
34 See below, Chapter 17.
35 See also below, Part III.
36 N. S. Burmistrov, op. cit., p. 14.
37 I. Blyumin, E. L. Granovskiy, G. M. Krzhizhanovskiy, M. I. Rubinshteyn, B. M. Tal' (eds.), *Tekhnicheskaya rekonstruktsiya narodnogo khozyaystva SSSR v pervoy pyatiletke* (1934), pp. 302–6.
38 V. Il'in, *Planovoye khozyaystvo*, no. 4, 1933, p. 103.
39 Cf. Sh. Ya. Turetskiy, *Vnutripromyshlennoye nakopleniye v SSSR* (1948), p. 110.
40 During the Plan unfinished construction increased faster than capital investments, with the largest percentage increase in construction (52·5) occurring in the final year of the Plan. (A. Notkin and N. Tsagolov, *Planovoye khozyaystvo*, no. 10, 1935, p. 111.)
41 N. D. Kondrat'ev, *Planovoye khozyaystvo*, no. 4, 1927, pp. 32–3. The subject of Kondrat'ev's critical article was primarily an article by S. G. Strumilin, and subsidiarily more specialized articles which were in approximate conformity with Strumilin's all of which had appeared in the preceding issue of *Planovoye khozyaystvo*. A volume of materials on the perspectives of the economy over a five-year period, edited by Strumilin, was published after Kondrat'ev's article was received for publication but before the latter was itself published.

7
PROGRESS AND CATASTROPHE: 1933–45

In 1933 an economic plan was drawn up for the first time for all industry, as distinct from only large-scale industry.[1] A Second Five-Year Plan was supposed to have begun in 1933, immediately after the First Five-Year Plan ended, but it was not confirmed until the following year, 1934. It ran until the end of 1937, i.e. for a full five years, if one dates its commencement from 1933. From an organizational viewpoint this was a less frenzied period than the previous Plan; however, year-to-year growth rates in industrial production were no less variable. As described by Naum Jasny, the period included 'three good years' (1934, 1935 and 1936), when industrial output increased markedly[2] (see Diagram III). In general, substantial progress was made. Rationing was ended in 1935. Agricultural output varied according to weather vicissitudes, 1937 being a good year. During this period, until 1939, foreign trade was declining.

The year 1935 is noteworthy for the birth of Stakhanovism. Alexey Stakhanov, a miner from the Donbass coal basin, achieved a striking increase in output through rationalizing his work process. His example was followed by pioneers in other industries who likewise achieved notable feats. The Party loved Alexey not only because his feat promised important rises in output without capital investment on a matching scale, but because it blew skyhigh a hangover from the days when there was any genuine workers' power in the factories — the trade unions had been bent to the Party's will in 1929–30, when their leader Tomsky had been overthrown — that there was some fixed norm which was all that a worker could be expected to perform.[3] Thereafter the authorities became preoccupied with turning Stakhanovism into a mass movement, and compulsion came much more to the fore.[4] The movement was followed by increases in workers' norms — the stipulated quantities of output per worker on which wages depended. These were raised by 15 per cent to 50 per cent, and there were inevitably some instances when wages were consequently reduced.[5] On the whole, however, this was a progressive development.

The Second Plan, like the First, had to bend in the direction of rearmament: the growth of heavy industry was speeded up at the expense of light industry.[6]
A Third Five-Year Plan, to cover the span 1938–42, was launched in 1938. In that year, as in 1933, it proved to be necessary to concentrate on completing works already in hand.[7] This Plan was interrupted by the war, and was never finished.

While it was extant, which was for 70 per cent of its allocated span (January 1938–June 1941), the economy's growth rate was rather low and this was due apparently to three circumstances: rearmament, the spy and sabotage trials and extensive 'purges' which are features of the period, and the war against Finland: especially the first two. Rearmament, which was now acquiring substantial proportions, impinged on the output of heavy capital goods, notably for transport purposes: more tanks were turned out instead of locomotives, and more naval craft instead of river vessels. The armed forces were built up, and in general attention was diverted towards strengthening the country's defences.[8] Largely due to rearmament, expenditure on the economy as a percentage of total budgetary expenditure declined from 70·6 in 1934 to 38·0 in 1938.[9]

There are curious features in the economic history of these years, such as that the output of ferrous metallurgy (pig iron, steel and rolled metal) was slightly smaller in 1939 than in 1938, which must have reacted unfavourably on the output of armaments *inter alia*. The decline is officially ascribed to 'inadequate business-technical direction and a weak organization of labour, and also an incomplete utilization of equipment',[10] but these allusions do not go to the heart of the matter, Management does not become worse for no reason. Another curious feature is that the number of production personnel in industry increased only very slowly in 1938 and 1939.[11]

Presumably the purges were responsible for these aberrations. Accusations of wrecking reached incredible crescendos in 1937–38. Charges were laid against foreign spies and diversionaries as well as against domestic traitors. Some of these accusations were sensational. Other alleged plots sound grotesquely humdrum to our ears.

> Experience has shown that one of the forms of wrecking by Japanese-German spies and diversionaries, who have penetrated into the food industry, was a reduction in the scale and a worsening of the quality of repairs.[12]

As an illustration of the wholesale nature of the purges, between 1938 and 1941 almost all the staff of Gosplan were replaced.[13] Besides industry and planning, transport too was affected.

One must also take into account the pernicious consequences of the unfounded mass repressions in relation to the staffs of railways and technical personnel. As was remarked at the XXIInd Congress of the KPSS, Kaganovich, making use of the 'theory of counter-revolutionary respect for outmoded norms' (*predel' chestva*) which he had thought up himself, organized a 'mass extermination of engineering and technical cadres'. Transport was deprived of many qualified specialists, their proposals to reinforce work in the technical reconstruction of transport were assessed as intending sabotage, attention to problems of reconstruction of the technical resources of transport was sharply weakened. This 'put a brake on the technical development of rail transport'.[14] Similar situation was observed also in water transport.[15]

As a result of the purges there appears to have been in 1938 an important shortage of business leaders for occupying commanding positions in the economy.[16] Doubtless, too, initiative was stifled by the fear of arrest if anything should go wrong. There ensued measures of a Draconian character to strengthen labour discipline. On the initiative, allegedly, of the All-Union Council of Trade Unions the working day was extended from 7 to 8 hours.[17] These measures will be described in detail in Part II.

In 1940, according to the latest available data, growth as measured by industrial output came almost to a halt.[18] This must be ascribed to the combined effects of the Finnish war and of rearmament.[19]

More people's commissariats were formed, and in 1937 also a co-ordinating body, the Economic Council (*Ekonomsovet*) which had authority also over Gosplan. The dissolution of the Economic Council has never been announced but it appears to have remained in existence until 1941. In April 1940 interdepartmental boards were set up, one for each of the six groups of commissariats.[20] During the 1930s the central economic superstructure ramified remarkably, the most complex branching-out taking place in 1939. The wartime period was not marked by comparably large changes in the nomenclature of commissariats although obviously the scope of their work did alter.

Between 1933 and 1940 collectivization became almost complete. The harvests of 1933, 1934 and 1935 were on the whole good, which contributed to favourable industrial results in the immediately following years through a raw-material linkage. Pressure to collectivize was kept up, and by 1 July 1935 nearly 83 per cent of all peasants had joined the collective farms. A year later the proportion was just under 90 per cent, and by 1940 it reached 96·9 per cent by numbers of householders, and 99·9 per cent by sown area. Evidently the percentage collectivized could hardly go higher, and instead it temporarily declined not owing to any change in policy but because the U.S.S.R., as presaged by the Non-Aggression Treaty signed with Germany in August 1939, now annexed new territories where farming was not collectivized. Within two years after their incorporation into the USSR these territories were invaded by the Nazis, and reorganization there of agriculture did not get properly under way until after World War II. The number of collective farms reached a peak in the whole country in 1935 (245,400). Thus, whereas at the outset of collectivization there were some 25·8 million peasant households, the number of basic units of agriculture with which the government had to deal had now been divided by a factor of 100. A quarter of a million was apparently thought to comprise a manageable number (this was recently also approximately the number of enterprises in Soviet *industry*) from the point of view of controlling the flow of grain from the countryside to the towns. Alternatively, it may be very tentatively suggested that this total was arrived at as it exchanged mir for collective farm approximately on a one-for-one basis: the number of mirs in all pre-Revolutionary Russia was 240,000,[21] which perhaps was not coincidental.[22] Thereafter (particularly since 1951) the number of collectives has been tending to decline[23] and their average size to be enlarged.

Despite privations and repressions, the population grew. The census of 1926 had recorded 147 millions, that of 1939 170·6 millions within the same borders. (The government was unpleasantly surprised by the slowness of the increase, about which more in Part V.) The annexation in 1939–40 of parts of Poland, Romania and Finland, and the whole of Estonia, Latvia and Lithuania, added about 22 millions, and it is estimated – though with a fair margin of error – that the population included within these widened frontiers rose to about 197 millions by June 1941.

The number of workers and employees in the 'national economy' (the whole State sector of the economy, including industry, transport and communications, construction, teaching, science, State administration, State Farms and Machine Tractor Stations[24]) rose from 10·8 millions in 1928 to 31·2 millions in 1940, i.e. it almost trebled. In industry alone the increase was from 3·8 millions to 11 millions. The proportionate increase in the industrial labour force was consequently no larger than in the state labour force generally. Industry *was* now contributing a larger share of the national income, owing to a bigger rise in labour productivity in industry than in other sectors.

The years 1939 to June 1941 are overshadowed both by the preceding Plans and by the war into which Russia was soon to be plunged. There is, however, a certain unity about this interim period. We can distinguish six respects in which it differed markedly from its predecessor:

(a) These were years when rearmament became substantial and a considerable hindrance to economic growth.

(b) This was a period of stocktaking, recruitment, dismissal, punishing and disciplining of the labour force. A census was taken; recruitment was rationalized; all supposedly unreliable executives lost their jobs, and worse; hours of work were lengthened.

(c) The ramification of industrial structure went much further, and control was centralized under the Economic Council.

(d) Location policy was altered, in the direction of considerably weakening the stimulus to industrialization of the remoter areas. (More about this in Part IV.)

(e) Foreign trade, predominantly with Germany, rose sharply.

(f) By annexing the Baltic States and parts of Poland, Finland, and Romania the Soviet Union acquired extra acres and citizens.

All this can perhaps be simply summed up. During the Second Five-Year Plan Russia had relied increasingly on her own resources: in economic development, technical improvement, managerial skill, in the potentialities of the Urals and Siberia. But now it must have seemed that her resources were too scattered; her managers too often incompetent or politically unreliable; her workers putting in too few hours; her technique still not matching that of Western Europe; the growth of her population falling behind expectations; her armed forces too ill-equipped; her rate of economic growth inadequate. Moreover, the Western world no longer presented such a wretched economic spectacle as it had done in 1929–32. In this predicament Russia shifted her attention towards Europe, and beyond her own frontiers. She looked abroad for assistance. For historical reasons, augmented by political miscalculations, she began an uneasy collaboration with the country which had long proclaimed itself the chief enemy of Bolshevism, but which now for the sake of securing the immediate objective of the destruction of Poland, swallowed its proclaimed intentions in regard to Russia, for the time being — with Nazi Germany. But now that time was running out.

Without warning, on 22 June 1941 the USSR was invaded by Germany and her allies. The invading forces relatively quickly occupied a huge area of European Russia: penetrating at length to Stalingrad (now Volgograd) which was over 1,100 km. east of the frontier. The occupied area had been inhabited by 45 per cent of the Soviet population, contained 47 per cent of its sown area, and produced 33 per cent of its industrial output. The existing economic plans had of course to be scrapped. The economy had to be placed at once on a war footing. It proved to be equal to the test.

There are only scanty statistics of national income or of total industrial or agricultural output for 1941–42. The Plan for 1941, the restricted version of which is available, shows output and other economic objectives for that year; this will be referred to in Part III in connection with planning techniques. We do not, however, know to what extent this Plan was fulfilled, but it must have suffered a heavy blow. The Gross National Product declined between 1940 and 1942; taking into account mobilization, war damage and occupation of territory, the decline must have been substantial. The national income declined by 34 per cent. Industrial output declined by 23 per cent in 1942 as compared with 1940.[25] After 1942 all indices registered some recovery.

Proportionate expenditures on investment and consumption naturally fell, by comparison with before the war, while military expenditures climbed, both proportionately and in absolute terms: according to Voznesenskiy military expenditures exclusive of the individual consumption of armed forces personnel increased from 4 per cent of the G.N.P. in 1940 to 17 per cent in 1942. The extent of industrial mobilization is shown by the fact that output for military purposes increased from 26 per cent of the total in 1940 to 68 per cent in 1942.[26] The capital stock of the economy was reduced in the second half of 1941, remained stable in 1942, and increased from 1943 onwards. The financial system was under strain, and deficit financing had to be resorted to in 1942 and 1943. A relatively large number of new big industrial undertakings were brought into operation during the war.[27] Costs of industrial production were reduced.[28] Rationing was strictly enforced. Prices of the more important rationed goods were fixed and remained stable, only prices of alcohol, tobacco and a limited circle of other items being raised;[29] however, the quantity and variety of goods on sale became more exiguous. Collective farm market prices were free to move, and actually rose 12–13 fold between 1940 and 1943;[30] but the market's share in total turnover was very small.

The Soviet Union suffered in the war great privations and enormous casualties and material losses. Until 1956 the human losses were not fully realized in the West; the Russians did not release complete figures of casualties, and for years afterwards did not allow visitors into the occupied areas. (This is, of course, understandable if they feared that the Western powers might take advantage of Soviet weakness if they realized the magnitude of the human loss). Apparently, the population was some 17 millions smaller in 1948 than in 1940. As, but for the war, the population ought to have increased during the period, the deficiency was considerably larger than this. Evidently Soviet human losses as a result of war, including notional losses due to the lowered birth-rate, were fantastically large.[31]

Voznesenskiy distinguished four kinds of material losses. These were: direct losses of property; direct war expenditures and other associated expenditures; losses of output and national income in the occupied areas; and decline in the national income during and after the war owing to the premature death of part of the population. This last is not normally accepted as a war loss, although certainly in a sense it is. It is not quantifiable, because the effect would extend into the indefinite future, nor of course is such a loss peculiar to the Soviet Union. Only a country which supposes its future growth to be entirely under its own control would dare to make such a calculation.

Direct material losses amounted, according to Voznesenskiy, to 679 milliard roubles or 128 milliard US dollars (prewar prices): this was stated to amount to two-thirds of the national property in the occupied areas. Total losses, including war expenditures and the decline in national income during the war, were stated to amount to 1,890 milliard roubles (357 milliard US dollars).[32] However, these totals are challenged by G. Warren Nutter who argues convincingly that *absolute* losses cannot have been anything like so large. A decline in national income due to the war is, of course, a hypothetical figure as what this would have been in other circumstances is unknowable. The destruction is more credible in proportionate terms: as much as a quarter of 'reproducible tangible' assets may have been destroyed.[33]

Statistics of the number of units physically damaged are probably more accurate than their valuation. Here is one simple check on the internal consistency of published sources. According to Voznesenskiy, 1,209,000 houses were destroyed or ruined. The occupied areas were inhabited by about 89 million people. In the city of Kursk, the population of which in 1941 should have been about 125,000, 440 houses were completely destroyed and 1,515 partially.[34] Kursk thus contained about 0·14 per cent of the population of the occupied areas, while the number of its houses destroyed or damaged was 0·16 per cent of the total. The proportions are very close, which tends to confirm the national total as the experience of Kursk was fairly typical: the city was occupied for just over 15 months and was more than once a battle-ground. However, one would like to continue the verification by checking personally on the city total.

In practice, the phrase 'completely or partially destroyed or looted' would cover such a wide range of situations as to become a scarcely meaningful description. Very large areas were involved: destruction could not have been complete and such cities as Kiev and Odessa retained many of their prewar buildings, although the port of Odessa was smashed. Ancient towns such a Novgorod still proudly exhibit their ancient monuments, although much rehabilitation of them has been carried out. Leningrad suffered appalling casualties among the civilian population, especially from starvation and cold; the city itself was seriously damaged, but never came under short-range artillery or mortar fire. Stalingrad, which is a thin ribbon stretching for dozens of miles along the west bank of the Volga, was sacrificed. Rural areas suffered relatively less than urban ones.

The capital stock of any country is equivalent to its national income over only a few years. The recuperative power of an economy is governed by the skills and powers of organization of its citizens much more than by its capital stock, much of which at any one time is obsolescent: as one sees clearly after the German 'miracle'. There may well be a correlation between the amount of wartime destruction and the present level of modernity, for example the French railways and the city of Cologne would score highly on both counts.

These qualifications apart, one can of course agree that the Soviet Union suffered very severely from the war, both in human and in material terms. (The extremely high human loss might lend plausibility to an estimate of very large material damage, but there would be no easily reckonable relationship between the two quantities.) It is common ground that part of the huge material loss was subsequently replenished by reparations, and that the USSR had received aid under Lend-Lease. Soviet and Western sources disagree sharply as regards the importance of Lend-Lease to the Soviet war effort; no prize is given for guessing which side minimizes its importance. As a proportion of the total war material manufactured in the USSR, the quantities were relatively small. Of course, the military importance of Lend-Lease may not have been precisely equivalent to its proportionate value. Soviet fighting potential may have been enlarged proportionately more.

The losses suffered by Russia during World War II were comparable with those she suffered during World War I and its aftermath. Her total human losses during the more recent ordeal were about 50 per cent larger but in proportion to the size of the population were not very different, although they were incurred within a slightly shorter period. The economy suffered more destruction than in 1914–21, but less disruption since the fighting fronts, although stretching on an immense arc through the populated heart of the country, were confined to the western and southern parts of European Russia. Because the disruption was less, the overall proportionate setback to the economy was less serious than in 1914–21. These results are generally in line with the propositions formulated earlier concerning the impact of war on an economy. Russia was, of course, not blockaded by the Western powers immediately after the war, although there was an unfortunate echo in the precipitate cessation of Lend-Lease deliveries.

The level of output in 1945, consisting as it did very largely of war equipment and munitions, would be difficult to compare directly with output in more normal years, when the military component would not have bulked so large. The comparison is consequently not very meaningful, but industrial output in 1945 is officially stated to have been 8 per cent below 1940; while in previously occupied regions it was 70 per cent below 1940. In 1946, as military output was curtailed, total output declined to 23 per cent below 1940.[35] Thereafter, it increased.

Agricultural output in 1945 was 40 per cent below the 1940 level; in this case there was less of a problem of reshuffling production assortments, but a severe drought in 1946, whose effects were aggravated by labour shortage and disorganization, delayed recovery. (By comparison with 1940 there were, however, fewer mouths to feed.) In contrast to the aftermath of World War I, when industrial output declined more than agricultural, World War II was followed by a proportionately larger decline in agricultural output. Over-population on the land had been very largely absorbed before and during the war, when women came to comprise almost three-quarters of all collective farmers, and no fragmentation of holdings occurred this time, while mechanization of some agricultural operations made agriculture more vulnerable to industrial disturbance.

The goods turnover of transport, which reflected the agonies of the economy, was nearly a quarter lower in 1945 than in 1940.

At the end of the war living standards had fallen to a very low level. Comparative statistics have been provided only during the past few years. According to data cited by Malafeyev,[36] State and co-operative retail trade (all trade except for the collective farm markets) in current prices declined from 175·1 milliard roubles in 1940 to 160·1 milliards in 1945, but in prices of 1940 it declined from 175·1 milliard roubles to 73·5 milliards, a reduction of 58 per cent. The index of prices in State and co-operative retail trade rose by 118 per cent between 1940 and 1945. Therefore, living standards of the urban population may have been cut by as much as a half between 1940 and 1945. It is amazing to relate that the output of 'cultural goods' was only half as large in 1945 as it had been in 1913. However, production of most producer goods was very much greater: of steel nearly 3 times, of coal 5 times, of electric power 22 times. Outputs of cement and of window glass were only about equal to 1913, so materials taken from demolished buildings must have been important in the early stages of restoration.

Notes

1 Gregory Grossman, *Soviet Statistics of Physical Output of Industrial Commodities, their Compilation and Quality* (1960), p. 45.

2 N. Jasny, *Soviet Industrialization 1928–1952* (1961), pp. 119–76.

3 E.g. B. Sukharevskiy, *Planovoye khozyaystvo*, no. 11, 1936, p. 123.

4 For example, the trouble-shooting People's Commissar of Heavy Industry L. M. Kaganovich ordered heads of Donbassugol' and Kuzbassugol' coalmining trusts to set about the practical organization of 'emulation'. (*Industriya*, 6 January 1938, p. 1.)

5 A. Baykov, *The Development of the Soviet Economic System* (1947), pp. 338–9. Baykov quotes *Za industrializatsiyu*, 30 June 1936, and *Pravda*, 20 June 1936.

6 V. Molotov, *Tretiy pyatiletnyy plan razvitiya narodnogo khozyaystva SSSR* (1939), p. 8.

7 A. Zelenovskiy, *Planovoye khozyaystvo*, no. 5, 1938, p. 16.

8 The *Pravda* leader of 6 April 1938 entitled 'Soviet Youth–Into Artillery Schools' expressed the sense of impending danger being justifiably aroused by the course of events in Europe.

9 C. Bettelheim, *La planification soviétique* (1945), p. 171.

10 G. S. Kravchenko, *Voyennaya ekonomika SSSR 1941–1945* (1963), p. 39.

11 Murray S. Weitzman and Andrew Elias, *The Magnitude and Distribution of Civilian Employment in the USSR, 1928–29* (1961), p. 61.

12 A. Gilinskiy, *Pravda*, 10 January 1938, p. 2.

13 A. Zelenovskiy, *Planovoye khozyaystvo*, no. 2, 1941, p. 17.

14 *Pravda*, 28 October 1961, p. 7.

15 B. P. Orlov, *Razvitiye transporta v SSSR 1917–1962* (1963), pp. 170–1.

16 A. Zelenovskiy, *Planovoye khozyaystvo*, no. 5, 1938, p. 24.

17 *Industriya*, 26 June 1940, p. 1, and 27 June 1940, p. 1.

18 See Raymond Hutchings, *Soviet Studies*, January 1969 (vol. XX, no. 3), p. 352, footnote**.

19 Among other curiosities in these years one notices a decline of almost two-thirds in the output of domestic sewing machines—from 510,000 in 1937 to 175,200 in 1940. (See the Appendix.) Presumably the capacity was turned over to war production. An alternative, but I think in this context much less likely, possibility is that the decline was due to a mistake by ordering agencies which exaggerated changes in popular demand. See in this connection P. Hanson, *The Consumer in the Soviet Economy* (1968), p. 191.

20 G. Bienstock, S. M. Schwarz, A. Yugow, *Management in Russian Industry and Agriculture* (1944), p. 6.

21 Clive Day, *Economic Development in Europe* (1942), p. 507.

22 Some doubt enters owing to the complexity of rural arrangements and terminology. This complexity is described by Y. Taniuchi, *Note*

on the Territorial Relationship between Rural Societies, Settlements and Communes, March 1966, Discussion Papers, Series RC/D, no. 3, Centre for Russian and East European Studies, the University of Birmingham.

23 Narodnoye khozyaystvo SSSR v 1958 godu (1959), p. 349.

24 Machine Tractor Stations were set up as an integral part of the collective farm system, to house, control and operate agricultural machines and to exercise various supervisory functions in regard to the farms' activities.

25 P. N. Pospelov et al., Istoriya velikoy otechestvennoy voyny, tom 6 (1965), p. 45.

26 Ibid., p. 46; N. Voznesenskiy, op. cit., p. 65.

27 Narodnoye khozyaystvo SSSR v 1958 godu (1959), p. 632.

28 N. Voznesenskiy, op. cit., p. 134.

29 A. Gordin, Sovetskiye finansy, no. 8, 1945, p. 7.

30 N. Voznesenskiy, op. cit., pp. 128–9.

31 See J. A. Newth in Soviet Studies, January 1964, vol. XV, no. 3, and my comment on this article in Soviet Studies, July 1966, vol. XVIII, no. 1.

32 N. Voznesenskiy, op. cit., pp. 161–2.

33 G. Warren Nutter, Growth of Industrial Production in the USSR (1962), pp. 214–15.

34 Kursk, ocherki iz istorii goroda (1957), p. 195.

35 Nutter estimates that in 1945 output was 17 per cent below the prewar level, and in 1946 over 40 per cent below (op. cit., p. 213).

36 A. N. Malafeyev, op. cit., p. 407.

8
SINCE 1945

After the war recovery was comparatively rapid, as it usually is in the reconstruction of a relatively advanced country, once orderly conditions have been restored and people can get down to work. In this case, there was much to be done. The claimed average rate of growth in industrial gross output was over 20 per cent yearly over the period 1947–50. These years were devoted mainly to repairs and rebuilding, or to extension of previously existing facilities with little entirely new development. However, during the latter half of the Fourth Five-Year Plan (1946–50), there was an abrupt change of mood: a series of ambitious, indeed grandiose, new projects were launched under the general name of the 'Stalin Plan for the Transformation of Nature' (launched 1948). Canals and hydro-electric plants were to be built, and extensive tree shelter belts to be planted to protect the north Caucasus, Ukraine and Volga regions from the dry south-easterly winds. It transpired only much later that most of the shelter belts perished. The canal-building section of the plan has been fulfilled only in part, the Volga-Don canal being completed in 1952. Very large dams and hydro-electric stations have been built at Volgograd and Kuybyshev, though Khrushchev – hardly choosing the most felicitous moment – remarked on the occasion of the completion of the Kuybyshev station that it would have been better to postpone such building till a later date, and there have been disturbing repercussions of the consequently shallowing water level in the North Caspian upon the caviare fisheries.

During the latter half of the Fourth Plan period there were violent alterations in prices. In 1949 wholesale prices were sharply raised; as a result, the system of payment of subsidies to heavy industry was abolished.[1] Reductions of wholesale prices were decreed in 1950.[2] Obviously someone had miscalculated, and it was in 1949 that Voznesenskiy, the Chairman of Gosplan and author of a much quoted short book, lost his post – and later his head. In 1950, there was a particularly large cut in *retail* prices, and living standards rose appreciably.

A Fifth Five-Year Plan was announced in October 1952, and was stated to have been fulfilled by 1 May 1955. As before the National Income and industrial output grew from year to year, but average annual increases were only half as great as those which had been achieved in the previous Plan period. Whereas in 1948 industrial output is claimed to have risen by 26 per cent, between 1952 and 1955 annual increases varied between 11 and 13 per cent. The deceleration was at least partly due to rearmament during the Korean War (June 1950–53), especially in 1951–52. In the fourth quarter of 1952 performance was unusually sluggish for the time of year, owing possibly to a larger number of arrests: this was a time of rising internal tension. Output began to pick up in the second half of 1953, as if responding to Stalin's death on 5 March; in a totalitarian state, multiple threads link the performance of the economy with the decisions and personal fates of its leaders. However, the high rates recorded in the Fourth Plan have not been reproduced since.

Six months before his death Stalin, who had long been out of the limelight as regards economic affairs, published an article[3] in which he discoursed on a range of theoretical and practical economic questions. The practical bent of his argument concerned in part agriculture. It was necessary, he claimed, to transform collective farm property gradually into national (*obshchenarodnuyu*) property, and barter of agricultural products had to be begun on a wide scale. Despite attempts by economists to write-up this last forecast,[4] it ran so directly across the main stream of evolution that it has sunk without trace. Stalin's essay correctly pointed to agriculture as an area where structural changes could be expected; however, actual changes have not in the main gone in the direction to which he pointed.

During the Fifth Plan 'work in connection with the peaceful use of atomic energy, and also in connection with atomic and rocket equipment, was developed on a large scale'.[5] The fruits of these labours became visible to the outside world later.

A Sixth Five-Year Plan was launched in 1956, to run until the end of 1960. It was ambitious: in agriculture especially Western observers thought it unrealistically hopeful. The industrial targets seemed more attainable. According to the official claim, industrial output had risen by 85 per cent between 1950 and 1955, and a further rise of 70 per cent was now projected.

In the upshot, this Plan was not proceeded with. It was decided in 1957 to abandon it (*supersede* was the word used) in favour of a Seven-Year Plan to cover the period 1959–65 inclusive. The officially quoted explanation was that the Five-Year Plan had not taken into account new possibilities of raising output, and that it was in certain directions too conservative. For instance, among fuels it allegedly laid too much stress on coal, too little on oil and natural gas; while new mineral deposits had been discovered in the meantime which it was expedient to begin to exploit. No doubt there was at least some truth in these explanations. However, the economy had not made a very good start in 1956: by the end of that year the outputs of some basic materials (e.g. cement) had been running well behind schedule. This may also have been taken into account in the decision to abandon the Plan, though this is not admitted. Now that 1960 is past, we see that though the grain target was not reached, industrial output levels actually reached in that year compare pretty well with those originally set in the Five-Year Plan. Yet there must have been serious reasons for the decision as a long-term plan had never before been abandoned in peacetime.[6]

This decision was announced late in 1957 when it was stated that a new Plan would start in 1959. Hence in the intermediate year, 1958, no integrated long-term plan was in operation. This makes a detectable although not very large difference in the result achieved in that year. Major reforms which were announced in 1957 (in industry and construction) and in 1958 (agriculture: collective farms permitted to buy agricultural machinery), together with major decrees affecting residential building and the chemical industry, all occurred during a sort of interregnum between two long-term plans.

One reason for choosing the longer period of seven years was probably so that more striking increases could be aimed at. Perhaps also 1965 was chosen as the terminal date so that thereafter five-year plans, ending in years which were multiples of 5, could be resumed. The next (Eighth) Plan was scheduled to end in 1970, being in fact five-yearly. This duration might facilitate statistical calculations, and would mesh in with the long-term plans of certain of the East European states. The Seven-Year Plan was in turn modified, a Two-Year Plan including the years 1964–65. A Ninth Five-Year Plan (1971–75) followed (a draft of the new Plan would be drawn up in August 1968 and made more precise during 1969–70)[7] and then a Tenth (labelled the 'Plan of Quality'), while the Eleventh (1981–85) has started.

Stalin's death closed an epoch in Soviet economic history during which extreme emphasis had been placed on developing heavy industry. By no means all improvements in living standards since the end of the war have taken place since Stalin's death. There had been notable gains before, for instance in 1950 by comparison with the previous year (as one gathers from people who were there at the time). There were large retail price cuts in 1950 and in some other years, although the retail price level has changed little since 1954–57. On the whole, between 1948 and 1954 there was a very striking improvement in living standards, although from a very low starting-point in 1945. Stalin's successors have minimized what was achieved under Stalin, rather as the Soviet régime minimizes what was achieved under Tsarism.

Although greater relative attention is now paid to light industry, heavy industry still receives the lion's share of funds and the emphasis formerly placed on it has been qualified but not removed. Moreover, defence expenditures, which after the Korean War had fallen, have since remained on a high level. (See below, Chapter 14.) Scientific spending has risen much more sharply than defence spending. Space research and artificial satellites, the first of which was launched on 4 October 1957, have doubtless made important inroads into other expenditures, without as yet producing anything significant in the way of spin-off, owing to internal secrecy barriers and the predominantly military orientation of these programmes.

Some benefits were distributed among the populace immediately after Stalin's death. Retail sales rose quite sharply in the second quarter of 1953, apparently owing to releases of government-held stocks, and there were substantial cuts in retail prices. Industrial output spurted upwards in the second half of 1953. In 1954 – owing perhaps to releases from labour camps in 1953 when certain classes of prisoners were amnestied – even the birth-rate rose. Government actions, and speeches of the new Premier, G. M. Malenkov, indicated that the government would place more emphasis than formerly on expanding supplies of industrial consumer goods. The shift actually achieved was very small,[8] and included a measure which in a Western country would be regarded as an expedient, but which is quite normal practice in the Soviet Union, of getting heavy industrial plants to manufacture consumer goods as a sideline. A programme of building iron bedsteads got under way, and some aircraft plants began to make babies' prams out of metal scraps! How far this switch of emphasis might have gone one cannot say, for in 1955 Malenkov was replaced as premier by Bulganin (though it had already become clear that Khrushchev was actually in command). However, agriculture must soon have taken priority before any sizeable expansion of industrial consumer branches.

Among other charges laid against Malenkov was an accusation of having abandoned the traditional (and ideologically obligatory) policy of expanding preferentially heavy industry. The output of Group B (consumer goods) actually grew faster than that of Group A (capital goods) during 1953, in sharp contrast to a normally higher growth rate of Group A. But Khrushchev in his turn began to emphasize agricultural development, then housing, and later the contribution which an expanded chemicals industry could make to consumer welfare.

Although since 1952 there has been a large expansion in the output of household consumer durables, private motoring continued to be held down to a very limited scale. Ancillary services were correspondingly skimpy: as late as 1959 there was only one petrol filling station between Moscow and Leningrad, a distance of 650 km.; furthermore, petrol was rationed and low octane. Community groups such as collective farmers often rode on lorries upon which were mounted rows of straight-backed wooden seats.

Since Stalin died very much more heed has been paid by the leadership to agriculture. It would not be true to say that agriculture had previously been wholly neglected. The creation of a tractor industry was one of the achievements of the First Five-Year Plan although this was also stimulated by the impromptu mass slaughter of horses, and tractors are used in forestry and building as well as in agriculture; some production capacity was also converted for making tanks in World War II. Mechanization of agriculture was ill-balanced: it touched some basic operations but not auxiliary ones, which still required large labour inputs. Fertilizers continued to be used on only a very small scale. Electrification, proclaimed with such fanfare, left the countryside almost untouched; indeed collective farms had not been allowed to hook up to the State electricity grid. The so-called 'Plan for the Transformation of Nature' envisaged agricultural improvement, and if successful it would have had an important effect. However, it failed. Little heed was paid to technical advances in other countries, and at home Lysenko's remarkable and pernicious biological theories held sway. Organizational initiatives were restricted to a political approach (collectivization, which was also applied in the territories annexed in 1939–40 and 1945, elimination of the kulaks, fiscal oppression); to barren decisions concerning the optimum size of farm labour unit (the *zveno*, i.e. 'link', versus the 'brigade'); and to pointless or politically-motivated prohibitions such as discouragement of not strictly agricultural, but very useful, occupations such as construction. A Plan was announced in 1949, to run until 1951, to expand the head of livestock, but this failed owing to shortage of fodder.

Peasant incentives were neglected. Farm incomes remained extremely low, and taxation discouraged any initiative. The collective farm system was treated as a political device for controlling the countryside, for mobilizing its food deliveries and maximizing them without regard to the effects on the farms themselves, and as a reserve of labour for which the State did not have to provide unemployment benefit. Agricultural statistics were not only extremely meagre, but misleading, for example grain harvests were quoted as the biological yield (what is standing in the fields, with no allowance made for harvesting losses which may run up to 30 per cent). Propaganda painted an excessively favourable picture of the agricultural situation.

The turning-point for the better was September 1953, when Khrushchev made a rather frank admission that nearly everything was wrong with Soviet agriculture. He pointed out that between 1940 and

1952 industrial output had grown 2¼ times but agricultural output by only 10 per cent. An announcement by Malenkov in 1951 (while Stalin was still alive and in command) that the grain problem had been 'solved' was later denounced by Khrushchev as a piece of deliberate deception. Ever since, Khrushchev devoted a large fraction of his time and voluminous public speeches to agricultural problems.

As one element in the solution of the problem of raising agricultural output, a huge new programme of ploughing up of 'virgin and idle' lands was launched in 1954. In the next three years 36 million hectares of virgin lands were ploughed up (this equals about the area of Japan or half that of New South Wales), mainly in Kazakhstan and Siberia. The new lands were sown chiefly with grain, above all with wheat. The virgin lands had an important effect on the grain harvest. This fluctuates very much from year to year, according to weather conditions, but the average of 1954–58 was 40 per cent higher than the average of 1949–53, and a considerable part of this increase was due to the virgin lands. Taking into account the growth of population, the Soviet grain situation would otherwise already have become serious. As we will later see, this rate of improvement was not maintained.

Other agricultural reforms were adopted, and contributed to this increase as well as to other gains in agricultural performance. First, important increases in prices paid for deliveries of agricultural products by collective farms and farmers were decreed, to furnish an incentive to the peasants to expand production which had previously been quite lacking.

The increase in prices, joined with increases in output and organizational reforms, brought about an important rise in farm incomes. Whereas, prior to these reforms, living standards of the peasantry were – as a matter of deliberate policy – well below those of industrial workers, part of this disparity has now been eliminated and although rural living standards in general remain low, some farmers are tolerably well off. This also has had repercussions on internal migration. Whereas prior to Stalin's death people moved in only one direction – from the countryside to the towns – since then there have been cross-currents although the prevailing movement is still townwards.

Khrushchev's agricultural initiatives were numerous. His maize campaign was obviously modelled on the agricultural pattern of the USA. In 1955 the area sown under maize for grain was doubled, and a large area was also sown under maize for fodder. Subsequently the maize campaign lost ground (in all senses) but the crop remained much more important than it had been before.

There were numerous changes in agricultural organization. The extremely centralized system of agricultural planning current in Stalin's day was dismantled (1959). Much more initiative began to be allowed to farms themselves (there had been none at all before). Since March 1958 collective farms have been permitted to own tractors and other agricultural machinery – a retreat from State ownership. The Machine Tractor Stations which used to perform mechanical operations on collective farms' land were abolished. Collective farms were encouraged to make 'advances' (somewhat similar to money wages) to their members, instead of confining themselves to an annual share-out in money and kind. The output of artificial fertilizers was increased, and more suitable types of machines began to be supplied.

In 1957 Khrushchev launched a campaign to raise the output of these items up to the point where the Soviet Union would produce more milk, meat and butter per head of its population than the United States. There have been large increases in production of milk and butter and the USSR now consumes more of these per head than Americans do. (Americans prefer margarine owing to its lower cholesterol content, and Soviet consumption of butter per head is much smaller than New Zealand's or Ireland's.) The head of cattle in the USSR has also risen, but it proved to be much more difficult to increase meat output than Khrushchev had imagined, and the US level of meat consumption has been nowhere near approached.

Although collective farms have become more prosperous, they are many fewer than they used to be (1937: 242,500; 1953: 93,300; 1960: 44,900; 1965: 36,900; 1970: 33,600; 1975: 29,000; at end-years).[9] This is partly owing to amalgamation, another development favoured by Khrushchev (it was theorized that a more advanced farm could help a less advanced one), and partly owing to the conversion of some collective farms into State farms (this, to some extent, offsetting the recoil from State ownership and management of agricultural machinery). Owing also to the fact that only State farms were set up on the virgin lands, the share of these farms in area and output increased sharply. At the end of 1975 there were 18,100 State farms, 3·7 times as many as in 1953. Their area under crops in 1975 exceeded 52 per cent of the total. There has been a good deal of new building in the countryside, chiefly but not only in the virgin lands.

Agricultural output has fluctuated sharply. A record grain harvest in 1962 was achieved only by further extensions of the sown area, not by any increase in yield, which had disturbing implications for the future as Soviet agriculture had already encroached on what would be marginal land in Western Europe or the USA. In 1963 there was a serious fall in the harvest of grain, and particularly wheat. The worse failure in wheat than in other grains was due to the concentration of wheat sowings on the 'virgin' lands, where the harvest was disastrous. The output of meat has fallen far below forecast. In 1963, more meat was procured than in the previous year, but at the cost of reducing the herds of cattle (other than cows), and of pigs and sheep. At the year's end there were 40·7 million head of pigs as compared with 69·7 million a year before. It was bound to take, at best, several years before the higher total could be regained, even if meat consumption remained meanwhile on a low level. By the end of 1966 the head of pigs had reached only 58·0 million.

Food prices have been altered jerkily in response to the situation on the farms, measured against rising popular demand. In June 1962 there was an increase of 30 per cent in prices of meat; eggs, canned goods and milk and dairy products were also affected. This sudden increase sparked off food riots in Novocherkassk.

Pensions were raised substantially in 1956. Collective farmers had not previously been eligible for State social insurance or pension rights. A law of 15 July 1964 provided for pensions to be paid to collective farmers at rates lower than, or equal to, those paid to workers and employees. Higher rates of minimum *wages* were fixed in 1956, 1965 and 1968. Certain increases in wages for workers in education, health, housing, and trade and other service branches, were announced in August 1964.

Following the 'stable environment for management'[10] created by the plenum of the Party Central Committee in March 1965, agricultural performance improved remarkably. While the grain harvest in 1965 at 121·1 million tons was lower than in 1960 (125·5 million), the 1970 harvest rose to 186·8 million. There was no harvest failure during this quinquennium, although 1967 was below par. Total agricultural output rose by more than a fifth.

The quinquennium 1971–75 did not maintain the impetus of growth of agricultural production that had been so markedly shown in 1966–70. Average annual production of grain and of milk were only 8·4 per cent above the average of the previous five years; potato production was 5·3 per cent below. Slightly less flax was produced, but more cotton and wool. Total agricultural production rose by 13·2 per cent, whereas the previous quinquennium had recorded a growth of 21·3 per cent.

However, reckoned over the full post-war span, Soviet agricultural production has scored very considerable successes. Average annual output in 1971–75, relative to 1946–50 (=1·00) amounted to the following: grain 2·56, milk 2·71, potatoes 1·13, cotton 3·31, wool 3·01, flax 2·03, total agricultural output 2·56. Thus on the whole over this long period foodstuffs and non-foodstuffs (as represented in each case by the products specified) have grown at not very different rates, although non-foods fractionally the faster. There is a much more conspicuous difference in the phasing of the growth of these categories, except that flax in *this* connection has to be included within the foodstuffs group. All the items in the 'foodstuffs' group recorded their largest percentage growth in 1956–60, relative to 1951–55, while their worst growth performance was in 1961–65 (usually), 1951–55, or 1971–75. By contrast, cotton and wool both achieved their largest relative growth in 1951–55. Thus, the impact of Khrushchev's agricultural polices was shown in the greatly accelerated growth of foodstuffs branches (and of flax) relative to that of cotton or wool, whereas post-Khrushchevian policies have tended to redress that balance.

Five-year averages are used in order to eliminate the impact of variations in individual years. In practice these variations are sizeable: the grain harvest, for example, can be up to 50–60 per cent larger in one year than in an adjacent year. In 1975 for instance the harvest was 140·1 million tons, but in 1976 it was 223·8 million. The ploughing-up of virgin lands in Siberia and Kazakhstan was intended to moderate these fluctuations, but actually has done little or nothing in that direction. Crops other than grain also vary, but usually their variations are of smaller amplitude although commonly in the same direction. Among irrigated crops, such as cotton, fluctuations are much smaller.

Industry and Construction

Second only to Khrushchev's attention to agriculture was his attention to industry and building.

A small number of skyscrapers in an extravagant 'wedding-cake' style had been erected in Moscow since the war presumably in imitation of New York, although Moscow lacks any economic justification such as the restricted land area of Manhattan Island. They were conspicuous because they were the city's first very tall buildings. Largest and most lavish was the new Moscow University building, which soars to 800 feet and cost 500 million pre-1961 roubles (= perhaps 20 million pounds sterling). With the possible exception of secret defence installations this probably made it at the time the world's most expensive building. Efficiency indices of several skyscrapers were discovered to be very low, and the style was in due course condemned by Khrushchev, since when only less extravagant, more prosaic and less lofty buildings have been erected.

This particular change, which affected directly little more than the skyline of the capital city and so was of architectural rather than economic interest, symbolized a change of more general significance in the direction of more careful reckoning of costs and losses before a project was undertaken. It came to appear less likely that grandiose schemes would be adopted – at least without a closer counting of the cost and a more thorough search for accompanying drawbacks. After Stalin's death there was a marked reaction against the very large-scale construction projects, including giant hydro-electric schemes, which had previously been favoured. However, the national traditions and the centralized economy and government predispose the system towards large-scale, grandiose solutions: if it does not plan and execute on a grand scale, such a system has no sufficient *raison d'etre*. A huge programme of irrigation and drainage, adopted in 1968, appears to share the same traits of grandiosity as have characterized several earlier schemes.

In July 1957 a new and expanded programme of residential building was announced. During all-out industrialization from 1928 onwards such building had been in great measure neglected. Some construction was unavoidable in order to accommodate the masses who flooded into the cities, and actual or planned expenditures on housing increased in absolute terms in the Second and Third Five-Year Plans. Even before the war, on 29 May 1939, it was decided to develop and modernize the building industry.[11] Some relief had also come from resettling workers in the mansions of émigrés.[12] As a result, and owing to the system of allocation of dwelling-space, accommodation must have been more nearly equalized than before the Revolution, especially in regard to families of different sizes. However, on the whole the cities became more crowded and average *per capita* dwelling-space shrank to improbably small areas. At the start of 1935, this average for workers in 'basic industry' (metallurgy, engineering, chemicals etc.) was only 5 to 6½ square metres,[13] that is to say one-third below what was regarded as the sanitary minimum.

In July 1957 a target was set to 'solve the housing problem' within 'ten to twelve' years. Under Soviet conditions, this meant to achieve a situation that every family had its own apartment (a flat, not a house). In 1957 it was normal for a family to share an apartment with one or two other families. The objective would therefore represent a very big advance on contemporary conditions. Dwelling-space was to be built partly by the State (i.e. by local authorities) and partly (mainly in the countryside) by individuals, who were to be granted loans to buy building materials etc. Individual house-building took place on a considerable scale, not only in rural areas but on the outskirts of towns: for instance in Kursk (then some 200,000 inhabitants) as I saw in January 1958, a great number of small and temporary-looking timber cottages had been built. In 1960, the policy of granting loans to individuals was discontinued and private house-building consequently fell sharply. Retail sales of building materials also slumped.

Khrushchev also had ideas about building materials. He promoted especially the more widespread use of prefabricated concrete sections. Bricks lost their prominence, many small brickworks being closed down. Following Khrushchev's fall from power bricks returned to favour.

Totalled over five-year spans, dwelling space (in millions of square metres) rose as follows: 1956–60 474·1; 1961–65 490·6; 1966–70 518·5; 1971–75 544·8. On the whole this shows a steady linear momentum, although most recently individual years show a levelling-off. A notable development of the past twenty years has been the revival of co-operative ('condominium') housing, which in the early 1970s was providing about 7 million square metres of living space annually; however, at that time the annual totals of condominium construction were no longer rising.[14]

Both construction and manufacture were affected by a major structural reform in 1957. During the 1930s the number of people's commissariats had multiplied as the variety of industrial output grew wider. This process continued, and by 1957 the number of ministries had reached 50. (The people's commissariats had been renamed 'ministries' in 1946, but this meant no change in substance.)

Khrushchev alleged that this multiplicity gave rise to various weaknesses. In particular, he claimed that the ministries functioned as virtually closed entities, and did not co-operate with other ministries, which led to duplication of effort and inefficiency. He proposed a drastic reshuffle involving the abolition of most industrial ministries, which would be replaced by regional economic councils. It is probable that Khrushchev also had a political motive in dispersing members of central government bodies round in the provinces. Malenkov, Molotov and other top leaders did not speak in favour of this change, and later on it was disclosed that Malenkov and Molotov had opposed it.

Khrushchev's 'theses' were 'discussed' in great detail in the press and were in substance adopted, except that the Gosplan was not made into an authoritative body as was first proposed. (It appears that no major point was modified as a result of the press discussion.) As from 1 July 1957, 25 ministries were abolished and their functions of controlling and regulating industries were transferred to 105 (later 102, and from November 1962, 47) councils of national economy or *sovnarkhozy*. The reform affected also construction to the extent that this had been managed by the now liquidated ministries. With some modifications (in particular, 'overlord' councils were set up in some republics, and other changes were made reverting towards centralization) this system lasted until October 1965.

A major decree in 1958 covered development of the chemical industry, which had lagged behind other industries, notably engineering and machine tools, and far behind the US or Britain. The programme outlined in the decree was extremely ambitious, especially as regards the quantity and variety of output of synthetic fibres.

The industry had been seriously damaged during the War. Subsequently it expanded a little faster than industry as a whole, but by 1957 its share in total industrial fixed capital was smaller than in 1940, while in total output it had fallen from fourth to sixth place (having been overtaken by fuels and ferrous metallurgy). This lag (which contrasts with a faster than average growth of chemicals in the USA and the UK) became the justification for awarding in 1958 a much higher priority to this industry. The change encountered obstacles such as planners' ingrained preferences for well-tried branches such as steel and engineering: Khrushchev spoke of 'metal-eaters' ensconced in the Gosplan and of planners who wore 'metal-blinkers'. Russia also lacked knowledge of some vital processes, such as how to produce terylene. Agricultural theory minimized the importance of fertilizers and insecticides: for example, the maize campaign (erroneously) envisaged that maize would not need fertilizer.

The priority for chemicals was intensified further in the Seven-Year Plan, yet the latter did not provide for an adequate level of investment. Main emphasis was now placed on expanding the outputs of mineral fertilizers, synthetic resins and plastics, and insecticides (any danger from excessive use of the latter being yet hardly appreciated). In 1963 investment in chemicals, among other branches, was increased, but it continued to prove difficult to accelerate output to the extent desired: between 1960 and 1965 output per unit of capital (*fondootdacha*) declined from 1·39 to 1·08. The Eighth Five-Year Plan (1966—70) provided, according to Kosygin, for a more realistic approach: the very high tempos aimed at in the Seven-Year Plan were slightly relaxed. Some very large proportionate increases were then achieved, such as an 81-fold rise between 1958 and 1965 in the output of polyethylene and polypropylene, while the total output of the chemical industry rose from 3·6 per cent to 5·4 per cent of all industrial output.[15]

The actual growth of chemicals production from 1965 to 1970 was 90 per cent, from 1970 to 1975 it was 68 per cent (as compared with 50 and 43 per cent respectively for total industrial output), so this priority has been generally maintained. The growth of output of mineral fertilizers has been especially striking: reckoned in conventional units, threefold between 1965 and 1977. This, of course, has considerably benefited agriculture.

Khrushchev's dismissal in October 1964 was followed by many revisions or reversals of policy, which showed that economic policy was still to a fairly big extent a 'personal' matter. Khrushchev, even more than Stalin, had an unlimited belief in the virtues of reorganizations. Kaleidoscopic structural changes since 1957 not only made it hard for Western students of the Soviet economy to keep track of what was happening; worse still, they confused the Russians themselves who had to try to make these systems work. In October 1965 it was decided to abolish the *sovnarkhozy*, including the 'overlord' councils and the central economic authorities set up after 1957. Except for territorial supply bases, the whole system established in 1957 has been superseded by a hierarchical system of industrial ministries, which essentially re-creates the network abolished in 1957. Other reforms were simultaneously introduced: a new emphasis on profits in guiding production; more autonomy for undertakings (a 'Statute of the Socialist State Productive Enterprise' was adopted);[16] a more satisfactory way of measuring performance than the 'gross output' index.[17] Great hopes were placed on the fixing of more correct prices by a newly formed State committee of prices.[18] New wholesale prices in industry were established in 1966–67,[19] and enabled subsidies to heavy industry to be reduced. But radical changes in the direction of permitting any general liberation of the economy from multiple controls have been avoided, and indeed the system has become more complicated.

The number of ministries has continued to increase, but much more slowly than total output or the production range; therefore, the size and complexity of ministerial systems has expanded further. Ministries and other bodies reporting their performance in the plan results for 1980 are listed below. On the whole, since 1965 the assortment of ministries has been very stable, but new ministries have been set up in several branches of machine-building (such as Heavy and Transport Machine-Building), the intended eventual beneficiaries also including consumer sectors, and within the latter, the supply of agricultural products. The list does not include ministries such as Defence, which do not report plan results. More State Committees also have been set up to head existing bodies, which signifies an elevation in their status (for example, the State Committee for Inventions and Discoveries and the State Committee for Material Reserves). At the all-Union level the total number of ministries, committees and State Committees whose existence has been made known approaches 100.

Ministries and similar bodies reporting 1980 Plan results
Electric Power and Electrification
Oil
Oil-Refining and Petrochemicals
Gas
Coal
Ferrous Metals
Non-Ferrous Metals
Chemicals
Mineral Fertilizers
Electric Power Machine-Building
Heavy and Transport Machine-Building
Electrotechnical Industry

Chemical and Oil Machine-Building
Machine-Tools and Instruments
Instruments, Means of Automation and Management Systems
Automobiles
Tractors and Agricultural Machine-Building
Machine-Building for Livestock Rearing and Fodder Production
Building, Road and Communal Machine-Building
Machine-Building for the Light and Food Industries and Household
    Appliances
Timber, Cellulose-Paper and Woodworking
Building Materials
Light
Food
Meat and Dairy
Fish
Procurements
Medicaments
Microbiological Industry (Chief Administration)

Changes in the size and number of economic bodies in the USSR have attracted less notice than the organizational reforms. Russia is becoming a country of very-large-scale economic organizations. Strumilin traced continuity in a trend of increasing concentration in metallurgical works without making any distinction in principle between pre- and post-Revolution.[20] As reported in 1929, 52 out of 11,400 industrial undertakings (*zavedeniye*) contained about 60 per cent of all industrial basic capital funds.[21] Most recently, between 1960 and 1963, concentration has been intensified: plants with an annual gross output of more than 5 million roubles comprised 10·9 per cent of all plants in 1960, but 15·8 per cent of the total in 1963; in 1960 these plants turned out 68·6 per cent of total output, but in 1963, 74·2 per cent.[22] Whereas at the end of the Fifth Five-Year Plan (1955) there were more than 200,000 State industrial undertakings (and over 100,000 construction sites[23]), by 1967 (possibly after some reclassification) the number of plants had declined to 45,000.[24] Although the numbers had been shrinking before, the rate of decline appears to have speeded up, due probably both to enlargement in the average size of plants (other than the very largest ones), and to amalgamation of smaller plants, partly by order of the *sovnarkhozy*.[25]

The process of concentration has continued following the formation of associations (*ob"edineniya*) especially after April 1973. The number of industrial plants peaked in 1972 (48,891) and has since declined gradually but continuously: in 1977, for instance, there were 43,788. Over about the same period the number of associations climbed from 608 in 1970 to 3,670 in 1977. The associations comprise about 40 per cent of the number of plants, and these account for slightly larger percentages of the total number of workers and of industrial output. It will be remembered that the number of collective farms had been reduced to 29,000 by the end of 1975.[26] Hence, while forms of organization still differ in agriculture and industry, in numbers of basic units these two major branches of the economy exhibit a strong tendency of convergence.

The share of 'national state property' in total ownership is constantly growing and now embraces over nine-tenths of all basic productive funds. Within industry this share was 92 per cent in 1955, 94 per cent in 1958, 97 per cent in 1960.[27] By 1977 all summary indices were registering 100 per cent.[28] However, as the percentage has risen its meaningfulness has declined. Actually, private production is still important in agriculture, and individual activity quite important in various consumer spheres.

Foreign Trade

Another major change since Stalin's death was to pay much greater attention to foreign economic relations. Under Stalin, the USSR concentrated its foreign trade on its satellites and on China. The USSR extracted from Eastern Europe more value than she provided in return (via reparations or excessively low prices paid, for example, for Polish coal). Since the Hungarian revolt in 1956, however, this relationship was altered and the Soviet Union extended important credits to Eastern Europe, especially per head of their populations to Hungary and Albania (before relations with the latter country were broken off). Economic relations with East Germany have been intensified, and East Germany is playing a large part in implementing the Soviet chemicals programme. Trade with Czechoslovakia is also important.

An economic grouping of Soviet bloc countries set up in 1949, CMEA (Council for Mutual Economic Aid, or Comecon) has been activated since 1954.[29] The further very extensive ramification of this network and activity, and of the Soviet Union's participation in it, constitutes a large and complicated subject in itself, and only highlights can be mentioned here. In 1971 a 'Complex Programme' of integration was adopted, and a number of important joint construction projects, concerned especially with raw materials supplies, have since been pursued. A further Agreed Plan of Multilateral Integration was adopted for 1976–80. Since 1971 the world economic climate has changed in directions not foreseen at that time (in particular, the oil crisis of 1973–4 and the shift in the correlation of prices of materials and finished products in favour of the former), which have tended to obstruct integration. Rates of growth within the group have declined, and little progress has been made towards convertability – which had been one of the objectives. Another fairly recent development has been the setting up of transnational economic organizations to which interested member-countries of CMEA (normally including the Soviet Union) belong: as reported in April 1981 there were 46 of these, primarily in engineering and transport.

Prior to 1955, the USSR did not pursue a forward policy in trading with the non-socialist world. Since then, it has used all possible means to expand trade dealings with underdeveloped countries, to which important credits have also been extended and experts seconded. Thus, since Stalin's death the USSR has pursued a more enterprising policy in foreign economic relations. This may even have been too enterprising: the abrupt withdrawal of Soviet scientists and technicians from China in 1960 was one of the causes of rupture between the two countries.[30]

The further expansion of foreign trade has been one of the most pronounced phenomena in Soviet economic development over the past twenty years: trade more than doubled between 1960 and 1970, and again roughly doubled between 1970 and 1980. Details will be found in Chapter 17.

Public Finance

Until the 1960s the post-war economy was not suffering from endemic financial problems. The monetary imbalance in 1941–45 had been put right by the currency reform of 1947, and during the Fourth and Fifth Five-Year Plans there were repeated cuts in retail prices. If in practice consumer demand was by no means always able to find satisfactory outlets, this situation was on the whole improving rather than deteriorating.

As from the period 1962 to 1965, the situation has changed rather radically. What has attracted particular attention in the West has been the enormous increase in the volume of saving, and consequently in the accumulated total of savings deposits, which increased more than 80-fold between 1950 and 1980. The reasons are doubtless mixed. They include urbanization, improved living standards, and the style of enrichment which encouraged consumers to save up to buy durable goods. The heaping-up of savings also must have resulted from imbalance between demand and supply. While it might not necessarily imply a situation of repressed inflation, in Soviet circumstances that is probably what it did imply. There is a possible connection with the growth of budget spending on the economy in excess of forecast, this excess having about the same order of magnitude as the accumulated savings.[31]

Total budget spending has certainly risen more rapidly since about

1965 than it had done before. This is especially visible in the republic section of the budget, which since 1963, except only in 1966, has invariably been overspent. As the union section of the budget is usually underspent but by a smaller proportion, and the two sections are of about the same size, from 1962 onwards (except only in 1972) total forecast budget spending has always been exceeded.

The 1965 reform of industrial and planning structure had been expected to result in a substitution of non-budget for budget spending on capital investment, and this did occur to some degree but apparently to an extent falling short of what had been expected.

Thus in the upshot, total savings, spending on the economy and total budget expenditure, either have risen faster and at a higher rate than previously since World War II, or if scheduled to decline have not done so to the anticipated extent.

Inequality

Under Khrushchev, and subsequently under Brezhnev, inequality in remuneration within professions has been reduced: engineers and technicians, or staff in scientific research institutions, naturally earn more than manual workers in the same branch, but the margin has been narrowed.[32] On the other hand, regional inequalities have grown wider: in the extreme range of national income per capita, Estonia was by this measure in 1960 2·1 times higher than Turkmenia, but in 1976 3·7 times higher.[33] Whether, on balance, nationwide inequalities have been diminished must on this showing remain an open question. The principal lever at the disposal of the authorities for reducing inequality via redistribution as between republics – the state budget – has not been used for this purpose to any substantial degree: more advantageous taxation conditions, or subsidies, to particular republics having clearly in mind primarily the contribution made by such special measures to the economic development of the USSR as a whole.

Trade and Services

At first view, the already mentioned considerable expansion of agricultural output does not square with continuing problems of supply of food products to the Soviet people, especially when recent signs of deterioration in that supply are taken into account. It must, of course, be borne in mind that the Soviet Union is an exporter of foodstuffs, though lately the share of foodstuffs in Soviet exports has declined (see Chapter 17). The explanation is to be found partly in the growth of the population (by about a quarter between 1959 and 1978); partly in unevenness of supplies from year to year; partly in interruptions in supply from week to week; partly in the lagging behind of output of higher-quality products, especially meat and other animal products; and partly in price inflexibilities. While in cities, for instance in the Gastronom shops, many delicacies including caviare are available, the other side of the coin is shown in the fact that in 1978 41 per cent of all vegetable sales in state and co-operative shops consisted of cabbage![34] On the whole, in calories, the diet is sufficient; whereas in composition, convenience and availability, for the mass of the population, it does not match the general economic level of the Soviet Union or its international position.

This brings us to consider trade, first of all in foodstuffs. This trade has expanded much faster than total consumption, due to the gradual contraction of self-supply as farmers have moved to the towns or have been incorporated in larger and more specialized units. The total volume of trade (state, co-operative and collective farm) reckoned in current prices has been roughly doubling each decade; the growth of state and co-operative trade by itself has been faster. Sales of non-food items via this network have expanded in recent years about twice as fast as sales of food products, with over a half of the total turnover in food and beverages; the shrinking self-sufficiency of the village is shown in the fact that the food/non-food proportions now scarcely differ as between town and country. Moreover, a large volume of buying by country folk is done in towns, where most shops are located. (In the 1950s peasants heading back to their villages could be seen at main railway stations of the capital, carrying with them large nets containing bread-rings.) Both in town and country, strong drink is usually in abundant supply. Public catering has grown more slowly than sales of food products, which seems surprising but is explained partly by the already large attendance at works canteens and partly by a shortage of restaurants, though more cafes were built especially in the 1970s. Besides the official markets, there exist a large number of smaller and unregistered markets.[35]

Consumer services (repairs, dressmaking, dry-cleaning, hairdressing, photography, etc.) have risen especially since 1963; varying somewhat as between republics, they still amount to only a very limited per capita sum. On the other hand, domestic service may still be quite widespread, but no statistics about this are published.

Environmental Protection

The Soviet Union has been caught up in the worldwide surge of interest and concern for conservation of natural resources, although Soviet pronatalist policy remains out of step with most of the rest of the world. Soviet circumstances are unfavourable to conservation in two respects: traditionally, resources have been regarded as virtually illimitable, and the whole organization of the State places immense impetus behind *production*. Moreover, conservation tends to be appreciated mainly at regional and local levels, but the Soviet system of economy is basically centralized. On the other hand, the same centralization should in principle permit co-ordinated remedial or preventive action. One observes now a new concern with the proper utilization of land, which traditionally had been regarded as inexhaustible, and with preventing further loss through erosion or unnecessary alienation.[36] In general, although great weight is still assigned to economic organization, more attention is being paid to resources, both human and non-human.

The growth of industry not matched by an equivalent development of automobile transport has been a main reason for the fact that pollution in the USSR affects water rather than air — the reverse of the situation in the United States. Naturally, landlocked or nearly land-locked water is the worst affected, in particular the Sea of Azov which has only a narrow outlet to the Black Sea. Lake Baykal, one of the world's principal reserves of fresh water, has had to be defended by conservationists against pollutants discharged from cellulose works built along its shores. In the vicinity of large cities water pollution has become a serious problem: for instance, by detergent foam (which I saw on the Moskva River near Kolomenskoye in 1971). A water resources law was adopted in December 1970, but its provisions were too weak.[37] An accidental nuclear explosion of unexplained origins, but evidently with serious effects, occurred in the Urals in 1957 or 1958; matching normal Soviet practice in not reporting accidents this was never mentioned officially, and was brought to light first by the émigré scientist Zhores Medvedev.[38] It provided confirmation that safety had been relegated to a low priority in military and scientific research.

The level of output of 41 items over the period 1913 to 1980 is indicated in the Appendix. There are gaps in the series, caused partly by the fact that a number of items were not produced at all at the earlier dates, and partly by lack of published information: only 1950 and 1960 show the complete range. The assortment displayed here was partly chosen to permit comparability with earlier dates; to some extent it could be called arbitrary, but the same might also be said of any other assortment and all the listed items are quite prominent in Soviet statistics. It is clear at once that proportionate increases have been extremely varied. In the forefront are items such as gas or electric power (more than 600-fold); at the other exteme possibly vodka, with very little increase. However, Russia continues to be quite well supplied with vodka. Electrification has been carried to significant lengths.

Besides changes in output volume one must mention such achievements as improving quality, mastering new techniques and processes, enlarging the variety of output. This aspect has received much less attention than the quantitative aspect; it is inherently even more difficult. Only a thorough analysis by technical experts in many different fields could adequately assess what has been achieved by the Soviet economy in these directions: and such an analysis is not to hand, although great strides have been made in studies at the University of Birmingham (in particular, *The Technological Level of Soviet Industry*, eds. R. Amann, J. Cooper and R. W. Davies, 1977), and by A. C. Sutton (in which connection see below, Chapter 18).

At this point the following observations, although disjointed, may perhaps be helpful:—

(1) The Soviet Union now turns out an enormously wide variety of items. For instance, at the start of the Seven-Year Plan, over 125,000 designations of machines, instruments and other articles were being produced.[39]

(2) As a rule, higher-quality goods are found among capital goods than among consumer goods. Some of the choicest items are probably among those which are not offered for close inspection by foreigners, such as military weapons.[40]

(3) All-union industry tends to turn out higher-quality items than local industry.[41] or than republic industry. These lesser categories are equipped with old machinery,[42] and perhaps do not receive the highest-quality materials.

(4) Mechanization has been carried out unevenly, essentially because it has been regarded as good in itself, whether or not it reduces costs.[43] As funds have not stretched far enough to mechanize *everything*, and there has been a lack of a clear criterion for where to stop, a halt sometimes seems to have been chosen arbitrarily. For example, mechanization has included harvesting but not stockbreeding or many auxiliary farm jobs, and very advanced machine tools but not materials handling.

(5) Probably for this reason the system admits big differences in the ratio of achievement to effort, as witness the marked differences in labour productivity in agriculture and large-scale industry.

In general, Soviet economic development exhibits many dimensions of unevenness: this is as basic to the pattern of development as it is to a system of economy where profit rates do not tend towards equalization. If we look beyond the economic scene, and contrast progress in economic affairs with stagnation in the political sphere we see that this unevenness has more dimensions still.

Notes

1 L. Mayzenberg, *Planovoye khozyaystvo*, no. 6, 1950, p. 60.
2 L. Mayzenberg. *Tsenoobrazovaniye v narodnom khozyaystve SSSR* (1953), p. 249, and F. Dobrynin and L. Kvitnitskiy, *Planovoye khozyaystvo*, no. 6, 1950, p. 57.
3 *Bolshevik*, no. 18, 1952.
4 E.g. N. Smolin, *Voprosy ekonomiki*, no. 1, 1953.
5 A. N. Yefimov (ed.), *Ekonomika SSSR v poslevoyennyy period* (1962), p. 21.
6 These may have included the rapid growth at the time of expenditures on science. See below, Chapter 14.
7 Ye. Ivanov and F. Kotov, *Ekonomicheskaya gazeta*, no. 30, 1968, p. 20.
8 See also below, Chapter 15.
9 The number of industrial establishments has also shrunk: see below, Chapter 11.
10 M. C. Kaser in Kaser and Brown (eds.), *The Soviet Union Since the Fall of Khrushchev* Second edition, 1978), p. 197.
11 D. I. Chernomordik (ed.), *Narodnyy dokhod SSSR* (1939), p. 151.
12 600,000 people had been accommodated in this way, according to W. Citrine, *I Search for Truth in Russia* (1936), p. 159. Housing policy was intended to serve a class purpose: former members of the 'bourgeoisie' were made to pay rents 20–25 times higher than those charged workers and employees (D. Buzin, *Problemy ekonomiki*, nos. 5–6, 1937, p. 180).
13 D. Buzin, op. cit., p. 188.
14 *Narodnoye khozyaystvo SSSR v 1974 g.*, p. 585; cf. J. Pallot and D. J. B. Shaw, *Planning in the Soviet Union* (1981), p. 193.
15 V. Bibishev, *Planovoye khozyaystvo*, no. 2, 1966, pp. 2–3.
16 *Ekonomicheskaya gazeta*, no. 42, 1965, pp. 25–9.
17 See below, Chapter 20.
18 Shubenko-Shubin and B Kulik, *Ekonomicheskaya gazeta*, no. 40, 1965, pp. 16–17.
19 See Gertrude E. Schroeder, *Soviet Studies*, July 1968.
20 S. G. Strumilin, *Chernaya metallurgiya v Rossii i v SSSR* (1935), pp. 289–90.
21 M. N. Smit (general editor), *Kontsentratisya fabrichno-zavodskoy i trestirovannoy tsenzovoy promyshlennosti* (1929), p. 54.
22 *Ekonomicheskaya gazeta*, no. 37, 1965, p. 3.
23 A. N. Yefimov (ed.) *Ekonomika SSSR v poslevoyennyy period* (1962), p. 29. The number of plants is given as 202,000 in *Narodnoye khozyaystvo SSSR v 1956 godu* (1957), p. 48.
24 *Voprosy ekonomiki*, no. 9, 1967, p. 45.
25 See below, Chapter 11.

26 See above, p. 80.
27 V. Semenov, *Ekonomicheskaya gazeta*, no. 2, 1962, p. 5.
28 *Narodnoye khozyaystvo SSSR v 1977 g.*, p. 38.
29 See M. Kaser, *Comecon* (1965). For most recent developments, see also V. Válek in *Mezinarodni vztahy*, no. 4, 1981, and J. Fingerland and B. Diakin in *Hospodárské noviny*, 6 November 1981; abstracts of these articles in English may be found in *ABSEES*, no. 67, May 1982.
30 Cf. in this connection Andrei Amalrik, *Survey*, Autumn 1969, p. 69, footnote 43.
31 See R. Hutchings, *The Soviet Budget* (1983), Chapter 11.
32 M. C. Kaser in Brown and Kaser (eds.), *The Soviet Union Since the Fall of Khrushchev* (Second Edition, 1978), p. 215.
33 J. Pallot and D. J. B. Shaw, *Planning in the Soviet Union* (1981), p. 209.
34 A. Nove, *Soviet Studies*, January 1982, p. 119.
35 Ibid.
36 E.g. K. Mitryushkin, *Ekonomicheskaya gazeta*, no. 15, 1968, pp. 28–9.
37 Brown and Kaser (eds.), *The Soviet Union Since the Fall of Khrushchev* (Second Edition, 1978), p. 201.
38 *New Scientist*, 4 Nov. 1976. See also his *Soviet Science* (1978), pp. 232–44.
39 A. N. Yefimov (ed.), *Ekonomika SSSR v poslevoyennyy period* (1962), p. 47.
40 Among the conditions possessed by the USSR for raising the quality of output the following was mentioned: 'the great experience of individual branches of industry (defence, aviation, rocket and others) in turning out articles of high quality'. (V. Tkachenko, *Planovoye khozyaystvo*, no. 7, 1965, p. 2.)
41 Cf. A. N. Sen'ko and N. N. Afanas'ev, *Mestnaya promyshlennost' i promyslovaya kooperatsiya v tret'ey pyatiletke* (1939), p. 26.
42 Cf. P. Studenski, 'Methods of Estimating National Income in Soviet Russia', in *Studies in Income and Wealth*, vol. 8, National Bureau of Economic Research, New York, 1946, pp. 211–12. Concerning the distinction between these categories, see below, p. 133.
43 Cf. I. V. Stalin, *Bolshevik*, no. 18, 1952, p. 23.

PART III

ORGANIZATION AND PLANNING

Any chronological account of Soviet development is obliged to turn aside in order to give explanations which do not easily fit within a chronological sequence. Consequently, in the remaining part of this book the material is classified primarily by subject-matter, although within each chapter the sequence is still in large part chronological.

Part III concentrates on particular topics related to organization and planning, as a preliminary to considering in Parts IV and V how and why development has occurred.

9

POPULATION AND LABOUR FORCE

A. Population

The first and main thing to be organized in the Soviet Union is people. One may consider Soviet population resources as given within a short period within unusually narrow limits, because except by extraordinary dispensation one is not allowed to emigrate from the Soviet Union; however, since 1960 and particularly since 1968 such dispensations have been granted much more often, especially to Jews and Germans, and about 250,000 and 60,000 respectively of these have left (*The Cambridge Encyclopedia of Russia and the Soviet Union* (1982), p. 61). The population has varied owing to frontier changes, at which point there is a link with territorial policy and international relations; it has also been decimated by wars and disasters.

The earlier history of population numbers has been traced in Part II; see also Table 3 in the present chapter. The 250-million mark was passed in 1973; the annual growth is more than two millions, but the rate of increase has declined.[1] The repercussions of lower growth will without doubt exert an important influence upon the history of the Soviet Union in the last third of the twentieth century.

Mid-way through the post-war period detailed information about population was provided by the census of 15 January 1959, when the total was 208·8 million. This total was made up of 100·0 million urban and 108·8 million rural dwellers, and of 94·0 million males and 114·8 million females. It included 114·1 million Russians (or 'Great

Russians'), 37·3 million Ukranians and 7·9 million Belorussians. These three groups, who speak mutually comprehensible languages, made up 76 per cent of the whole population. In all, 72 major nationalities were listed, besides minor sub-divisions.

From an economic viewpoint the qualifications of this huge mass of people are also very relevant. Between 1939 and 1959 the number of people having had higher education increased from 1,777,000 to 3,778,000, and having had secondary education from 14·7 million to 54·9 million. Thus, over twenty years the number who had had some secondary or higher education more than trebled. The great majority of these had had an 'incomplete secondary' education (lasting seven to ten years), and except among people who had received a 'complete higher' education there was a larger number of educated women than of educated men. Male wartime losses must have been one of the main reasons for this difference. By comparison with 1939 the number of students at higher schools as a proportion of the total population had more than doubled, while those at specialized secondary schools had risen by one-third.

Other tables illustrate the territorial distribution of educational qualifications. In spite of notable advances since 1939, one would still have only one chance in five in the countryside as compared with in the towns of meeting a stranger who had had a 'complete higher' education, and one in two of meeting one who had had 'secondary or incomplete higher' education. Of course, as compared with 1897 there had been a vast change, for instance the achievement in the countryside of a level of literacy little short of that reached in the towns; although the literacy figures apply not to the whole population but only to those aged 9–49 in 1959. Among those, 1·5 per cent described themselves as illiterate.[2] There is no doubt that much success was achieved in the literacy drive which was one of the Bolsheviks' first mass projects.

There are still quite wide variations in the educational qualifications of the various republics. Estonia and Latvia, which were among the most highly educated republics in 1939 – when they had not yet been incorporated in the Soviet Union – remained near the front. They were surpassed only by Georgia, which held a decisive lead in the proportion of its citizens who had had a higher education. Other particularly well-educated republics were Armenia and the Ukraine, while Lithuania and Moldavia (which had not been favourably placed in 1939) tied for bottom place. Their large rural populations presumably reduce average standards in the last two republics mentioned. Despite the clustering of many educated people in Moscow and Leningrad (which are the principal centres of culture, science, and industrial· design as well as of government), the Russian Republic does not emerge as one of the most highly qualified republics, perhaps because it contains throughout its length and breadth such a diversity of nationalities.

The difference in numbers of persons having higher or 'secondary or incomplete' education per 1,000 of the population in the various republics was quite wide, for instance those with a higher education numbered 38 in Georgia and only 10 in Moldavia or Tajikistan. Those having a 'secondary or incomplete' education varied from 344 per 1,000 in Latvia to 175 in Lithuania. These differences were not, however, so wide as they had been in 1939. *Russians* did not emerge from the statistics as particularly well educated.

Officially it is claimed that all regions and all peoples of the USSR have access to enlightenment and culture. However, Russians did and probably still do occupy a more than proportionate share of posts requiring intellectual attainments. This would be in a considerable degree a legacy of the Tsarist period, when Russians were intellectual leaders in the country (Georgians, Armenians and Jews excepted).

As regards the quantity of quality of current education many visitors to Russia have been impressed – as indeed I have myself – by the scale of technical education and widespread acquaintance with technical matters. About the time of the First Five-Year Plan all reports said that Russians were technically incompetent, did not look after machinery etc. Russians have not had the long technical background of the English-speaking peoples and among country folk one will find a lower technical competence than in the towns. Manual workers (painters, decorators etc.) are generally less skilled than their American or British counterparts. But where theoretical knowledge is required there is no inferiority.

In the Soviet Union, supposedly a state of workers and peasants, manual work carries no prestige. As the salary scales show, vastly bigger rewards go to the scientist, expert technician, researcher. Placards carry pictures of manual workers, whose status is higher than before the Revolution, especially in relation to the peasantry. But anyone who is able to choose between being a worker and an 'intelligent' would choose the latter without a moment's hesitation. The way to get ahead is to go to college. This was always required for an academic career, but (as in the United States) it is now much more necessary than before if one seeks any kind of managerial post. It is even more necessary in the Soviet Union than in the United States because of the absence in the USSR of almost all opportunities for private enterprise.[3]

B. Labour Force Composition and Recruitment

This leads to a complex of questions such as: how is the labour force recruited, is there really no unemployment, what if any is the role of forced labour? Basically, there is freedom to choose one's occupation. Yet this right is qualified or diminished in several ways. The fact that one cannot start up one's own business is the most obvious limitation. Sex barriers are less of a problem. Equal pay is paid for equal work, and men and women are to a fairly large degree interchangeable in the economy. Three-quarters of all doctors and an even higher proportion of dentists are women, while women technicians and engineers are no rarity. One seems to find little if any trace of any feeling among men that they would prefer not to be subordinate to a woman. Yet extremely few women have occupied the *highest* posts, such as of minister or chairman of a State Committee. There are certain bars to female employment in some jobs, such as in underground coalmining,[4] but the vast majority of jobs are, at any rate in theory, open to women on an equal footing with men. However, although there are many advertisements for both males and females, enterprises sometimes advertise jobs specifying males only.

Soviet women may and do work at much physically tougher jobs than is normal in the West. They lay bricks and sewer pipes, chip away ice from pavements, labour at many farming jobs, drive tractors. They sometimes seem to do the harder work. This at least is more conspicuous in the Soviet Union than in any *Western* country. One needs to avoid assuming that this is necessarily bad: Russian women are often physically strong, and after the War many were left without husbands or children to look after; the necessities of postwar reconstruction and the equal opportunities afforded to women as regards education must also be remembered. But in the later 1960s the opinion began to be voiced that the participation of women in heavy physical work was an unsatisfactory state of affairs, which ought to be altered — which is in contrast with the previous attitude that the high percentage of women in occupations of nearly all sorts illustrated women's emancipation under Soviet rule.[5] The percentage of women employed in the most rugged occupations, such as building, has in fact declined slightly since 1965.

Government policy, social attitudes and the numerical preponderance of women in the population generally have the result that women form a large proportion of the labour force. The percentage of women in all branches of the State-owned economy (excluding collective farmers and individuals working on their own account) was in 1967 50 per cent. This percentage has increased slightly since 1960, owing probably to the incorporation of co-operatives into the State economy in that year (see below, pp. 103 & 112). Before, this proportion had been very stable, having been 48 per cent both in 1952 and in 1962. It varied in different branches, from 85 per cent in the health services, 74 per cent in trade, 66 per cent in communications, 58 per cent in state and business administration, to 47 per cent in industry, 28 per cent in construction, 24 per cent in transport.[6] In rural localities generally there had been 52 per cent in 1939, 71 per cent in highly abnormal wartime conditions in the beginning of 1943. It is likely that women still make up about half of all collective farmers, although owing to their home duties they work fewer 'labour days' per person than the men do.

As a rule, a married woman will go out to work partly because her husband will not earn enough to pay for any extras, and partly because going out to work is the accepted thing to do in the society. She is much less likely than in the West to gain any reflected glory from her husband's career.

The subject of women in the Soviet economy obviously cannot be dealt with in a few lines. This subject has been studied in detail by Dodge.[7] One might note in addition: (a) the Communists' proclaimed intention of freeing women from the drudgery of the kitchen sink; (b) the inadequate provision of kindergartens, houseroom and other home amenities; (c) the supposition that virtually all time not occupied by labour at one's place of work is free leisure time,[8] which only recently has been realized officially in the USSR to be nonsense; (d) Soviet women, having as a rule to go out to work as well as look after their home and help bring up their children, definitely enjoy less leisure than Soviet men.[9]

Apart from Hobson's choice of growing up as a man or woman, there are two major alternatives: to grow up in a peasant family or in the family of a town worker, and to grow up as a Russian (including a Ukranian or White Russian) or among one of the other nationalities.

It is a drawback to be born into a rural family. Educated people are fewer here, automobiles few, city lights distant. Educational opportunities are inferior. A survey of 10 per cent of middle-school leavers in Novosibirsk oblast in 1963 found that 10 out of 100 leavers whose parents were agricultural workers continued their education, whereas 82 out of 100 leavers whose parents belonged to the urban intelligentsia did so. The percentage who had wished to continue had been respectively 76 per cent and 93 per cent.[10] Apart from the limited scope offered by agriculture, all possibilities of advancement are found in the towns, but opportunities for moving there are limited by dwelling restrictions. However, as the government has had to rely on the peasantry to furnish a sizeable proportion of the labour required for industrialization, a bright boy or girl is likely to get the chance.

In the countryside, the main opening is to be found in agricultural mechanization. In the past this proceeded alongside gross waste of labour resources: certain functions were mechanized while others were not. Moreover, operational control of all heavy machinery was restricted to the Machine Tractor Stations, though many collective farmers were employed in driving machines.

If born into a Russian-speaking family one starts off with a linguistic advantage, comparable perhaps to that of belonging to an English-speaking family in Australia or America rather than to a non-English-speaking one. One will be more likely to be eligible for any post with a national security significance, a very important consideration in the USSR where security-consciousness penetrates to extraordinary limits.[11] Some at least of the smaller nationalities have secured their full share of the highest posts, such as Stalin (a Georgian), or Mikoyan (an Armenian). But a member of a nationality which is considered insufficiently 'Russianized' could probably not rise to such heights. It would be as disadvantageous to be born within a small, obscure nationality as it would be within any other large country and for similar reasons. However, no single racial group is so distinctly divided off from the rest as coloured people in the United States or South Africa.[12]

The non-Russians do not on an average participate as yet in the industrial labour force to the same extent as the Russians, but their participation is increasing.

Social status plays a certain role. Property or money may be inherited.

Peculiar advantages of an important position are that the incumbent's family is more likely to reside in Moscow, or perhaps in Leningrad or Kiev, where cultural facilities are much more abundant and accessible than they are elsewhere; while the family will be allotted better living quarters and very possibly will own an out-of-town summerhouse. In the better-off family the mother can also look after the younger children herself during the day, instead of leaving this to an aged grandmother or impersonal kindergarten as most families have to do. Another advantage is dietetic. Such a family can afford to make bread and potatoes less important items of diet.

Good family connections are probably not important in job-seeking generally. Among politically significant posts, however, one notes such phenomena as the promotion of Adzhubey, a son-in-law of Khrushchev, to the editorship of *Izvestiya* − and his dismissal soon after Khrushchev himself. The decentralized system of appointment and dismissal to minor posts creates strong possibilities of nepotism, which was illustrated in 1936−37 when the arrest of executives was generally accompanied by the arrest of their subordinates.[13] All appointments to important positions (those listed in the *nomenklatura*) have to be approved by the Party, this being one of its main instruments of control of the society.

Immediately after the Revolution a sort of social status in reverse operated: it was advantageous to belong to a 'proletarian' family and disadvantageous to have had 'bourgeois' connections. Little trace of such attitudes has survived. Very many families have had one or more of their present or past members imprisoned or otherwise punished for alleged anti-State activities, and perhaps subsequently 'rehabilitated' (which means as a rule that they are no longer alive).

It is claimed that because of the nature of the economic and social structure there are no exploiting or idle classes. Such a state of affairs is contrasted with the alleged existence of a large and wholly parasitical class in 'capitalist' countries. In the Soviet Union there are some idle *individuals*: very wide differentiation of incomes, coupled with very low rates of income tax and death duty, has created a situation where the children of the richer groups would not need to go out to work, although the majority of them probably do so, especially since laws have been introduced which impose stiff penalties on 'parasitical' elements in the population.[14] The ideological justification for such laws is the slogan 'he who does not work shall not eat'.

A good brain, thorough training and good health and stamina are as important in the Soviet Union as in most other countries, but in some posts political conformity and reliability are required more than intellect. It is very advantageous to be born with a tendency to conform, or to acquire such a tendency. Here, there are two possibilities. One is to be an enthusiastic and unquestioning Marxist-Leninist, then one will never feel the enveloping restrictions. The other alternative is that one's talents should lean towards fields which are not naturally susceptible to ideological interference. Obviously, economics is about the worst to choose from this point of view. Sociology would be equally bad. Best would be some highly technical subject, for instance, how to design gearwheels, about which Marxism-Leninism can have nothing to say. (Though, in theory, Marxists regard all sciences as being governed by the principles of dialectical materialism.) This consideration probably turns many Soviet students towards the technical sciences, which also serves the Party's purpose in that it strengthens the economy while leaving their ideologists a near-monopoly of the whole social science field.

Nowadays, Soviet citizens are anything but revolutionary-minded. Young students often show an independent spirit, but this is usually short-lived as considerations of career gain the upper hand. All persistent protesters against the regime find their paths to advancement blocked, and if they attempt any public protest are arrested and imprisoned.

After graduating at a university one must serve for three years in a place designated by the State, in accordance with one's speciality. Usually, a choice of three places is given. After this term has expired one may work where or how one likes, although these words have to be understood within the context of the normal circumstances of living in the Soviet Union. One may not employ others for gain,[15] buy anything with the intention of reselling it, export or import on one's own account, or own capital equipment. The only form of permitted non-State business organization has been the 'co-operative'. This type of business used to operate in a fairly wide variety of fields, but typically involved a particular (perhaps localized) skill, such as a handicraft co-operative; or performed work which was not physically very exacting (e.g. cloakroom attendants), or was concerned with making repairs. The technical equipment of a co-operative was generally much inferior to that of a State organization. Like the Israeli *kibbutzim*, the co-operatives found it difficult to function efficiently without employing hired labour, and they might in fact employ up to 20 per cent of their own strength.[16] This category was reduced in size in 1956 and was largely absorbed into State industry in 1960, with the probable exception of some highly specialized art or craft co-operatives.[17]

It is theoretically possible to work independently, but the opportunities for doing so are extremely limited, owing to the impossibility of buying any kind of capital equipment apart from simple tools, and as every cultural field is highly organized while all organizations are Party-dominated.

While recruitment of labour in general is now free, up to 1953–1955 forced labour played a fairly substantial part in the economy. For a long time apologists did not wish to believe in the existence of forced labour in the USSR. A 'confession against interest', as a reliable voucher for the apparently circumstantial stories brought back by individual victims, was lacking. There is no shred of doubt left now, of course, after the publication of Solzhenitsyn's 'A Day in the Life of Ivan Denisovich' and other memoirs.[18]

A historical approach to the question shows that the onus of disproof should have been laid on those who denied the existence of forced labour in the Soviet Union rather than on those who affirmed its presence, because forced labour is indeed nothing new, either in Russia or in North America or Australia. Until little more than a century ago forced labour – then called serfdom – comprised the very basis of the Russian State. Soviet researchers have recently turned up new data which show that earlier accepted percentages of the extent of serf labour in Russian industrial output in the eighteenth and nineteenth centuries had been understated. The now accepted percentages among the total workforce in Russian factories are as follows:–[19]

Year	Per cent
1767	91
1804	73
1825	66
1860	44

Thus, even just before the emancipation in 1861 nearly half the industrial workers were serfs. Subsequently, exile to Siberia was a commonly imposed punishment. One walked: the trek took about twelve months.[20]

An authoritative history of forced labour in the USSR has not been and cannot be written, owing to the lack of systematic published information. However, even before the more recent revelations Soviet sources made occasional reference to 'corrective labour'. A decree of 4 August 1933 declared 12,484 persons 'freed from further measures of social defence', while 59,516 more were to have their sentences shortened, and 500 were to be reinstated with rights of citizenship.[21] This followed the completion of the Baltic – White Sea Canal, which was achieved

> by White Sea Construction under the direction of the OGPU[22] by forces of criminals, sentenced for various terms, in exclusively difficult geological and hydro-technical conditions in the record short period in the practice of hydro-technical construction of 20 months.[23]

The Chief Administration of Camps, GULAG, is mentioned in other decrees.[24] Dal'stroy, literally 'Remote Construction', responsible for mining operations in eastern Siberia, also is mentioned occasionally in decrees, being listed next to GULAG.[25] The 1941 Plan shows that the contribution of the NKVD to capital construction in that year was to have been very important: it was put down for 6,810 million out of 37,650 million roubles' worth of capital works,[26] or roughly as much as total investment in the coal, oil and chemicals industries put together. About one-third of this was ascribed to GULAG and other parts to highway and railway repairing, while part was left unspecified.

The NKVD was also listed as engaging in industrial output. In some cases this was evidently to be performed by forced labour, such as 150,000 tons of chromite ore to be mined by GULAG and 5,325,000 tons of coal ascribed to the NKVD.[27] Some other items listed under the NKVD included steam-rollers, scrapers, Brinell presses (for measuring hardness), even stockings (2½ million pairs).[28] It seems much less likely in these cases that forced labour was involved. Possibly some free labour was also administered by the NKVD. The NKVD was put down for 1,969 million roubles' worth of industrial output,[29] which was 1·2 per cent of total planned output.

One problem has been to distinguish between several distinct categories of forced labourers. For instance, for infringement of certain rules workers might be sentenced to a type of involuntary labour with reduction of 25 per cent in wages, but they remained at their normal place of employment or in its neighbourhood. One might also be exiled to remote places where the only workplace was a single factory or mine. There was also forced labour in camps of the 'classic' type.

An article 'Forced Labour in the Soviet Bloc'[30] summarized various estimates of numbers of forced labourers. These estimates have ranged at different times from 3·3 million to 8, 12 or even 20 million. Jasny estimated 3½ million in application to 1941 but thought that the actual figure might have been 'even smaller'.[31] Swianiewicz believed this number to be too low: his estimate was about 6·9 million.[32] Clearly, big problems would be raised by even minimum maintenance (food, shelter, clothing etc. under Russian climatic conditions) of great numbers of people in remote areas. There would also be a problem of providing useful employment, although this would be diminished if only rudimentary tools were provided, while huge numbers of people could be employed on such laborious tasks as earth-moving. These problems would be further reduced if a substantial proportion of the total were stationed in more inhabited or accessible areas. Certainly, there are many remote corners even of European Russia, but these include regions which are served by rail links although they are not visited by foreigners. Problems of supply would be eased by standardization of rations, by ordering in bulk and perhaps by other simplifications.

The problem of maintenance would also be eased by a high mortality rate. If very large numbers are involved one would expect that there would have been a large reaction on birth-rates and death-rates, and in this connection we have noted that the population did not increase between 1926 and 1939 as much as the planning authorities had expected; furthermore, in 1954 the birth-rate rose, presumably owing to the release of some categories of prisoners in the previous year.

One also readily sees that the total of forced labourers could run into millions, considering: the 'liquidation' of the kulaks, and deportations of some nationalities (certain Crimean and Caucasian nationalities, allegedly for treasonable conduct during the war: this was condemned in Khrushchev's secret speech in 1956 about Stalin's crimes). The location of all members of national groups is not ascertainable from the 1959 census. Western investigators agree that the extent of forced labour has varied at different times.

Its origins were threefold. There was Russia's historical background of servitude, already noted. Secondly, there was the Marxist notion that there was wage-slavery in capitalist societies, which would suggest that militarization of labour would not make any great difference. Indeed, Trotsky argued in favour of militarization of labour, which he described as 'the essential and unavoidable means of organizing labour . . . in accordance with the wants of a socialistic society during the period of transition from Capitalism to Communism'.[33] But Trotsky's viewpoint was not generally adopted among the Bolsheviks. Thirdly, there was the notion that former capitalists had to be re-educated in order to crush out their capitalistic leanings.

The system expanded to engulf numbers of peasants swept up in forced collectivization when government policy collided with the established rural structure. During the later nineteen-thirties, forced labour fed on purges and persecutions of intellectuals and of the managerial class, both in business and in the armed forces. During the war there were fresh deportations of members of the indigenous nationalities from the Baltic States and Poland (though many Poles were later allowed to leave the USSR, and provided first-hand accounts). In 1953 and 1955 amnesties of several categories of prisoners were proclaimed, and forced labour is believed to have been sharply reduced. It still exists as a judicial category; and while it probably no longer has any substantial importance in economic life, traces remain, such as the chessmen carved by Gerald Brooke.

The practice at certain periods of forced labour on a vast scale must obviously modify our view of Soviet economic history. Forced labour deterred or stifled opposition to government policies which might otherwise have emerged: it thus facilitated implementation of such policies as giving priority to investment in heavy industry and armaments, reorganizing agriculture for mixed political, ideological and economic motives, and whatever else the Party decided or might decide. Work was consequently performed in fiercely cold and inhospitable regions without the need to pay the very high wages, and make the heavier investments in social capital, which otherwise could not have been avoided. The use of manual labour on a large scale made it possible to economize on providing mechanical equipment. From this angle, forced labour would figure among the factors that promoted Soviet industrial development. But the practice also damaged the economy, in that it provided no incentive to modernize certain branches, lowered labour productivity, probably encouraged an excessive attention to development of the remoter and more inhospitable areas, tied up tens of thousands of guards, and held back the growth of the population. These negative aspects probably outweighed the positive ones, even if humanitarian considerations are entirely disregarded.

One published memoir (on the attempted construction of a railway from Salekhard to Igarka between March 1949 and March 1953) includes the following comment on the suggestion that the use of prisoners in constructional projects was relatively cheap:

> It merely seems so, after all the prisoners have somehow to be fed, shod, clothed and guarded, and guarded well: special areas have to be constructed, provided with watch-towers for the sentries, guard-houses – yes, and for that matter the maintenance of the guards is a costly matter. Then there are the operational, cultural-educational and[34] ... sections which existed nowhere outside the camp. ... In fact a sizeable establishment. Then there are those again who have to fetch the water for them, wash the floors and heat the baths. After all there are a lot of things that living human beings need. Then in the columns and camps there are also many duty officers and cooks, the hewers of wood, and drawers of water, the clerks, carpenters, and other 'scabs' as they are called in camp! So that if one averages it out you must reckon one and a half ancillary persons for every one who actually works. But the main thing is that the guards cannot deploy the labour force as it ought to be: either one is not allowed to use the necessary machinery, or else the foremen and superintendants, who are prisoners themselves, simply have no time to stop and think about how to organize the work because of the consequent parades, inspections and all the other mess.[35]

After Stalin's death this line, the signals and everything that had been erected by great numbers of forced labourers from their camp sites spaced out 15 kilometres along the line, were left to rust in the snow.

Its construction had been started to give effect to a remark by Stalin that the 'Russian people had long dreamed of having a safe outlet onto the Arctic Ocean from the Ob' river'. Later it was decided that the line would have to be extended to Igarka. Cost was to be no object. This of course was not a rational economic decision, and more generally forced labour in spite of its varied economic aspects cannot be regarded as purely an economic phenomenon. It seems to be a characteristic of a totalitarian state at a certain stage in its evolution.

Labour compulsion in this extreme form has never been the typical form of employment in the Soviet Union. In a lesser degree, there is labour direction of graduates. Lesser still, there is the *orgnabor* system. Like forced labour, *orgnabor* was considered to have a useful educative effect.

All these data bear witness to the revolutionary role played by Soviet labour law as an instrument of organized recruitment of labour power for industry in regard to the re-education of collective farmers and the crushing out among collective farmers, induced into the ranks of the working class, of petty bourgeois, petty-ownership survivals.[36]

As noted below (Chapter 16), before the war a system of regional allocation was in operation. The 1941 Plan contains rather detailed information about numbers of workers to be recruited from particular regions for particular ministries. The various regional and Party authorities would doubtless have been blamed for any underfulfilment of the specified total. Probably a mixture of publicity, cajolement and coercion would be employed.

Another form of recruitment is the 'communal call-out' (*obshchestvennyy prizyv*). This is used when labour is being recruited for 'heroic' tasks in specially rough conditions for which it would otherwise be too costly to recruit a workforce, or which glow with patriotic or ideological appeal. Perhaps the best example is the initial recruitment to plough up the virgin lands in Siberia and Kazakhstan. A typical source for such recruits would be a university. A sort of high-powered publicity campaign backed by the Party, Komsomol,[37] all official student organizations, the press and radio, and all the other publicity and propaganda organs, would be launched. Still, by digging in one's heels one might contrive not to go, but otherwise might well find oneself going. Return would be discouraged, though if one were determined it could probably be managed. In launching a 'communal call-out', the authorities rely on a force of persuasion which is not opposed by any rival body, although it contrasts with the ethos of a society where sectional charitable appeals have no place, and cannot evoke any glamour of labour abroad under the banner of a 'Peace Corps'. Owing probably to fears over security and that 'liberal' ideas would be injected, little use has been made of foreign student volunteers.

Another form of labour direction was made a collective responsibility. On 2 October 1940 each urban and collective farm centre was required to send a quota of boys to technical schools, who after graduating were to serve as directed for a five-year period.[38] Since 3 March 1936, there has been an obligation of collective farmers and individual peasants aged from 18 to 45 (men) or from 18 to 40 (women) to do road work on six days a year.[39]

Finally, certain demobilized army units have been transferred almost *en bloc* to work on some particular project or to set up a State Farm. The impossibility of objecting to unfair competition greatly facilitates this employment, of course. One occasionally used to see uniformed soldiers working at simple manual civil tasks.[40] Presumably it would be more efficient to demobilize them and employ individuals according to their personal qualifications – if any.

These various kinds of extraordinary recruitment have one thing in common, namely that they involve migration to the place of work. If labour is being recruited for local projects, or to fill particular slots in existing organizations, none of these means are used and the Soviet labour market is at the present time approximately as voluntary as most others.

However, job-changing is still discouraged. In Western countries there are in normal circumstances no *official* barriers to changing one's job. Other deterrents do exist, such as that uninterrupted service with a given organization may be a condition of promotion: 'a rolling stone gathers no moss'. Contributory pension schemes às a rule stipulate continuity of employment. However, the disadvantages to the economy of such inflexibilities are increasingly realized. Automation and other technical developments demand more flexible employment patterns. For its part, the State provides unemployment benefit and a national system of employment exchanges. In contrast, in the Soviet Union all official emphasis has been on the need to reduce 'labour fluidity' and to retain workers in given jobs.

'Labour fluidity' – flitting from one job to another – emerged as a phenomenon of the early industrialization period and the problem has never been long dormant. It was combated by discriminatory action in regard to vacations, and by the introduction (1938) of a Labour Book system, which recorded any change of occupation.[41] Then, on 26 June 1940, a decree 'forbade all employees of state enterprises and institutions to leave their work without permission, save in a few narrowly defined instances (e.g. qualifying for old-age pension, being the wife of a person sent to work in another town, etc.)'.[42] Absenteeism, or lateness for more than 20 minutes, was to be severely punished. The timing of this law was presumably influenced by the threatening international situation, but at the time it was not presented as such (this was the heyday of Soviet-Nazi collaboration). It remained on the books until 1956 although it seems not to have been enforced after 1952.

Workers may now give notice and leave without meeting any legal obstacle, but they are still strongly discouraged from so doing. Khrushchev threatened to deprive workers who quit of their annual holidays; but such a measure would be contrary to the Constitution, for what it is worth (and hitherto the Constitution has been much more scrupulously observed in its economic than its political clauses), and it has not been adopted. One must, however, appear before a trade union committee and justify a wish to leave. It is still assumed by most

Soviet commentators that the quitters are the irresponsible ones, but dissentient voices are beginning to be raised: the simplicitude of supposing that all quitters leave because they want to earn 'a long rouble' is at long last being exposed. Automation and other changes are likely to induce a change in the direction of greater liberality, but questions of creating permanent cadres and of 'liquidating their fluidity' (!) remain on the agenda.[43]

Meanwhile, tightness in the labour market has resulted in one forward step. In December 1966 it was decided to set up state committees on the employment of labour resources in the republics. It was planned to set up employment and information agencies in all towns of over 100,000 people which had a need for them.[44]

Another way in which the labour market has been regulated has been through manipulation of the working week. Although Sunday is Sunday, the government may or may not decide to make it a rest-day. In 1929 a continuous working week was decreed and spread to more branches in 1930: one laboured four days and then rested one,[45] but there was no universal rest-day. The drawbacks of a system which was liable to lead to 'depersonalized' machine-tending and so led to careless maintenance, and which only by accident gave relatives or friends the same day off, led to its abandonment conclusively with the reintroduction in 1940 of a seven-day working week, with Sunday to be observed as the rest-day. Subsequently (1968–69) a five-day working week in the more normal sense has been introduced.

The exception of unemployment pay from the normal range of social insurance payments is supposed to be justified by the absence of any unemployment in the USSR. As already noted (Chapter 6) it is officially claimed that there has been no unemployment since 1930. What apparently happened was that as soon as the rural population had been organized into collective farms, whose members shared the surplus product (if any) of the group, a framework was cast within which rural underemployment could increase indefinitely: unemployment began to decline and disappear as the speed of collectivization exceeded a certain critical figure.[46] Completion of the collectivization process should (other things being equal) have begun to generate unemployment, which even if not officially admitted might show itself indirectly, less in the cities (owing to restrictions on dwelling there, except to the extent that these were evaded), or in villages (as these are physically situated on the territory of the collective farms), as in the smaller towns.

A much larger increase in employment did occur in 1959–65 than the Seven-Year Plan had foreshadowed, yet pools of 'surplus labour' additionally appeared in middle-sized and smaller towns: at the 23rd Congress of the Communist Party in March 1966 delegates from Tajikistan, Uzbekistan and various areas in European Russia disclosed the presence of unemployed labour in their respective constituencies, whereas labour was said to be short in Moscow and Leningrad, and in Siberia generally. Labour was generally surplus in Europe and in the Urals, and so it was proposed to build in these areas mainly enterprises belonging to labour-intensive branches; to increase shift-working; and generally to utilize existing equipment more fully. New enterprises were to be built chiefly in middle-sized and small towns, only new service enterprises in large cities.[47]

On the whole, the labour market might be described as both organized and unorganized: it has been organized macroeconomically but not microeconomically, whereas in market economies the situation is approximately the other way round. The absence until lately of labour exchanges for facilitating job-changing must have made it easier for the government to ensure participation in organized recruitment. Against this, a heavy demand for labour, resulting from pressure to fulfil the plans and from the planners' proclivities to make too optimistic forecasts of increases in labour productivity, had the result that it was easy to find a new job. To counteract what it saw as an undesirable extent of flitting from one job to another the government consequently had recourse to artificial impediments, such as the Labour Book system and other obstacles to labour movement. Administrative measures were thus used to combat economic stimuli which themselves stemmed only slightly more indirectly from government policy.[48]

On the whole, the link between the size of the population and that of the labour force is more direct in the Soviet Union than in a number of other countries. This is due to such features as the absence of income from investments and the large extent of female employment. Besides the low wage-rates already mentioned, various aspects of the society combine to produce the result that a high proportion of the able-bodied and non-student population goes out to work: (a) living space per person is small, and so does not require as much attention as a larger house or apartment; moreover, very few urban dwellings have separate gardens; (b) cares of looking after children are reduced by: the small size of the average family, State arrangements for intermittent training or recreation of children, such as Pioneer camps; and ubiquitous grand-mothers.[49] On the other hand, the following factors would strain the closeness of the link between the population and labour force: (a) cares of looking after children are enhanced by: the relatively late school-starting age (7 years); difficulties and inconveniences of shopping; the usual lack of a family car; (b) the student group is large (one-third of the population is undergoing some form of full-time or part-time education, not counting children of pre-school age); (c) presumably there are, as an aftermath of the war, a considerable number of invalid cases;[50] (d) the pensionable age is rather low, though recently fresh inducements have been held out to encourage people to go on working longer.

C. Labour Force Trends in Relation to Population

Table 3 shows average yearly totals of persons employed in the 'national economy' and in collective farms. The statistical handbooks provide reasonably complete data only for the State sector: however (c) and (d) together should convey the trend over time of the whole labour force fairly accurately, except during any periods when substantial transfers from the non-State sector to the State sector (or, for logical completeness, vice versa) are being made. In column (c), to preserve comparability over time, members of handicraft co-operatives have been added throughout, although these (as regards at any rate their vast majority) were finally incorporated within the State sector only in 1960. This eliminates one possible course of distortion. As in 1940 the gathering into collective farms of peasants living in the recently annexed areas had not been completed, column (d) in that year should be enlarged to take account of this difference: the addition would perhaps amount to a few millions.

Even making allowance for such an addition the ratio of the labour force to the population as defined by (c) + (d)/(b) rose between 1940 and 1953. Apparently, wartime losses did not depress this ratio: as if the economy had not suffered then such a great depletion of labour power considered in the abstract without reference to particular individuals, as one might have supposed. This is in conformity with what was written earlier concerning the impact of war on an economy.[51] Since 1953 this ratio has gone on rising, between about 1963 and 1973 even at a faster rate — the annual rate of population growth having declined from 1·2 per cent in 1968 to 0·9 per cent from 1971 onwards.

The continual rise in the column (d) percentage means, of course, that the labour situation is becoming very tight. This was foreseen a long time ago; for instance as noted in 1966 Leningrad industry, according to the secretary of its Party committee, was expected to be short of 100,000 workers by the end of 1969.[52] As yet, relatively few workers have been redistributed in an organized way on account of technical progress,[53] but this nettle will have to be grasped, and in general, ways must be found to utilize the available labour force more effectively. Labour organization is one field where procedural, possibly even structural, changes can be expected.

Table 3

Population and Labour Force, 1940–77 (millions)

	Population January of each year (a)	In 'national economy' (av. yearly totals) (b)	In collective farms (including fishing) (av. yearly totals) (c)	$\frac{(b) + (c)}{(a)}$ (d)
1940	193	33·4	29·0	32·3
1945	170–175	28·6		
1950	178·5	40·4		
1951	181·6	42·3		
1952	184·8	43·8		
1953	188·0	45·3	25·6	37·7
1954	191·0	49·0		
1955	194·4	50·2	24·8	38·6
1956	197·9	51·7		
1957	201·4	54·3		
1958	204·9	55·9		
1959	208·8	57·9	24·5	39·5
1960	212·3	62·0	22·3	39·7
1961	216·2	65·9	20·7	40·1
1962	219·7	68·3	20·0	40·2
1963	223·2	70·5	19·4	40·3
1964	226·4	73·2	19·2	40·8
1965	229·3	76·9	18·9	41·8
1966	231·8	79·7	18·6	42·4
1967	234·4	82·3	18·4	43·0
1968	237·2	85·1	18·1	43·5
1969	239·5	87·9	17·5	44·0
1970	241·7	90·2	17·0	44·4
1971	243·9	92·8	16·5	44·8
1972	246·3	95·2	16·2	45·2
1973	248·6	97·5	16·1	45·7
1974	250·9	99·8	15·9	46·1
1975	253·3	102·2	15·4	46·4
1976	255·5	104·2	15·0	46·7
1977	257·8	106·4	14·6	46·9

Gaps indicate that information is not published.

Notes

1 See in this connection my article 'Declining Prospects of Soviet Population Growth', *The World Today*, December 1968.
2 *Itogi vsesoyuznoy perepisi naseleniya 1959 goda, SSSR (svodnyy tom)* (1962), Table 25, p. 88.
3 Cf. Joseph S. Berliner, 'Managerial Incentives and Decisionmaking: A Comparison of the United States and the Soviet Union', *Comparisons of the United States and Soviet Economies*, Joint Economic Committee, Congress of the United States, Part I (1959), p. 351.
4 It appears, however, that this has not altogether prevented the employment of women underground.
5 E.g. N. Voznesenskiy, *Voyennaya ekonomika SSSR v period otechestvennoy voyny* (1946), pp. 92–3.
6 *Narodnoye khozyaystvo SSSR v 1967 g.* (1968), p. 654. These were the 1967 proportions; there are slight variations from year to year.
7 Norton T. Dodge, *Women in the Soviet Economy* (1966).
8 From which has naturally followed official inattention to provision of adequate shopping facilities, demands to attend political meetings etc.
9 Time-budgets' prepared by the well-known economist S. G. Strumilin demonstrated this difference, which it is possible to regard as an inheritance from conditions of peasant life in a highly seasonal form of agriculture, where the women but not the men, work all the year round (see his *Izbranniye proizvedeniya, tom 3* (1964), pp. 167–249).
10 V. N. Shubkin, *Voprosy filosofii*, no. 5, 1965, pp. 65–6.
11 Cf. O. V. Penkovsky, *The Penkovsky Papers*, p. 255.
12 There are extremely few Negroes in the Soviet Union; very many Soviet citizens probably have never seen one.
13 Margaret Dewar, *Industrial Management in the USSR* (1945), pp. 53–4.
14 See R. Beermann, *Soviet Studies*, April 1964. A common punishment for 'parasitism' is exile to Siberia. As a result, some women in Novosibirsk region complained about an influx of 'parasitic girls' from Leningrad. They pointed out that if Leningrad was unable to cope with such girls, their village could scarcely be expected to reform them; and how could they protect their husbands?
15 Note that there is not a complete ban on employing others: one can employ a housemaid, for example, but the person employed must not be creating 'surplus value', i.e. by producing anything material.
16 A. Nove, *The Soviet Economy, An Introduction* (1961), p. 44.
17 The share of total industrial output which was produced by co-operatives dropped from 6 per cent in 1959 to 3 per cent in 1960 (*Narodnoye khozyaystvo SSSR v 1960 godu* (1961), p. 213). There appears to be no later figure.

18 See for example Boris D'yakov, *Oktyabr'*, July 1964.
19 Jerome Blum, *Lord and Peasant in Russia from the Ninth to the Nineteenth Century* (1961), p. 324.
20 This is illustrated in the East German film *Velikiy podvig* (The Great Exploit).
21 *Sobraniye zakonov i rasporyazheniy SSSR*, 1933, no. 50–294.
22 Secret Police.
23 Reference as footnote 21, no. 50–295.
24 See for instance *Sobraniye zakonov i rasporyazheniy SSSR*, 1935, no. 61–488.
25 Ibid., 1933, no. 33–195 (decree of 21 May 1933).
26 *Gosudarstvennyy plan razvitiya narodnogo khozyaystva SSSR na 1941 god, Prilozheniye k postanovleniyu SNK SSSR i Tsk VKP (b) no. 127 ot 17 yanvarya 1941 g.* (1941), p. 484. Cf. J. Miller, *Soviet Studies*, April 1951, pp. 380–1.
27 *Gosudarstvennyy plan razvitiya narodnogo khozyaystva SSSR na 1941 god, Prilozheniye k postanovleniyu SNK SSSR i Tsk VKP (b) no. 127 ot 17 yanvarya 1941 g.* (1941), pp. 17 and 13.
28 Ibid., pp. 29, 49, 71.
29 Ibid., p. 10.
30 Franklyn D. Holzman (ed.), *Readings on the Soviet Economy* (1962), reprinted by permission from *Trends in Economic Growth: A Comparison of the Western Powers and the Soviet Bloc*, prepared for the Joint Committee on the Economic Report by the Legislative Reference Service of the Library of Congress (1955), pp. 234–46.
31 N. Jasny, *Journal of Political Economy*, October 1951, p. 416.
32 S. Swianiewicz, *Forced Labour and Economic Development* (1965), p. 31.
33 S. N. Prokopovitch, *The Economic Condition of Soviet Russia* (1924), p. 31.
34 Abbreviation not understood.
35 Statement by Selivanov, as reported by A. Pobozhiy in *Novyy mir*, August 1964, p. 155.
36 Z. Grishin, *Sotsialisticheskaya organizatsiya i distsiplina truda i voprosy sovetskogo trudovogo prava* (1934), p. 25.
37 Junior Branch of Communist Party. The Komsomol was itself an important source of recruits: between 1956 and 1960 it sent 1,230,000 volunteers to 'shock construction sites' in Siberia, the Far East and Kazakhstan (N. I. Shishkin (ed.), *Trudovyye resursy SSSR* (1961), p. 170).
38 John N. Hazard in H. Zink and T. Cole (eds.), *Government in Wartime Europe* (1941), pp. 135–6, quoting *Vedomosti Verkhovnogo Soveta SSSR*, no. 37 (100), 9 October 1940, p. 1.
39 M. V. Kolganov in D. Chernomordik (ed.), *Narodnyy dokhod SSSR* (1939), p. 166.
40 Cf. O. V. Penkovsky, *The Penkovsky Papers*, p. 211.
41 W. W. Kulski, *The Soviet Regime* (1963), p. 228.
42 A. Nove, *The Soviet Economy, An Introduction* (1961), p. 119.

43 E.g. *Ekonomicheskaya gazeta*, no. 25, 1968, p. 13.

44 K. Novikov, *Kommunist*, no. 13, 1969, as reported in *Soviet News*, 21 October 1969, p. 29. This piecemeal approach is typical of the Soviet approach to problems which are awkward to reconcile with official propaganda, in this case concerning the alleged absence of unemployment in the USSR.

45 In some branches, five days of work were followed by one rest-day. On this whole subject, see Solomon M. Schwarz, *Labor in the Soviet Union*, (1953), pp. 268–77.

46 See my article in *Soviet Studies*, July 1967 (vol. XIX, no. 1).

47 Raymond Hutchings, *The World Today*, August 1966, p. 357.

48 E.g. *Industriya*, 21 June 1940, p. 1, which complained that although Labour Books had been introduced, in the existing situation of labour shortage many plant directors did not look at them.

49 More controversially and tentatively, I would add: the still common swaddling of babies like parcels and the consequent docility of young children.

50 These are not particularly in evidence in Moscow, either because they are discouraged from living in the capital (restrictions upon dwelling in Moscow, and various other cities, are still in force), or because most limbless veterans have been fitted with artificial limbs, so that their disability is not ordinarily apparent.

51 See above, Chapter 5.

52 G. Romanov, *Ekonomicheskaya gazeta*, no. 17, 1966, p. 4.

53 M. Sonin, *Ekonomicheskaya gazeta*, no. 2, 1966, p. 29.

10
AGRICULTURAL ORGANIZATION AND POLICY

At the present time approximately 37 per cent of the Soviet population live in rural areas, while about 21 per cent are engaged in agriculture; whereas in 1917 the corresponding proportions were about 82 per cent and 70 per cent. Agricultural organization and policy have therefore been of direct concern to the majority of the population. Indirectly, of course, they have been of concern to the whole population, owing in part to the relationship between agricultural and industrial performance.

The alternation of government policy with regard to agriculture and the assault upon the established rural structure and its catastrophic consequences were described in Part II. The present chapter is confined to a brief discussion of the factors which have influenced agricultural organization and policy.

As Katkoff well puts it,

> the organizational structure of Soviet agriculture is primarily the result of the interplay of three basic factors: the historical servitude of Russian peasantry, the nature and topography of the major agricultural regions of the Soviet Union, and the Marxian doctrine of ownership of means of production and its adaptation by Soviet agricultural policy-makers.[1]

The Soviet régime inherited a backward agriculture, which still mainly used primitive tools. In relation to the low yields obtained per acre the density of population on the land was high. After serfdom had been abolished, the countryside was ruled by the communal village organization, the mir. There was little of a tradition of independent farming, but this little had been encouraged by Stolypin and began to flourish after World War I, after the peasants had seized the land they regarded as rightfully theirs. During and after the war the mir experienced a revival.[2]

Prior to 1929 the Bolsheviks had not effected any major change in arrangements in the countryside, apart, of course, from placing themselves at the head of the upheaval which enabled the peasants to expropriate the big landowners. On the other hand, the change brought about by collectivization was more drastic than was the subordination of industry to the Soviet government. For the nationalization of industry did not diminish the freedom of the Soviet worker *as* a worker. The workers did not become share-holders in the nationalized factories, but then they had not been before, Except during the earliest stages of spontaneous nationalization the participation of the worker in ownership of his factory was not affected, for it was nil in either case; although some small degree of workers' participation in decision-making, in relation to both production and welfare, has been achieved.

Collectivization of agriculture, on the other hand, snatched away from the kulaks their share of ownership, which they fiercely resented. This resentment did not threaten the régime, because it was essentially local in viewpoint and was not expressed through any national political body.[3] However, such was the size of the agricultural sector that even its blind, uncoordinated actions brought repercussions through the economy. This resentment indeed took forms which obliged the Soviet government to restore this share of ownership in some measure, by permitting the peasants to retain small private plots and to sell their small surpluses of produce on the collective farm markets.

However, the collectivized peasantry were left in an inferior position as compared with the industrial proletariat. They, for example, received no minimum wage or guaranteed remuneration. They did not belong to trade unions. Educational and all other facilities in the countryside were inferior to those of the towns. The city working class or proletariat was, at any rate in theory, the class that exercised authority.

A Collective Farm Charter was adopted in 1935. In theory the farms were voluntary organizations, managed democratically by their members (everyone over 16 years of age). In practice, the farm chairman who was in charge of the farm generally, was nominated by the local Party organization. What farms should grow, when they should sow and carry out other stages in the agricultural cycle, how they should organize their work, were laid down in minute detail from above (the Ministry of Agriculture at the apex), and were enforced by the local government and Party organizations.

The well-being of farm members was neglected. Indeed, the government did not accept responsibility for this, although it had fixed the organizational framework which would largely determine whether a farm prospered or not. Payments to the Machine Tractor Stations, which were responsible for all work with heavy machinery, and compulsory deliveries ('procurements') to the State and allocations to the 'Indivisible Fund' took precedence over any distributions to members. The amounts distributed in the form of an annual share-out might be much or little: usually they were little, and sometimes extremely little. The sums paid for deliveries to the government furnished little or no incentive to expand output, so that low output compounded the results of low payments per output unit. As farms did not pay rent, the better-situated farms gained an advantage over the worse-situated ones. The rigidity of the pattern allowed of no automatic adjustment or movement of workers or resources, or alteration in crop patterns in response to differing rates of profitability. Instructions emanating from Moscow paid insufficient attention to local peculiarities in soils or otherwise. The system was in fact adapted to a single end: ensuring that a sufficiently high proportion of what was produced was received by the towns and industrial areas.[4]

One major change effected already in Stalin's day was the mechanization in a substantial degree of the *principal* agricultural processes, such as ploughing and reaping. Mechanization was, however, very uneven and often it did not lead to any reduction in the numbers employed. The system of payment for members of collective farms, based on relative numbers of 'labour-days' earned, the 'labour-day' being a conventional unit which was defined in physical terms, allowed the actual value of a 'labour-day' to be infinitely elastic. There was, accordingly, no incentive to a farm to economize in 'labour-days' and thereby raise labour productivity. True, the government was concentrating attention on other sectors of the economy, and one important reason why productivity was low was overpopulation on the land — a legacy of the past.

Besides the collective farms, there were State farms. These were State agricultural factories, whose workers received wages. Their numbers varied but until Stalin's death they did not occupy as much as a tenth of the total sown area.

The fact that socialization of the means of production in agriculture had not in reality been fully achieved left an ineradicable imprint on Soviet policies towards agriculture. Since in industry full socialization had been achieved,[5] any increase in production could only strengthen further the socialist sector: therefore, State policy could uninhibitedly recommend and pursue policies of maximizing output. But in agriculture such policies risked strengthening the private sector as much as, or more than, the socialist sector. State policy in regard to agriculture had thus to ride two horses at once: to strengthen the socialist sector, and to raise and diversify output.

This might not have caused embarrassment if reliable means had been at hand to stimulate collective production. However, the priority awarded to developing industry imposed one limitation on the means available for this purpose. This priority meant both that resources 'ploughed back' into expanding agriculture would necessarily be limited, and that agriculture must continue to furnish manpower for industry and for other sectors of the economy. Another limitation stemmed from the smaller amenability of agriculture than of industry to central planning. Here, much more depends on local conditions, including soil, while the number of units is far too large to be managed by a central authority. Issuing extremely detailed instructions defeated its own ends. Much more depends on the vagaries of the weather, and generally on the natural environment.

Given these limitations, the possible initiatives of the Soviet government were reduced to the following, each of which has been implemented:

(1) measures which both raise output and raise the degree of socialisation of agriculture;
(2) measures which would raise output, but would lower the degree of socialization of agriculture;
(3) measures which would raise the degree of socialization of agriculture, but would lower output;
(4) measures which would raise output and were neutral as regards the degree of socialization of agriculture; and
(5) measures which would raise the degree of socialization of agriculture and were neutral as regards increasing output.

It is clear that a shift of emphasis towards increasing the degree of socialization would lead to emphasis upon (1), (3) and (5), while a shift of emphasis towards raising output would lead to emphasis upon (1), (2) and (4). Evidently, (1) has a double chance of being implemented. Presumably such measures should have been taken first, and if at a later date any still remained to be implemented, this would be because the opportunities had been neglected.

(1) The virgin lands campaign may be placed in this category. Khrushchev accused the previous government of neglecting this important reserve. The campaign launched in January 1954, which led to an increase of about one-quarter in the cultivated area, was a measure preeminently suitable to be conducted by the Soviet *government*, which alone could within a short time mobilize hundreds of thousands of farmers to go to work in remote and inhospitable conditions; provide for expanded production of agricultural machines and their diversion to the virgin lands instead of to traditional agricultural areas; or contrive to build new railways and roads to carry away the anticipated harvests. As the virgin lands were to be cultivated with a much higher ratio of machines to manpower than the European farmlands, the role of the government as supplier of these machines was also enhanced. Finally, of the two main forms of agricultural organization the State

farms were clearly the best adapted to bringing under cultivation new masses of land not included within the land grants of existing collective farms. The campaign would, therefore, enhance agricultural socialization while raising output. As the measure satisfied both criteria it is not surprising that this campaign was one of the first to be initiated, and that it received the loudest publicity and the largest State backing.

(4) Naturally, reforms of this type (which raise output and are neutral as regards the degree of socialization) were also among the first to be implemented by the Khrushchev government. Most prominent in this category are the increases in procurement and purchase prices for agricultural products announced in 1953. These prices had been minute before, except for a few special crops such as cotton. However, while the peasants' greater prosperity would not by itself detract from socialization, the more prosperous collective farmers became the more able they might be in due course to supplant the public sector in agriculture. Besides, to increase the purchase prices paid to farmers meant to raise their prosperity by comparison with the industrial workers, who were regarded as the mainstay of the régime; and the government also did not wish to upset the traditional townwards migration. However, further increases in procurement prices had to be made later – these were among measures announced at a plenum of the Party in March 1967 – the delay being due to economic weakness in conjunction with the view that enough had already been done in this direction.

The introduction in 1966 of guaranteed rates of pay for work done by collective farmers[6] is a major step in the direction of improving the attractiveness of work in agriculture, and of consequently raising labour productivity.

Most technical changes, or recommendations, exhortations or instructions to plant one crop rather than another, also belong to this ideologically neutral category. Khrushchev advocated a variety of these, in particular: extension of the area sown to maize and planting according to the square-cluster system (which permits cultivation from two directions). Central government action can be fairly effective in these respects; for instance, if a very large shift in the sowing pattern is required, only a government authority can ensure that the shift correctly emphasizes the crops in greatest demand and does not allow the production of others to fall too low. Taking the maize campaign as an illustration we find this to date from 1955; i.e. the year following the virgin lands campaign. Changes of this nature bore an idiosyncratic character as long as Khrushchev was in command – this is typical of an autocratic régime – and have largely been modified since his downfall.

One is slightly doubtful whether the reform of agricultural administration decreed on 9 March 1955 should or should not be classified under (4). Since 'democratic centralism' is an integral part of socialism as it is understood in the USSR, whatever undermines centralism can be understood as diminishing socialization. The decree, entitled 'Changes in the Practice of Agricultural Planning', cited a number of deficiencies which resulted from inept centralized decisions: it criticized over-centralization and attempts to prescribe everything from above. The extremely centralized system of administration whereby literally everything was decided by the Ministry of Agriculture in Moscow was dismantled. In its place, Machine Tractor Stations were ascribed a more important role in agricultural planning. This enhancement of the position of the MTS was short-lived, which also sheds doubt on the beneficial effects of the decree in so far as it related to the MTS. The Brezhnev government, indeed, restored the Ministry of Agriculture to its former position of authority, while the 'territorial production administration' was abolished and the Communist Party, which Khrushchev had divided into industrial and agricultural wings, was again reunited.

Starting in 1959, the whole system of planning output of agricultural machinery was also changed: plans of output were to be drawn up on the basis of orders from *kolkhozy* and *sovkhozy*. A special organization for supplying equipment (*Soyuzsel'khoztekhnika*) was later formed.[7]

The aim of making agriculture more efficient, as exemplified by the transfer of State farms to a self-supporting (*khozraschot*) basis, announced in April 1967,[8] may also be included under this heading although its direct effect might be to reduce costs; a reduction in inputs per unit of output should, however, make possible a rise in output.

(2) Measures which raised output but weakened socialization in agriculture have naturally been undertaken with reluctance and after a long delay, and where possible they have been balanced by measures which belong to categories (5) or even (3) (which raise socialization while being neutral or even detrimental as regards output).

By far the most important entry in category (2) has been the 1958 reform which abolished the MTS and allowed their machinery and tractors to be purchased by collective farms. This change reversed the decree of 1955, regarding the MTS. It came four years after the virgin lands campaign and three years after the maize campaign; though this interval was doubtless required not only in order to make the proposal acceptable to the ideologists, but so that farms could prosper sufficiently to allow them to pay for the machinery they bought. Actually, however, they had not prospered so much that purchasing machinery did not place a heavy financial burden on them. The change represented a retreat from State ownership in this sphere, although of course it was not represented as such. Khrushchev was forced to argue that collective farms were just as good socialist forms of agricultural organization as

State farms. Yet the decision was not a complete innovation, for according to Stalin a decision had been taken in 1930, but was later cancelled, to sell the MTS to the collective farms.[9] Reductions in prices of machinery, announced in March 1965, compounded the subsequent benefit to the farms of the reform.

Another measure of this type relieved collective farmers of the requirement to make compulsory deliveries of many kinds of agricultural products.

These measures were, however, balanced by others which were intended presumably to maintain or enhance socialization. The sale of machinery to the collective farms meant that the farms reimbursed the exchequer for the machinery (although apparently at low prices). In general, it seems to have been expected that during the Seven-Year Plan collective farms could begin to meet a larger proportion of the costs of investment in agriculture. The results in terms of productivity did not come up to expectations, but the Khrushchev government decided against making further large investments out of State funds.

While collective farms became somewhat better off and began to own their own equipment, their numbers declined owing to two other organizational trends: of amalgamation of collective farms into larger units, and of conversion of collective farms into State farms. The latter move was evidently intended to enhance the importance of the State sector. Apparently, it used often to be the less prosperous farms which were converted (and may have had to receive subsidies from the budget after conversion); however, the number of State farms has since increased so rapidly that it becomes harder to maintain that any special principle of selection is applied. As regards amalgamation, while one object was that 'advanced experience' could be passed on from one farm to another, another may have been to make the farms more amenable to regulation and advice from the centre: the number of talented and politically suitable farm leaders is always limited, and a reduction in the number of farms enables their authority to be stretched further. Similarly, a reduction in the number of farms raises the proportion in which there is a Party organization.[10]

Also under (5) (measures that raise socialization but are otherwise neutral) may be listed whatever measures have been taken to increase the participation of collective farm members in the work of the farm, as opposed to their working on peasants' individual plots. Minimum work requirements were laid down in 1939 (centrally) and these minima were raised in 1942 to 100–150 labour-days annually; collective farmers had also to work a minimum number of labour-days during each season of the year. These provisions remained in effect after the war.[11] In 1956 the 20th Party Congress suggested that general meetings of farms should re-evaluate labour-days. The intention apparently was that farm administrations (under pressure from Party organizations and others) would fix higher effective minima. This, of course, should benefit the socialized production of the farm but would – at any rate in theory – take labour away from tending the private plots. In practice, the latter are so productive in relation to their size that one would expect their owners to do their level best to tend them adequately.

(3) A few measures of category (3) have been taken, for instance collective farmers have been recommended to sell their cows to the collective farm administrations: in places pressure has been applied, though this has been reproved by the press. The government also watched for any abuses which enabled the peasants to profit from some aberration of the official policy, for instance peasants have fed bread purchased from the State shops to their cattle instead of trying to grow more fodder:[12] this was prohibited as soon as the authorities got wind of what was happening, but it obviously is difficult to prevent as long as price relationships are out of line. Under the later Khrushchev government a general squeeze was directed at the private plot; this policy was reversed by the successor government.

Other Agricultural Measures

A decree of February 1961 reorganized State purchasing of agricultural products. Starting with 1961, purchases should be made by contracts ('which represent orders to *kolkhozy* and *sovkhozy* for the products needed by the State') over two to five years.

Generally speaking, since Stalin's death much more has been done to aid agriculture and the approved measures above all stimulate agricultural output. Whether these tend to increase or decrease socialization has appeared to be a secondary consideration. The response of agriculture has been positive, but not sufficient. The system is always changing as the Party strives for more effective solutions to the farm problem: for instance, in March 1962 a Union Committee on Agriculture was set up. The day has long since passed when the Soviet leaders can determine agricultural organization without reference to anything but securing an adequate level of supplies for the towns. But the latter remains an essential consideration, and the post-Stalin and post-Khrushchev Soviet governments have gone much further in the direction of expanding their base of State farms which furnish an increased proportion of required foodstuffs, particularly grains, than Stalin ever did. Since the downfall of Khrushchev various criticisms have been levelled against his agricultural policy. It is said, for example,[13] that 'planned and proportional' development was not achieved, and that policies failed to produce the required degree of conformity between the personal and the social interest; that material incentives did not receive enough attention; that there were too many administrative reforms; that too many stereotyped directives were issued from the centre without due heed to natural conditions and local experience; that some farms had become too large to be manageable; and that the collective farm charter was frequently violated. Brezhnev said that there had been a harmful tendency to balance the books at the expense of agriculture.[14]

Since Khrushchev's departure, agriculture has received more attention than he gave it, in funds although not in words. However, policy is still not consistent. The government pursues a stop-go policy in its financing of agriculture: in 1968, for instance, the signs indicated go, in 1969 stop, in 1970 they indicated go again. There is obviously controversy behind the scenes: some leaders would like to contract the moneys devoted to agriculture, while others stress that agriculture has not yet reached such a secure position that any relaxation would be justified. A setback to progress in 1969, due to weather difficulties, justifies this more cautious assessment. Organizationally, policy has been more consistent: the State farms have finally been given their head. The day is not distant when it may be possible to look upon the collective farm system as a transitional one, and there is no sign that the collective farms will offer such a stubborn resistance as peasant cultivation did. Whereas, however, it seemed a few years ago that the collective farms might disappear physically, it now seems more likely that differences between collective and State farms will become so small[15] that the difference in name will no longer amount to much in substance.

It is clear that since 1953, and even more since 1964, when a minimum wage and pensions for collective farmers began to be introduced, Soviet agriculture has been approached with a new spirit. An exclusively political approach had nearly proved to be its ruin. Even a mixture of political and economic approaches has failed to assure an adequate rate of progress. The constant migration of young people away from the villages has now become a serious problem especially as a shortage of agricultural labour already hampers performance.[16] In maximizing procurement and in creating conditions where whoever could would quit the countryside, Soviet policy succeeded only too well. The need now is to discover and implement policies which will counteract the consequences of past policies which succeeded in compelling agriculture to contribute everything for the sake of industrial development.

The problems of Soviet agriculture have arisen partly from organizational weakness or, more exactly, unsuitability, and partly from shortage of appropriate machinery, spare parts and other needed supplies.

As regards the first, the Brezhnev period has seen fewer changes than the Khrushchev period, and this on the whole has undoubtedly been beneficial. Brezhnev, in March 1965, had already announced that the Ministry of Agriculture would be restored, campaigns abandoned, and procurement prices fixed for years ahead. In 1965, and again in 1970, the prices paid for agricultural, especially livestock, products were raised. Now partially within the scope of State pensions, collective farmers have also received internal passports (enabling them to move about more freely). Their remuneration has risen faster than that of State-employed workers, although the private sector of agriculture has not expanded.[17]

Some impressive successes of Soviet agriculture over the past twenty years have been noticed in Chapter 8 and, moreover, these have been achieved with a declining labour force. Is it not time to make a re-appraisal of Soviet agriculture?

This reappraisal was attempted by Durgin, who laid stress on the positive achievements of farming in the USSR in a noteworthy essay.[18] Admitting that agricultural plans had often failed, he pointed out that the plans of US farmers could never be known, but in a number of cases, what happened to them obviously could not have been planned. The USSR is the world's largest producer both of milk and of cotton. Also of substantial interest is the appraisal of Soviet agriculture from a variety of viewpoints in a book edited by Shaffer.[19]

It is impossible to summarize in a few words the very complex issues involved; however, the assessment of Soviet agriculture depends essentially upon whether one is concerned with measuring *output* or *productivity*. In total volume and variety of output (either its absolute level or its growth over time) Soviet agriculture has performed quite well. By contrast, the productivity of Soviet farmers is far below that of US farmers, although here one should take into account the less favourable climatic and soil conditions and the fact that over time there has been a substantial improvement.

The post-war trend of budget spending on agriculture is to some extent unexpected: as a percentage of total budget spending on the economy it doubled between 1948 and 1954, but by 1959 had declined again to the lowest level since 1946–47. Subsequent increases have only partly recovered the lost ground, although the proportion is now fairly stable from year to year, at about 16 per cent.[20] The absolute totals have, of course, increased greatly. In recent years total investment has been of the order of 25–30 milliard roubles annualy (depending on the categories of expenditure included); in 1975 to 1977 inclusive this comprised 27 per cent of all investments in the economy.[21] Such a high proportion is rather hard to believe, but if approximately correct it raises at once the question of whether agricultural development has not been achieved at exorbitant cost.

Notes

1 V. Katkoff, *Soviet Economy 1940–1965* (1961), p. 164.
2 M. Lewin, *Russian Peasants and State Power* (1968), p. 26.
3 Ibid., pp. 471–2.
4 Cf. *Komsomol' skaya pravda*, 14 July 1964, p. 3.
5 With the partial exception of the handicraft co-operatives; these, however, had an inferior status by comparison with State industry.
6 Roger A. Clarke, *Soviet Studies*, October 1968 (vol. XX, no. 2), p. 162.
7 A. N. Yefimov (ed.), *Ekonomika SSSR v poslevoyenniy period* (1962), pp. 252–3.
8 *Pravda*, 15 April 1967, p. 1.
9 I. V. Stalin, *Bolshevik*, no. 18, 1952, p. 48.
10 MTS were comparatively few and large probably for similar reasons of efficacy of central control. See N. Jasny, *The Socialized Agriculture of the USSR* (1949), p. 277.
11 Harry Schwartz, *Russia's Soviet Economy* (1951), p. 274.
12 See A. Plastinin, *Trud*, 24 December 1955. I am indebted to the late Mr. P. Gent for his admirable translation of this amusing *feuilleton*.
13 These follow J. F. Karcz, *Soviet Studies*, October 1965 (vol. XVII, no. 2).
14 L. I. Brezhnev, *Pravda*, 30 September 1965, p. 2.
15 Aspects of what might be called the 'convergence' of collective and State farms are described by Roger A. Clarke, *Soviet Studies*, October 1968 (vol. XX, no. 2), pp. 176–7.
16 K.-E. Wädekin, *Soviet Studies*, January 1969 (vol. XX, no. 3).
17 This brief statement relies largely on A. Nove, 'Agriculture', in Brown and Kaser (eds.) *The Soviet Union Since the Fall of Khrushchev* (Second Edition, 1978).
18 Frank A. Durgin, Jr., 'The Inefficiency of Soviet Agriculture versus the Efficiency of US Agriculture', *The ACES Bulletin*, Fall–Winter 1978.
19 Harry J. Shaffer (ed.), *Soviet Agriculture: An Assessment of Its Contributions to Economic Development* (1977).
20 R. Hutchings, *The Soviet Budget* (1983), Chapter 7.
21 *Narodnoye khozyaystvo SSSR v 1977 g.*, p. 356.

11
INDUSTRIAL STRUCTURE

A. Introduction

On 1 July 1957 there was a major reorganization in the economy which affected industry in particular. However, many features of the earlier system were carried over, and this earlier system would in any case be of interest and importance from the viewpoint of explaining how Soviet industry has evolved; moreover, since October 1965 a large element of this structure has been re-created. First, then, about Soviet industrial organization before the 1957 reform. This organization has had its own history, indeed there has been a rather detailed and complicated sequence of changes.

In pursuing their political and economic objectives the Soviet leaders enforce plans, the attempted implementation of which places industry under strain. This may lead to such phenomena as non-fulfilment of plans, production of wrong assortments, disruption of supplies etc. As a rule, the government then reacts not by lightening the burden on industry but by making organizational changes with a view to – or in the hope of – enabling these difficulties to be surmounted. Because strain has been a recurring phenomenon, frequent changes have been necessary; yet such changes often turn out to be less basic than they seemed at first sight. Given that industry is socialized and functions according to a comprehensive plan, the main lines of which are drawn up and approved at the centre in accordance with relatively stable priorities, certain principles of organization are already determined. The precise forms are by comparison of secondary importance. In short, Soviet industrial structure is changeable, and yet seems to be inherently stable, in that if pushed off balance it will tend to return to the previous pattern.[1] Even in wartime no substantial modification needed to be made in the system – in which respect the Soviet industrial system differs sharply from a capitalist one.[2]

The 1957 reorganization too was not so much of a revolution as some commentators suggested. In order to illustrate this, I shall first list features which are applicable both to pre-1957 and post-1957 industrial structure and then list the features which the 1957 reorganization altered.

B. Features that Remained the Same

1. State ownership of industry

This obtains and has obtained universally except for some foreign concessions (during NEP only), and up to 1960 except for handicrafts and very minor rural industries. These exceptions are not important, and I shall focus on State-owned industry.

2. Government direction of industry

That is to say, industry takes its orders from the government as to what to produce, how to produce it, what levels of costs to observe, and so on in tremendous detail. In practice this means that various controlling, planning and supervising agencies must exist.

3. No unitary direction of industry

That is to say, no single body represents or governs industry. In this respect industry has differed from agriculture, for example (the Ministry of Agriculture represented at any rate the entire collective farm sector), or from the health services. However, this situation has been true only since 1932. Between 1917 and 1932, the Supreme Economic Council (VSNKh) did control at least the larger part of industry. But in 1932 VSNKh was abolished, apparently for two reasons: it was tending to duplicate the function of Gosplan and, according to some Gosplan officials, was 'quietly sabotaging' the latter's work; and the expansion and diversification of industrial output made unitary direction no longer practicable.

4. Principle of subordination

Within State-owned industry, every plant is included within some larger grouping, and is subordinate to the authority placed at the head of that grouping; there are no freelance organizations. This is quite analogous to a military organization. Above the industrial structure proper, authority resides in the government.

The exact pattern of hierarchical units and their nomenclature have varied. In general, the number of intermediate authorities has increased in step with the expansion and diversification of output. Exact numbers are not often given, but there were, for example, 28 coalmining trusts in 1936, 60 in 1941 and at least 75 in 1947. In the

RSFSR there were in 1938 325 trusts of republic subordination and 809 of local subordination, and in 1939 correspondingly 513 and 1,081.[3] There has also been a weaker tendency to multiply the numbers of intermediate stages. In the whole economy, the number of intermediate controlling industrial organizations runs into several thousands. The principal designations of these have been: chief administrations (*glavki*), associations (*ob"edineniya*), combines (*kombinaty*), trusts (*tresty*). At the bottom is the plant or enterprise (*predpriyatiye*).

The pattern varies a good deal in different branches of industry, and the most important enterprises have tended to be subordinate directly to a ministry (pre-1957 or post-1965) or between 1957 and 1965 to a *sovnarkhoz* department.[4]

5. Principle of inequality of rights

This is also analogous to a military pattern, and means that a higher authority may issue binding instructions to lower level units within its system. 'An organ of State administration is endowed with authoritative functions, and orders issued within the bounds of its competence are obligatory.'[5]

The work programmes of lower-level units are consequently not based on 'agreement' between them and higher organizations or on the latter's 'co-ordination' but formally on the authority of the higher level. This is at any rate true in a formal sense. The opinion of a plant manager will certainly carry weight higher up but this does not affect the formal relationship between plant and superior organization.

A corollary of this principle is that lower levels do not conclude contracts with higher levels. A contract (in the USSR or elsewhere) implies formal equality of rights which would directly contradict the principle of inequality of rights. Despite these guidelines it is possible that plan and contract may in practice clash.[6] The inclusion among factors controlling industry of both plans and contracts is a complicating factor in Soviet industry as compared with an ideal type of free market economy, although of course in actual Western economies businessmen have to accommodate themselves to public constraints, as well as to other obligations.

Infringements of contract used to be very common, because the financial penalties were slight. After the 1965 reform the penalties were made much heavier.

6. Production (and distribution etc.) is carried out only by basic lower-level units

That is to say, people's commissariats (since 1946 ministries), combines, trusts etc., confine themselves to organizing, controlling and supervising functions. This again is analogous to a military pattern — headquarters and general staffs do not take part in battles.

A separate hierarchical structure is called a 'system'. The authority at the head of each 'system' undertakes approximately the following functions: administration, supervision and inspection by higher levels of lower levels; transmission or initiation of instructions downwards, requests upwards, and queries and information in both directions; reception, further elaboration and onwards transmission of plans and projects; assignment and reassignment of working capital, supplies etc.; collecting and paying taxes, including deductions from profits, an subsidies; and maintenance of links with other 'systems', particularly in arranging supplies and sales.

7. Goods not despatched along lines of subordination

Because higher-level bodies do not produce, they do not receive consignments (except for their own administrative needs, of course). Unless, therefore, a plant is producing everything it needs and consuming everything it produces — an inconceivable situation — it must be receiving components or other supplies from some other lower-level units and despatching semi-finished or finished products to other ones. These latter may belong either to the same or to another 'system'.

8. Basic units conclude contracts with each other

How does a plant keep in touch with other plants, or control what they do? Basically the answer is that plants have equal rights (*predpriyatiye* being a legal category) and they consequently may and do conclude contracts with each other. Such contracts are similar to contracts in the Western world in that they provide for certain obligations to be performed by each side, such as specified quantities of certain items to be delivered at such and such intervals, or payment to be made at so much per unit, also in a defined procedure. They are also similar in that society (the courts) will enforce the contract, supposing that this does not contain any illegal provisions. But Soviet contracts differ from contracts made by Western firms in that (i) contracting plants are obliged by their respective higher organizations to conclude the contract, and that (ii) the main provisions of the contract are already determined by agreement between the higher organizations, leaving only details to be worked out by the plants themselves.[7] This means in effect that the concept of illegality, making the contract invalid, extends much more widely. For instance, a contract which embodies prices which exceed those shown in price-lists is regarded as invalid.[8]

However, contracts are not made invariably between supplying and

consuming plants, if for instance a sales department of the higher
authority is handling all matters to do with supplies and sales. Business
contracts are apparently in most cases concluded for a period of one
year.[9]

9. Plants have no independent access to the market, and in general are
   not allowed to determine the prices charged for the goods they make

In general, lower-level organizations are not permitted to substitute
alternative supplying or receiving organizations, or to alter the amounts
stipulated for delivery or the unit prices charged. Prices do not move
spontaneously: they are influenced by supply and demand but are
formed directly under instruction from higher authority.[10]

10. Basic units are required to fulfil plans both in physical and in
    financial terms

These units must, in other words, be financially accountable. This
has not always been the case. The requirement that *plants* (as distinct
from some higher-up grouping) should be financially independent dates
from 1929. The Russian term for financial accountability, *khozraschot*,
has in fact a more complicated meaning. A plant which is placed on
'full *khozraschot*' (as most are) has placed at its disposal definite
resources (both material and monetary); has a definite (though limited)
degree of autonomy; makes extensive use of monetary accounts; is
legally empowered to conclude contracts with other bodies which enjoy
equal rights; and has an obligation to become self-supporting (not to
rely on subsidies from the budget) and to earn profits (most of which,
however, it must remit to the budget).

These ten points are equally applicable to the organization of Soviet
industry before or after 1957, and for the most part, before or after
October 1965.

C. Features that Changed

Basically, what changed between 1957 and 1965 was the arrangement
of the upper levels of the industrial superstructure (the plant being at
the bottom). Up to 1957, the number of ministries increased almost
year by year. The Malenkov administration, probably for political
reasons – in order to gather all main guiding lines of economic
administration into a small number of pairs of hands – attempted to
check the trend, by ordering mergers of a number of ministries.
However, this did not last: within a year approximately the same
pattern of ministries that had existed previously was restored (for
instance, metallurgy was redivided into ferrous and non-ferrous). It is

difficult to say whether this was chiefly because the larger number of ministries was really a more efficient pattern or because the vested interests of the existing ministries opposed an effective resistance. At all events it appeared that this pattern was rather strongly resistant to changes imposed from outside.

However, there was also a long-standing tendency to decentralize, in the sense of increasing the relative importance of republic and local industry, as opposed to all-union (federal) industry. A triple division of industry among federal, republic and local systems goes right back to War Communism and this triple division was preserved through many vicissitudes. From time to time attempts were made to extend the relative importance of the republic and local groupings. One such movement occurred in 1933–34, and another in 1953–54. The relative importance of 'union' industry (all-union plus union-republic) seems to have reached a peak in 1952 when it accounted for 70 per cent of all output. Thereafter this proportion declined, for example to 53 per cent in 1955.

Ministries which had their headquarters in Moscow were of the all-union or union-republic type. The distinction between these was that all-union ministries controlled plants directly irrespective of where they were located, while union-republic ministries controlled plants indirectly, through the agency of similarly named ministries at republic level which controlled only plants located in their particular republics. There was also a tendency to convert all-union ministries into the union-republic type, for example oil and coalmining were so converted. But the number of central ministries of one category or another continued to increase, and in 1957 there were 50, 28 of which were concerned with industry.

This system of administration had certain strengths and certain weaknesses. Of course, at the time of the reorganization and for some time afterwards one heard most about its weaknesses. Criticism of the ministerial system was not rife in the years prior to the reorganization. One can trace certain criticisms far back in the specialized literature, but it was not until the winter of 1956–1957 that these criticisms began to be widely aired.

In theory, each ministry was held responsible for a branch of industry. In theory, too, the type and purpose of the final products turned out by the ministry were dominant features in deciding where a dividing line should be drawn between it and other ministries. The nature of the technical process, its technical basis, any particularities of the raw materials used, and the type and qualifications of the labour force, also had in practice some importance,[11] so that there was no single basis for division. In the electrical industries, for instance, the common feature was the link with electricity, not that any special or distinct raw materials were used (e.g. the raw material for making an insulator could equally well be used in the making of a porcelain jar).[12]

In practice, ministries produced much wider varieties of things than their names (such as Ministry of Heavy Industry or Ministry of Aviation Industry) would suggest. Many consuming ministries controlled their own sources of supply. Thus, the Ministry of the Coal Industry did not control all coalmines, but did control some engineering works. Similarly, steel and rolled metal were turned out not only by the Ministry of Ferrous Metallurgy but by a number of other ministries as well. Many ministries turned out consumer goods as a sideline, for instance planned production of the People's Commissariat of Heavy Industry in 1938 included domestic hardware and crockery.[13]

Although a considerable degree of co-operation necessarily occurred, there was a strong tendency for ministries to try to become as self-contained as possible, and to grow into economic empires spread all over the extensive territory of the Soviet Union. On the other hand, the ministries did not find it difficult to give national interests their due weight as compared with those of particular localities. The ministerial system, although containing a multiplicity of units, was basically simple in that it comprised the same basic structures with the apex located always in Moscow (except in the case of industries of republics or local significance only, which were centred in republic capitals or cities). The ministries, in short, provided many of the advantages of centralization. The system allowed resources to be concentrated on favoured projects, even if to the neglect of others, and thus enabled the Party to pursue its industrialization schemes comparatively undistracted by protests from particular regions.

However, in 1956–57 the ministries were accused of favouring their own interests to the detriment of others, and in particular it was charged that they neglected regional co-ordination and permitted excess haulage of goods and other resources from one end of the country to the other; while too much time was lost and too many initiatives were curbed by the need to refer always to Moscow. Khrushchev proposed a fundamental reform which would abolish the ministries and set up in their place regional economic councils. His 'theses' for doing so were published on 30 March 1957. They became law (with some changes) on 10 May of that year and the reorganization was to be complete already on 1 July 1957. A breakneck pace.

Out of the 28 industrial all-union and union-republic ministries, all but three (chemicals, electric power and probably nuclear weapons) were abolished. According to Katkoff, a total of 141 ministries of all categories (all-union, union-republic and republic) were abolished.[14] In place of the ministries, two things were done at once, and two more things a little later.

The two things that were done at once were to set up regional economic councils (plural=*sovnarkhozy*), and to strengthen the Gosplan. The two things that were done subsequently were to set up in the largest republics *sovnarkhozy* on a superior level to the regional economic councils *within* that republic, and to set up in Moscow more and more State Committees to look after particular industrial branches.

Initially, 105 'economic administrative areas' were set up, each one being placed under a *sovnarkhoz*. These divided up the entire country between them. The boundaries between them were so drawn that there was some tendency to equalize volumes of industrial production; thus, in Siberia where there was little industry a single *sovnarkhoz* covered a vast area whereas another one was responsible solely for Moscow city. However, this tendency was not fully carried through, and some *sovnarkhozy* operated on a much larger scale than others. Whereas the average annual output of a *sovnarkhoz* was 7½ milliard roubles, individual *sovnarkhozy* ranged from 28 milliard roubles in Sverdlovsk and 'some tens' of milliards in Moscow oblast to less than 1 milliard in Kustanay − a range of perhaps 40 to 1.

When the reform was under discussion, a variety of different principles of division were mooted, such as in order to maximize the economic self-sufficiency of individual areas. As it turned out, however, the *sovnarkhoz* areas in most cases simply duplicated the existing administrative divisions into republics and oblasts. Evidently it was thought too risky, difficult or complicated to suppress the ministries without having the established administrative divisions to fall back on. Under Soviet conditions, which require a great deal of knitting together of plans in the source of composition and of checking up on their fulfilment, it might be unworkable to have two distinct territorial systems of division.

In general, the *sovnarkhozy* were granted the ordinary rights (analogous to those of a ministry) of managing undertakings for which they were responsible. They were not permitted to alter basic plan quantities, or to infringe the provisions of the budget, the wages fund or the revenue plan. Central control over wages and prices was maintained. These therefore may be added to the list of circumstances that remained the same, except of course that the *sovnarkhozy* supplanted the ministries in being competent or not competent to take the corresponding decisions.

The new councils were made responsible for about three-quarters of all industrial production. The remainder was retained under central control under the three industrial ministries, plus a few smaller groups such as underground gasification of coal, or was retained or placed under local or municipal control.

The *sovnarkhozy* established themselves apparently without serious dislocation, though there were temporary difficulties. Their first steps were in the direction of ordering mergers of undertakings and of rationalizing the distribution of tasks as between undertakings which had belonged to different ministries. They began to surround themselves with technical-advisory councils, apparently with a view to rendering themselves self-sufficient in this respect.

In some respects the scope of the reform seems to have been less than was originally intended, but in other respects the *sovnarkhozy* gained increased powers at the expense of factory directors, such as over transport schedules, while owing to plant amalgamations some managers were dismissed. Some difficulties arose in ensuring supplies from one *sovnarkhoz* to another, there being at first no authority lower than the Council of Ministers competent to settle disputes between them (apart from any which might go to arbitration).

Now concerning the strengthening of the Gosplan. Khrushchev at first intended to combine planning and administrative power in one body, which was still to be called the Gosplan. However, this intention was abandoned. The final decision left the Gosplan without executive power, purely as a planning body, as it had been before. However, the Gosplan was reassigned responsibility for long-term and short-term planning. Prior to the reform there were two organizations concerned with planning, the Gosplan concerned with long-term plans (over one year's duration) and the State Economic Commission with plans of shorter duration. The latter was abolished and its functions transferred to the Gosplan. Divisions of Gosplan gained increased prestige, and probably were enlarged in terms of personnel. Several former ministers became heads of divisions in Gosplan, and heads of divisions were granted ministerial rank.

In practice the Gosplan, probably in the person of these divisions, sometimes tended to act as if it had executive authority. There are occasional references to factories being 'subordinated' to divisions of Gosplan, though in a literal sense this cannot have been so. One can easily imagine that ministers who now found themselves divisional heads of Gosplan could suppose that nothing really had changed, and that they would exercise their habitual authority over the heads of the newly formed inexperienced *sovnarkhozy* to which factories were nominally subordinated. In particular, the Gosplan took over at the all-union level many of the supply functions of the former ministries. Their disappearance had apparently left a gap which the *sovnarkhozy* could not immediately fill.

A considerable number of State Committees were created. These proliferated (e.g. Chemicals Industry, Aviation Technology, Fuels and

Metallurgical Industries), which made one suspect that they were performing certain tasks which used to be performed by the ministries: yet they were not administrative bodies and were supposed to be mainly concerned with new techniques and with research. One criticism of the 1957 reform was that research ought not to be dissipated among a number of territorial organizations. (As basic research was not numbered among the functions of the *sovnarkhozy*, these functions were more restricted than those of the ministries.) The truth of this criticism was later admitted.

Problems of co-ordination continued to be encountered. In 1960 super-*sovnarkhozy* were set up in the three largest republics – the RSFSR, Ukraine and Kazakhstan – to co-ordinate all *sovnarkhozy* within these republics. Most of the other republics included only one *sovnarkhoz* each. In November 1962 the number of *sovnarkhozy* was reduced to 47. As there still did not exist at a national level any body besides the Council of Ministers of the USSR competent to resolve disputes between *sovnarkhozy* that were not amenable to arbitration, in November 1962 a *Sovnarkhoz of the USSR* was established. The superstructure was crowned in March 1963 by the establishment of a Supreme Council of National Economy. The *Sovnarkhoz of the USSR*, the *Gosplan* and the Gosstroy (which controlled construction, analogously to the way the *Sovnarkhoz of the USSR* controlled industry) were made formally subordinate to this Supreme Council. However, the basic pattern of administration still remained territorial. The revised system had by this time become rather more complicated than the one that it had superseded in 1957.

As they had tried a branch and a territorial form of structure and had found both of them wanting, it seemed possible that the Soviet leaders might reach the conclusion that the major defect was not the shape of the Soviet industrial structure so much as its built-in rigidity – that it had a shape at all, one might say. Any weakening of this rigidity cannot be achieved so long as industry generally functions like one huge combine; it would be achieved only if factory managers were granted much more freedom of initiative, but this would mean freeing enterprises from hierarchical obligations and allowing them to determine their own activities in accordance with a market system of prices. Such a reform – having affinities to the Yugoslav system – would go against the grain in Russia where government had always been all-powerful. But a supreme power can also relinquish power and if it decided to do so this one would not be hampered by any private-property rights.

A tentative start has been made. Since 1962 'firms' have been set up: these consist of a group of undertakings, headed by one of them, which have some autonomy in deciding what to produce and where and how to sell it. The experiment started in Lvov and spread to Leningrad and

Moscow. These are not firms in the Western sense, in that they have no independent access to capital or market, or untrammelled freedom to grow, but they are a step in that direction.

However, one of the principal aspects of the 1965 reform was a reaffirmation of the importance of structure, and this in fact regained approximately the pre-1957 pattern. In all, 24 out of 28 titles of reconstituted ministries were either identical with or similar to previously existing titles.[15]

If one considers the 1957 reform to have amounted to decentralization (which as indicated above would be rather an over-simplification, but would be essentially correct), then recentralizing moves became very visible from 1960 onwards and these in a formal sense reached their culmination when the Supreme Council of National Economy was created. The essence of the October 1965 reorganization is neither decentralization nor centralization but a shift from centralization based on a territorial structure to centralization based on a branch structure. However, while recentralization was not the essence of the 1965 reform, it was achieved incidentally as the number of controlling economic administrative bodies was reduced from 47 *sovnarkhozy* to 28 ministries, which were re-established in Moscow – the seat of the Government and Party. At the other extreme, more independence was devolved to enterprises. Some authority was therefore drained from the middle reaches of the hierarchical system.

The post-1965 set-up may also be superseded in due course, but meanwhile there is no evidence that it is regarded by the leadership as merely interim. It would seem that a relatively highly centralized branch system of administration has been reinstated because it has been found by experience that it works best under Soviet conditions. A territorial pattern of administration is evidently not very suitable for Soviet conditions, apparently for a combination of circumstances. The development of territorial planning in the USSR has lagged behind that of central planning,[16] certainly in part owing to the greater weight of tradition and experience behind central as compared with regional initiatives in Russia. Some geographic reasons were mentioned in Chapter 1.[17]

The regional dimension appears to be the critical one which planning techniques cannot at present grasp. If, for example, quantities are sub-divided to the *rayon* level (the territorial unit immediately below the *oblast*), by comparison with the all-Union total all quantities must be sub-divided by a factor of up to 4,000. But this of course is not merely an arithmetical problem: the unequal sizes, differing climatic conditions and perhaps cultural peculiarities of the *rayony* should also be considered, although due to the adoption of a 'Soviet culture' transcending in a limited degree national cultures, and to the absence of critical religious or other tensions, this last problem is more soluble than it would be in most territories of a comparable size. The alternative to working out a territorial breakdown in such detail is for transport to be overloaded, but here the consequential economic costs will not be astronomical and the whole system will still work, although not optimally. One can also seek some simplification by promoting foreign trade to supply directly remote parts of the USSR such as the Far East provinces, as has in fact been done. A need for territorial planning will not disappear under a ministerial system, but its efficiency can be less whereas under the *sovnarkhoz* system relatively efficient territorial planning was obligatory.

A more immediate reason for the reform, and perhaps the most conspicuous one at the enterprise level, was the great difficulty under the previous system of implementing a unified technical policy. The *sovnarkhozy* were not competent to perform this very complex task because they were not built around a particular branch of industry— despite their efforts to equip themselves with advisory 'technical-economic councils' which sometimes enrolled several hundred members. The State Committees which proliferated after 1957 were likewise unable to fill the gap.[18] In general, increasing heed is being paid to technical issues when questions relating to the economy, including its organizational structure, are decided.[19]

The system of industrial administration did not change fundamentally between 1965 and 1981. There was, indeed, no other possible direction of fundamental reform, apart from dismantling the hierarchy altogether. Instead, a variety of directions of reform, each of a partial nature, was and is being pursued. A recent useful survey lists these under five headings: planning, organization, incentives, computerization, and miscellaneous.[20]

As regards reorganization – the time-honoured direction of reform – the operative year was 1973, when the course was set to form 'associations' (*ob"edineniya*), either 'industrial' (comprising former chief administrations), 'production' or 'science-production' (the latter, naturally, incorporating some research participation). The last two types are usually reported as a single total, which since 1970 has increased as follows:–

1970	1971	1972	1973	1974	1975	1976	1977
608	879	1101	1425	1715	2314	3312	3670

Source: *Narodnoye khozyaystvo SSSR v 1977 g.*, p. 119.

As the number of plants has not increased simultaneously, and indeed it has been declining slowly, the associations have taken over a larger share of industry. In 1977, reckoned either by output or by employment, this share was about 45 per cent. This proportion is scheduled to rise further. The associations exhibit a territorial-production profile, that is to say they combine both the branch and the territorial principles of grouping.

The reasons underlying the other category of measures adopted in 1965, which comprised measures for improving planning and strengthening economic stimuli and the initiative of plants, are somewhat more complicated than those which relate to the reform of hierarchical structure. As the essential background to understanding them is an acquaintance with Soviet economic planning generally, this forms the next subject to be covered.

It would seem that there operates under Soviet conditions, at least, a law of 'decreasing returns to reorganization'. In the short term, reorganization may lead to the overcoming of abuses which had become obvious and notorious, but this reserve is soon used up and then the negative effects of the reorganization become apparent. The continual growth in size and complication of the whole system causes attrition of any universal organizational solution, while making any further reorganization still more complicated and consequently less effective.

Notes

1 The presence of 'elements of permanency' in industrial organization was noticed by C. B. Hoover almost fifty years ago (C. B. Hoover, *The Economic Life of Soviet Russia* (1931), p. 42).

2 Changes which took place during the War were: the granting of rights to people's commissariats to distribute or redistribute all resources including 'basic funds' (fixed capital) among their constituent plants, and of certain rights in the disposition of plants' current accounts, and the granting of rights to plants to sell surplus material resources via the selling organizations and without the consent of the people's commissariats (G. Kozlov, *Khozyaystvennyy raschot v sotsialisticheskom obshchestve* (1944), p. 32). Cf. A. V. Venediktov, *Gosudarstvennaya sotsialisticheskaya sobstvennost'* (1948), p. 728. 'The war did not introduce any substantial changes into the system of administration of state industrial enterprises created in recent years.' There was only a certain adaptation, especially an enlargement of the circle of plants which were directly subordinate to the commissariat and stricter economy in administration.

3 Reference as in my thesis, op. cit., p. 106.

4 See below, Section C.

5 I. L. Braude, *Dogovory po kapital'nomu stroitel'stvu v SSSR*

(1952), p. 85.

6 Some Soviet economists were therefore hoping for the creation of an 'organic link' between plan and contract: e.g. N. P. Lebedinskiy, *Ekonomicheskaya gazeta*, no. 25, 1968, p. 9. See below, p. 155.

7 If there is disagreement as to implementation of the contract, the matter can go to arbitration: there is a network of arbitration courts.

8 S. Rubinshteyn and I. Tsypkin, *Sovetskiy kredit (Chast' III)* (1933), p. 49.

9 Sh. Ya. Turetskiy, *Vnutripromyshlennoye nakopleniye v SSSR* (1948), p. 283.

10 In regard to price-fixing see below, Chapter 13.

11 A. I. Rotshteyn, *Problemy promyshlennoy statistiki v SSSR* (1936), tom I, pp. 76–7.

12 Cf. I. Korostashevskiy, *Planovoye khozyaystvo*, no. 1, 1929, p. 240.

13 *Industriya*, 4 August 1938, p. 2.

14 V. Katkoff, *Soviet Economy 1940–1965* (1961), p. 121.

15 See my article in *Australian Outlook*, April 1966 (vol. 20, no. 1), p. 57.

16 See for example A. Korobov, *Planovoye khozyaystvo*, no. 1, 1939, p. 62.

17 See also my 'Geographic Influences on Centralization in the Soviet Economy', *Soviet Studies*, January 1966.

18 A. N. Kosygin, *Pravda*, 28 September 1965, p. 3.

19 Attention is also being paid to the influence of prices in technical progress. See V. P. D'yachenko, *Planovoye khozyaystvo*, no. 1, 1966, p. 94.

20 National Foreign Assessment Center, *Organization and Management in the Soviet Economy: The Ceaseless Search for Panceas* (ER 77–10769, December 1977), p. 1.

12

ECONOMIC PLANNING

Soviet economic planning is based on State ownership of natural resources, large-scale industrial equipment and other means of production. This situation is reached after the nationalization (socialization) of natural resources etc.; often it does not obtain in Western economic planning, which the Russians have therefore been prone to dismiss as unreal, although they no longer do so as dogmatically as they once did.

How to define a planned economy is an interesting and far from merely academic question. If collective ownership of means of production is the criterion, this assumes some substantial degree of control over the physical world.[1]

In the Western view, the opposite of a planned economy is not an economy where there are no plans, because such a situation is inconceivable: in every economy innumerable individual and corporate plans are being pursued. In a 'planned' economy, however, co-ordination of plans is effected consciously and *ex ante* by some central authority, whereas in an 'unplanned' economy co-ordination is effected only *ex post*, through a market. This is a convenient distinction if we do not understand it to apply rigidly to existing societies: 'unplanned' economies also execute national plans of partial scope, while certain variables are in a 'planned' economy, including the Soviet one, left to be co-ordinated by market forces, or even are not co-ordinated.[2]

Various types of plans can be distinguished. Plans may be less or more authoritative: long or short, coterminous or overlapping. Until recently, it has been tacitly assumed in the USSR that plans have to be authoritative (following heated debate of this point in the late 1920s), of both long and short duration, and coterminous (i.e. all current plans of a given duration to begin and end on the same dates). The most readily recognizable feature of Soviet planning has been the long-term (usually, five-year) plans. One must not prejudge whether these exist as really effective instrumentalities, and this is examined further below.

These were, of course, not formulated from scratch: the present being taken as a starting-point, a plan indicated directions and magnitudes of further development. Plans were drawn up purposefully, specifying both objectives (targets) and the means to achieve them.

Long-term plans were intended to be modifiable. All such plans *have* been altered during their lifetime, either (such as the Third Five-Year Plan) under the impact of external events, or (the Sixth Five-Year Plan) because new possibilities of growth have allegedly been discovered. Changes are made by the government without recourse to any constitutional procedure (though a *new* plan has normally been confirmed by the Supreme Soviet, following adoption of Plan Directives by a Party Congress). Once confirmed, the plan is called a *law*, which – in theory – must be fulfilled.

However, long-term plans have not usually been published, or confirmed, at the start of the period to which they are supposed to apply. The First Five-Year Plan commenced retroactively; the Second Five-Year Plan was confirmed in 1934 although its starting date was 1933. No general long-term plan was in operation in 1958, or probably in 1951–52.

The procedure most recently followed has been for a draft plan to be published: this is then 'discussed' nationwide in the press and finally in Moscow and a slightly modified version is soon adopted. This procedure pays some attention to democratic procedures although any modifications effected in the plan are only minor.

A fulfillable plan has to be internally consistent. For example, if a particular increase in production capacity is to be achieved, the necessary funds must be provided to finance this increase. Once these have been agreed and incorporated in the Plan, this as it were reserves (in Russian one uses the more vivid 'armours') the funds for that purpose (though the actual process of supplying those funds may be long drawn out). While a new plan is being concocted there is therefore intense activity, pressure and lobbying, to get one's favourite projects included, as will be examined further in Chapter 15. Although a plan that is internally consistent is obviously superior to one that is not, there is no particular reason why it should be optimal, i.e. the best possible plan. To arrive at an *optimal* plan one would need to follow another kind of route, which included comparisons of alternative plans and decided at each stage which was superior. Although the First Five-Year Plan was drawn up in two variants, subsequent long-term plans until the Eighth Five-Year Plan have been drawn up in one version only, thus precluding even a choice of two alternatives.[3] Of course, to arrive at a true optimum one would need to compare not merely two but a very large, or perhaps infinite, number of variants. Yet it is out of the question to construct even a large number of internally consistent variants.

For some time there have been signs of divergence from the traditional 'ideal' type of Soviet plans. The emphasis now placed on the long-term plans as all-embracing, authoritative expressions of the national purpose is now much less than it used to be. The German invasion in 1941, which interrupted the Third Five-Year Plan, harshly ushered in the new trend. Important disconnected initiatives were launched during the Fourth Five-Year Plan — Stalin's 'Plan for the Transformation of Nature' (1948) and the Three-Year Livestock Plan (1949–51) — although both of these were ultimately unsuccessful. The leadership may have drawn from this, and from the episode of the Korean War (which also demanded alterations in the Plan), the conclusion that interruption of long-term programmes might be normal rather than abnormal. A more pragmatic attitude to long-termness was also expressed when the Sixth Five-Year Plan was superseded by a plan of seven rather than five years' duration,[4] and in the modification in its turn of the Seven-Year Plan. Moreover, continuously operating plans were suggested. A decree of December 1960 demanded improved planning procedures which would involve drawing-up principal targets of economic development for the last year of each current five-year period so that there would be a continuously operating five-year plan.[5] A subsequent book on continuity of planning emphasized the need for linking together the plans of two adjacent years,[6] and in 1964–65 such a two-year plan was in operation. These changes must have made adherence to any programme of long duration very difficult, and taken in conjunction with other evidence[7] they suggest that although in name long-term plans were continued after the war, their effectiveness and coherence were diminished by comparison with the three prewar plans. It is now intended to place greater emphasis on long-term plans and to convert them into more real and effective instruments.

The long-term plan is supplemented by plans of shorter duration which, chronologically, are included within it. As a rule there have been annual and quarterly plans. During World War II *monthly* plans were confirmed by commissariats for outputs of the most important products and for transport, the aim being flexibility in meeting changing demands from the battlefront.[8]

The annual plans are the operative ones. The first year of a FYP should be merely a division of the longer plan, set out in more detail. As regards later annual plans, since these are compiled later the long-term plan can be altered appropriately. Such modifications are introduced not only annually but in compliance with decrees issued during the year, or with other decisions. Enterprises will try to 'overfulfil' the plan if possible, because plan targets are, ordinarily, minima rather than exact objectives. Overfulfilments in some sectors will multiply demand in cooperating sectors and so will (or may) force related changes in other plan objectives (this is analogous to, though not identical with, a multiplier effect in a market economy). However, what subsequent annual plans can prescribe with any hope of fulfilment is necessarily restrained by what has been achieved in previous years. Soviet planning includes, besides the economy, cultural development and education etc. Even economic planning could not otherwise be comprehensive. However, less attention is paid to the social content of a plan than to economic relationships. This is one important reason why Soviet planning has been generally unsuccessful in regard to agriculture, which is a complex social-economic problem.[9]

How can a plan be directed at specific aims when the development of the whole economy and society is affected, and when interrelationships between different sectors are almost infinitely complex? This difficulty has not been solved, but 'leading' or priority aims, to be achieved if necessary even at the expense of others, have been chosen. Typically, heavy industry and defence have shared this top priority, these being interrelated in that their production assortments are to some degree interchangeable.

How can plans be implemented in a way which allows adequate room to take account of unforseen events while still aiming at the original objectives? This problem has been in some respects not as complex as would face the planning agency in a more highly developed country – the United States for example – which sets itself more varied objectives.

In the early stages the Soviet leaders do not seem to have thought of demand as being governed by price. Rather, they apparently thought of demand as something absolute – we would say inelastic – like the demand for foodstuffs: as if all consumer goods were equally necessary.[10] As an economy becomes richer it needs become more diverse. The Soviet one does not try to produce anything like so much in the way of novelties, just for the sake of novelty, as capitalist economies do: and this simplified the planning problem. (The latter is, however, much more complex than in a country like China.) Until not so long ago, most things in Russia had been in short supply. Goods were needed for their basic qualities rather than to score off someone else. Conspicuous consumption was by no means characteristic of the society, indeed an almost uniform style of dress was once the rule, as it is still in China; although conspicuous investment *has* been characteristic.

The slimming down of foreign contacts surely tended to restrain wants which might otherwise have been stimulated. Such foreign imports as were admitted were (with a few exceptions) not of a kind which would make those deprived of them conspicuously worse off than those who could obtain them. The absence of uncontrolled advertising helped to limit popular demand to things which were really needed. But this simplification has been in a large degree offset by the pursuit of self-sufficiency, which has demanded production of a wide assortment of engineering and military items: so that while economic plans have been simplified, technical and scientific problems have been enhanced.

The economy is faced with one problem which is not consciously faced by an 'ideal' capitalist economy and which, in an actual capitalist economy, is 'solved' (of course not necessarily optimally) by the combined decisions of industrialists, investors and others, including the central or Federal and State governments: namely the problem of what share of the national income to devote to investment. In a socialist economy, this is necessarily an arbitrary proportion.[11] In practice in the USSR the highest achievable rate of investment consistent with an adequate defence posture has been aimed at: even the social structure and the growth rate of the population have been sacrificed for the sake of supporting a heavy investment burden. Capital investment is a function predominantly of industry, and here the fundamental doctrine has been that production of capital goods should grow faster than production of consumer goods, as has in fact been the case. To allow for this, a second fundamental tenet has been that labour productivity should grow faster than money wages.

A number of other major questions have to be decided before the broad lines of the plan can be mapped out. These include the speed with which various regions are to be developed; the amount of attention to be devoted to developing agriculture, as opposed to industry and other sectors; and export and import policy. (More about the last in Chapter 17.)

Once 'political' questions such as these have been decided, composing the plan becomes a technical problem of enormous complexity. First, there is the problem of organizing the planners themselves. The history of this is itself complicated. The mutual relations of bodies which deal with plans of shorter-term and longer-term duration have been unstable, with changes in organization and function announced every few years, or even more often. Currently, the Gosplan is responsible for all planning. Earlier, Gosplan had been restricted to plans of up to one year's duration while the State Scientific-Economic Council dealt with plans of longer duration. Earlier still, the situation had been just the opposite: Gosplan had been responsible for plans of more than one year's duration while *Gosekonomkomissiya* had been responsible for shorter plans. There has been a series of such changes, which are connected with trends in the industrial structure:[12] the motive forces are that long-term planning is less urgent than short-term, a fact which encourages dividing the two organizationally in order that long-term planning shall not be squeezed out; and on the other hand since all planning is for the future, it is artificial and liable to become unworkable if the concoction of plans of different duration is made organizationally too distinct. In practice, names and formal subordinations are probably affected much more than the actual personnel engaged or the mode of work. Specifically, this appears to have been true when in March 1963 the Gosplan was made subordinate to the 'Supreme Economic Council'.

Under Gosplan, there are republic Gosplans, between 1957 and 1965 planning departments of *Sovnarkhozy*, and planning departments of industrial enterprises, State farms and other State undertakings. Gosplan has direct authority only over its own subordinate planning units.

As regards general relationships between planning and organizations, 'any organ of management in industry fulfils at the same time also functions of planning on the basis of "all state plans" '.[13] The history of the interaction between industrial planning and central direction testifies to the desirability of retaining a separate and specialized planning organization but also to the inconveniences caused by duplication or overlapping of authority at the summit.

Next, let us look at the composition and integration of the Plan. The procedure for composing plans has been as follows. The Gosplan sends *down* to inferior authorities, and eventually to the enterprise, control figures which the latter then considers as regards the section which applies to itself,[14] and suggests improvements and increases in them; the modified figures are then passed *upwards*, being included in larger and larger totals; these latter are finally considered and co-ordinated by the Gosplan and are incorporated in the comprehensive plan; this is confirmed by the Supreme Soviet and becomes law; the totals are then divided by lower authorities and remitted *down* to individual plants to implement. This is, in fact, a rather idealized picture. Possibly in some cases the earliest stage is omitted. The precise procedure may vary according to the sector of the economy. In engineering, for instance, the 'historical meaning' of the down-up-down sequences was that it revealed reserves of production capacity, and prepared the way for the transition from *promfinplan* (industrial-financial-plan) to *tekhprom-finplan* (technical-industrial-financial-plan).[15]

As regards the integration, ideally everything has to be kept in balance. Several types of balance have to be kept:
(1) Output goals should be fixed so that all available or prospectively available productive factors are employed (no more and no less). To require less would involve under-employment and fail to maximize output; to require more would cause failure to fulfil the plan, or at any rate strains, probable interruptions in supplies and a lopsided final result. This equality should hold good for all factors of production

(labour, transportation, basic materials, power etc.).

Any discrepancy in the target for a particular item may be very complicated to correct, since many other items (components) may need to be altered simultaneously. Gosplan tries to avoid this by requiring that output should be increased *without* supplying additional materials; this sounds unreasonable, but is sometimes achieved thanks to economizing and 'mobilizing' of reserves – these latter often being substantial owing to plants' desires not to be left short, and to loopholes in financial restraints on overstocking. If cuts have to be made in aggregate allocations these are likely to be made in sectors, where production does not affect other output sectors. This is probably one reason that consumer goods have tended to have a low priority: if less of these are produced only consumers suffer directly. (Of course, some individual consumers are also producers; these in times of shortage are likely to be allotted bigger rations than non-producers.)

(2) Production takes place in space: so planners must decide where output is to be produced, avoid unnecessary haulage, ensure availability of manpower. Regional planning has lagged behind branch planning, and one of the motives of the reform of industrial organization in 1957 was to improve it. As recently as 1968 the complaint was heard that territorial planning essentially consisted simply in adding together the indices for that particular area.[16]

(3) Physical and financial indices must match each other, for example, supplies of consumer goods must keep pace with money incomes, and inflation or deflation should be avoided (though these have different results in the USSR than in a market economy), unless one or other is necessitated by other policy objectives.

(4) The output of finished products and that of their components must stay in balance (for example, output of automobile tyres must keep in step with that of automobiles). This again is difficult to achieve.

> In addition, in the practice of planning capital investments in transport the indicated tasks were not co-ordinated in the required degree with the possibilities of supply of materials and equipment. Thus, for example, the prewar programme of producing steam locomotives and wagons foreshadowed outputs of rolling stock and locomotives in larger quantity than was permitted by the volumes of outputs of wagon wheels, wheel-sets for locomotives, equipment for automatic coupling and other things.[17]

(5) When outputs of components of related factors are being expanded, plans must be so drawn that the related quantities remain in balance at different stages of development, for example, an expansion of iron-

ore mining must keep in step with expansion of production of goods which require iron and steel. These running balances should ideally apply to particular regions as well as to the whole economy.

(6) Physical (and value) quantities must be brought to the notice of who actually is to do the producing and distribution.

(7) There is the problem of securing fulfilment of the plan – of conveying instructions to responsible bodies and of ensuring that these instructions are carried out. In general, accounting indices are wider than plan indices.[18] Indices of fulfilment of long-term and of annual plans are badly co-ordinated.[19]

(8) Since it would overload the centre beyond endurance for all quantities to be planned centrally, a division must be made between those which are to be planned centrally and those which are not.

Production assortments are divided into two groups, which are planned in a more centralized procedure and in a less. The exact form has varied. Prior to 1957 materials were classified as 'funded' or 'non-funded'. 'Funded' supplies were allocated in the more centralized procedure, for a specified period (usually a year), the quota being annulled if not claimed within that period. According to the latest pre-1957 data, something under 1,000 funded items were being centrally planned by the Gosplan. In May 1968 Gosplan was distributing about 2,000 named items of production to 120 fundholders, although a large proportion of these received only very tiny quantities.[20]

Ministries themselves planned the production and distribution of non-funded items. This category bridged the gap between the complexity of the complete production programme and the simplified material balances drawn up on a national scale. For example, in 1946 plan and balances in ferrous metallurgy enbraced some 70 items, whereas the then Ministry of Ferrous Metallurgy issued instructions about producing several thousand items. Again, the plan indicated only the total number of ball-bearings to be produced, whereas the number of individual specifications of ball-bearings reached some 750. Prior to 1957 non-funded production was becoming more diverse relative to funded.

After 1957 the division between funded and non-funded vanished. The USSR Gosplan was to determine inter-republic deliveries in respect of 1,200–1,500 types of materials and equipment. Items which had a 'limited sphere of consumption and were less deficitary' were to be planned by republics (3,000–3,200 names), while distribution of the remaining items should devolve on *sovnarkhozy* directly.[21] Following the re-creation of ministries non-funded production or its equivalent is probably again planned by ministries.

As a general guide one may say that each year a plan of materials supply is drawn up by Gosplan, which makes preliminary estimates of availability, using as a guide past availabilities and present plans. Using input norms' (standard rates of consumption), plants then reckon up their needs and these are considered, modified, totalled, by superior organizations (between 1957 and 1965 by *sovnarkhozy*, but now again by ministries), and forwarded to the republic Gosplan; these then forward estimates of requirements to the all-union Gosplan which compiles a national balance for each funded item. The totals are then distributed to republics, then down to intermediate units and so to individual plants.

(9) Congruity must be ensured between the long-term plans of the whole economy and the plans of individual plants. Hitherto, long-term plans have not been drawn up for the latter. Some economists think that this is possible only by business corporations (*khozyaystvennyye ob"edineniya*), in which plants are included.[22]

(10) There is the problem of ensuring congruity between long-term plans and still longer-term plans ('general' plans). Clearly, a plan should fit within a matching series of plans of longer duration. Strumilin complained already in 1927 that composing the Five-Year Plan was made more difficult by the fact that the GOELRO 'general' plan, compiled in 1921, was out of date while a new one was not yet ready.[23] As reported in 1968, a 'general' plan up to 1980 was being worked out. For improving long-term planning, it is regarded as very important to work out long-term prognoses, especially of scientific and technical development, population growth and use of natural resources.[24] As this list illustrates, the further ahead one looks the more meta-economic factors have to be considered.

The fact that some elements of the economy are more easily planned than others is a major handicap. The least readily planned elements are foreign trade and agriculture: consequently the long-term plan is always reticent about foreign trade, and although agriculture is included and specific plans are apparently laid down, these are not meant to be fulfillable in the same precise sense as the industrial production plans are. Industrial output, capital construction, and transport comprise the more readily and reliably plannable segments of the whole, and these consequently are spelled out in the greatest detail.

Apart from the sectoral division, plans embrace the various means by which, it is hoped, the plan can be implemented. Here, too, the reliability is uneven. Neither the productivity of labour nor that of capital can be planned with any assurance of exactness, especially if new techniques are to be introduced;[25] the precise time when new techniques will begin to yield their full effect is no less difficult to predict. Even experience cannot easily eradicate these weak points in the planning process, except by showing in what directions forecasts are liable to err. As reported in 1968, the Gosplan had recently begun to characterize the effectiveness of social production by reference to summaries of expenditures on the 'three basic factors' – living labour, material expenditures and the output/capital ratio (*fondootdacha*)'.[26] Since 1962, there has been lively discussion concerning the most efficacious indices for measuring industrial performance. Industrial performance must be measured so that fulfilment of the plan can be calculated, but how should this be done? The trouble is that whatever measurement is adopted has the result of injecting a bias into the work of the undertaking. If, for instance, value of total output is the criterion, the undertaking may be tempted to violate the prescribed assortment of output by using more expensive materials. If the criterion is weight, it will produce unduly heavy items. For example, planning the production of steel tubes by weight is disadvantageous.[27] This is the 'success indicators' question, as it is called by Nove. It is a permanent and inbuilt feature of the economy, which is frequently referred to in Soviet writing.[28] However, besides the relationships of formal subordination, which must not be infringed too crudely, there are contractual obligations to be met; restrictions on supplies and technological barriers also modify the operation of the principle. Analogous problems are faced in Western countries when ordering military equipment, but are marginal whereas in Russia they are nearer to being central. In Russia a number of different solutions have been proposed. One was to introduce a 'standard fabrication value' (*normativnaya stoimost' obrabotki*).

A major defect in a system of judging performance by plan fulfilment is that an apparently favourable result can be achieved by actions which are opposite to each other in economic effect: either through over-fulfilment of a given plan or through getting the plan reduced. The former is indeed the more attractive to an ambitious manager, especially if his factory then gets the green light to expand and/or his own promotion is secured. However, the latter offers the easier way out, especially as planners have always been inclined to estimate what a plant can do by reference to what it has done before, so that good performance can result in an even stiffer task being set next year.[29] If this built-in defect of the planning system could be removed, a major source of weakness would go with it. The radical suggestion of Professor Liberman of Kharkov was to measure a plant's performance not by its plan fulfilment but by the percentage by which its output rose from year to year; but this suggestion was not adopted. What was done was to replace the 'gross production' (*valovaya produktsiya*) index as a measure of performance.

Already in the mid-1930s the then People's Commissar of Heavy

Industry had spoken in favour of adopting an index of commodity production (*tovarnaya produktsiya*):[30] this at first was calculated only in order to compare it with total sold production, in regard to trusts. In 1936, however, the index was designated for characterizing the fulfilment by *enterprises* of their tasks in turning out *completed* production. As described in 1936, on 1 October of that year commodity production became the 'basic index' of production planning.[31] All output destined for outside the enterprise was included, not omitting its housing construction or internal capital investment.[32]

Despite this, as described in 1940 the 'basic index' continued until that year to be gross production.[33] The national economic plan then established tasks both in gross production (in 1926/27 prices) and in commodity production (in current prices).[34] The change seems to have been timed to accompany the contemporary splitting up of commissariats and formation of new ones. A commissariat had now to rely to a greater extent on other commissariats, i.e. on their commodity production, and the index was altered appropriately.[35]

The difference between gross and commodity production is that the latter does not record changes in stocks of semi-fabricates or the incomplete production of any raw material supplied by the client.[36] The choice of reporting unit is also significant. The smaller the reporting unit, the closer commodity production approximates to gross; the two can even be identical.[37] The new index differs from commodity production in that it refers to sold rather than to saleable output, and so is more clear-cut. The difference is mainly relevant to branches where a substantial proportion of output had previously remained unsold.

It was generally agreed by Soviet (as well as by Western) economists that plan indices needed to be simplified. The more numerous the indices, the more likely they are to be mutually inconsistent, in which case a plant can fulfil certain criteria only by violating others. It must consequently *choose* which to fulfil, so that paradoxically the attempt to strengthen control from the centre over the plant has the contrary result of compelling the latter to exercise some freedom of choice.[38] The plant also now becomes more tempted to simulate fulfilment, either by preferring qualities which are stressed by the reporting indices at the cost (in all probability) of neglecting others, or by pretending to have achieved better results than it actually has.

The greater stress now on profitability too has antecedents which go very far back. This trend began before 1929, when enterprises were granted a status of 'economic accountability' (*khozraschot*). A reform of the credit system in 1931, which abolished barter, reinforced the trend, as did the system of business contracts when this was introduced.[39] The trend was reaffirmed during the Second Five-Year Plan

(1933–37) and later, when the heavy and light branches of industry ceased to be subsidized.[40] Turetskiy listed a series of developments which allegedly comprised a 'single system of measures which promote the full utilization of such levers of capitalism as price and money in the interest of socialist construction'.[41] However, the continued use of 1926/27 prices, which occasionally became a virtually fictitious category, obstructed this trend. The 1926/27 prices became far more important than 'unchanged prices' usually are in statistical practice. As they were the main indices of plan-fulfilment, planners and business leaders fixed their eyes on them to the neglect of costs and revenues.[42] A restriction of the number of plan indices to which enterprises had to conform was announced in 1955.[43] In 1965, further progress was envisaged in both these spheres.

Before October 1965 a plant had to fulfil 20–30 indices.[44] The reform reduced the number of indices fixed from above to eight, which was an important simplification yet hardly left a huge field for directors to manoeuvre independently.

While means were explored to reduce the number of decisions taken by controlling authorities, especially by those at the centre, means were also explored to rationalize and mechanize such decision-taking as must still remain. The problem here is to improve the method of 'balancing' inputs and outputs. Balances have become wider in scope; for instance, the First Five-Year Plan included no balance of equipment, whereas the Second Plan did.[45] However, despite decades of practice the method of economic balancing seems to have remained, until lately, on a primitive technical level: it has been an aim rather than a method. The input-output scheme of analysis was developed indeed by a Russian, Wassily Leontiev, but he emigrated to the United States where his work found its first application. Only during the past few years has the Party overcome an ideologically-based aversion from the use of mathematical methods in economics. An input-output table with 73 entries was published in 1961,[46] and a more detailed one in 1968. Great attention is now being paid to such theoretical tools as input-output analysis and linear programming (a mathematical method to find the optimum solution to a problem, where there are many possible solutions). The Soviet authorities are not even averse from learning from Western techniques of management, although it is less clear whether these techniques can be applied within such a different kind of society.

How far may these innovations eventually modify organization and methods in Soviet industry? Co-ordination within its various branches is likely to be improved, and cross-hauls and other irrationalities may be diminished. The willingness shown in trying out new methods and jettisoning ideological handicaps is moderately encouraging for the future progress of Soviet industry and for the economy generally, although a much more adventurous spirit has been shown elsewhere in Eastern Europe. The fundamental clash between a Party-dominated industrial system and mathematical methods – for to admit the primacy of the latter would be to dethrone the political aspect of 'political economy' and so to strike a blow at Marxism – has not really been overcome. The Party will use mathematics to discover the most efficient ways to accomplish its policies, but will certainly not allow mathematics to dominate policy.[47] As before, industry will continue in a given course of action, unless and until a change of course is ordered.

Whereas *plans* are laid down for some standard and simply definable period, such as for one year or for three months, *campaigns* are launched covering more irregular periods, for example every year a campaign is launched to ensure that tractors are in good repair in time for the start of field work in the spring. These campaigns may be tied to fulfilment of the plan but they acquire a momentum of their own. Other campaigns are launched at irregular intervals and apparently without reference to the sequence of plans, for example a campaign in 1951 to speed up the rotation of circulating capital. In 1957, Khrushchev launched a longer-range campaign to overtake the United States in production of meat, butter and milk per head of the population. He pursued many other campaigns to get agriculture to grow particular crops, or in particular ways.

A large number of decrees and other ordinances in economic matters are issued.[48] This aspect is about the most obvious to strike one whenever one opens a Soviet newspaper and it has been curiously late in gaining recognition in textbooks, which still largely concentrate on economic plans.

In short, an image of an economy governed by plans is very far from being a complete picture of Soviet economy. There are plans, but these are often implemented in a far from rhythmic manner and with a campaign mentaility; an unusually integrated financial system;[49] and a very wide repertoire of administrative measures. Soviet experience does not show that an economy that is goverend by plans alone can work because the Soviet economy is not of such a type.

Part of the reason why plans cannot assume the whole burden of running an economy is that they cannot be altogether complete or free from error and internal inconsistency, even if compiled on the basis of all currently available data. The probability of error is compounded as more time elapses since the inception of the plan, as new relationships or coefficients, or more efficient methods, are discovered which were not known before.

One of the directions of post-1965 reforms was to upgrade the status and strengthen the role of long-term plans. There was also to be an improvement in planning methods, involving novel methods as already discussed. As regards incentives, the objectives have been greater efficiency and higher quality. This latter is partly a matter of materials and of the design of the finished product, to which much keener attention has been paid since about 1962.[50] At the production level, quality of output demands appropriate criteria for incentive payments, with sufficient flexibility to allow them. Higher temporary prices for better-quality goods have been one of the adopted expedients. Computerization is another objective: in the vast, fundamentally centralized, mathematically highly-educated Soviet Union very ambitious programmes would inevitably be adopted. Most prominent in this connection are the ASU or automated management systems. It is planned to establish nationwide information processing and transmission. Other measures have included, in particular, enhanced attention to the role of contracts. These, in principle, already offered some counterbalance to excessive deference to the letter of plan provisions. Since 1974, adherence to delivery contracts has been stipulated if output plans are to be regarded as fulfilled.

The Second Economy

As yet, our subject has been planning, organization and administration on a grand ('macro') scale. On a small ('micro') scale planning and organization tend to be weak. This has been true of the labour market, as previously noted. It is no less true of day-to-day arrivals of goods in the shops, of the availability of services or spare parts, or of arrangements for swapping city accommodation.

In the capital city almost all lodgings are municipal or institutional and in order to move, for instance, to another district, one must find someone with whom to exchange. Although a bulletin is published to facilitate such exchanges, which are not immune from legislation,[51] many people find it necessary to supplement the official channels by informal arrangements.

Almost all services, such as repairs or house painting, have typically been performed with delays or difficulty by the official network and therefore it has been common to have recourse to having work done privately. Instead of approaching a co-operative as a whole, one might approach one of its members. In many cases the materials used in such work, or for work such as private building, are probably taken out of the public or co-operative stock.[52] Another illustration of private use of official resources is to be seen in the streets: drivers of official vehicles, being not fully employed at their official job, are often willing to pick up random passengers and take them to their destinations — as on two occasions that I well remember. Such earnings will of course not be reported, and so one can only conjecture their total, but this must be fairly considerable. One other sizeable field of semi-legal collective endeavour is rural building, which apparently is often performed by collective farm building teams on behalf of other organizations. Certain of these activities seem to be officially tolerated, or although they are illegal the prohibition is not strictly enforced. It is definitely illegal to hire a private car (or an official car off-duty), but probably few cases where this is done wind up in court. However, other offences such as 'speculation' (buying by an individual with the intention of selling) are punished, sometimes very heavily. (Touting of tickets outside the theatre seems to be exempt, perhaps because it would be difficult to prove the intention.) But where there is a flagrant violation or large sums are involved the law may be invoked in its full ferocity. Since 1961 at least 200 people have been shot for economic offences.[53] One must suppose that the response is proportionate to the anxiety, or perhaps alarm, felt by the authorities; and more indirect evidence points to the same conclusion. More than one British smuggler of drugs has been apprehended by the Soviet Customs; quite possibly their capture was a by-product of a larger operation which was directed also against smuggling by Soviet citizens.

If the judicial system is invoked, this is in order to catch and punish offenders who are in effect trying to profit from the shortcomings of the system itself. Private initiative finds an interstice to fill that has been left by the concentration on heavy industry, or on production rather than services. Some handicrafts may even have been enabled to survive because of the lack of competition from the State sector. One might conclude that alongside the officially admitted and schematized economic system there exists in symbiosis with it an unofficial and semi-legal or definitely illegal system. Although the official system predominates the second is not negligible, and some acquaintance with it is necessary for living at all comfortably within the society.

The 'second economy' – the name given to these unofficial arrangements by Western commentators during the past decade – certainly exists on a larger scale than used to be realized by most non-Soviet writers on Soviet economic affairs. I have been convinced of its importance since 1963, when during one short spell in Moscow I set out to discover on how little I could live. With a hotel room already paid for and spending nothing on clothing, transport, or the many other usual, and generally unavoidable, calls on one's purse, and confining myself therefore to food purchases – and very basic foods at that – I nevertheless found it most difficult to spend, on average, less than 3½ roubles a day. Yet the average monthly wage in 1965, not including social remuneration or holiday pay, was 90 roubles,[54] and neither earnings nor retail prices would have changed significantly between those dates; or, if anything, earnings had *increased*. I was therefore spending only on the most basic foods, and purely on myself, slightly more than was on average earned by wage-earners, and which must have been spent by them on various things in addition to food. The equation does not match, and the conclusion must be that many people were gaining a not negligible income from unrecorded sources.

Obvious objections to this conclusion are easily refuted. For example: I did not know the right things to buy? Incorrect; I had already lived in the USSR for about three years and knew this quite well. Prices may be higher in Moscow than elsewhere? On the contrary, actually they are lower. One could probably economize on purchases of clothing, for instance? Actually clothing and shoes are expensive, and warm (though not fashionable) varieties of both are indispensable for getting through the Moscow winter. Doubtless it *is* less economical to live as an individual than as a member of a family, but economies under this heading would not be sufficient to close the gap. Access to low-cost canteen meals may be placed in the same category. Fishing and hunting (the latter remarkably widespread) also help (hunting in particular being on a scale that damages the environment), but these last are included within the 'second economy', at any rate to the extent that privately culled fish or game is marketed.[55]

However, it would be quite mistaken to suppose that whatever is not done through the official hierarchy *is* done, more or less well, by private enterprise. Although the semi-legal or illegal arrangements may work on a larger scale than one would at first expect, the limits of what can or will be done along these lines are quickly reached. As a rule, whenever a particular necessary decision is not taken through the official system, at a rather high level, nothing will be done either at any lower level or by private enterprise to remedy the omission. A spirit of individual initiative in economic matters is alien to the Soviet Union: for the most part, people accept that nothing can be done if the centre takes no action. Items go on being produced or not produced long after the need for a change of course becomes clear. The absence of market mechanisms pervades the economy. When considered from a distance, the Soviet economy may seem to be more highly organized and better co-ordinated than a capitalist economy. When one sees it in close-up one gains a different and largely contrary impression.[56]

Notes

1 Thus, it is claimed that Communism 'raises to a great height the mastery of human beings over nature, gives the possibility of managing her anarchic forces to an ever greater degree' (*Nauka i zhizn'*, no. 11, 1965, p. 34). Cf. E. Sollertinskaya, *Planovoye*

khozyaystvo, no. 5, 1946, p. 55.

2 Cf. E. Zaleski, *Planification de la croissance et fluctuations economiques en URSS, tonne I, 1918–1932* (1962), Introduction.

3 A. A. Arzumanyan in *Stroitel'stvo kommunizma i obshchestvennyye nauki* (1962), p. 48.

4 Alec Nove was told that the Sixth Plan was scrapped for political reasons. (A. Nove, *An Economic History of the USSR* (1969), p. 342.) I have no evidence which would support that the motive was in fact political.

5 H. Levine in *Dimensions of Soviet Economic Power* (1962), p. 58.

6 B. L. Goncherenko, M. I. Petrushin, G. I. Somborskiy, A. S. Tolkachev (eds.), *Nepreryvnost' v planirovanii i pokazateli gosudarstvennogo plana* (1962), pp. 28–9. Cf. also pp. 7, 46, 49, 51, 52 and 60.

7 This is presented in the very interesting and original article by Kyril Fitzlyon, 'Plan and Prediction', *Soviet Studies*, October 1969 (vol. XXI, no. 2).

8 *Planovoye khozyaystvo*, no. 5, 1946, p. 18.

9 G. M. Sorokin, *Ekonomicheskaya gazeta*, no. 25, 1968, p. 12.

10 Cf. R. L. Hall, *The Economic System of a Socialist State* (1937), quoting Lorwin and Abramson, *International Labour Review*, January 1936, p. 33.

11 Some attempts, which I cannot examine here, have been made to show the contrary.

12 See Part II, Chapter 6. Similarly, the redivision of ministries between August 1953 and April 1954 called forth various measures to relieve the Gosplan of detailed functions of fixing norms of material expenditures (*inter alia*).

13 Sh. L. Rozenfel'd, *Organizatsiya upravleniya promyshlennost'yu SSSR* (1955), p. 17.

14 Margaret Dewar, *Industrial Management in the USSR* (1945), p. 12.

15 G. V. Teplov, *Planirovaniye na mashinostroitel'nykh zavodakh* (1949), p. 40.

16 A. T. Tayliyev, *Ekonomicheskaya gazeta*, no. 25, 1968, p. 13.

17 B. P. Orlov, *Razvitiye transporta v SSSR 1917–1962* (1963), pp. 170–1.

18 A. Arakelyan, *Planirovaniye narodnogo khozyaystva SSSR* (1952), p. 29.

19 A. A. Arzumanyan in *Stroitel'stvo kommunizma i obshchestvennye nauki*, op. cit., p. 49.

20 V. M. Lagutkin, *Ekonomicheskaya gazeta*, no. 26, 1968, p. 9.

21 N. Gal'perin, *Voprosy ekonomiki*, no. 7, 1958, p. 45. Cf. P. Karpov, *Planovoye khozyaystvo*, no. 7, 1958, pp. 18–19, and M. C. Kaser, *Soviet Studies*, April 1959, pp. 325–6.

22 A. N. Yefimov, *Ekonomicheskaya gazeta*, no. 25, 1968, p. 13.

23 S. G. Strumilin, *Planovoye khozyaystvo*, no. 3, 1927, p. 19.

24 N. P. Lebedinskiy, *Ekonomicheskaya gazeta*, no. 25, 1968, p. 9.

25 Sh. Ya. Turetskiy, *Planovoye khozyaystvo*, no. 2, 1935, p. 140, in relation to planning labour productivity.

26 N. P. Lebedinskiy, *Ekonomicheskaya gazeta*, no. 25, 1968, p. 9.

27 *Ekonomicheskaya gazeta*, no. 10, 1968, p. 11.

28 E.g. I. Mayevskiy, *Planovoye khozyaystvo*, no. 3, 1966, pp. 15–16.

29 For example, see *Ekonomicheskaya gazeta*, no. 20, 1968, p. 12.

30 S. Ordzhonikidze, *Po-stalinski borot'sya za protsvetaniya nashey rodiny*, p. 46, cited in D. Chernomordik (ed.), *Narodnyy dokhod SSSR* (1939), p. 55.

31 B. Sukharevskiy, *Planovoye khozyaystvo*, no. 11, 1936, p. 132.

32 D. Savinskiy, *Kurs promyshlennoy statistiki* (1944), pp. 98–9.

33 Sh. Ya Turetskiy, *Sebestoimost' i voprosy tsenoobrazovaniya* (1940), p. 136.

34 Ibid., p. 133.

35 Ibid., p. 137.

36 B. A. Vvedenskiy (chief editor), *Entsiklopedicheskiy slovar', tom II* (1964), p. 507.

37 As cited in S. M. Kutyrev, *Balans dokhodov i raskhodov khozyaystvennoy organizatsii promyshlennosti, kniga vtoraya, chast' tret'ya* (1941).

38 Cf. E. Liberman, *Sovetskiye finansy*, no. 12, 1945, p. 10.

39 Sh. Ya. Turetskiy, *Planovoye khozyaystvo*, no. 9, 1935, p. 96.

40 Sh. Ya. Turetskiy, op. cit., pp. 27 and 122, and Yu. Shenger, *Plan*, no. 15, 1937, p. 27.

41 Reference as footnote 39.

42 Sh. Ya. Turetskiy, *Sebestoimost' i voprosy tsenoobrazovaniya* (1940), p. 133.

43 D. Sankin, *Planovoye khozyaystvo*, no. 4, 1955, p. 79.

44 Gregory Clark, *Australian Outlook*, April 1966 (vol. 20, no. 1), p. 45.

45 A. Arakelyan, op. cit., p. 35.

46 *Narodnoye khozyaystvo SSSR v 1960 godu* (1961), pp. 103–44.

47 The conservative view was clearly expressed by Baybakov, the Chairman of Gosplan, at an economic conference in May 1968 (*The Times*, 29 May 1968, p. 5). However, the conservatives were under strong pressure from two directions. First, the progress of the economy had been slowed and the introduction of mathematics into policy-making might well help to cure the malaise. Second, mathematics has a particularly high prestige and importance in Soviet science.

48 See in this connection Z. Frank and J. Waelbroeck, 'Soviet Economic Policy since 1953: A Study of its Structure and Changes', *Soviet Studies*, July 1965 (vol. XVII, no. 1).

49 This is described in Chapter 13.

50 See in this connection R. Hutchings, *Soviet Science, Technology, Design* (1976), pp. 177–81.

51 As reported in 1939, permission to effect the exchange might be refused if certain conditions were not fulfilled, including if as a

result of the exchange tenants would be accommodated in less than 5 square metres per person. (J. N. Hazard, *Soviet Housing Law* (1939), pp. 91–2.)

52 E.g. M. Kozeko, *Pravda*, 9 February 1968, p. 3.
53 I. Lapenna, *Soviet Penal Policy* (1968), p. 90.
54 *Narodnoye khozyaystvo SSSR v 1965 g.* (1966), p. 566.
55 See in this connection B. Komarov, *The Destruction of Nature in the Soviet Union* (1978), p. 86.
56 Concerning the subject of this section see Gregory Grossman, 'The "Second Economy" of the USSR', in M. Bornstein (ed.), *The Soviet Economy, Continuity and Change* (1981), pp. 71–93, and other sources mentioned therein.

13

THE FINANCIAL SYSTEM

Financial planning is less developed than planning in physical terms. No financial plans or budgets have been composed for a five-year period. When annual plans are compiled, the accounts are based on current prices. While a summation of productive indices is included in the economic plan, there is only a partial inclusion in it of monetary incomes and expenditures.[1] However, plants are required to fulfil plans in financial as well as in physical terms. Plans compiled in physical indices and plans compiled in physical terms are now to receive an approximately equal emphasis: for instance, starting in 1968 the Gosplan would compose balances of machinery and equipment in both physical and value terms.[2] Historically, planning in physical indices has been the dominant aspect. There has been a persistent tendency to attach more weight to financial indices – to cost calculations, for instance, rather than to fulfilment of plans at any cost, and recently to profitability. This trend has not yet reached a point where finance governs behaviour as directly as it does in a market economy, nor is such a final result likely.

The Soviet financial system shares a number of features and trappings of the financial system in a market economy. There is a monetary system, a State budget, a Ministry of Finance, and a State Bank (Gosbank). Differences are that: (1) there is only one bank (other than for construction or foreign trade), and this bank enforces stronger and more universal controls than any bank in a free economy; (2) a much larger proportion of the Gross National Product passes through the State budget; (3) prices are fixed by authority rather than by a market.

(1) Financial relations between the Gosbank and individual enterprises are regulated according to the principle that every enterprise must have an account at the Gosbank, and must depend on the Gosbank for part of its working capital. In other words, a Gosbank loan is the only legal form of short-term credit. An enterprise is also provided with a sum of working capital which is called its 'own', but this is

purposely made insufficient to cover its needs at all seasons of the year. Seasonal variations in output and sales are still considerable, owing to intermittent supplies and other causes (such as demand variations, climatic variations, icing-up of waterways, transport bottlenecks, seasonal migrations, vacations), so this limitation is important (particularly, of course, in branches where seasonal variations are large, such as timber haulage and food processing).[3] Among other arrangements conducive to control is the fact that all except insignificantly small payments must be made by State enterprises to each other by draft, through the medium of the Gosbank (cash payments not being allowed). The use of cash by State organizations is therefore restricted to the payment of wages, buying agricultural products, and other small sums.[4] The Bank has also other controlling functions, for instance it is required to report if any prices charged in transactions which are accomplished through its medium exceed permitted levels. Like other institutions, the Gosbank has its plan to fulfil, including a 'Credit Plan' and a 'Cash Plan' (the latter relating to currency issue, also a bank monopoly). The Bank is the recipient and reservoir of budget funds, although decisions connected with the national finances are the preserve of the Ministry of Finance.

(2) A budget is presented to the Supreme Soviet annually, although not always at the beginning of a year (as extreme examples, the 1950 budget was presented in June of that year and the 1953 budget even in August). More recently, December of the preceding year, sometimes even as early as October, has been the usual month of presentation. Reported discussion of the budget in the Supreme Soviet is perfunctory, and the published budget is indeed from most angles very uninformative.

Prices, or precisely what is included in categories, are not published. Besides being incomplete, the types of information which are made available vary from year to year, which makes interpretation of the budget by anyone who does not have access to confidential data extremely difficult.

The budget includes most payments relating to the socialist sector of the economy, i.e. to defence, capital investment, subsidies, education, social security and communal services, and State administration. It excludes collective farm investments and personal consumption.

The Soviet budget covers a much larger proportion of total national expenditures than the budget of a Western country does. This is partly owing to the fairly large share of social security and communal expenditures, but mainly owing to the inclusion within the budget of almost all investment spending. The budget distributes, or redistributes, approximately half of the GNP. Because it claims a larger share of total expenditures, defence makes up a relatively smaller share of it. This enables the Russians to point out that the United States budget consists mainly of defence expenditures, whereas less than one-tenth of their own does. The difference in coverage largely nullifies the comparison.

The budget has revenue and expenditure sides. The federal (all-union) accounts, and consequently the consolidated budget, show a surplus of revenues over expenditures, which gives the appearance of a budget surplus. However, in most years this has not been a true surplus: it is stated to have been utilized for extending credits to industry, agriculture or trade, or as a central reserve, and this is confirmed by the evidence of the totals.[5] If it were a real surplus, astronomical sums would by now have piled up (in fact, they could not have piled up in any real sense). Extra leeway has thus been provided for diverting expenditures to untraceable purposes. However, the amount of this surplus has been declining. Unlike their all-union counterparts, the revenue and expenditure estimates applying to individual republics or to localities do balance. The republic accounts are confirmed later than the federal (consolidated) budget, which appears to leave the former no margin of variation outside the permitted total.

The utilization of this surplus has been, to some extent, a question mark. If the credits extended in any one year exceeded the announced surplus, this would imply inflationary financing. This was resorted to during World War II, and the consequences had to be corrected by a monetary reform of December 1947 when a large part of personal savings was wiped out. Since then there have occasionally been rumours of another impending reform. None has occurred, although in January 1961 a new and heavier rouble was adopted (1 new rouble equalling 10 old ones), while at the same time the *external* rouble was in reality devalued (although the operation was described more euphemistically).

The main items of revenue are Turnover Tax (TT) and Deductions from Profits (d.f.p.). Naturally, both ultimately are paid by Soviet citizens.[6] In form, they are paid by the socialist sector (TT is paid when goods pass into the wholesale trade network whereas dfp is paid by plants). The concept of shifting tax incidence, familiar to every economics undergraduate in Britain, is not alluded to in the USSR. The two taxes are identical in that both are employed to finance expenditures generally, but varying amounts received as TT are allotted to individual republics. Co-operative producer societies have paid lower rates of TT than State establishments.[7]

TT is a tax on sales. Individual tax rates have been only occasionally published and no year-to-year series is available, but the average level appears often to have been of the order of 100 per cent (on top of factor costs inclusive of d.f.p.).[8] Since 1930, when it replaced a total of 61 taxes,[9] TT has provided the bulk of budget revenues, though the percentage is declining. Deductions from profits are reckoned as a percentage of gross profits of industrial organizations and this item has been increasing in importance.

A clause 'mobilization of the resources of the population' provided 17·9 per cent of revenues in the First Five-Year Plan and was meant to provide 12·5 per cent in the Second Plan.[10] For about 30 years a significant contribution to revenues was made by popular subscriptions in the form of State Loans. In form voluntary, these subscriptions were in fact compulsory according to a decree of 2 July 1936.[11] Personal taxes (income tax and the like) are comparatively unimportant and were to be discontinued by 1965, but this decision was later rescinded, which was one of the charges laid against Khrushchev.

The main expenditure headings are: (a) 'Finance of National Economy' (abbreviated here FNE): this is mainly capital investment (financed chiefly by outright grants) and partly subsidies; (b) 'Social and Cultural Measures' (SCM) (education, health services and physical culture, children's and unmarried mothers' allowances and state insurance, no unemployment benefits); (c) 'Defence' (DEF); and (d) 'Administration' (including cost of non-commercial government bodies). The main items of expenditure, usually in that order, are FNE, SCM and DEF.

One may also divide up the budget according to whether it is federal, republic or local (oblast etc). Over time, certain shifts in revenues and expenditrues can be noted. The evolution of budget quantities will be examined in Chapter 14.

At the time that the budget is made public, certain non-budget expenditures too are forecast. These consist of payments made from enterprises' own funds and are destined mainly for financing the 'national economy', especially capital investment. In 1962, for example, budget expenditures on the national economy were forecast at 32·47 milliard roubles, whereas total budget and non-budget expenditures on the national economy were forecast at 56·50 milliard roubles, or 74 per cent greater.

If budget plans are scantily reported, little is reported either about their fulfilment. But one notices appreciable deviations from planned totals in both revenues and expenditures, which hint at changes of direction during the year or at difficulties or additional opportunities which emerged.

(3) In fact, the annual budget is only one means of financial control by the authorities over the economy. Besides determining expenditures from enterprises' own funds, the government has the power to alter prices. Clearly, if a plant needs a subsidy, this is because it is not allowed to shut down, or to charge an economic price for its output, or to alter its production profile. Its need for a subsidy arises, in other

words, from government decisions. What the budget signifies can consequently be ascertained only when any relevant changes in prices and costs (for example, wages payments) are also taken into account. Whether or not Turnover Tax is included is highly relevant, in view of the heavy rates which may be payable but from which some institutions may be exempt.[12]

In general, *prices* within the State sector are not determined by supply and demand directly but only to some extent under their influence. They are fixed directly by price-fixing organizations, with approval by the Ministry of Finance, and may not afterwards be changed. The government values highly its ability to fix prices: 'Price is a most important, sharp and effective lever of the Soviet State.'[13] Although recently there has been much discussion of how rational prices should be arrived at, up to the present at least the fixing of prices from above is a fixed point in the Soviet economic system, like the State monopoly of foreign trade. One can in no way agree with proposals to go over to anarchic market prices, was how the Chairman of the State Committee for Prices expressed it.[14]

In some cases, prices are allowed to be lowered independently, but not raised; but it is rare for any Soviet producing or selling organization to lower its prices voluntarily — as was shown at the time of the 'scissors' crisis of 1923. Only in a few special instances — unique items and new items during the first six months of producing them — are selling and purchasing organizations permitted to concert prices jointly. This loophole has probably tended to lead to an upwards drift over time of certain prices, and to simulated or actual novelty of product.[15]

The price-regulating mechanisms — reacting against inflationary tendencies — have been employed to keep prices down, or to prevent them from rising too fast, and while this need has been especially acute in such tense periods as the First Five-Year Plan, it is a continuing preoccupation. But these mechanisms have not been able to do the job on their own. Although setting up the State monopoly of foreign trade was the cornerstone of the system of price regulation, in turn administrative pressure, control over stocks, a currency reform, industrialization and expansion in the State sector of the economy, and finally taxation policy, had to come to the aid of the price-regulating agencies. Another reaction of the government to upward pressure on prices in certain periods has been to strengthen the price-regulating machinery.[16]

Prices must, of course, cover costs, unless a subsidy is to be admitted. They are related to average rather than marginal costs: if alternatively wholesale prices were to be based on marginal costs (i.e. on the performance of the worst enterprises) this according to the Chairman of the State Committee for Prices would necessitate raising wholesale prices by more than 30 per cent and would lead to serious social consequences.[17] As subsidies are payable to some but not all branches, prices can and do vary widely relative to costs; while the range of costs within a given industry is, in turn, rather wide (having grown wider during the period 1927/28 to 1935),[18] owing to the reluctance of the planners to withdraw plant from service until it is physically worn out and to the practice of turning over equipment which is replaced in all-union industry to local industry. The market is consequently very imperfect and actual profit rates diverge very widely from the average.

Various 'social benefit' considerations are also taken into account. Wholesale prices were supposed to stimulate production of the most important items, the replacement of deficit items by others which are more abundant, import-replacement, and so on.[19] Similar considerations apply among retail prices, although if one contemplates the high price of vodka, one might conclude that revenue-raising had been remembered no less than the desirability of discouraging its consumption. There may possibly be more recondite and sinister connections too: it has been asserted that alcohol was hoarded for the missile programme, which caused a shortage of vodka;[20] in 1962 the price of vodka was in fact increased. The mechanisms of price formation and price structures are quite different for Group A and Group B items[21] – in particular, the latter pay TT whereas the former do not.

According to Hanson, however, differences in TT incidence do not help to explain differences in the Soviet price structure as compared with that of the United Kingdom between major categories of items. Hanson (like myself) finds that Soviet retail prices of food are high in relation to Soviet prices of durable consumer goods; also, he points out, they are high by comparison with the corresponding price relationships in Western Europe, Czechoslovakia and East Germany.[22] However, differences in TT incidence apparently do not reduce retail food prices relative to those of consumer durables, while within main groups of consumption goods there is a moderate correlation between relative prices and turnover tax rates.[23] As regards major categories, Hanson concludes that the explanation of relative prices must be found primarily in relative cost-structures. The entire industrial sector is perhaps operating on a lower cost level than the agricultural sector, which absorbs a large proportion of consumption expenditrues.

During NEP, prewar prices still exerted a good deal of influence, as did import prices, although any automatic link between prices at home and abroad had been cut by the setting up of the State monopoly of foreign trade. Towards the end of the Second Five-Year Plan import prices ceased to exert any influence in price-formation.[24]

As a rule, price changes have occurred rather infrequently and also erratically, as if prices were manipulated by some vast combine or oligopoly. As major changes in prices would affect many elements in the budget – this is in fact the sequence, TT being in theory not price-determining but following from prices fixed by the plan[25] – there is inertia tending to keep things as they are. The price-fixing system is inflexible as regards movement in detail. (This is true both as regards wholesale and retail prices.) The degree of stability of retail prices since 1954 is noteworthy. Probably one main explanation of it is budget flexibility.[26] The central authorities have at their disposal an unusually wide range of levers for controlling the economy. It is also owing to this wide repertoire that they can maintain fairly stable programmes of capital investments, by manipulating if necessary other parameters.[27] Another explanation is the prohibition of 'speculation', which as Ware points out enables the planned price to be slightly lower than the market would bear, so that there is market stability without equilibrium.[28] Collective farm market prices are a safety valve and therefore also part of the explanation.

Within the collective farm market, prices are ruled by supply and demand, although the latter is naturally influenced by the level of prices in the State sector. Soviet commentators assume that a reduction in State prices will induce a reduction in market prices; it may even be implied that there will be no change in the distribution of expenditure as between the fixed and the free sectors.[29] One can imagine circumstances – although it would take us too far afield here to explore them – when the result might be the contrary.

While economic plans are drawn up in respect of periods stretching ahead for months or years, the financial system comprises primarily a month-to-month, even day-to-day system of supervision and control. This is largely routine work: the State Bank functions from day to day, the budget comes round every year. The recurring cycle partly conceals the fact that the financial system has functioned as an instrument of central control much more effectively in some periods than in others.

Notes

1 D. Kondrashev, *Balans dokhodov i raskhodov predpriyatiy i ob"edineniy promyshlennosti* (1948), pp. 5–6.
2 A. M. Lalayants, *Ekonomicheskaya gazeta*, no. 26, 1968, p. 8. Cf. P. D. Podshivalenko, *Ekonomicheskaya gazeta*, no. 28, 1968, p. 11.
3 See Raymond Hutchings, *Seasonal Influences in Soviet Industry* (OUP for RIIA, 1971).
4 G. Shvarts, *Sovetskiye finansy*, nos. 9–10, 1945, p. 5.

5 Over the period 1941—52 inclusive the accumulated net budget surplus (surpluses minus deficits) was 151·6 milliard roubles, while between 1940 (end-year) and 1952 credit investments of the Gosbank amounted to 148·0 milliard roubles. (For sources, see my Ph. D thesis, op. cit., Tables III and IV, pp. 263 and 266.)

6 See Leon L. Herman, 'Who Pays the Taxes?', *Problems of Communism*, vol. 8, 1959, pp. 21—6, reprinted in Alex Inkeles and Kent Geiger, *Soviet Society, A Book of Readings* (1961), pp. 389—95.

7 M. I. Bogolepov, *The Soviet Financial System* (1945), p. 14.

8 Concerning Turnover Tax rates see also below, p. 166.

9 M. Bogolepov, *Planovoye khozyaystvo*, no. 4, 1935, p. 98.

10 Ibid., pp. 94—6.

11 C. Bettelheim, *La planification soviétique* (1945), p. 177.

12 Thus, Malafeyev notes that all wholesale purchasers paid TT except the war department, the OGPU and Exportkhleb (op. cit., p. 180).

13 Sh. Ya. Turetskiy, *Vnutripromyshlennoye nakopleniye v SSSR* (1948), pp. 323—4.

14 V. K. Sitnin, *Ekonomicheskaya gazeta*, no. 28, 1968, p. 11.

15 Producing bodies have also attempted to exploit other opportunities to raise prices, such as the annual signature of contracts.

16 See my 'The Origins of the Soviet Industrial Price System', *Soviet Studies*, July 1961 (vol. XIII, no. 1).

17 Reference as footnote 14.

18 Sh. Ya. Turetskiy, *Planovoye khozyaystvo*, no. 8, 1936, p. 96.

19 Sh. Ya. Turetskiy, *Sebestoimost' i voprosy tsenoobrazovaniya* (1940), p. 119.

20 O. V. Penkovsky, *The Penkovsky Papers* (1965), p. 252.

21 V. V. Yevdokimova, *Ekonomicheskaya gazeta*, no. 28, 1968, p. 12.

22 P. Hanson, *The Consumer in the Soviet Economy* (1968), pp. 111—17.

23 Ibid., p. 114.

24 Reference as footnote 19 in this chapter, p. 120.

25 M. I. Bogolepov, *The Soviet Financial System*, p. 11.

26 See my article 'Some Behavior Patterns in the Soviet Post-War Budget', *The ASTE Bulletin*, Fall 1962.

27 See below, Chapter 15.

28 H. A. Ware, *Bulletins of Soviet Economic Development*, no. 4 (1950), p. 22.

29 E.g. the decree on reduction of retail prices of consumer goods in March 1949.

PART IV

LEVERS OF DEVELOPMENT

In economic history no hard and fast line can be drawn between the organization of an economy and the means that are used to devise or promote its development: both are passive or active according to the policy which infuses them. One can, at the most, direct attention to particular means, whose relevance to the developmental process is more close or more directly perceivable than the more static elements of the environment. Five such means, or levers, are examined in this Part. The selection presupposes a State-controlled economy and an adequate availability of resources. The latter were largely derived from the agricultural sector: in terms of labour power and unequal exchange which enabled the necessary funds to be generated.

14

THE BUDGET

This chapter is based entirely on official published data: principally the annual budget debates and laws, statistical annuals, and articles each year by the Minister or Deputy-Minister of Finance in Finansy SSSR. Exact sources are seldom given, as – especially when a table is made up from many different sources, as is often the case – these would be very complicated, and by no means proportionately useful to the great majority of readers.

A. Main Items of Expenditure and Revenue

From whatever angle one approaches the problems of economic development, the mechanism by which funds are accumulated and mobilized for expenditure comes very high in importance. In the Soviet Union this function has been performed by the State budget. The bare bones of the budgetary system were described in Chapter 13. In the present chapter its components are examined more closely with the aim of discovering how and why they have altered over time, and how they are interrelated with each other and with other aspects of the economy or trends in its development.

Table 4

Prewar Budget Expenditures
(milliard pre-1961 roubles)

Years	FNE	SCM	DEF	Total Expenditures
1928/29	3·7	2·8	0·9	8·8
1932	24·8	8·3	1·3	38·0
1937	43·4	30·9	17·5	106·2
1940	58·3	40·9	56·7	174·4

Table 4 gives a bird's-eye view of the prewar growth of budget expenditures in milliards of pre-1961 roubles.[1] Unfortunately, the upward movement in these series is exaggerated by the contemporary rise in prices for which one cannot make any precise allowance. The percentage shares of these components in total expenditures altered as in Table 5.

Table 5

Prewar Budget Expenditures
(percentages)

Years	FNE	SCM	DEF	Total of the three columns on the left
1928/29	42	30	10	82
1932	65	20	3	88
1937	41	29	16	86
1940	33	23	33	89

We observe a rise in Finance of the National Economy (FNE) between 1928/29 and 1932 and then a very considerable rise in Defence spending (DEF) between 1932 and 1940 with the simultaneous squeezing of Finance of the National Economy. Social and Cultural Expenditures did not fluctuate so sharply as either of these in proportionate terms, but had to yield ground to FNE between 1928/29 and 1932 and to DEF between 1937 and 1940.

Since 1940 the main percentage components of actual expenditure have altered as in Table 6, which discloses larger but less sudden shifts in proportions as compared with 1928/29 to 1940. FNE has climbed to about 55 per cent, substantially more than its 1937 proportion,

Table 6

Post-1940 Budget Expenditures
(percentages)

Years	FNE	SCM	DEF
1946	31·1	26·1	23·6
1950	38·2	28·3	20·1
1955	43·2	27·3	19·9
1960	46·6	34·1	12·7
1965	44·2	37·6	12·6
1970	48·3	36·2	11·6
1975	51·6	35·9	8·1
1979	54·8	33·6	6·2

while SCM too stands higher than in 1937. On the whole, the proportionate sizes of the main expenditure components in 1937 and in 1963 were rather alike, but since 1963 have spread further apart.

The average growth rate of total budget expenditures has been much smaller since 1940 than it had been between 1928/29 and 1940. The deceleration has been mainly due to a slackening of the price inflation, but also the rate of growth of the economy has slowed down and in some recent years at least the budget may have declined in relation to total national spending. Between 1946 and about 1958 the budget rose approximately in a linear trend,[2] whereas since 1959 and especially from about 1965 its increase has been somewhat faster.

Actual budget revenues and expenditures almost always differ from the forecasts of them, and the divergence is sometimes fairly substantial, as in 1948 (a shortfall of 17·1 milliard pre-1961 roubles in expenditures) or 1958 (an excess of 15·0 milliards).

Budget revenues have generally grown roughly in parallel to budget expenditures, although the former increased marginally faster between 1946 and 1950. According to Zverev, currency emission to balance a budget deficit has been practised sparingly and reluctantly,[3] although it had to be resorted to during the war as expenditures exceeded receipts in 1942 by 18·9 milliard (pre-1961) roubles, and in 1943 by 7·3 milliard.[4] However, under Zverev's successor Garbuzov the situation may have altered; the provenance of a large portion of revenues is unclear.

The principal itemized components of budget revenues have remained throughout Turnover Tax (TT) and Deductions from Profits (d.f.p.). During the 1930s an overwhelming reliance was placed on Turnover Tax. Since 1946, and particularly since 1950, d.f.p. have become more important, and in the early 1970s were comprising slightly the larger revenue source. At present (1982) each of these items is contributing just under one-third of total revenues. In the table, the proportion contributed by d.f.p. is consolidated: since 1965 this item has been re-labelled Payments out of Profits, and it is split three ways: into payment for productive funds, rent, and levies of free profit margins. The chief aim of this change was to encourage more economical capital investment.

Table 7

Budget Revenue Items

Years	TT	d.f.p.
1928/29	35·6	6·3
1932	51·5	5·3
1937	69·4	8·5
1940	58·7	12·1
1946	58·5	5·0
1950	55·8	9·6
1955	43·0	18·2
1960	40·6	24·6
1965	37·8	30·2
1970	31·5	34·6
1975	30·4	31·9
1979	31·4	29·9

The largest expenditure item is usually Finance of the National Economy and this is also the one that chiefly concerns us. Table 8 indicates amounts spent under this heading between 1940 and 1967. It reveals two peaks, in 1951 and 1959–60, and one nadir, in 1953; there was one abrupt rise, 1954–55. Whereas the two crests are synchronized with the commencement of long-term plans – respectively the Fifth and the Seven-Year – and are, I believe, genuine movements, the nadir in 1953 and the abrupt rise in 1955 reflect changes in *total* budget expenditures in those years. These latter changes are, I believe, not genuine (more later on this score).

Social and Cultural Expenditures have remained more stable: in recent years the only eventful year was 1957, when there was a substantial rise due partly to an increase in pension rates but in all probability partly also to a transfer of some items from Defence to the sub-category Science.

Defence expenditures declined sharply in 1946 and then more slowly until 1948, when they rose until 1952 (Korean War), thence declining until 1960 when they again began to increase, reaching a peak in 1963; and since then have fluctuated, reaching a record level in 1970–73. What is revealed here is determined mainly by national security considerations, though also with an eye to the propaganda impact of a particular total or trend, and outside observers have no direct check on the truth or completeness of the published figure, which is not broken down in any way. It is widely thought that other defence spending is located elsewhere in the budget, and/or that the overt total is reckoned at artificially low prices.[5]

These three items always account for a very large proportion of total expenditures, and moreover since 1946 this proportion has increased (Table 9). Subsidiary items, such as payments in connection with State loans, have dwindled, as have the opportunities for concealing budget expenditures outside these three major components, i.e. within the right-hand column in the table. Let us therefore concentrate on the detailed composition of these three items.

B. Finance of National Economy

The two wings of this item are budget and non-budget. There has been, if anything, a slight tendency away from budget financing of the national economy. The transition to the new system of industrial administration after October 1965 enhanced this trend.

The budgetary components of this item can in certain years be split up in a sixfold division:

Capital—Industry	Capital—Agriculture	Capital—Residue
Non-capital—industry	Non-capital—Agriculture	Non-capital—Residue

Let us now try to fill these boxes. *Forecast* figures are given in all cases.

The relative sizes of capital investments financed from the budget and of budget allocations to FNE cannot usually be calculated, as capital investments are financed also from other clauses, particularly from SCM. A simple comparison of the two series, which is presented in Table 10, is therefore, strictly speaking, illegitimate: the ratio of capital investments *within* FNE to FNE would be lower, and in fact was to have been 34·0 per cent in the Ninth Five-Year Plan.[6] If this caveat is borne in mind, the trend of this ratio can still be meaningful. As shown in the table, for certain years it reached a peak of 56·0 per cent in 1954, sagged but rose to another peak in 1962, then fell to a low point in 1972, and since then (according to available information, which is

Table 8

Budget Expenditure Items

(milliards of roubles and percentages of total expenditures)

Years	FNE		SCM	DEF	
	Amount	Per cent	Per cent	Amount	Per cent
1940	5·84	33·5	23·5	5·68	32·6
1941	5·16	27·0	16·4	8·30	43·4
1942	3·16	17·3	n.a.	10·84	59·3
1943	3·31	15·8	17·7	12·50	59·5
1944	5·37	20·3	19·4	13·78	52·2
1945	7·43	24·9	21·0	12·82	42·9
1946	9·57	31·1	26·1	7·26	23·6
1947	13·27	36·7	crest 29·5	6·64	18·4
1948	14·75	39·8	28·5	6·63	17·9
1949	16·19	39·3	28·1	7·92	19·2

Year							
1950		15·79	38·2		28·3	8·29	20·1
1951		17·94	40·5	crest	26·8	9·34	21·1
1952	decrease	17·88	38·9		26·7	10·86	23·6
1953	only very small increase	18·10	35·2	nadir	25·0	10·78	20·9
1954		21·33	38·5		25·6	n.a.	n.a.
1955		23·31	43·2	sharp rise	27·3	10·74	19·9
1956		24·52	43·5		29·2	9·73	17·3
1957		26·70	44·0	new pensions	32·6	9·12	15·0
1958		29·03	45·2		33·3	9·36	14·6
1959		32·37	46·0		32·8	9·37	13·3
1960		34·10	46·6	crest	34·1	9·30	12·7
1961		32·61	42·7		36·0	11·60	15·2
1962		36·2	43·8		34·9	12·6	15·2
1963		38·8	44·6		35·6	13·9	16·0
1964		40·6	44·0		36·1	13·3	14·4
1965		44·9	44·2		37·6	12·8	12·6
1966	only very small increase	45·2	42·8		38·6	13·4	12·7
1967		52·8	45·8		37·8	14·5	12·6

scanty) has remained stable or risen slightly. The fall in this ratio from 1962 to 1972 in large part reflects the effect of the 1965 economic

Table 9

FNE, SCM and DEF

	Combined Percentages	Residue
1940	89·6	10·4
1946	80·9	19·1
1950	86·5	13·5
1955	90·4	9·6
1960	93·4	6·6
1965	94·3	5·7
1970	96·0	4·0
1975	95·6	4·4
1979	94·6	5·4

Table 10

Capital Investments (a) and FNE (b) from the Budget

(milliard roubles)

	(a)	(b)	(b)/(a) (%)
1952	9·81	18·04	54·4
1954	12·11	21·63	56·0
1960	18·03	32·85	54·9
1962	19·7	32·47	60·7
1965	23·5	42·36	55·5
1970	25·8	63·48	40·6
1972	31·5	82·63	38·1
1975	40	102·63	39·0

reform, which announced a broad policy of change from grant, to loan, financing of capital investment. This fall also reflects an expansion of subsidies, both for agricultural products and very possibly also to Defence, in compensation for the unnatural stability of the officially reported total for Defence expenditure.

The previous table offers a horizontal division. One can also offer a vertical one as between industry and non-industry (Table 11), of forecast spending from the budget alone (col. 1) and from all sources (col. 2). Proportionate spending from the budget alone was declining until 1970, but since then has been rising again and has almost regained the 1960 level. Spending on industry from all sources exhibits the same switchback, but at a higher level. The larger proportion of spending from all sources than from the budget alone illustrates the fact the industry is better able than most branches of the economy to finance its own development. (Data for forecast spending from all sources are available only from 1960 onwards.)

In most years budget spending not on industry has been planned to exceed budget spending on industry, but in particular years this relationship has been reversed.

Although budget capital expenditures do not rise every year, their growth has been a shade more regular than that of budget non-capital expenditures: between 1952 and 1969 budget capital expenditures increased in 11 years and decreased in 4 (2 being unknown) while non-capital expenditures increased in 10 years and decreased in 5 (2 being unknown). Also, budget spending on industry increases more regularly than budget spending not on industry: spending *on* industry increased in 9 years and decreased in 1 (6 years being unknown) while spending *not* on industry increased in 7 years and decreased in 3 (6 years being unknown). Combining these two results, we find that capital expenditures within industry are the most stable component of planned budgetary FNE. This brings us to the same result as other approaches, that the Soviet government sets the firmest priority on capital investment in industry.

Table 11

Forecast Spending on Industry as a Percentage of Total Spending

	(1)	(2)
1946	62·4	
50	60·6	
55	50·3	
60	46·2	53·4
65	48·6	52·9
70	37·7	50·0
75	41·2	52·5
80	45·7	54·0

Would these trends be offset by contrary trends within *non-budgetary* spending? Would we, for example, find that *non-budgetary capital* expenditures increase specially strongly at the start of long-term plans? A general answer to this question is not available, but this would have been the case in the year 1963 (*not* a commencing year): the budget was then concentrating on an increase in non-investments, non-budget sources on an increase in *investments*. It is hard to see how the economy could accommodate sharp changes from year to year in *total* capital or non-capital expenditures, so one inclines to think that some such compensatory variation must occur.

In commencing years of the Sixth Five-Year Plan (1956) and of the Seven-Year Plan (1959) the budget concentrated on financing non-industry, whereas in the commencing year of the Eighth Five-Year Plan (1966) it concentrated on financing *industry*; hence there is a trend to intensify budget financing of industry at the start of long-term plans. This seems to be a purposeful trend but variations from year to year remain quite marked. A somewhat similar trend is visible in the sequence of budget non-capital expenditures (industry and non-industry: see Table 11); as a proportion of total expenditures these increased very slightly in 1956, by much more (3·2 per cent of total expenditures) in 1959, and by more still (3·5 per cent) in 1966; although the latter increase was one of a series, the reasons for which are not clear.

We would wish to divide budget spending not on industry into narrower slices. Unfortunately, this is possible only up to 1962 and in 1965–66, when spending not on industry can be broken down into agriculture and residue. The increments in residue are much more erratic than the increments in agriculture, and there may be a connection with the timetable of long-term plans: residual spending rises especially sharply in certain initial years of long-term plans.

FNE tends to vary inversely with DEF. In percentage terms this is normally (although not always) the case, this reflects the fact that SCM is normally the more stable quantity and that these three items take up most (and now nearly all) of budget expenditures. However, the fact may be worth emphasizing: if the USSR spends more on defence it will normally spend less on its economy, at any rate from the budget, and vice versa. Whereas it *could* logically happen that SCM, rather than FNE, diminished when DEF rose, more often it is FNE that recoils.

Moreover, the alternation of FNE and DEF is not chronologically random. There has been a definite tendency for FNE to be relatively higher at or near to the start and end of five-year plans, and of DEF to be relatively higher near to the plans' mid-points. The reciprocal alternation is most clearly seen in the Eighth Five-Year Plan (1966–70).

Subsequently this relationship appears to have become weaker, but this may well be due at least in part to the fact that Soviet sources now provide only a single total for DEF, that is to say, the actual figure is always reported as equal to the forecast figure. This is so unlikely that it has to be disbelieved; deviations surely occur, but are accommodated elsewhere.

Why should the FNE cycle be 'concave'? The most likely general reason is that spending on the economy is enlarged at the start of the plan to get the plan off to a good start, and towards the end of the plan to bring it home to a successful conclusion. Any expenditure that dovetails with spending on the the economy must, of course, adopt the opposite rhythm. A time-lag connects this sequence with the sequence of rates of growth of industrial output, which as will be shown (below, Chapter 21) varied markedly at different moments in the timetable of certain five-year plan periods. This may not be the complete explanation, but very possibly it is a large part of it.

In the cycle as envisaged, expenditure on FNE is the independent variable and on DEF the dependent variable. The assumption here is of circumstances that are not interrupted by any national emergency, or perceived emergency. *If* such an interruption occurs, *yet* there is time for larger spending on Defence to take effect, spending on Defence will no doubt regain the priority.

The fact that FNE does not grow smoothly must modify our appreciation of the consequences of the impulses towards over-investment which are analysed in Chapter 15. These impulses have to yield to *force majeure* in the shape of the claims of national defence. However, it remains true that sums allocated for capital investment fluctuate within narrower limits than those allocated for non-capital purposes.

At times of a national emergency, of course, SCM can be diminished. However, the contraction in SCM during the War is partly explicable by by the diminished population in the unoccupied areas by comparison with the total prewar Soviet population. In recent years, especially since 1953, the expansion in SCM has been impressive.

C. Social and Cultural Measures

However, SCM is a complex category. Its main components are: Education, Health and Physical Culture, Social Security, State Social Insurance, and Allowances to Mothers with Many Children and Single Mothers. These five elements have comprised the following percentages of total actual budget expenditures on SCM since 1950 (selected years):

Table 12

Components of SCM

Years	Education	Health and Physical Culture	Social Security	State Social Insurance	Allowances to Mothers
1950	48·5	18·0	18·8	11·1	3·4
1955	46·8	21·1	17·7	10·9	3·4
1960	41·3	19·2	26·1	11·2	2·0
1965	45·9	17·6	23·8	10·5	1·3
1970	44·3	16·6	22·8	13·1	0·8
1975	42·6	14·9	23·6	15·4	0·5

The table brings out the dominant share of Education, followed at some distance by Social Security, and now by Health and Physical Culture. The increased share of Social Security after 1955 reflects the pensions rise in 1957. State Social Insurance is more stable, while Allowances to Mothers decline after 1955, matching the contemporary decline in the birth-rate.[7] We can break down the largest element, Education, further:

Table 13*

Education (less Capital Investments)

(percentages of components)

Years	General Education	Cultural Enlighten- ment Work	Training of Cadres	Science	Art and Radio	Press
1950	53·6	3·3	31·9	9·2	1·1	0·8
1955	48·7	3·7	33·7	12·0	1·1	0·9
1960	48·5	3·5	23·3	22·5	1·0	0·7
1963	49·1	2·2	21·1	25·3	1·8	0·5
1965	51·1	2·5	19·7	24·4	1·8	0·5

* The year 1967 is excluded as the components do not add up to 100 per cent.

Clearly, General Education is dominant here, and there is a jump in Art and Radio in 1963 which was perhaps due partly to the setting up of a design institute (VNIITE) in 1962. However, the main item to watch here is 'Science', which has grown to about a quarter of total spending on 'Education'. The fact that Science has grown particularly at the expense of Training of Cadres (higher education, including universities) is noteworthy. This growth has probably had other repercussions too.

To get a complete picture one must allow for expenditures on SCM from outside the budget. The relationship has been as shown in Table 14.

Table 14

SCM

(milliards of post-1961 roubles)

Years	From Budget (a)	From all Sources (b)	$\frac{(b)}{(a)}$
1950	11·7	13·0	1·111
1955	14·7	16·5	1·122
1960	24·9	28·3	1·137
1963	31·0	35·5	1·145
1965	38·2	45·3	1·186
1967	43·5	53·7	1·234

The relative importance of non-budgetary SCM expenditures was rising slowly over this period. Among the items partly financed by extra-budgetary contributions is Science: the budget has normally contributed about 70 to 71 per cent of the total and non-budgetary sources 29 to 30 per cent. The budget contribution consists of an all-union (or federal) element and a republic element (which is divided among the fifteen republics of the USSR). Within the republic element of Science the clearest trend is the big increase in capital expenditures in construction. These rose from 3·4 per cent of the total in 1950 to 19·3 per cent in 1960.

D. Other Expenditure Components

Defence cannot be broken down into components.

Administration cannot be sub-divided either. Until 1965 this clause was relatively stable from year to year, despite the growth in scale of complexity of the economy and society, but subsequently it has increased.

State Loan Expenditures used to be a regular (although not large) item.

Budget Residue

A usually unitemized residue (not to be confused with the *surplus* of total revenues over total expenditures) is left. The size of this residue does not depend on the size of the total budget: after 1954 it decreased owing probably to a reduction in expenditures on the secret police, but has since stayed fairly level in absolute size, and so has decreased as a proportion of the increasing total. Except in 1940—41 the final residue has always fallen short of the estimated one, as if part of it had been already earmarked for supplementing one of the named major expenditure clauses, but which clause had not as yet been decided. This probably *is* a large part of the explanation.[8]

E. *Federal and Republic Budgets*

The other major cross-section of the budget is between the Federal (or Union) and the Republic divisions. The percentage share of the Republic division declined from 24·2 in 1940 to a low of 12·1 in 1942. It then rose continuously until 1948, then declined (with some wavering) to 20·7 in 1953, rose more steeply to another much higher peak (59·7) in 1961, and since then has been declining. These movements can be related to the following broad developments in the economy:

(1) The comparative importance of DEF. As DEF is financed entirely from the Federal budget, a rise in the percentage share of DEF in total expenditures is likely to be accompanied by a decrease in the share of the Republic division. (See Table 15.)[9]

Table 15

DEF and Republic Division

Years	Per cent of DEF	Per cent of Republic Division
1940	32·6	24·2
1946	23·6	20·5
1950	20·1	23·2
1955	19·9	26·2
1960	12·7	58·8
1963	16·0	58·6
1965	12·6	57·5
1967	12·6	48·5

(2) The comparative importance of SCM. The larger the share of SCM the larger is likely to be the share of the Republic division. (See Table 16.)[10]

Table 16

SCM and Republic Division

Years	Per cent of SCM	Per cent of Republic Division
1940	23·5	24·2
1946	26·1	20·5
1950	28·3	23·2
1955	27·3	26·2
1960	34·1	58·8
1963	35·6	58·6
1965	37·6	57·5
1967	37·8	48·5

(3) General trends of financial centralization or decentralization, as in 1957 when the Republic division rose from 31·2 per cent to 47·0 per cent (decentralization), or declined in 1966 from 57·5 per cent to 51·0 per cent (centralization).

As noted, the Republic division has a nil share in DEF. Its percentage share in FNE has been:

Years		
1940	14·4	
1946	14·7	*
1950	14·1	
1951	12·4	
1952	11·9	†
1953	14·6	
1959	72·3	
1960	72·4	‡
1961	62·8	§
1961	62·5	
1962	67·0	‡
1963	65·8	

(For notes to this table see foot of following page.)

Because this proportion is not systematically published a different constellation of years has to be quoted, but one clearly distinguishes an earlier period, when only about one-seventh of total FNE was from the Republic division, and a later period, when this proportion had risen to about two-thirds. The steepest gradient was probably in 1957. According to Aleksandrov, writing in 1961, republic budgets were financing three-quarters of total capital investments.

The Republic division's share in total SCM has been large: for example in 1951 it was 54·4 per cent, in 1953, 54·0 per cent,[11] in 1961 over 70 per cent.[12]

The Republic division can be broken down into republic budgets, budgets of autonomous republics, and local budgets. One can also make a territorial separation into the budgets of particular republics, wherein the same threefold division into republic, autonomous republic and local can be effected. Schematically, the double division may be envisaged as follows:

Republic Division

	RSFSR	Ukraine	Belorussia	Uzbekistan	Etc., etc.
Republic					
Autonomous republic					
Local					

Budgetary evolution is most clearly illustrated by the history of the first principle of division. The local budgets component of the Republic division decreased its share from about two-thirds in 1953 to one-third in 1958, the biggest reduction occurring in 1957 (see below). This reveals the essence from a financial viewpoint of the 1957 reform of industrial structure and planning (and of the complementary earlier decentralization); the devolution of additional rights to republics, but not to lesser provincial divisions.

---

* K. N. Plotnikov, *Ocherki istorii byudzheta sovetskogo gosudarstva* (1954), p. 441.

† Ibid., p. 535.

‡ Eugene Zaleski, *Le budget et les finances sovietiques en 1963, l'URSS., tome II (Extrait)* (1964) Tableau XII, p. 245. Refers to budget estimates.;

§ A. M. Aleksandrov (ed.), *Gosudarstvennyy byudzhet SSSR* (1961), p. 42.

Years	Local Budgets as a percentage of the Republic Division*
1940	71·4
1950	68·5
1951	69·1
1952	69·7
1953	67·2
1954	58·6
1955	55·6
1956	50·0
1957	35·5
1958	32·6

* *Mestnyye byudzhety SSSR* (1960), p. 4.

From a viewpoint of territorial location and from an internal political one the division among particular republics is the more interesting. However, little systematic work has been done on this. Here are statistics for one Stalin and one post-Stalin year:

Table 17

Republic Budgets

Republic	(milliard roubles)		(%)	
	1951*	1965 (forecast)†	1951	1965 (forecast)
RSFSR (including Karelo-Finland)	55·7	315·5	56·1	57·9
Ukraine	18·0	92·8	18·1	17·0
Belorussia	3·7	16·6	3·7	3·0
Uzbekistan	3·5	18·4	3·5	3·4
Kazakhstan	4·2	39·8	4·2	7·3
Georgia	2·7	9·5	2·7	1·7
Azerbaijan	2·0	9·3	2·0	1·7
Lithuania	1·6	7·7	1·6	1·4
Moldavia	1·2	5·1	1·2	0·9
Latvia	1·4	5·6	1·4	1·0
Kirghizia	1·1	5·3	1·1	1·0
Tajikistan	1·1	4·9	1·1	0·9
Armenia	1·2	6·0	1·2	1·1

Republic	1951*	Table 17 cont. 1965 (forecast)†	1951	(%) 1965 (forecast)
Turkmenia	1·0	4·6	1·0	0·8
Estonia	1·1	4·1	1·1	0·8
Totals	99·3	545·3	100·0	99·9

* K. N. Plotnikov, op. cit., p. 537.
† *Pravda*, 12 December 1964.

The table discloses a greater-than-average increase in Kazakhstan, and a number of lesser relative changes. Recently, Kazakhstan and Turkmenia have been receiving subsidies from the Federal budget.

F. Budget Plan and Actual

To what extent are budget forecasts implemented? As a rule, only a single forecast is published: this may differ very slightly as between the Finance Minister's speech and the Budget Law which is adopted a day or two later, in which case the Law figure is adopted here as definitive. Subsequent alterations in budget provisions are rarely made explicit, but in retrospect (comparing actual performance with the target implied by the percentage of claimed fulfilment), it can be discovered that changes must sometimes have been made. For example, the 1959 and 1961 initial expenditure plans appear to have been subsequently lowered, whereas that of 1962 appears to have been subsequently raised. Revisions seem to be made about the middle of the calendar year. No further attention is paid here to these mid-course alterations; results are compared with the *initial* (published) estimate. It is also common for the final results to be subsequently revised downwards by small amounts.

For most main clauses results are available for 1954 to 1979 inclusive, a period of 36 years. Total budget revenues and (in particular) expenditures have been more commonly overfulfilled than underfulfilled, but here it is essential to distinguish between the Union and the Republic components of the budget. The Union section of budget expenditures is usually underspent (by about 4 per cent) whereas the Republic section invariably since 1953 onwards, except only in 1967, has been overspent; the excess is now normally 10 per cent or more. In the total budget, FNE is normally exceeded, while in years (up to 1962 only) when any difference was allowed to show between forecast and actual, DEF normally fell short.

Applying the same method of comparison to budget expenditures on Science, we find that the estimate has been much more commonly overfulfilled than underfulfilled.

The postwar period splits into two spans, Stalin (1944—53 inclusive) and post-Stalin (1954 onwards). One notices in the post-Stalin period a strong tendency for Republic revenues and expenditures and for SCM to be overfulfilled whereas previously they had been more often underfulfilled, and a weaker tendency for *total* revenues and expenditures to be more commonly overfulfilled. Republic revenues and expenditures exceeded forecasts in several years by very wide margins, although the freak result in 1957 (47 per cent above forecast) is attributable to the reform carried out half-way through that year of the industrial and planning structure.

Is the estimate for a given year based on the estimate or on the results of the previous year? To investigate this, let us examine sequences of under- and overfulfilment. If plans are based on results (or expected results, according to current performance), we should expect to find no tendency for underfulfilment or overfulfilment to repeat themselves consecutively; conversely if plans are based on estimates we *should* expect to find such a tendency.

In a random arrangement with only two possible states one would expect a given state to follow its like on an average half of the times. This is almost the case for FNE and DEF, which suggests that forward planning in these cases is based on a mixture of estimate and fulfilment, although mainly on the former. However, among total budget revenues and in particular, total budget *expenditures*, including their Union components, and also SCM, it is markedly more common for underfulfilment to follow underfulfilment or for overfulfilment to follow overfulfilment. This strongly suggests that in these cases forward planning is based on the estimate rather than on actual or predictable fulfilment, while the Residue seems to be based entirely on the estimate and not at all on the previous year's fulfilment. The short-term feedback mechanism is in these cases weak, and in the case of the Residue even non-existent.

It does not seem very sensible to draw up the total budget for next year without a close reference to the results to be expected for the current year. One is led to conclude that the annual periodicity is rather conventional and is not inherently necessary. That others thought so is suggested by the fact that in 1964—65 as an innovation, budgets were drawn up for two consecutive years at once, although neither FNE nor DEF for 1965 were specified at the earlier date; which again confirms that these quantities are planned more carefully than others, with attention to current performance as well as to forecast.

Even among these items plan and actual sometimes diverge quite widely. DEF should presumably be the more sensitive to the international climate of political relations, but in fact its average divergence has been rather smaller than that of FNE (see Table 18).

Table 18

Percentage Deviations of Actual from Plan

	Years	FNE	SCM	DEF
Stalin	1944	+20·1	−0·2	n.a.
	1945	+14·8	−5·1	−7·0
	1946	−6·4	−3·3	+0·6
	1947	+0·7	−0·6	−0·9
	1948	−1·0	−9·2	+0·3
	1949	+6·2	−2·7	+0·1
	1950	−4·0	−3·2	+4·4
	1951	+0·5	−1·6	−3·1
	1952	−0·9	−1·6	−4·6
	1953	−6·0	−0·8	−2·2
Post-Stalin	1954	−1·4	+0·5	n.a.
	1955	+4·9	+0·1	−4·2
	1956	+3·4	+1·8	−5·1
	1957	+9·1	+5·2	−6·7
	1958	+12·9	+0·9	−2·8
	1959	+4·8	−0·4	−2·5
	1960	+3·8	+0·5	−3·2
	1961	−3·8	+0·9	+25·4
	1962	+11·5	+0·5	−6·0
	1963	+12·3	±0·0	+0·1
	1964	+4·9	+1·8	±0·0
	1965	+6·1	+2·1	±0·0
	1966	+3·2	+1·2	±0·0
	1967	+12·6	+1·4	±0·0
	Averages (irrespective of sign) of 24-year period	6·6	1·9	3·6

The deviations of SCM are smaller still. The relative stability of SCM as a proportion of total expenditures is thus complemented by a high level of predictability. The appreciable fluctuations in FNE would not suggest an economy that is free from disturbing (probably, cyclical) movements. It is possible that deviations in DEF are not publicized (are, perhaps, minimized) from a national security motivation. The large rise in 1961 was doubtless publicized for the sake of its international impact: it was in August that the Berlin wall was erected.

Earlier increases were perhaps not reported at the time so that the rise when eventually announced in 1961 would appear more formidable. Enhanced secrecy is probably the explanation for the span 1964–67, when no deviation at all is admitted.

One might expect that in years when FNE was underspent from budgetary sources it would be overspent from extra-budgetary sources, or vice versa. Unfortunately, although systematic statistics are published of the fulfilment of SCM from sources outside as well as inside the budget, they are not in respect of the fulfilment of FNE. In 1960, at any rate, underfulfilment was probably compensated in this way. The curious feature of this year was that two different totals were successively quoted for fulfilled FNE: first 31·0 (milliards) and then 34·1. The lower total would have been below actual spending in the previous year, yet capital investment was reported to have been 11·5 per cent larger in 1960 than in 1959. Apparently, a larger share of total investment was financed from non-budgetary sources, which in later published reports were added to the budget account.

If more were spent by non-budgetary sources than had been planned, unless these latter also earned extra-large sums they would have less to pay into the exchequer, which might show up as a shortfall in Deductions from Profits. In 1960 these deductions did reach only 19·0 milliards as compared with a planned 20·3 milliards. Comparing over and under in this item with over and under in budget financing of the national economy we find over the period 1944–67 an inconclusive but slightly positive correlation.

G. Discrepancies and Other Difficulties

One would also expect to find a positive relationship between capital investment and spending on the economy. Unfortunately, elucidation of this relationship is very difficult, owing to: the publication only of budget capital investment provisions, not of actual investments; the non-availability of budget figures expressed in unchanged prices, whereas statistics of actual investments *are* given in unchanged prices; the absence of detailed published reports of expenditures broken down by source of funds; and minor differences in coverage of reported totals.

Price changes evoke other difficulties. Occasionally it is mentioned that particular allowances ought to be made to compensate for price changes: for example, that defence spending declined more in real than in monetary terms in 1947, owing to a rise in prices of foodstuffs and in servicemen's pay. Reductions in heavy industrial wholesale prices and freight rates occurred on 1 July 1955, which appears to have been reflected in the 1955 actual (but not the plan) figures and in both sets of figures for 1956; this possibly helps to account for an unusually large increase in FNE residual allocations in 1956. In 1953 and 1954 a novel and probably unique procedure was adopted by the Malenkov government: instead of being recorded as a reduction in revenue, certain benefits gained from tax reductions and increases in government buying prices were recorded as an increase in expenditure, as if they represented a subsidy. Owing to these additions, the 1953 and 1954 budget totals are not directly comparable with those of previous years. In 1955 these amounts were withdrawn and the practice has not been revived. Above all, subsidies and differences in relative prices distort the comparative size of different expenditure components. This is particularly relevant in international comparisons. A regional analysis would be interesting. One would expect that the more advanced regions of the USSR would have contributed more than proportionately to financing the national development, but this has been documented only in the case of the Ukraine, where the surmise seems to be true.[13] Whether regions such as the Ukraine have contributed more than their *fair* share is a more complicated question and one which cannot be resolved here.

H. Conclusions

The budget's reliance on revenues from the State sector, and the huge expenditures on the State sector, show that to a considerable extent this sector of the economy pays for its own development. In this connection, Kaser pointed out that recent policy had been to dismiss so far as possible the private ownership sector from the plan model,[14] although as noted above the proposal to abolish income tax was itself rescinded. In any case, the size of the State sector is variable by command of the government, although this size is also influenced by geography and history. According to Strumilin, out of 34–39 milliard roubles to be invested in the economy during the Five-Year Plan not less than 24 milliards would be obtained from profits and rent received by the State by its rights of ownership from the nationalized undertakings, woods and lands;[15] this would have left about 10–15 milliards which was to be financed otherwise. Taking into account the artificially low prices paid for agricultural produce a large share of the burden of development has been borne by the peasantry. In one way or another, directly or indirectly, the economic development of the Soviet Union has been paid for by the Soviet population.

On the whole it may be claimed that despite difficulties and complexities of interpretation, the trend of budget revenues and expenditures appears to reflect evolution at many points in the economy. The prominence of the Finance of National Economy item indicates that the budget has been an important lever of Soviet economic development, although there seems to be an element of tradition and convention in the adherence to an annual budget sequence.

Notes

1 In other tables, post-1961 roubles are used. Ten pre-1961 roubles equal one post-1961 rouble.
2 See Raymond Hutchings, 'Some Behavior Patterns of the Soviet Post-War Budget', *The ASTE Bulletin*, Fall 1962.
3 A. G. Zverev, *Zapiski ministra* (1973), p. 176.
4 N. A. Voznesenskiy, *Voyennaya ekonomika SSSR* (1946), p. 133.
5 See also in this connection Raymond Hutchings 'Soviet Defence Spending: Towards a Reconciliation of Different Approaches', in F. -L. Altmann (ed.), *Yearbook of East European Economics*, vol. 9 (Munich, 1981).
6 V. A. Yevdokimov, *Kontrol' za ispolneniyem gosudarstvennogo byudzheta SSSR* (1974), p. 141.
7 See, above, Chapter 9.
8 See also later section on budget fulfilment.
9 By Spearman's ranking correlation, R = −0·720, a fairly high negative correlation.
10 By Spearman's ranking correlation, R = 0·643, a fairly marked positive relationship.
11 The Republic contributions are given in absolute terms in K. N. Plotnikov, op. cit., p. 537.
12 A. M. Aleksandrov (ed.), op. cit., p. 42. Refers to budget estimates.
13 See Z. L. Melnyk, *Soviet Capital Formation Ukraine, 1928/29−1932* (1965).
14 M. C. Kaser, *Soviet Studies*, April 1959, p. 333.
15 S. G. Strumilin, *Sotsial'nyye problemy pyatiletki, 1928/29−1932/33*. Second Edition (1929), pp. 39−41.

15
INVESTMENT PLANNING AND PRACTICE

Since 1931, when credit financing was replaced by budgetary,[1] capital grants have been made to producing enterprises in response to claims that they themselves make and – until 1965, when a change was announced – predominantly as non-returnable and interest-free grants from the budget; there has been no charge to the producing organization to which the grant was allotted. Investment projects have been at least for preference included within nationwide long-term plans of finite length.

The sequence of composition of investment plans is similar to that of planning output, but in addition lists of projects ('title-lists') to be accomplished during a given period have to be prepared. The procedure of confirming acceptance of projects depends on their scale: those larger than a specified limit have to be confirmed in a more centralized procedure. Together with its production programme a plant submits 'a claim for raw materials, fuel, working capital and capital investments in magnitudes necessary to carry out the programme'.[2]

At first sight one might suppose that capital investments, which are often conspicuous, and whose planning (the composition of estimates, detailed drawings, etc.) is often protracted, must be meticulously controlled by the Soviet government. However, this has not always been the case. The planning and economics of capital investment lag significantly behind other sectors of the economy.[3] Decentralized influences have not been unimportant.

If in a competitive economy capital grants were provided without charge, every firm would set out to secure as much as it could. Within the Soviet system inter-firm competition has been damped down, yet, although weakened, a competitive urge to expand is by no means eliminated. There is, in the first place, a connection between the urge to invest and the system of output plan targets. A planned output target has an asymmetrical effect on the performance of an enterprise, because it encourages overfulfilment of the output plan while discouraging underfulfilment of it. Conveniently, there is a matching structural asymmetry: legally an enterprise can be more easily expanded than contracted. Dissolution is excluded, because by the law of 10 April 1923, and subsequent legislation, distraint cannot touch the fixed capital of an enterprise. The latter perhaps will not flourish, but its survival is assured and barring revolution or enemy action it can go on growing.

Claims for investment grants are naturally drawn up on a generous scale, and in terms which are meant to leave no doubt that the proposed works are indispensable and non-postponable. The onus of comparing projects, weighing their respective merits, and then (almost inevitably) trimming them down so as not to exceed permitted maximum expenditures, is borne by higher levels. As a Soviet economist wrote in 1936:

one can say beforehand that the needs of industry in the field of capital construction surpass the possible resources of the economy. This is confirmed every year in connection with the composition of new projects of annual control figures and industrial-financial plans. In spite of a strict limit upon investments, the claims of associations with respect to 'absolutely necessary works' surpass the people's commissariat limits by 50 per cent or more, and factories' claims surpass in corresponding proportions the demands of associations.[4]

This ratio of claims to agreed proposals of about 2 : 1 or 2¼ : 1 (i.e. 1½ x 1½, an association being an administrative stage in between factory and people's commissariat) is supported by a report of a discussion of proposals to develop the Kuybyshev hydro-electric power complex, a plan which was finally carried out after the war.[5]

The demand for additional capital allocations is prominent in the annual budget debates. Here is Finance Minister Zverev's summing-up of such proposals when presenting the budget for 1956 to the Supreme Soviet:

It is necessary to report, Comrade Deputies, that during the discussion of the State Budget of the USSR for 1955 in the Council of the Nationalities and the Council of the Union, Deputies introduced proposals for the allotment of additional appropriations for capital construction and other needs of the Union Republics. The Government of the USSR examined these proposals and allotted 1,386,500 thousand roubles to the Republics in 1955 over and above the sums approved for the 1955 budget, including: 881,500 thousand roubles for housing, school and hospital construction, 330,300 thousand roubles for the construction of the Stalingrad hydro-electric power station, 112,700 thousand roubles for the Novosibirsk hydro-electric power station, 53 million roubles for the Karakum, Samur-Divichinsk and Verkhno-Karabakh canals.[6]

Only comparatively minor changes are effected in budget proposals laid before the Supreme Soviet, although in absolute terms the additions just mentioned were not small. But it is an equally significant feature of the proceedings that the deputies always press for higher and not for lower allocations. The situation resembles the 'queue of members asking to have atomic power stations in their constituencies' to which the then British Minister of Fuel and Power referred in June 1955.[7] It is much like the contest in Washington for Congressional appropriations – and no doubt something similar goes on in Canberra. Party units, as well as business and republic organizations, have been accused of asking for additional capital investments without sufficient reason.

Just how much force is generated by this pressure is difficult to gauge. To some extent the planning organizations allow for it and automatically cut down the requests submitted to them; but against this, requests are liable to be inflated in the expectation that they will automatically be reduced. But one cannot mistake the direction of the pressure. If not restrained by the government the total of capital investment must have been greater than it actually was.

Sums derived by other means than simply asking for them are also enlarged by the claiming body, which uses whatever other expedients or stratagems seem appropriate. For instance, a portion of funds usable for capital investment is designated 'amortization'. Their total volume depends, among other things, on the value attached to the capital stock, which consequently tends to be exaggerated.

The sums granted tend to be spread among a large number of projects, so that no single one gets very much. The claimant's motivation here is that once work has been begun on a particular project this establishes its 'place in the sun', because once started it must go on being built or the resources already sunk will become a sheer loss; so that leverage is secured for obtaining a larger total grant than would probably have been secured if all funds had been devoted to only one or two items. If every project gets only a little at a time its completion will be delayed, which also supplies a good argument for asking for a larger sum later on in order to complete it. The *granting* body is inclined to acquiesce both because it wants its subordinates to become more numerous (which will enlarge its own prestige and importance), and because being one or more stages removed from the scene of action it cannot very well judge which projects are most meritorious, and so finds it safer and less liable to provoke discontent to give equally to each.

Various organizational tendencies support the same conclusion:

Organizations to which funds are allotted often start building in advance of any detailed project that has been confirmed in the approved manner. It is most likely that the project will be only crude and rough at the moment when construction begins.

Enterprises have shown a preference for organizing construction themselves, rather than by engaging a contracting body which has been the arrangement normally preferred by the government. In the former case the work is more closely under control of the producing body, even though it may be done less well.

Investments are preferentially angled so as to guarantee or extend the self-sufficiency of the recipient organizations, i.e. there is an urge towards vertical expansion and against horizontal specialization which would entail 'co-operation' with many other enterprises, although this latter solution is again the one ordinarily preferred by the authorities.

Even in advance of building, enterprises typically accumulate the equipment to be installed once it becomes ready, so that at any one moment in the whole country very large quantities await installation.

Once the project is inscribed in the list of accepted titles, and work begins, it will very likely turn out to cost more than was originally estimated. Costs will rise not only as early estimates are made more precise but still more noticeably while the actual work is under way.

Enterprises try to reallocate funds granted to them so as to maximize the advantage to themselves. Particularly, they prefer to hold assets in a relatively illiquid form: this was especially the case during the period up to 1936 when many industrial branches were subsidized.[8] Occasionally this predilection was carried to a point that jeopardized current operations.

In Germany also, in the nineteen-twenties, there had been some diversion of short-term loans to finance capital investment. The possibility of borrowing stimulated extravagant expenditure by public bodies, such as municipalities, from which they would otherwise have been forced to refrain.[9] One essential difference was that in Germany loans were often derived ultimately from abroad (particularly the United States), whereas in the Soviet Union borrowing was from an *internal* source. For this reason, and because the Soviet economic system was better protected against world economic fluctuations, the Soviet phenomenon (unlike the German) was unaffected by the Great Depression of 1929–32. After the Second World War some West German firms used the same method of building up their assets.[10] Readiness to convert short-term loans into fixed assets is a point of similarity between dynamic socialism and dynamic capitalism.

These various kinds of behaviour have all been unwelcome to the Soviet government, which has taken such measures as to segregate funds destined for investment in circulating capital as distinct from in fixed capital, to insist that schemes not provided with projects confirmed in the approved manner be not financed, to inweigh against 'frittering away', and to take other economic and judicial measures to enforce its authority. Despite all this, investment plans are overfulfilled, costs become inflated and heroic reductions have to be called for,[11] the growth of basic capital put into operation tends to fall short of budget allocations for capital investment,[12] unfinished construction consequently remains on a high level or increases,[13] while the proportion of funds devoted to new construction is nearly twice as large as in the United States.[14]

The aim of introducing payment for capital funds, announced in the reform of October 1965, was of course to stimulate economy in their provision and exploitation. Although credit-investments had been made before, and were becoming more important,[15] they still comprised only a small proportion of total investments. Such an obvious step as greatly to extend their scale was not taken before, presumably owing to an ideological objection to a practice that seemed redolent of capitalism; to apprehension that investments would be directed away from the less profitable capital goods towards the more profitable consumer goods; and to the greater complexity of a loan system than of a grant system.

Currently, these objections are rated less important than the achievement of investment economies, a need which has been underlined by a recent increase in the capital/output ratio.[16] The rate of payment for credit should be raised, according to a Deputy Minister of Finance.[17] Judging by past experience, excessive investment will not be discouraged solely by fiscal means.

The system is consequently always tending to overrun, essentially for three reasons: the State is in effect giving away money, and naturally the recipients want as much as they can get; as the whole economy operates under strain because ambitious aims are being pursued, the output of individual productive units has generally to be maintained in the national interest; and as one acknowledged object of capital investment is to enable production to rise continuously, it seems inconsistent to erect barriers against additional investment which would be expected to make possible an even more rapid increase.

Once capital investment plans have been fixed these prove to be relatively stable components of the plan, or more precisely, it is very hard to *reduce* them. In capitalist economies or in semi-planned economies which practise public works capital investment – especially its time-scheduling – is liable to be a somewhat variable item, whereas consumption in the mass is more difficult to alter. In the USSR the emphasis is different, almost the contrary. Once activity starts at . construction sites this virtually governs the direction of work for years to come, since periods of construction are typically long, partly owing to the short annual building season. Although the government *can* halt construction, and an emergency may compel it to do so,[18] in practice it has been reluctant to adopt this course. It is much less unwilling to declare a moratorium on new starts — for instance, Khrushchev proposed such a moratorium in 1962 — but such a moratorium is difficult to enforce for reasons flowing from those already discussed. In contrast, consumption and other non-capital expenditures are more controllable than in normal circumstances in market economies, because the Soviet government has additional powers over prices and over the economic structure, has complete control over advertising, and has to hand militia and armed forces capable of suppressing any disorders. (This is not to say that no disorders have occurred.[19])

The inertia that is exhibited in plans for capital investments generally extends also to its distribution among different sectors, as shown in Table 19. As we see, since 1 October 1928, except during the war, industry has always received between 34·4 and 41·1 per cent; agriculture, always between 10·8 and 20·1 per cent; housing, always between 12·8 and 23·5 per cent. However, it has only recently been admitted that *before* 1928 the share of housing was immensely larger: 64·3 per cent, whereas the percentage previously given (and cited in the first edition of this book) had been 22·2 per cent. The share of housing fell dramatically after NEP, and this must be reckoned *the* most important single shift in the direction of investment following the entry into the era of five-year plans. The rise in the share of housing in 1956—60 shows the effect of the housebuilding decree of 1957, but this impetus has not lasted. There are certain other variations, such as the unusually high shares of industry in 1951—55 and of transport and communications in 1933—7. Within industry, Group A has always gained between 28·5 and 36·5 per cent, Group B between 4·5 and 6·8 per cent, which puts into proportion much-vaunted shifts from time to time in these proportions; Stalin's death led indeed to a bigger share for Group B. Changing attitudes to agriculture are also seen to have had considerable importance. As one would expect, the period of World War II exhibits the biggest deviation from more normal proportions, although one that is not especially marked at this level of aggregation.[20]

Inertia in the distribution of investment, to the extent it is exhibited, is due partly to ideology, which lays stress on Group A output and on its growth priority; this was held up against Malenkov during this short-lived spell of accentuating production of consumer

Table 19

Percentage Shares of Total Capital Investment in Various Sectors of the Economy

Sector	1918 to 1 Oct. 1928	First FYP	Second FYP	1938 to 1 July 1941	1 July 1941 to 1 Jan. 1946	Fourth FYP	Fifth FYP	Sixth FYP	Seventh FYP	Eighth FYP	Ninth FYP
(1)	16·8	38·0	37·3	34·4	42·9	38·6	41·0	35·7	36·5	35·2	35·0
(2)	11·5	31·7	30·5	28·5	39·5	33·4	36·5	30·4	31·7	29·9	30·2
(3)	5·3	6·3	6·8	5·9	3·4	5·2	4·5	5·3	4·8	5·3	4·8
(4)	0·2	1·1	0·8	1·1	1·9	2·9	3·0	3·1	2·7	3·4	3·8
(5)	3·1	15·6	11·8	10·8	9·4	11·8	14·2	14·3	15·5	17·2	20·1
(6)	11·1	17·7	21·4	18·9	16·2	12·8	9·7	9·2	10·1	9·6	10·8
(7)	8·8	10·2	10·5	10·7	11·6	7·7	4·9	3·4	3·2	2·7	2·6
(8)	64·3	15·4	12·8	17·0	15·0	19·4	19·8	23·5	18·6	17·2	15·3
(9)	4·5	12·2	15·9	17·8	14·6	14·5	12·3	14·2	16·6	17·4	15·0
(10)	0·7	2·6	4·8	4·2	1·9	3·4	3·8	4·9	6·2	6·0	5·2

(1) = All industry
(2) = including Group A
(3) = including Group B
(4) = Building industry
(5) = Agriculture
(6) = Transport and Communications
(7) = including Rail Transport
(8) = Housing Construction
(9) = Construction of Trade and Communal Enterprises, Enterprises of Forestry and Procurements, Institutions of Science, Culture, Arts, Education, Health
(10) = including Construction of Enterprises of Science, Arts, Culture, Education

Note that (2) and (3) are included in (1); (7) is included in (6); and (10) is included in (9).

Source: Narodnoye khozyaystvo SSSR v 1979 g. (1980), pp. 366–7.

goods. The institutional expression of this predilection has been the Party Congresses, which at irregular intervals have issued general directions regarding economic development. Nearer to the actual unfolding of events, an institutional explanation may be found in the pattern of people's commissariats (or ministries): the more prestigious are these, and the longer-lasting, the more assuredly and successfully they press their claims for investment grants.

A tendency of ministries to concern themselves with all aspects of their employees' existence (ministries have owned and administered blocks of flats for their employees, market gardens, crèches and hospitals, and have even reserved seats at the ballet) is another expression of this assurance and success. Unmistakable signs of lavishness in the construction plans of the more entrenched ministries, such as the Ministry of Railways (for instance, an ornately decorated new station at Sochi), point to the same conclusion.

No doubt, too, a kind of logic of interrelation of various branches and sectors in the economy has added its weight to the institutional inertia. In this connection, Table 19 leads us to consider other biases in industrial development which are associated with investment policy.

(1) As we see from the table, heavy industry is very markedly favoured, if necessary at the expense of light industry. Like over-investment, this is due to initiatives both from the centre and from the periphery. The heavy category was at first favoured by the Party and government for reasons (economic, power-political and ideological) set out above in Chapter 6, and which were institutionalized by the ministerial system as noted above. This priority can nevertheless be, in part, understood as a response to the propensity of the system to expand its material supplies insufficiently in relation to the output of machinery; because in order to combat this propensity, in circumstances of wide geographic dispersion of mineral deposits and of industries requiring supplies, very large investments are liable to be required.

(2) The output of materials has in fact consistently risen more slowly than that of machinery; materials are thus typically in short supply, and engineering output has to be restricted. For example, as described in 1935 the quantity of output of ferrous metals was governed mainly by the capacity of available equipment, whereas the output of machines depended largely on the supply of metal: the existing engineering capacity could have doubled or more than doubled its output if only it had got metal enough.[21] For the same reason the postwar growth rate of industries which use large quantities of metal has been relatively low.[22] An analogous situation was reported in 1966: shortage of metal was a main reason which prevented the achievement of a higher ratio of output to capital in machine-building. Likewise, the supply of fuel and raw materials lagged behind the growth of manufacturing

industry.[23] One main reason for this discrepancy is that, when requirements are totalled up, indirect ones are not taken into account.[24] This would be due to shortcomings in planning method, especially to the attempt to balance supplies against needs without resorting to the more advanced methods of input-output analysis.

(3) The propensity to accumulate large stocks is very firmly rooted. This practice appears to have been especially pronounced during and soon after the war. During the decade before 1957 the volume of stores seems to have been reduced. A variety of reasons have been advanced by Soviet economists to explain the phenomenon, including: shortcomings in planning; uneven and badly assorted despatch of materials and equipment; the lack of necessary assortments at bases and warehouses of sales organizations, which compelled purchasers to order (for the convenience of the railways) quantities which might be larger than they really required; changes in the assortment of production and of materials which were needed; and infringement of conditions and specifications in despatch of materials.[25]

The use during postwar reconstruction of materials taken from demolished buildings, the value of which was not declared or was understated, with the result that big excess funds were allotted to building organizations,[26] illustrates the general point that any departure from ordinary circumstances makes control more difficult and offers opportunities to get the better of the exchequer.

Besides, Soviet enterprises (basically owing to the size of the USSR and to the nationalization of land) are often spread over very large areas. This gives them ample room to heap up stores, although sometimes in the open air which leads to spoilage and waste.

Finally, Soviet industry is orientated towards achieving an imposing production result rather than producing for a market (whether the latter happens to be composed of individuals or of other organizations). As a result, problems of supply must often be solved within a given 'system'. In particular, ministries and enterprises often put in inflated claims for supplies, doubtless reasoning that they will not get all they ask for,[27] and that any surplus can be exchanged for other things which they do want.[28] The most fundamental reason is that there does exist a mechanism and a channel by which one can submit a claim for a free-of-charge increase in working capital. This being so, all manner of conditions and restrictions cannot remove the *propensity* to ask for as much as possible.

That enterprises tend to over-invest is, indeed, only one aspect of a more general tendency for producing bodies to demand maximal quantities of *all* inputs. As regards labour, for example, territorial bodies have inflated their demands by various subterfuges, such as adding together all the seasonal peaks, or quoting an incorrect ratio of the (conventional) agricultural 'labour day' (*trudoden*') to an actual working day. To block this manoeuvre, economists suggested that the ratio of 'labour day' to actual working day should be fixed to at least two decimal places. All-union plants' requests for labour often exceeded their real requirements by 1½–2 times or more.[29] Some branches of the Gosbank had sent in unjustifiably large claims for cash in circulation.[30]

(4) Factories tend to grow very large, so that the degree of concentration is very high. The style of planning during the First Five-Year Plan contributed to the result that very large works were built (the plan left more scope for enlarging individual projects than for increasing their numbers, which latter required more elaborate justification). In fact, such projects as DneproGES combine, Kharkov tractor works and Stalin (now *imeni Likhacheva*) motor works in Moscow were constructed on a larger scale than the First Five-Year Plan had envisaged. In general, it was easier to surpass the plan in the direction of building bigger than to gain approval for an entirely new scheme. Besides, Russians love to build objects as large as possible! The consequence was 'gigantomania' which begins to be officially denounced in the nineteen-thirties. A Party Conference in 1934 issued instructions for a 'decisive struggle' against gigantomania. 'In the field of building, wreckers intentionally dispersed and immobilized resources passing into capital constructions, implanted "gigantomania" and artificially prolonged periods of construction.'[31] After the war the phenomenon continued to be denounced, though in soberer terms.

Although 'gigantomania' was ascribed to wreckers, we will scarcely find difficulty in explaining this phenomenon as part and parcel of a tendency of lower organizations to ask for maximum amounts of allocations. If in these circumstances planning procedures present a greater obstacle to inclusion of a quite new project than to enlarging an existing one, a tendency to build bigger inevitably follows.

Since the war, larger than ever projects have been tackled, yet the word 'gigantomania' has passed out of currency. The reason may be that the post-Stalin government *abandoned* a few major projects quietly, as a rule (such as the Grand Turkmen canal).[32] More recently, however, Khrushchev observed that the giant hydro-electric plants on the Volga had been constructed too soon, and opinion has veered in favour of building larger numbers of *thermal* power plants instead. This is connected with a new approach to the question of investment versus operating costs.

The choice of how much to invest, and thus – assuming a close link between these quantities – of what growth rate to aim at, is in the essentially one of economic-political strategy. The comparative advantages of different variants of a given investment project are then weighed partly in terms of social advantages, e.g. air transport might be preferred to road as being a more progressive form of transport, as requiring smaller consumption of gasoline, not requiring mass construction of garages, etc. The use of formulae enters at a late stage, but apparently these assist in determining the relative merits of alternative variants. Such variants seem to occur in modern economies most often in transport, where there might be a choice between a tunnel and a bridge (as in the question of how to link the two sides of the English Channel). After 'social' considerations have been taken into account (in this case, for instance, these would include whether ships might crash into a bridge), the 'redemption period' of each variant is taken into account. If x equals the first investment costs, and y the annual saving in running costs as compared with a situation if the fixed investment cost had not been incurred, the project will be chosen for which x/y is a minimum.

If, for example, one takes three variants with the following comparative data:

(1) x = 500 million roubles
y =   25 million roubles
Then $x/y = 20$

(2) x = 300 million roubles
y =   20 million roubles
Then $x/y = 15$

(3) x = 175 million roubles
y =   10 million roubles
Then $x/y = 17½$

In this case project No. (2) would be chosen, other things being equal.

Although this formula, the 'redemption period' (*srok okupaye-mosti*), is sometimes employed, indeed as described in 1946 was habitually used,[33] we do not know how widely or what weight is ascribed generally to the method. This is the only method of comparison that we do *know* to be used.

One readily sees that the formula takes no account of losses resulting elsewhere in the economy which may be directly due to the length of the period of construction. If for instance, in the above illustration, project (3) could be completed much earlier than the other two projects, this might benefit the economy even if the other projects saved more on running costs proportionate to the initial cost. Thus, the 'redemption period' concept might reinforce other tendencies which already induce towards undertaking large-scale projects, and thus might lead to longer construction periods. According to a recent comment:

The evaluation of the effectiveness of capital investment in transport from the standpoint of the redemption period (*srok okupayemosti*) was one-sided. It did not take into account the final advantages for the economy that capital investments in new railway construction would give in a perspective of several years – growth of the national income owing to development of production in regions where the new lines would exert their power of attraction, improvement in the distribution of production, rationalization of transport, economic connections, improvement in conditions of supply for the population, replacement of less effective types of transport by more economic ones, and so on.[34]

Construction periods in Soviet projects have tended to be very prolonged. One illustration of this is the very large number of projects – in the neighbourhood of 100,000 – under construction at any one time. Another is the very large stocks of equipment on hand at any one time, waiting to be installed.

The government is often trying to concentrate capital investments among fewer projects. In the later stages of the Khrushchev régime – this is the new approach mentioned above – much more attention was paid to the time element in building. This was illustrated in the emergence of a preference for building thermal power stations, despite their larger running costs, as compared with hydro-power stations which take much longer to build. 'The maximum gain in time in the competition with capitalism' became one of the approved slogans, which after Khrushchev's dismissal has, like he himself, fallen from favour.

The planning of investment exhibits in an enhanced degree the problems of combining central direction and decentralized response. Although a powerful lever in the hands of a determined government it should not, therefore, be regarded as a passive one. There is a perpetual tendency to over-invest, which is of service to the State in facilitating ventures of great size and prestige value, such as the programme of space exploration, or a maximum rate of expansion of heavy industries; but which at times gets out of hand and is liable, unless checked, to create an overstrained and distorted economy.

Whether this tendency must continue is an interesting – and important – question to which one cannot at present give a definite answer. Our analysis relates mainly to the system of State financing of investment which prevailed between 1931 and 1965. It may well prove difficult to supersede this system, in which all business organizations apart from the exchequer have a vested interest; but there are signs that its opposite, wage inflation, is beginning to make its appearance. This is a less familiar phenomenon in the Soviet economy, and consequently adequate preventive measures have probably not been devised, whereas elaborate, although not always effective, measures *have* been built up for controlling investment.

Wage inflation, carried far enough, might counterbalance or even outweigh the investment pressures described in this chapter, especially if these latter are simultaneously weakened as a result of a general abandonment of the system of financing investment by means of budget grants.

Notes

1. S. Rubinshteyn and I. Tsypkin, *Sovetskiy kredit (chast' III)* (1933), p. 17. It became clear in 1925/26 that capital investment would have to be financed predominantly out of the State budget.
2. Ya. A. Ioffe, *Proizvodstvennaya programma promyshlennosti* (1940), p. 57.
3. B. Smekhov, *Planovoye khozyaystvo*, no. 4, 1951, p. 82.
4. N. S. Burmistrov, *Ocherki tekhniko-ekonomicheskogo planirovaniya promyshlennosti* (1936), p. 206.
5. *Planovoye khozyaystvo*, no. 5, 1938, pp. 159–61.
6. A. G. Zverev, *Pravda*, 29 December 1955, p. 3.
7. *The Times*, 14 June 1955.
8. Sh. Turetskiy, *Plan*, no. 18, 1936, p. 25.
9. C. W. Guillebaud, *The Economic Recovery of Nazi Germany, 1933–1938* (1939), p. 12.
10. *The Economist*, 18 October 1952, p. 212.
11. The plan of investment in the whole economy was overfulfilled in the Fourth Five-Year Plan (1946–50) by 22 per cent. In 1950 the Council of Ministers of the USSR called for a reduction of 25 per cent as from 1 July 1950 in the costs of construction (B. Smekhov, *Planovoye khozyaystvo*, no. 4, 1951, p. 82).
12. *Planovoye khozyaystvo*, no. 6, 1967, p. 27.
13. This is liable to apply to auxiliary works (rail transport, communications, or power generation, for example) in particular, owing to the tendency to meet rising costs of a main item by assigning to it funds previously assigned to auxiliary works (A. Zinchenko, *Ekonomicheskaya gazeta*, no. 19, 1968, p. 26).
14. As reported in 1966, about 80 milliard roubles would be needed to finish all constructions being worked on, whereas lately about 18–19 milliards had been assigned annually for building productive objects according to the State plan (I. Mayevskiy, *Planovoye khozyaystvo*, no. 3, 1966, p. 17).
15. A decree of 21 August 1954 set a task of increasing credit investments in order to expand the output of consumer goods (V. Madayev, *Den'gi i kredit*, no. 12, 1955, p. 24).
16. A. N. Kosygin, *Pravda*, 28 September 1965, pp. 1–2.
17. I. V. Guzhkov, *Ekonomicheskaya gazeta*, no. 28, 1968, p. 9.

Cf. V. A. Vorob'ev, op. cit., p. 10.

18 Such as the halting in 1941 of the construction of a large building in Sadovo-Samotechnaya Ulitsa, Moscow, across the boulevard from where I was living in 1957–59.

19 See above, Chapter 8.

20 The relationships between investment and output will be considered in Chapter 21.

21 N. S. Burmistrov, op. cit., pp. 10–11.

22 A. N. Yefimov, *Ekonomika SSSR v poslevoyenniy period* (1962), p. 52.

23 A. Arakelyan, *Planovoye khozyaystvo*, no. 3, 1966, p. 26.

24 A. Nove, *The Soviet Economy, An Introduction* (1961), p. 207.

25 M. Eydel'man, *Vestnik statistiki*, no. 4, 1950, p. 89.

26 E. Tul'chinskiy, *Sovetskiye finansy*, nos. 1–2, 1945, pp. 21–2.

27 Cf. P. Pod''yachikh, *Vestnik statistiki*, no. 5, 1951, p. 3.

28 Cf. Z. Atlas, *Sovetskiye finansy*, no. 9, 1943, pp. 16–17.

29 B. Babynin, M. Sonin, S. Trubnikov, *Planovoye khozyaystvo*, no. 4, 1940, pp. 58, 63–4.

30 *Den'gi i kredit*, no. 5, 1955, p. 9.

31 A. Zelenovskiy, *Planovoye khozyaystvo*, no. 5, 1938, p. 17.

32 See above, Chapter 8.

33 S. G. Strumilin, *Izvestiya akademii nauk*, no. 3, 1946, p. 199.

34 B. P. Orlov, *Razvitiye transporta v SSSR 1917–1962* (1963), p. 186.

Postscript

Among recent studies of tendencies towards investment overheating in socialist economies, tendencies which in regard to the USSR are the main theme of this chapter, just as they were of my unpublished Ph.D. dissertation 'Studies in Soviet Industrial Development' (University of London, 1958), see in particular the interesting article by Imre Barta in *Közgazdasági Szemle*, no. 3, 1982, concerning Hungarian experience. An abstract (by Ervin Soós) of this article in English is appearing in *ABSEES*, September 1982. Considerable amplification of the present chapter may be found in the above-mentioned dissertation.

16
LOCATION POLICY

A vital element in investment policy is location policy. As noted in Chapter 2, before the Revolution Russian industry had been concentrated overwhelmingly in European Russia, and especially in the St. Petersburg, Moscow and Ivanovo areas and in the Ukraine. Leningrad, which like the Chinese treaty ports[1] (or Australian State capitals) was most readily accessible from overseas, suffered on the eve of the First Five-Year Plan from the absence of local deposits of iron, which had to be brought from the south (mainly) or from the Urals.[2] The city suffered also from inadequate supplies of local fuel and electric power.[3]

According to a pronouncement made in 1927, one aim of industrial development was to bring Soviet industry 'nearer to its bases of raw materials and power, on the one hand, and to districts which consume the product, on the other . . .'[4] This posed two problems: relocating industry and shortening haulage distances.

In the immediately ensuing period, between 1930 and 1939, when industrial output was growing rapidly, the government concentrated on the first objective – on relocation – rather than on the second. One can distinguish three planks in this programme.

1. In 1930 a system of railway freight charges was introduced which tapered to as little as 25 to 30 per cent per ton-kilometre of the initial rate. This facilitated the industrialization of the remoter parts of the Union, while minimizing its calculable disadvantages so far as these were measured by freight charges, by comparison with a situation where freight charges had remained unchanged.

2. Before 1939 people's commissariats were allocated regions from which they had exclusive rights of recruiting labour under *orgnabor*, a system which led unavoidably to 'superfluous mass transfers by rail of manpower, and sometimes cross-movements'.[5] This development too fits into the picture of paying relatively little heed to transport costs.

3. Also fitting into this picture was the lack of any progress between 1930 and 1939 in price-fixing in order to afford an incentive to economize on transport. Prices fixed f.s.n. (*franko stantsiya naznacheniya*,

i.e. inclusive of costs reckoned to the station of destination) afforded sellers a stronger incentive to economize on transport than prices f.s.o. (*franko stantsiya otpravleniya*, i.e. reckoned from the station of depart-ure).[6]

It was probably from about the beginning of the 1930s that the average rail haulage distance began to lengthen. This statistic is not published for all years, but in 1913 it had been 496 kilometres and apart from frontier changes little had occurred by the start of the First Five-Year Plan to alter this. By 1940 it was 700 kilometres, which raised by over 40 per cent the strain put on the railways in transporting a given weight of goods. A major cause of this lengthening was the building of the Urals-Kuznetsk combine, which required overland hauls of coal to the unexampled distance of over 2,000 kilometres (over 1,200 miles).

Because the railways provided nearly all east to west transport, the founding of new industries in the east led to the result that in 1932 the railways accounted for 77·5 per cent of all freight transport but by 1940 for as much as 85·1 per cent. Freight moved by water hardly increased during this period. Between 1937 and 1940, river transport gained at the expense of sea transport, apparently owing to the cutting of canals within the USSR during the late nineteen-thirties and the out-break of war at sea between Germany and the Western powers. There was no appreciable change in the average haulage distance by water.

Thus in general, during the nineteen-thirties heavier and heavier burdens were piled on the transport system, and especially on the rail-ways. This was a formative period when the centre of gravity of industry was shifting eastwards. But nothing had been done to shorten haulage distances; indeed, the trend was strongly contrary.

There was an increasingly serious phenomena of cross-haulage and of unnecessary hauls. A number of causes contributed to this result. One was the proliferation of people's commissariats in conjunction with the fact that they individually controlled plants which might be scattered all over the USSR. Each people's commissariat system was already beginning to act like a sort of semi-independent economic empire. New plants had been built on a basis of specialization, which increased haulage requirements. Some types of production were concentrated within a single area. There was no single plan of distribution (e.g. furniture) or if there was one it was disregarded (e.g. cement). Finally, funds were allocated in the absence of a regional breakdown (i.e. central planning had run ahead of regional planning).

The various measures making long-distance transport not unattrac-tive obviously encouraged local authorities to 'import' items from far off instead of making them themselves. The volume of 'irrational transport' was estimated at 20 milliard ton/km. in 1937, out of total transport of about 400 milliard ton/km. (indicating a surplus of 5 per cent).

Low transport charges encouraged the setting up of industries near to the existing industrial centres, on the principle of 'external economies'; thus, local industry developed mainly around Moscow and Leningrad and in the Ukraine. Works were established in large cities (Moscow, Kiev, Kharkov) apparently contrary to a decision in 1931 of the Party Central Committee, and compared with plan too large a percentage of local industry in the RSFSR was concentrated in the Moscow and Leningrad areas. Ninety per cent of *rayon* industrial output was produced in the RSFSR, with Moscow and Leningrad alone accounting for two-thirds.

Soviet policy with respect to specialization of enterprises and to their preferred size is rather intimately linked with location policy. The less heed is given to transport requirements, the smaller are the objections to building very large, specialized works serving the whole of the USSR. Conversely, the more heed is given to transport requirements, the more one will favour building a larger number of smaller works, designated for supplying only regions adjacent to themselves.

The nineteen-thirties were therefore a period during which specialization was being pressed to the utmost and so when very large works were built. As regards machine-building, the First Five-Year Plan had proposed to build specialized works involving mass production. It was not until 1938–39 that the disadvantages of extremely narrow specialization in ferrous metallurgy were recognized (in a decree of 3 April 1938, and by a decision of the XVIII Congress of the Party in 1939 to build duplicate works, this decision stemming partly from a defence motivation).

In 1939 policy was changed.

1. A more moderate gradient of tapering of freight charges was introduced: to not less than 45 per cent of the initial ton/km. rate. Also, an 'average rational distance' was fixed for each item (for example, 500 km. for ores and firewood, 3,000 km. for salt). Up to this point ton/km. charges declined, but beyond it they remained stationary or even rose.

2. The labour recruitment system was supplemented by an arrangement by which areas where labour was short were allotted other areas in order of priority, recruitment from the more distant areas being permitted only for certain occupations.[7]

3. Prices f.s.n. (see above) were introduced for cement and scrap metal (which are very heavy in relation to their value). Already before the war prices f.s.n. applied to all main items of personal consumption, especially foodstuffs.

Thus, immediately before the war, policy shifted in the direction of encouraging a reduction in haulage distances.

The reasons for this change of policy are not altogether clear. At this time international tension was increasing and it would be natural to suppose that location policy would respond to the visibly increasing threat from Nazi Germany. In that case, however, one would expect that the movement of industry into more easterly regions would be intensified, whereas in fact this movement was slackened. Against this, Koropeckyj argues that precisely such a change was justified even from a defence angle, as output in general could be increased more quickly in the central areas than if attention continued to be focused on development deep in the interior.[8] This tricky question cannot be resolved here, although I should have thought that the aggravation of the burden placed on the railways, the result of emphasizing growth in the Urals and Siberia, could by itself be an adequate explanation of the revision of policy. Furthermore, the de-emphasizing of development in distant areas fitted in with the westwards-turning of the Soviet Union in 1939, already mentioned.[9]

The net result of location changes since the beginning of all-out industrialization was to leave the eastern areas dependent on the western ones for many consumer goods, but to raise substantially in the east the capacity to produce coal, steel and other heavy goods. 'As regards the metal-working and chemicals industries, the output of the Soviet Union's eastern areas exceeded pre-Revolutionary Russia's total production by tens of times.'[10]

When Russia was invaded in 1941 location policy had of course to be revised. During the war, the centre of gravity of industry shifted sharply eastwards. For this, one can distinguish three reasons stemming from the German advance: the loss of factories in the occupied areas, evacuation of plants (mainly war plants) eastwards, and the fact that new construction was carried out only in the east.

The occupied areas were producing at the time of the German attack some two-thirds of all Soviet industrial output (e.g. 63 per cent of coal, 58 per cent of steel). These plants were not recovered until nearer to the end of the war, and in nearly all cases they were heavily damaged. According to Voznesenskiy only 13 per cent of prewar enterprises survived the occupation.

The second half-year of 1941 was marked by the evacuation to the east, largely to the Urals, western Siberia, Central Asia and Kazakhstan, of more than 1,360 large enterprises. Millions of workers, tens of thousands of machine tools, turbines, motors etc., were moved. These established themselves and began to produce from about March 1942 onwards.[11] After the war, many of these plants, with their workers, returned to their old haunts, but some remained in the place to which they had been evacuated (there are no comparative statistics).[12]

Capital investments continued to be made in the unoccupied areas. The immediate effect of the invasion was to diminish the annual volume of investment in all branches of the 'national economy' by about a half. After 1943, however, investment climbed rapidly and it was nearly as large in 1945 as in 1939. A regional breakdown is not available but Voznesenskiy states that 'centralized' capital expenditures during the four years of war economy in the eastern areas were on an average 23 per cent higher than the prewar average. New capacity put into operation included coalmines with a total capacity of some 30 million tons and about 2·5 million tons of steel-making capacity. A particularly large mileage of new railways was constructed during the war years. The urban population of the eastern regions grew by nearly 5 millions between 1939 and 1945. The growth in investment was especially large in the Urals area (55 per cent above the prewar average), which during the war became the main industrial area of the country. Particularly large additions were made to metal-working and engineering capacities in the eastern regions. On the whole, the prewar tendency of these regions to develop as heavy industrial centres was intensified.

During 1944 and 1945, as the Soviet armies rolled westwards, the centre of gravity of industrial production began to move westwards as well. Rehabilitation of formerly occupied areas was proceeding in 1944 and 1945. Their rehabilitation was also the main task of the Fourth (Postwar) Five-Year Plan. The major schemes launched during the period in connection with Stalin's 'Plan for the Transformation of Nature' (announced in 1948) affected mostly the south-east of European Russia rather than Asia. The failure of this project was mentioned earlier. Another spectacular failure was of a project to build a railway between Salekhard and Igarka, in the latitude of the Arctic Circle.[13]

The vulnerability of the western areas, which the war had demonstrated, seemed hardly to influence the government's determination to rebuild there. After all, it was not the first time that Russia had been invaded. Minsk, capital of White Russia, has more than doubled its population since 1939, and in recent years some of the highest rates of annual increase in industrial production have been recorded in the Baltic republics. In fact, these three republics (Estonia, Latvia and Lithuania) showed the highest of all rates of increase among Soviet republics in industrial production between 1940 and 1960. White Russia has also improved its industrial prospects. The predominance of the central region in *rayon* industry was even more marked in 1947 than it had been in 1940.[14] Only in a few cases have the brakes been applied, most notably in the case of Leningrad, whose exposed situation had been realized long before the war (it was one of the circumstances leading to the Soviet invasion of Finland in 1939).

In 1949 and 1950, among a number of measures taken in price-formation, transport charges according to rational distance were differentiated more consistently.[15]

During the Fifth Five-Year Plan (1951–55), although there was some change, the relative weight of the eastern regions in total industrial output changed only slightly. In July 1955 Marshal Bulganin complained that works were still being set up in the central regions instead of being more widely distributed. He observed that many industries

> continued to follow the incorrect practice of concentrating the construction of new enterprises in inhabited areas, where industry is developed already, without taking into account whether enterprises under construction can be supplied with local raw material and fuel.
>
> Why – reason some heads of ministries and ministerial departments – build enterprises somewhere in Siberia, which is far away and hard to reach? It is much simpler and easier to build new works, or expand existing ones, somewhere near the centre of the country or better still in Moscow or Leningrad.
>
> Despite the repeated instructions of the Party Central Committee and Government regarding cessation of new building or reconstruction and expansion of existing enterprises in Moscow, Moscow oblast and Leningrad, many ministries and ministerial departments try in every possible way to evade these instructions and on one pretext or another to put up new industrial buildings, or to reconstruct and expand existing enterprises in the above-mentioned central areas.[16]

This propensity was presumably helping to cause a fuel shortage (coal and électric power) in regions of European Russia, about which there were reports in 1955 and 1956[17] and which it was expected that the hydro-electric constructions at Kuybyshev and Stalingrad would relieve: 60 per cent of the power which they generated was to be diverted to Moscow.[18]

Geological discoveries continued, including that of diamond pipes in a remote region of Siberia, near the Vilyuy river, in 1954. The amnesty of various categories of prisoners, announced in 1955, probably affected a number who had been engaged in mining in the east and so tended to reduce the share of those regions in total output. Industrial production in Magadan oblast declined by one-seventh between 1952 and 1955, at a time when production generally was increasing.

On the whole, the regions beyond the Urals enlarged their relative importance between 1940 and 1956: thus, during this period the RSFSR raised its industrial output 3·5 times, but eastern Siberia by 3·7 times and western Siberia by 6·3 times.[19] Western Siberia, the Volga area and the Urals recorded the largest proportionate increases during this period. Phenomenal rates of increase in gross industrial production were claimed for certain republics, for example in Kazakhstan 33 times and in Armenia 41 times, between 1913 and 1955.[20] When evaluating these reports, one must remember that the industrial output of these areas in 1913 would have been extremely small. The *Far East* recorded a smaller than average increase.

From 1954 onwards, the cultivation of virgin lands raised the relative importance of *agriculture* east of the Urals.

An enhanced attention to regional planning probably helped to motivate the industrial/constructional reform of 1957. However, the boundaries of the newly set-up *sovnarkhozy* usually coincided with the oblast boundaries. Earlier suggestions that a rational pattern of divisions should be demarcated according to purely economic criteria were not taken up, and the *sovnarkhozy* were inconveniently numerous for effective regional planning. However, in April 1961 the creation of 17 large economic regions was announced. These were not administrative regions; they were supposed to recommend guiding lines for the development of that particular area. These regions were much larger than those of the *sovnarkhozy*, and they were based on purely economic criteria.

The reform of 1957 appears to have been beneficial as regards haulage distances. It was to have been followed by a rearrangement of supply links in the direction of making these more rational, but this did not occur. However, attention has been given to linear programming techniques which may eventually help to relieve the problem. It is said that haulage could be reduced by 10 per cent as a result of adopting distribution patterns based on linear programming solutions.

The first draft of the Seven-Year Plan (1959–65 inclusive) showed that more emphasis would be given to developing the eastern regions. This emphasis was, however, slightly watered down in successive drafts. The latest intention was to invest in the east about 40 per cent of the total. Capital investment (not all of it in industry) was to grow especially rapidly in Tajikistan, Uzbekistan, Kazakhstan and Kirghizia. The biggest share of the total sum was allocated to Siberia and Kazakhstan, especially for developing oil and allied industries. A rapid development of fuel, power, chemicals, and engineering was envisaged. Siberia was expected to raise its share in the total output of the RSFSR from 16 per cent in 1958 to 25 per cent in 1965.

The development of resources in the east is spread over a wider area than those of European Russia and the choice can therefore be more selective. Only the richest deposits need be worked. The problem in all cases is not any lack of abundance of deposits but climatic extremes, difficult communications, absence or scantiness of social capital. Siberia is still very empty and undeveloped. Among the very large projects which have been tackled are hydro-electric power stations at Bratsk, Angara and Krasnoyarsk which provide large amounts of electric power for making aluminium and other non-ferrous metals.[21] The only rival in scale in European Russia to the Siberian deposits of basic ores is the 'Kursk Magnetic Anomaly' iron ore body to the south of Moscow (in the Kursk-Belgorod area). This is now being developed energetically, a course which possibly helped to diminish the relative weight assigned at first during the Seven-Year Plan to investment in Siberia.

Looking back, one can thus distinguish three periods when special emphasis was placed on developing the Soviet east: the 1930s, 1941–43 and (tailing off) 1959 onwards. Tackled discontinuously, the problem of dispersing productive capacities more evenly has continued to haunt the Soviet leaders. As compared with 1913, a very important measure of dispersion has occurred. A comparable dispersion has not been achieved in planning, projecting, designing, or research, though Khrushchev began to tackle the problem of dispersing research organizations more widely.

Although a fair measure of dispersion of production has been achieved, which is important from a military point of view and also for the sake of exploiting more fully the country's natural resources (always a keenly felt preoccupation), the aim of bringing Soviet industry 'nearer to its bases of raw materials and power, on the one hand, and to districts which consume the product, on the other', set in 1927, has not yet been reached. However, considering the far-flung extent of the country and its correspondingly dispersed resources, one may argue that such an objective is not attainable. Experience also teaches that haulage distances are responsive to the form of industrial structure. After 1957 they were shortened, but from 1965 onwards the average length of railway haulage again increased: from 807 km. in 1965 to 812 km. in 1966 and 830 km. in 1967.[22] In fact, location policy cannot be pursued independently of other objectives in industrial organization – hence independently of other economic objectives.

In the west, location theory has been dominated by Weber, who introduced the distinction between weight-losing and weight-gaining branches. In order to minimize transport costs, branches of industry in which weight is lost in manufacture tend to locate themselves nearest to the source of materials, whereas branches (such as ink or beer) in which weight is gained in manufacture tend to settle nearest the consumer. For this reason, and also because products after the final stage of manufacture are often at their most fragile and perishable, consumer goods industries often locate themselves nearest their markets whereas primary manufacturing processes, involving for example reduction, crushing, smelting or the use of large quantities of fuel, settle nearest to material and fuel sources. On these criteria,[23] it is rational for heavy industry to be located nearest to the sources of materials and/or fuel, as has occurred in Siberia, but not rational for consumer industries to be concentrated in any particular area. Whenever location policy comes up for discussion in the USSR, it is the restricted extent of the local facilities in various outlying regions for producing household necessities that comes under fire.[24]

Soviet economists[25] are acquainted with Weber, and doubtless also with more recent additions to location theory in the west. Their application in Soviet conditions is opposed by the Party, which alludes to a need to satisfy social considerations of a possibly unquantifiable nature.

By comparison with powers to hand in Western countries, the Soviet authorities have two additional variables at their command:

1. Regional differences in wages can be altered by central government decision. There have been substantial regional wage differentials in different regions, wages being highest in the north and Far East and generally in the more remote areas. This, other things being equal — though actually these areas have other drawbacks too — would tend to deter business organizations from opening new industries there. Khrushchev inveighed against big regional differences, alleging that Siberia had been slandered: it was actually rather pleasant there, and there was no need to pay extra wages as an inducement to people to move there. However, following Khrushchev's dismissal his policy of attenuating regional wage differences has been reversed. Obviously, wage policy in this field has to take popular preferences into account.

2. Within limits, the Soviet authorities can found not only new industries but new consuming districts. Sometimes a construction site becomes the home of a permanent town: such as Volzhskiy, on the left bank of the Volga near to Stalingrad (Volgograd), where the dam builders lived, some 35,000 of them. Under Russian climatic conditions permanent houses must be built if construction is to continue during cold weather, and there consequently arises a question of what to do with the completed facilities. (Especially as, in Volzhskiy, a large neo-Classical 'Palace of Culture' had been erected.) It was planned that the builders (those at least who were not highly specialized) should remain in the town and that new industries would be established there. The specialized dam builders were doubtless transferred to new scenes of action, including Siberia and, at the other climatic extreme, the Aswan High Dam in Egypt.

One should not exaggerate either the rationality of location policy or the degree to which this is pursued consistently. Until now, to quote a Latvian Party secretary, enterprise building sites have often been chosen on the principle of who shouted the louder.[26] Krivoy Rog town has been built on top of an iron ore mine, and has to be moved[27] – which is just about the situation of the town of Yallourn, in Victoria, Australia, which sits on top of valuable brown coal deposits.

Though to some extent the authorities can shift consuming districts, in practice mobility is limited by the hostile climatic conditions in Siberia, the absence of east to west waterway communications, the need to create social capital in proximity to producing works which are removed from inhabited places, and the ingrained preference of the ministries to build nearer to Moscow or other large cities in European Russia. Following the re-creation of the ministries in 1965 there is also every reason to suppose that their typical vices are again being manifested.

Besides domestic political and economic considerations, foreign policy has evidently exerted some influence. The proximity to Europe of the western regions no doubt contributed largely to the decision to build the Urals metallurgical base, and we saw that the easterly shift had to be intensified during the war. In addition to these obvious and direct repercussions one may trace at least a vague influence upon location policy of general emphasis in foreign policy. Whereas in the nineteen-thirties and in 1941–43 Russia was repelled by Europe, in 1940 and from 1943 onwards Russia was re-establishing herself in Eastern Europe: her frontiers were pushed forward, engulfing new territories and populations. Not unnaturally, at these times attention was concentrated on construction in the west rather than in the east. Even the second thoughts about the Seven-Year Plan might be related to a renewed determination to accomplish particular goals in Eastern Europe, relating especially to Berlin and East Germany. Indeed, the rise of East Germany as a trade partner of the Soviet Union in effect modifies the location of industry that is directly geared to supplying the needs of the Soviet economy.

This last consideration, when applied to the present strained relations between the Soviet Union and China, has appeared to make it more doubtful whether the gradual eastwards shift of the centre of gravity of the Soviet economy would be maintained, at least as regards areas in propinquity to China.[28] As seen from the perspective of 1981 and judging by the trend of comparative sizes of republic budgets – although this is a rather coarse measure – the eastwards shift has come to a halt.[29]

Soviet location policy can be discussed, as has been done in this chapter, primarily in terms of easterly or westerly movements. Problems of movement in a northerly or southerly direction have been less prominent. One must note certain important exceptions to such a rule: the mining of nickel, gold and other important metals in the Far North, and the development of Uzbekistan as the primary cotton-growing region of the USSR with accompanying industrial development and the construction of the Turk-Sib railway to link Central Asia with Siberia. Although the Soviet Union has no 'north-south problem' of *sharply* differing living standards, there are differences between republics which often fall into three groups: the RSFSR, Estonia and Latvia (top); Kazakhstan, Lithuania, Ukraine, Armenia, Belorussia, Georgia (middle); Kirghizia, Azerbaydzhan, Moldavia, Turkmenia, Uzbekistan, Tadzhikistan (bottom).[30] Interrepublic differences are even widening, owing in part to the much more rapid growth of population in Central Asia and Transcaucasia than in the USSR as a whole.[31]

The extension of cultivation northwards, into climatically harsher regions, has been a constant preoccupation of Soviet agronomists. To some extent, the easterly movements already described have also involved penetrating into more northerly areas, such as in the discovery of diamonds in Siberia. Arctic and sub-Arctic deposits now supply substantial fractions of Soviet outputs of a number of important minerals, such as nickel, oil, gold and tin; during the Tenth Five-Year Plan, the Tyumen' region accounted for 90 per cent of the rise in natural gas output. No other country has made a comparable effort in the Arctic.[32] The penetration of the north is important also from the scientific and military viewpoints. The same is even more true of exploration into the third dimension, upwards into space!

Notes

1 Cf. K. L. Mitchell, *Industrialization of the Western Pacific* (1942), pp. 100–2.
2 Z. A. Osvenskiy, *Metall*, no. 4, 1931, p. 77. He wrote that this dependence created many difficulties.
3 A. S. Vaynshteyn (ed.), *Voprosy sebestoimosti promyshlennoy produktsii* (1935), p. 139.
4 *Materialy k pyatiletnemu planu razvitiya promyshlennosti SSSR* (1927), p. 176, cited in S. G. Strumilin, *Problemy planirovaniya v SSSR* (1932), pp. 468–9.
5 A. Aristov, *Planovoye khozyaystvo*, no. 11, 1939, pp. 95–6.
6 See in this connection my 'The Origins of the Soviet Industrial Price System', *Soviet Studies*, July 1961 (vol. XIII, no. 1), pp. 10–11.
7 See above, Chapter 9.
8 Iwan S. Koropeckyj, *Soviet Studies*, October 1967 (vol. XIX,

no 2), pp. 239–240.
9 See above, Chapter 7.
10 N. Voznesenskiy, op. cit., p. 47.
11 Ibid., pp. 41–3.
12 An evacuation of industrial enterprises to the east was carried out also in the First World War. Over 1,000 large factories were evacuated, although it is not known how many actually established themselves elsewhere. The evacuation was carried out hurriedly and without any plan. (P. Lyashchenko, *Istoriya narodnogo khozyaystva SSSR, tom II* (1956), pp. 589–90.) It is not surprising that a more systematic approach could be adopted the second time.
13 See above, Chapter 9.
14 P. Yevseyev, *Planovoye khozyaystvo*, no. 4, 1948, p. 55. .
15 L. Mayzenberg, *Planovoye khozyaystvo*, no. 6, 1950, p. 62.
16 N. A. Bulganin, *Pravda*, 17 July 1955, p. 5. Cf. V. Kostennikov, *Izvestiya*, 27 September 1955, pp. 2–3.
17 V. F. Vasyutin, *Pravda*, 30 August 1955, p. 2. Fuel and power supplies were very critical in the European USSR and the Urals (Ya. Feygin, *Trud*, 8 February 1956). Also S. Tokarev, *Planovoye khozyaystvo*, no. 2, 1956, p. 78.
18 *Voprosy ekonomiki*, no. 10, 1951, pp. 6–7.
19 V. Katkoff, *Soviet Economy 1940–1965* (1961), p. 507.
20 S. Tokarev, *Planovoye khozyaystvo*, no. 2, 1956, p. 76.
21 There is also an aluminium works at Stalingrad (see press, 20 December 1960).
22 *Narodnoye khozyaystvo SSSR v 1967 g.* (1968), p. 518.
23 Location theory is also influenced by the positioning of junction points and other desiderata, but these will not be explored here.
24 E.g. P. Yevseyev, *Planovoye khozyaystvo*, no. 4, 1948, p. 57.
25 E.g. V. Troitskiy, *Puti industrializatsii*, nos. 5–6, 1931, p. 44.
26 V. P. Lein, *Ekonomicheskaya gazeta*, no. 25, 1968, p. 12.
27 V. Travinskiy, *Literaturnaya gazeta*, no. 10, 1968, p. 10.
28 Most commentators argue that Russia would wish to 'fill up' the territories adjacent to China, in order to establish a better claim on them. However, Russia cannot by any imaginable means establish a demographic presence in these territories which would be equal to China's. It seems equally, or more, likely that Russia will prefer to maintain relatively few economic installations in regions adjacent to China, and thereby will limit her own vulnerability to a Chinese attack.
29 See R. Hutchings, *The Soviet Budget* (1983), Ch. 6.
30 H.-J. Wagener, *Osteuropa-Wirtschaft*, no. 2, 1969, p. 114.
31 See my article 'Declining Prospects of Soviet Population Growth', *The World Today*, December 1968.
32 T. Armstrong, in a presentation at the annual conference of NASEES, Fitzwilliam College, Cambridge, 29 March 1982.

17
FOREIGN TRADE

A. *Introduction*

While it is perhaps not essential to link the subject of Soviet foreign trade with that of location policy, a country's trade is obviously influenced by its accessibility to trade routes. Whereas the United States and Australia were first settled along the ocean coast-line and then pioneers pushed inland, the Russian heartland is the interior. As they expanded outwards, the Russians discovered new outlets to the ocean, which naturally affected trade patterns: for example, the Pacific shoreline renders the Far East conveniently supportable now by imports of grain from Canada. Again, the USSR extends over such a huge area that some international routes conveniently pass through it, such as a back-door route to Afghanistan when a few years ago transit to that country was barred through Pakistan, or to Iran, Romania or Czechoslovakia.[1] It may be convenient for the USSR on geographic grounds to export and import the same commodities, if these are in surplus in some regions of the country but in deficit in other regions. The USSR can also more conveniently export certain products than transport them to distant regions within its own borders, for example timber from Arctic forests can be more conveniently sent to Western Europe than to the Ukraine.

Statistics of Soviet foreign trade are now available both from Soviet sources and from those of other countries. It is possible — though very laborious — to compare the two sets of statistics. There is a reasonable degree of conformity between them, although not an exact conformity: the foreign trade statistics of different countries rarely do match exactly, for reasons which are often not clear.

Soviet foreign trade statistics are expressed usually in roubles, but occasionally in US dollars. The roubles are not the same as the roubles used in calculations within the USSR: they are based on US dollar statistics, converted into roubles at the prevailing rouble/dollar exchange rate. This rate, which is fixed by the Russians, has from time to time been altered. When it is altered, so are the statistics expressed in roubles; for example, total Soviet foreign trade in 1958 was given as 34,589 million roubles at the pre-1961 exchange rate but as 7,783 million roubles at the post-1961 exchange rate.[2]

For a long period, under Stalin, the USSR did not publish statistics of its foreign trade. The Russian example of secrecy was imitated by the satellites, and one of these, Romania, maintained secrecy for much longer. The first hard information about the structure of Soviet trade was couched in percentages and appeared in 1956. Much more information has appeared since, and it is now the rule for a statistical handbook on foreign trade to be published annually. This handbook lists countries with which the USSR trades and provides a fairly detailed breakdown of traded commodities and values.

Invisible items are not included. Tourism into or out of the Soviet Union is on a notoriously small scale, while shipping services until lately were small, but now (including foreign exchange earnings from a large tonnage for passenger cruising) have become quite substantial. Trade statistics are stated not to include goods delivered as unrequited assistance to foreign countries and other goods which do not bear a commercial character. It is not clear from this whether arms deliveries are included in the statistics. They are at any rate not itemized, but may well be included in the global totals of trade with particular countries.

B. Foreign Trade History

Soviet trade has had its ups and downs; its fortunes have indeed been erratic. The totals in various years, in current prices expressed in terms of the present rouble/dollar exchange rate, have been as shown in the table on this page (milliard roubles). These particular years, except 1960 and later, mark turning-points in the trend. One may comment as follows on the series.

1913	2·3	1970	22·1
1919	almost nothing	1971	23·6
1924	0·5	1972	26·0
1930	1·6	1973	31·3
1935	0·5	1974	39·6
1939	0·3	1975	50·7
1945	2·8	1976	56·8
1946	1·3	1977	63·3
1960	10·1	1978	70·2
1965	14·6	1979	80·3

Before World War I Russia conducted a quite substantial foreign trade. During the war this shrank, and by 1919 when Russia was being blockaded by the allies trade was virtually nil. It revived especially following the Treaty of Rapallo (1922), making a big jump in 1925 and reaching a new peak in 1930, yet this reached to only three-quarters of the prewar level, After 1930 it declined, by more than two-thirds between 1930 and 1935, and by almost another half between 1935 and 1939. In 1940 there was some improvement. The foreign trade annuals pass over the war period 1941–44 in silence. According to Voznesenskiy, between 1940 and 1943 Soviet imports rose nearly fivefold while Soviet exports decreased by more than two-thirds. If in 1940 the Soviet trade balance was, as it is claimed, approximately in balance (according to Soviet statistics, an approximate balance is kept between exports and imports, except in the years affected by Lend-Lease), in 1943 the ratio of imports to exports must have been about 15 : 1. What is exhibited here is, of course, allied deliveries, especially Lend-Lease supplies. In 1945, according to Soviet statistics, the ratio of imports to exports owing to the same cause was over 10 : 1. Thus, out of the total foreign trade in 1945 of 2,757 m. roubles, over nine-tenths were imports. The termination of Lend-Lease caused a sharp decline in trade in 1946. Thereafter there has been an increase from year to year, and in 1967 the level of trade was nearly thirteen times that of 1946, or more than seven times that of 1913.

These statistics are in current prices, which during certain periods were rising rapidly. Consequently, trade reckoned in fixed prices rose much more slowly than these figures indicate. Whereas, for example, the increase in trade between 1937 and 1955 was in monetary terms rather more than ten times, the volume of trade is claimed to have increased only by slightly more than twice. The trade turnover (exports plus imports) reckoned at 1960 prices, or after 1960 in terms of the index 1970 = 100, is stated to have increased as shown in Table 20. Thus in comparable prices trade in 1960 was 9·12 times larger than in 1938, while in 1979 it was 37·24 times larger.[3] This rapid increase must not, however, be accepted as characterizing the growth of trade throughout the Soviet period, as there had been a very marked shrinkage during the 1930s.[4]

C. Countries With Which the USSR Trades

The USSR was claiming in 1963 to trade with over 90 countries (as compared with 59 in 1955), which was most of the world's countries; the 1967 handbook listed 82 countries, including West Berlin as one. The 1979 handbook stated that trade was carried on with 131 countries, but the roster had meanwhile continued to lengthen, due to

Table 20

Growth of Foreign Trade

1938	100		1972	115
1946	129		1973	132
1950	280		1974	142
1955	501		1975	157
1960	912	48	1976	168
1965		68	1977	177
1970		100	1978	194
1971		104	1979	196

decolonization. The USSR does not trade with South-Korea or Taiwan, for the obvious reasons that she supports, politically, North Korea and (in relation to Taiwan) Communist China. Soviet trade with Albania, which had been sizeable for Albania's population, was chopped off after 1960 and has not been resumed. Trade with Israel was broken off after Suez (1956). With many countries, such as Burma, Kuwait, Kenya, Senegal, even Mexico, trade is very small, and the great bulk of Soviet trade is carried on with rather few partners.

Much more trade is conducted with bloc than with non-bloc countries, a situation which dates only from 1945, there being no Communist bloc previously. The proportion is roughly 7 : 3 (in 1959, for instance, 74·4 per cent). However, this share has been falling (in 1979, only 67·9 per cent). Soviet trade per Communist head is 4—5 times Soviet trade per non-Communist head.

Within the bloc, until the Soviet break with China, East Germany or Communist China were in first place. Since 1960 this place has been held by East Germany, whose lead can now be challenged only (perhaps) by Poland, if the Polish economy recovers from its severe setback in 1981. In 1967 the GDR accounted for nearly 16 per cent of all Soviet trade, in 1979 for 10·1 per cent. Obviously, this is an important tie between the two states. Following the GDR and Czechoslovakia (10·7 per cent of the total in 1967, 8·2 per cent in 1979) the next three places in 1967 were occupied by Poland, Bulgaria and Hungary. Poland soon overtook Czechoslovakia as the USSR's second biggest trading partner. After Hungary followed Cuba, then Romania. In 1967, only after these eight did any non-bloc country start to figure: Japan, Yugoslavia and the United Kingdom each registering about 2·8 per cent. West Germany's share in that year was only 1·9 per cent, but by 1979 West German trade amounted to 5·3 per cent or 4·2 milliard roubles, a 13-fold gain turning West Germany into the seventh largest trading partner of the USSR (just below Cuba, which sends to the Soviet Union almost exclusively sugar, receiving in return an extremely wide range of items). The West German advance is the chief change in the direction of Soviet foreign trade over the past 10–15 years. The second most important has been the enlargement of trade with the United States. Whereas in 1967 Soviet trade with the US was only about one-half to one-third as large as Soviet trade with Mongolia, North Korea or North Vietnam, hence was quantitatively negligible to either partner, in 1979, following a 31-fold expansion, trade with the US had reached 2·8 milliard roubles; though still short of West Germany, more than with France. It was very unbalanced, imports from the US predominating. Out of 2·5 milliard roubles' worth of imports from the US in 1979, grain comprised 1·5 milliard; machinery and equipment 0·34 milliard.

Soviet trade with the developing countries, apart from those belonging to the Soviet bloc (Mongolia, Cuba, North Korea, Vietnam), and excepting also the UAR, India and China, has remained small. Between 1969 and 1979 trade with 'industrially developed capitalist countries' rose by 6·7 times; trade with developing countries rose by only 4·7 times. Trade with such countries as India or China, although not negligible in absolute volume, is extremely small on a per-head basis. Per-head of the other trading country, Soviet trade with Finland is hundreds of times larger than Soviet trade with India or China. Vietnam now absorbs a quite large volume of Soviet imports, but sends back only one-third as much, and so has become an appreciable burden for the Soviet economy.

D. Types of Traded Commodities

Many hundreds of separate items are traded; for instance, a full list occupied 29 printed pages in the 1963 trade handbook. The most general possible breakdown is into 9–10 groupings of commodities. In 1913 Russia exported chiefly vegetable and animal raw materials, including foodstuffs, and food products: especially grain, and timber and timber products. Her exports of other raw materials, metals, or machinery or equipment were extremely small, although there was a small trade in handicrafts. She imported primarily vegetable and animal raw materials, e.g. raw cotton (mainly non-foodstuffs), machinery and equipment, and some consumer goods, food products (fish, fruit, etc.), fuel, metals and rubber. Fifty years later, among exports, machinery and equipment had moved up into first place, followed by fuel and by vegetable and animal raw materials. These increases had been more than offset by a decline in the export of foodstuffs raw materials. Other bulk commodities such as crude oil, ores and concentrates, and metals had increased their share, whereas the percentage of exports of industrial consumer goods had fallen. Among imports, machinery and equipment had, as among exports, moved up into first place; they were followed by industrial consumer goods, vegetable and animal raw materials (including foodstuffs), food products, and ores and concentrates. The transition from a food exporting country to a machinery and equipment exporting country holds up a mirror to Russian economic development. However, in any given year imports of machines still exceed exports of them. Among the dates listed in Table 21 the disparity was greatest in 1938 and had diminished by 1950, but since 1958 it has widened again. In 1963 the difference between percentage shares of machinery and equipment in imports and exports, 15·2, was approximately the same as in 1913 (15·6). Despite industrialization, the net machinery and equipment balance is still very markedly inwards (see below).

The commodity composition of the *value* of Soviet exports has altered substantially over the past decade, owing to the oil crisis of 1973 and the subsequent repeated rises in world oil prices. In 1970, liquid and solid fuels comprised 15·6 per cent of the value of Soviet merchandise exports, but in 1975 these comprised 31·4 per cent and in 1979 even 36·0 per cent (see Table 21). This rise would have been even more sudden, had not the USSR at first adhered to her long-term agreement to supply the East European countries at prices which followed world prices only on average and after a time-lag. Visible too, though less striking, has been the declining share of Soviet foodstuffs exports as the domestic food situation has become more strained; this is, of course, also in line with the expansion of grain imports from the US or (when President Carter banned grain exports to the Soviet Union following the Soviet incursion into Afghanistan) from Argentina.

The other principal change in the item – composition of exports, although not demonstrable from Soviet official statistics (in which respect the USSR is not much more secretive than other arms-exporting countries) has been the immense expansion of Soviet arms exports. Arms may now make up something like 40 per cent by value of Soviet exports to Third World countries. According to data gathered by the Stockholm International Peace Research Institute (SIPRI), Soviet exports of 'major arms' (comprising warships, armoured fighting vehicles, aircraft and missiles, which are categories that make up less than half of total arms exports to the same group of countries) grew about 66-fold between 1950 and 1975, since when there have been further increases, up to a total of over US $4,000 M in 1978 reckoned in dollar prices of 1975. While a five-year moving average of this series exhibits an almost steady linear increase, between 1955 and 1970 the annual totals of Soviet 'major arms' exports to all Third World coun- tries arrange themselves in a cyclical sequence which approximately matches the timetables of the Soviet five-year plans. During this period arms exports tended to be highest in the second or third year of the contemporary five-year plan (1961–65 being reckoned here as a 'Seventh Five-Year Plan').[5] This cycle satisfying statistical tests of non-randomness,[6] it must apparently be concluded that the timetable of the five-year plans has exerted an influence on the timing of Soviet arms exports, and therefore – very possibly – upon the timing of various important events in post-war international relations. The less regular sequence since 1970 may be presumed to reflect such circumstances as the participation in Third World conflicts of Cuban and other Soviet bloc forces. The Soviet Union retains the ability to enlarge arms exports further wherever the opportunity emerges.

As regards the value composition of imports: machinery and equipment made up in 1979 38·0 per cent, as compared with about 34 per cent during the 1960s; this is down slightly from 1978 (42·0 per cent), which was probably an all-time high. Imports of foodstuffs too have expanded their share (1960, 6·4 per cent; 1970, 15·0; 1979, even 21·9), whereas the percentage share of imports of industrial consumer goods has fallen back almost to its level in the 1950s.

A more detailed breakdown of major traded commodities shows that out of 54 listed in 1965, 46 were both exported and imported.[7] For example, the USSR both exports and imports cotton goods (the USSR having a net export balance), oil (also a net export balance *from* Romania: *to* Finland and Iceland), and sugar (a net import balance). However, there are real differences here: thus, Egyptian raw cotton, which the USSR imports, is long staple, whereas Central Asian cotton is short staple: while the imported and exported cotton goods are not identical with each other. There are probably few, if any, common items among machines which are both imported and exported. It is sometimes alleged that the Soviet Union buys equipment in the West which it then sells to developing countries, but it is extremely unlikely that this happens on any significant scale. The machinery acquired from the West is as a rule more sophisticated than that which the USSR itself exports, particularly to developing countries.

The somewhat chaotic composition of Soviet foreign trade is well shown by a comparison of quantities of exports and imports with home production of the corresponding items. Any detailed survey of this relationship would, of course, form the subject of a whole book. We can notice here only a few of the more striking relationships. In 1965, for example, imports were especially important in relation to production in the following items: rail passenger carriages (54·4 per cent of home production), tea (43·0 per cent), main-line and industrial electric locomotives (39·3 per cent), wool (24·2 per cent), sugar (19·3 per cent), caustic soda (16·0 per cent), *papirosy*[8] and cigarettes (10·6 per cent), and raw cotton (10·0 per cent), while exports were especially important in the following: cameras (29·0 per cent of home production), raw cotton (24·9 per cent), *balansy* (short logs from which paper is manufactured) (20·9 per cent), newsprint (18·9 per cent), crude oil (17·9 per cent), iron ore (15·7 per cent), manganese ore (13·2 per cent), tea (13·2 per cent), wool (12·1 per cent), sticky veneers (11·1 per cent), and motor graders (10·7 per cent)[9]

Soviet trade still has many features of a developing country, such as the predominance of imports of machinery and the still substantial importance of exports of raw materials (including crude oil, ores and concentrates). However, the simultaneous prominence of machinery and fuel exports shows that this is a developing country of a peculiar kind.

This is the trade balance of a country which is mainly situated in high latitudes: thus, the USSR imports tropical food products such as citrus fruits, tea (though some tea is grown in Georgia) and coffee, and also tobacco, and exports timber from its northern forests. Even mammoth tusks are now being exported! (*Daily Telegraph*, 24 July 1982)

The item-pattern of trade confirms the predominance in output of capital goods, although the increased share of imports of industrial consumer goods, and the decreased share of exports of industrial consumer goods since 1950, are both noticeable − the overall flows in both cases being very markedly inwards.

An extremely important aspect of Soviet trade is the facilities which are obtained for furthering technical progress, through the importation of more advanced items than are currently being produced in the Soviet Union and in general for the acquisition of technical knowledge, as an accompaniment to imports.

E. Comparative Importance of Political and Economic Considerations

The question arises whether political or economic considerations are uppermost in Soviet foreign trade policy. One can only answer that both are important. The initial switch of Soviet trade towards the socialist countries was no doubt in large part politically motivated, like the sudden support offered to Cuba after Castro came to power (Soviet trade with Cuba increased by 23·4 times in 1960!) and the cutting off of oil deliveries to Israel after Suez. The reduction of Soviet trade with China after 1960 has been variously interpreted by the USSR and China, each claiming the other was wholly to blame. But once a country has been assigned to either the Communist or the non-Communist camp, the extent of trade depends primarily on economic considerations of comparative advantage, accessibility and availability.

Table 21

Structure of Soviet Exports and Imports (including Re-exports)
(percentages)

	1913	1938	1950	1960	1963	1970	1975	1979
EXPORTS								
Finished products	36·0			60·7	60·2	64·9		
including:								
machinery and equipment	0·3	5·0	11·8	20·5	19·7	21·5	18·7	17·5
liquid and solid fuels	3·4		3·5	11·2	11·8	15·6	31·4	36·0
food products	18·9		6·8	4·0	6·4	8·4	4·8	3·4
industrial consumer goods	4·7		4·9	2·9	2·6	2·7	3·1	2·6
Raw commodities	64·0			39·3	39·8	35·1		
including:								
crude oil	0·0	0·5		0·4	5·0	5·9		
ores and concentrates	1·3			2·2	4·4	4·0		
metals	1·1			3·5	6·4	5·5		
vegetables and animal raw materials	25·6			17·6	12·6	10·9		
foodstuffs raw materials	35·1			13·8	9·1	6·5		
IMPORTS								
Finished products	56·3			60·2	69·6	73·7		
including:								
machinery and equipment	15·9	34·5	21·5	29·8	34·9	35·1	33·9	38·0
liquid and solid fuels	7·1		11·3	3·9	2·7	2·0	4·0	3·8
food products	9·7		7·8	6·4	5·7	15·0	23·0	21·9
industrial consumer goods	11·1		7·4	17·2	18·3	18·3	13·0	11·4
Raw commodities	43·7			39·8	30·4	26·3		
including:								
ores and concentrates	0·1			5·9	5·6	4·2		
metals	3·3			3·7	3·5	1·9		
rubber	2·9			3·5	3·2	2·6		
vegetable and animal raw materials	24·7			14·8	10·3	8·2		
foodstuffs raw materials	9·4			9·6	5·7	7·1		

Sources: *Narodnoye khozyaystvo SSSR v 1963 g.*, pp. 551–2; *Vneshnyaya torgovlya SSSR za 1963 god*, p. 36; *Vneshnyaya torgovlya SSSR v 1970 g.*, p. 19; *Vneshnyaya torgovlya SSSR v 1975 g.*, p. 17; *Vneshnyaya torgovlya SSSR v 1979 g.*, p. 18.

One cannot say even then that exclusively economic considerations are involved, because non-bloc and, doubtless, bloc countries as well enforce various restrictions on goods they deem to be strategic. One hears most about non-bloc controls, but this is because any discussion of such restrictions enforced within the Communist group would not be published. The Western powers from the outset embargoed the export to the USSR of atomic energy materials. At the time of the Berlin blockade (1948–49) other controls being imposed by individual Western countries were co-ordinated, and since January 1950 this has been done by a committee (COCOM) which now includes 14 NATO countries (all except Iceland), plus Japan. In 1950 a virtual embargo was imposed on exports of industrial and major raw materials to countries of the Sino-Soviet bloc. The lists as regards European member-countries of the bloc only were reduced in 1954 while the differential as regards China was abolished in 1957. Various revisions and adjustments have been made subsequently. In 1965 the list included 146 items, 54 of which were electronic.[10] Relaxations were announced by President Johnson in October 1966, but following the Soviet incursion into Afghanistan controls have been strengthened.

In general terms, such restrictions can be expected to retard progress in the particular spheres where exports were denied, but to stimulate a search for substitutes, the discovery of which would eventually begin to overcome the retardation, though only at the cost of having diverted research resources from other fields. Hence the most general result would be to encourage still further the pursuit of self-sufficiency, which the USSR has been inclined to pursue in any case. As progress is made towards this goal, the justification for embargoing particular items disappears, but such justifications are liable to be perpetually renewed by differentials or believed differentials in the rates of advance by either side into new spheres which are regarded as of strategic importance. In recent years this is exemplified by the case of the pipe-lines. The USSR embarked on ambitious schemes of building networks of large-diameter pipelines to carry oil or natural gas within its borders and also across them, into Eastern Europe (the 'Friend-ship' pipeline). Current domestic production of large-diameter pipelines was insufficient and so the USSR attempted to import them, but countries which followed the American lead in regarding these as of strategic importance refused to supply, whereas others did. The deal to exchange Soviet oil for Italian pipelines assisted the rise in Soviet-Italian trade between 1959 and 1962.[11]

In the main, however, economic considerations are dominant, so that despite very bad political relations Soviet trade with West Germany has consistently remained fairly high, while the USSR continued to buy rubber from Malaysia although verbally supporting Indonesia over 'confrontation'. Countries or firms which have for sale what the USSR wants can thus expect to achieve in due course some success (although firms which are established in this field have the substantial advantage of being already acquainted with the peculiar conditions and of having made personal contacts).

F. Trade Balances

Against this, it is sometimes claimed that the USSR attempts to maintain particular relationships between its exports to and its imports from individual countries. The evidence is inconclusive, but it is note-

Table 22

Soviet Trade Balances with Particular Countries

$$\frac{\text{Imports}}{\text{Exports}}$$

	A	B	C	D	E	F	G
1960	0·88	1·08	1·76	1·68	0·88	0·56	0·97
1965	0·94	1·12	1·03	0·93	0·69	0·52	1·14
1970	0·90	1·03	2·28	1·43	1·48	0·53	1·05
1975	0·89	0·94	1·61	2·24	1·24	0·62	0·91
1976	0·86	0·96	1·19	1·81	0·66	0·49	1·00
1977	0·84	0·91	1·10	1·43	0·72	0·39	1·07
1978	0·93	1·02	1·16	1·42	0·77	0·78	1·18
1979	0·93	0·95	0·84	1·12	0·67	0·74	0·77
SD of above ratios	0·033	0·069	0·445	0·381	0·286	0·121	0·123

A = East Germany; B = Czechoslovakia; C = France; D = West Germany; E = Italy; F = United Kingdom; G = Finland.

Source: Soviet statistics.

worthy that British exports to the USSR regularly reach only about 50–60 per cent of Soviet exports to Britain. This might be because of the UK's special position as banker of the Sterling Area: some sterling earned in exporting to Britain is spent elsewhere in the Sterling Area. In Soviet trade with other countries, it is often possible to estimate the prospective ratio of imports to exports within rather wide limits: for example, the USSR ordinarily has an active balance with East Germany but a passive balance with Czechoslovakia. On the other hand, the relationship of imports to exports in Soviet trade with France has been erratic, but the origin of these differences has probably been economic rather than political. (See Table 22.)

Given the more stable political relationships and the existence of an almost complete network of bilateral trade agreements, one might expect that Soviet trade with bloc countries would be more stable than its trade with non-bloc countries. However, analysis of the available figures shows that the variability has scarcely been greater from year to year in the one category than in the other. (See Tables 23 and 24.) Presumably the propensities to conclude long-term trade agreements

Table 23

Soviet Trade with Bloc* and Non-bloc Countries

(millions of post-1961 foreign exchange roubles)

Year	Bloc	Non-bloc	Total	Annual Increments Bloc	Non-bloc
1946	698	582	1280		
1950	2373	552	2925		
1952	3862	904	4766		
1955	4627·8	1208·4	5836·2		
1956	4919·2	1583·7	6502·9	+291·4	+375·3
1957	5517·6	1970·5	7488·1	+598·4	+386·8
1958	5754·3	2028·1	7782·4	+236·7	+57·6
1959	7122	2341	9463	+1367·7	+312·9
1960	7210	2861	10071	+88	+520
1961	7621	3022	10643	+411	+161
1962	8523·7	3613·7	12137·4	+902·7	+591·7
1963	9077·2	3820·7	12897·9	+553·5	+207·0
1964	9678	4198	13876	+600·8	+377·3
1965	10049·6	4560·1	14609·7	+371·6	+362·1
1966	10023·1	5055·5	15078·6	−26·5	+495·4
1967	11089·2	5277·4	16366·6	+1066·1	+221·9

* Including Cuba and Yugoslavia

also with capitalist countries, to trade especially with larger firms and consortia, contracts which specify performance over a period, possibly the more vital character for the USSR of trade with capitalist than with socialist countries, and the much larger number of non-bloc than of bloc countries (which multiplies the alternative sources of supply and so tends towards greater quantitative stability of the total), approximately offset any extra rigidity of the formal structure of long-term bilateral trade agreements and annual protocols with bloc countries.

Table 24

Percentage Increases from Year to Year in Soviet Trade with Bloc and Non-bloc Countries

Year	Bloc	Non-bloc
1956	+6·3	+31·1
1957	+12·2	+24·4
1958	+4·3	+2·9
1959	+23·8	+15·4
1960	+1·2	+22·2
1961	+5·7	+5·6
1962	+11·8	+19·6
1963	+6·5	+5·7
1964	+6·6	+9·9
1965	+3·8	+8·6
1966	−0·3	+10·9
1967	+10·3	+4·4
range	−0·3 to +23·8	+2·9 to +31·1

Source: previous table (which is based on official statistics).

In one respect, however, Soviet trade relations with bloc countries *are* unusually stable: there is relatively little variation from year to year in the ratio of Soviet exports to a bloc country to Soviet imports in the same year from that country. This is fairly clearly seen in Table 22: the Standard Deviations of the ratios of Soviet imports to Soviet exports are much lower for the two bloc countries, East Germany and Czechoslovakia, than for the five non-bloc countries. Trade with the United Kingdom and Finland is, however, more stable than with France, West Germany or Italy.

With all countries together an approximate balance is maintained between visible exports and imports, a passive balance in one year tending to be replaced the following year by an active balance. However, the USSR displays no particular capacity to increase its exports by a larger margin than normally in order to pay for greater than expected imports within a given year. Indeed, the relationship between percentage increases in exports and imports fluctuates quite markedly: since 1956 increases in exports have varied from −2·0 per cent to +26·6 per cent, in imports from −1·8 per cent to +18·0 per cent. The largest increases in exports or in imports occur when 'ready products' increase their share in total exports or imports most markedly: thus, in 1962 'ready products' grew from 59·5 to 63·6 per cent of exports and from 68·3 to 74·6 per cent of imports. This then is the more dynamic component and 'raw commodities' the more inert one. Among particular items, grain imports vary more than grain exports: the latter have been kept at as high and stable a level as possible in order to maintain trade exchanges with the East European countries which cannot feed themselves.[12]

G. The Link with Gold

To cover deficits on its trading balance the USSR may sell gold, which is mined in the USSR mainly for its value as foreign exchange.[13] It is apparently sold in order to meet a particular deficit that happens to have arisen rather than that any advance programme of gold exports is followed. According to apparently reliable estimates, Russia's sales of gold between 1953 and 1964 were substantially greater than her output, resulting in a depletion of reserves by a value total approaching US $1,000 m., i.e. by about one-third.[14]

Because the USSR exports gold, it is naturally interested that its price should be relatively high and from time to time Soviet voices are heard which advocate a rise in the price of gold. This attitude is in sharp contrast to remarks made by Lenin about gold ('When we conquer on a world scale, I think we shall use gold for the purpose of building public lavatories in the streets of several of the large cities of the world'). The retail prices of items made from gold on the Soviet internal market are very high and recently the 'Torgsin' (trade with foreigners) shops, which accept only foreign currency or precious metals, have been revived (now under the name 'Beryozka'); greater attention has also been paid to expanding gold output.

There is a legal provision requiring 25 per cent gold backing of the currency. There would appear to be no rational reason for such a requirement in a country where transactions between State organizations are effected by bank transfer, where there is no free convertability into gold, and where all foreign trade and financial transactions are State controlled. The provision seems a rather absurd hangover from times past, but it is not inconsistent with other orthodox trappings of the Soviet financial system, such as the insistence on a budget surplus. One might interpret the 1961 10-for-1 exchange of the currency, and the simultaneous devaluation of the gold content of the rouble by $4^4/_9$ times, as having the effect of raising the proportion of the currency which was backed by a given weight of gold, and thus as freeing a larger quantity of gold for export. Soviet sales of gold did actually rise in 1961 and were larger on an average during 1961–64 than during the previous four-year period.

Since 1956 the USSR has become much more willing to sell gold, even to the extent of raiding its reserves, than was the case before 1956. Under Stalin, and for some while thereafter, sales of gold were probably below output whereas subsequently sales of gold have probably been above output. Other studies indicate that Soviet reserves of *grain* had been allowed to dwindle to almost nothing by midsummer of 1964. Evidently Khrushchev's government pursued a more active and enterprising, but from another point of view more reckless, policy in its dealings with the State's gold reserves. One may, of course, make the rejoinder that it was much more rational to sell the gold than to hoard it and keep secret the amount of the hoard (in which case one would not even gain the benefit of a stronger credit-worthiness). The move away from using forced labour (gold is largely mined in the viciously cold north-east of Siberia) may also be remembered.

H. Foreign Trade Planning

Forecasts of trade with particular countries can occasionally be compared with results. Such comparisons for 1960 in relation to 1959 are shown in Table 25. The estimate of the increase in trade with the entire world proved to be fairly accurate. Forecasts for particular countries were less uniform and on the whole less accurate, but those in respect of Poland, Romania and Czechoslovakia turned out to be quite near the mark. The Chinese result was obviously affected by the political difficulties between the two countries which erupted in 1960. The fact that volumes of trade with particular countries are reasonably well predicted suggests that policy or possibility fluctuates rather than performance, at least in trade with the European bloc.

References to foreign trade in the long-term plans are always very scanty. Final decisions as to magnitudes of trade with particular countries in particular years are no doubt made deliberately more flexible than the internal economic plan, as these decisions must be influenced by factors such as world prices, attitudes of foreign countries, and other political developments, which are partly or wholly

Table 25

Forecast and Actual Increases in Soviet Trade with
Certain Countries 1959–60

(percentage changes)

	Anticipated	Actual
Poland	+11	+9·3
Romania	+9	+12·2
Czechoslovakia	+8 or +15½*	+8·4
Bulgaria	'well above 1959 level'	+14·0
China	+10†	−19·0
North Vietnam	+ almost 50	+34·2
World	+5·4	+6·4

* Czech statement.

† Relative to amount stated in protocol for 1959. Actual trade in 1959 exceeded expectation.

outside Soviet control. The Soviet side stresses bilateral relations, doubtless with the aim of achieving a predictable pattern of foreign trade, and official pronouncements (such as by Khrushchev) have stressed the necessity of buying more from the USSR if one wants to sell more to it. At times, attempts have been made to foist bilateralism on individual Western exporters. A foreign company which can both sell to and buy from the USSR has an advantage over one which can only sell, a fact which places the larger and more diversified firms in a relatively favourable position by comparison with smaller or more specialized ones.

I. Principles of Trading

No theory of foreign trade has emerged within Marxist-Leninist economics. In practice, the USSR tried to become as self-sufficient as possible, only modifying this principle as a 'socialist market' was created and only more recently going so far as to admit that the USSR might renounce production of individual items in the general socialist interest. When the 'socialist market' was created, Soviet trade was channelled as far as possible within this and overflowed to the outside world only where necessity dictated. The simplest possible rule of trading was already to hand: the USSR should import what it did not possess itself (and which the Plan decided was needed) and pay for it with whatever could find a market, with little regard to repercussions within Russia herself: during the First Five-Year Plan, Khrushchev claimed, grain was being exported while people were dying of starvation (as had, of course, also occurred before the Revolution).

The traditional element in trade patterns is indeed quite strong. This is not surprising, since the 1913 volume total remained for a long time unsurpassed (and much longer than the level of industrial output or other quantitative indices in industry, as already noted), and considering that there was no such clear-cut objective in foreign trade as in industrialization. Moreover, the export staples (timber, grain, etc.) rested on the fact that Western Europe's consumption needs were in excess of its home domestic production, or on the Russian need for tropical products in return for the products of a northerly country – situations which were inevitably perpetuated. However, the Bolsheviks' economic objectives included making Russia more economically independent of the outside world which would imply making her more self-sufficient. The alternative, and logically possible, course of developing agricultural exports in order to pay for imports of industrial finished products had been rejected. The chosen course of building up domestic industry required massive imports of machinery which, especially in the circumstances of building up 'socialism in one country', could only be paid for by the traditional (agricultural) exports.

Immediate self-sufficiency tends to be sacrificed for the sake of production potential (e.g. agricultural exports to pay for machinery), i.e. for future self-sufficiency. The correct choice of items in which to seek self-sufficiency is therefore very important. Foreign trade might be expected to diminish at least as a proportion of GNP as this objective was approached, and certainly foreign trade declined very markedly as a percentage of GNP, compared with 1913, up to the end of the 1930s; since World War II, on the other hand, there has probably been little change in this proportion. The goal of self-sufficiency is constantly being approached, but it recedes almost as fast, owing to the emergence of new wants or technical deficiencies (machinery for making synthetic textiles, uranium ore, etc.), or owing to the enlargement of domestic demand. The USSR is now certainly nearer to a goal of self-sufficiency than Russia was in 1913, but it remains still quite far from such a goal. Moreover, since 1945 it has become possible to pursue self-sufficiency within the wider context of the socialist bloc, the only obstacle being the growing ambitions of economic independence, including a larger measure of self-sufficiency, of those countries themselves.

The principles so far enunciated do not take one far (apart from leading to detrimental results) and the next step on a ladder of increasing rationality (which almost certainly would point the way towards a rather different trade pattern) should be to act according to a principle of comparative advantage. This, however, can be reckoned only by reference to a price system, but as Soviet economists themselves admit, no rational system of Soviet prices has been constructed. As a result, it has been difficult or impossible for Soviet planners to determine the comparative advantage of importing some item as compared with making it at home, or of exporting it by comparison with home consumption, and seriously irrational decisions must have occurred. On the whole, perhaps an excessive attention has been paid to exporting good foreign-exchange-earning items. For example, it might have been wiser to spread more fertilizer on the fields, instead of exporting phosphate fertilizers (on the scale of about 2½ m. tons annually), and then needing to import grain. Why, too, should the USSR export its motor-cars to the already oversupplied world market when at home there was a chronic shortage of cars and the waiting list was years long? True, as Nove points out,[15] such irrationalities should not be compared with some imagined ideal observance in the West of a comparative costs principle, but with existing far-from-perfect arrangements involving semi-monopolistic quotas, different duties, special privileges, subsidies to particular industries, etc. In determining the commodities to be traded in and the amounts to be exchanged the USSR may thus be said to adhere to no clear or ascertainable principle.

J. Foreign Trade Organization

Against this, the *organization* of foreign trade may be said to observe *too* rigidly the principle of a State monopoly of foreign trade which was one of the first measures adopted by the Bolshevik government. There currently exist in this connection (a) a Ministry of Foreign Trade which oversees all transactions, concludes trade treaties and protocols, etc., and (b) a number (about two dozen) of foreign trade corporations.[16] One might wonder why there should be two organizations: the answer is to be found in the legal status of the corporations, which are not in theory State organizations. Obviously this is a fiction, the object of which is to enable the Soviet government to disclaim responsibility (as it does) for any breach of contract by the corporation for which it might otherwise be held liable. At the same time, the government retains the right to overrule the corporation (by *force majeure*) in implementation of its general foreign policy. The cutting off of Soviet oil deliveries to Israel after Suez showed this mechanism in operation. (This is, of course, a right reserved by all nations.)

The corporations arrange imports, exports, or both, of anything classifiable within a specified rather broad group of items. This arrange-

ment is in principle rational and easily surveyable, by comparison with
the jungle of exporting or importing organizations in a capitalist
economy, although problems of demarcation are sometimes encountered. The corporations are an additional stage between seller and user:
the eventual consumer of an item may very well not be known to the
foreign supplier, who is obliged to receive instructions through a less
technically expert intermediary. Against this, the system confers some
benefits to the Soviet side of monopsony (or monopoly): where there is
only one Soviet foreign trade corporation and several possible foreign
suppliers the corporation can, and does, try to play off one against the
other. It is commonplace for a head of a Soviet purchasing corporation,
when on a foreign tour, to announce that he can obtain better terms
in some other country, though no one is much deceived by such
announcements. The obvious answer from the foreign point of view
is for firms to unite into larger groupings for the purpose of trading
with the USSR, and some consortia have been formed for this purpose.
An interesting question[17] is whether the Soviet corporations have a
plan, e.g. an import plan, to fulfil. If they had and one knew what it
was some arm-twisting could be indulged in. Sometimes they can be
seen to be aiming at a particular goal of importing, for example, large-
diameter pipelines.

The amounts available to spend on imports appear to be fixed on a
year-to-year basis, so that if a foreign trade corporation exhausts its
quota for a given year it has to wait until the New Year before undertaking fresh commitments. No clear correlation can be seen between
increases in trade turnover and the timetable of the long-term plans,
although the contrast between 1958 (no long-term plan in operation –
increase of 4·0 per cent) and 1959 (initial year of long-term plan –
increase of 21·6 per cent) is somewhat striking and perhaps shows this
effect in operation.

K. Conclusions

It is sometimes asserted that foreign trade is 'marginal' to the Soviet
economy. It is hoped that this chapter has shown that foreign trade is
in fact an integral component and that changes in foreign trade
relations are intimately linked with other fundamental changes in the
economy. There is a particularly close relationship to foreign policy, via
such channels as arms exports. Organizationally, however, it is rather
more correct to call Soviet foreign trade marginal: its planning cannot
reach even the levels of approximation that are achieved in domestic
planning, and the actual business of exporting and importing is still
held at arm's length from the functioning of other sectors of the
economy. This has not impeded a very large expansion of the total

volume of trade.

Given the avidity with which Russians shop abroad, such as at ports like Gibraltar, one must wonder why the government does not give a free rein to individual caprice in imports, so as to make up for the shortcomings of the planning mechanism by exploiting the capability of non-socialist economies to produce whatever might be wanted in the way of superfluous variety. In that event, centralization would have promoted commerce, as it did in Russia's early history. To a degree this actually happens, for certainly the top Party layers have profited from extraordinary access to foreign currency; such as Khrushchev with his Italian suits. In broad lines, however, foreign trade had to be harnessed to the needs of development, because Russia continued to depend on foreign imports of many types of machinery and other things needed for her own industrialization.

Considering the Soviet period as a whole, it appears difficult to reconcile the irregular course of Soviet foreign trade with a rational approach to the needs of development. At times, evidently, aims of maximizing self-sufficiency have been pursued – and always abortively. Since 1945, by contrast, the expansion of trade seems unnaturally large, because trade has been used as a lever to bolster not only economic but political relations with other countries of the Communist bloc.

The most important changes since 1913 have been the promotion of machinery and equipment exports, and the transition from a food-exporting to a food-importing country. Yet, on balance, Russia appears to have become less self-sufficient in machinery and equipment. This result may seem somewhat surprising. One could not explain it if industrialization had been the only major process in Soviet economic history to occur during this period. It underlines once more that no simple formula will serve as a model of Soviet economic development: this can only be understood as a complex process involving socialization (particularly here enforcement of the State monopoly of foreign trade), which enabled the government to pursue particular conscious foreign trade policies; collectivization; industrialization accompanied by geographic dispersion and a commencing of exploitation of new mineral deposits; and population growth; all these trends being framed within broader trends in the world outside, including since 1945 the creation of the 'socialist market' within which Soviet foreign trade is still mainly concentrated.

Notes

1 *Vneshnyaya torgovlya SSSR za 1962 god* (1963), p. 19.
2 *Narodnoye khozyaystvo SSSR v 1958 godu* (1959), p. 799. *Nar-*

odnoye khozyaystvo SSSR v 1960 godu (1961), p. 748.

3 *Narodnoye khozyaystvo SSSR v 1967 g.* (1968), p. 764

4 A volume index of Soviet foreign trade is calculated by M. Kaser, *Soviet Studies*, April 1969 (vol. XX, no. 4); see also *Soviet Studies*, July 1969 (vol. XXI, no. 1), p. 130. Kaser's index is, however, stated to involve a weight-to-value paradox, which perhaps at this moment justifies caution.

5 R. Hutchings, *Osteuropa-Wirtschaft*, June 1978, pp. 182–202; and R. Hutchings, *The World Today*, October 1978, pp. 378–89. The most recent SIPRI source drawn upon here is the *SIPRI Yearbook 1979* (1979), pp. 172–3.

6 A. Abouchar, *Osteuropa-Wirtschaft*, June 1981, pp. 147–8.

7 *Vneshnyaya torgovlya SSSR za 1967 god* (1968), pp. 52–3.

8 *Papirosy* are cigarettes which have a cardboard mouthpiece.

9 Based on *Vneshnyaya torgovlya SSSR za 1967 god* (1968), pp. 52–3.

10 *The US Department of State Bulletin*, 1 February 1965, the Battle Act Report, 1964, 17th Report to Congress, Excerpt, pp. 148–50 and especially Appendix B.

11 See the article 'East-West Trade 1 – In the world economy', *Aspect*, February 1963.

12 Totals in certain years have been as follows:

Years	Grain exports	Grain imports
	(millions of post-1961 foreign exchange roubles)	
1959	438·5	14·3
1960	422·6	15·3
1961	426·4	41·7
1962	476·5	3·1
1963	379·9	194·8

13 Cf. *Izvestiya*, 25 December 1963.

14 K. Bush, *Soviet Studies*, April 1966, pp. 490–1.

15 A. Nove, *The Soviet Economy, An Introduction* (1961), p. 192.

16 A small amount of trade in consumer goods, especially agricultural products, is also conducted by national co-operative organizations. This has some historical roots (e.g. trade between *Tsentrosoyuz* and the Scottish CWS goes back to at least 1925) and some significance from the aspect of international co-operative relations, but only minor economic importance. The decree granting independent rights to *Tsentrosoyuz* was dated 13 March 1922. Between 1935 and 1955 *Tsentrosoyuz* ceased to direct any foreign trade relations. It resumed doing so in 1955: trading links were established with co-operative organizations and firms in 31 countries. As reported in 1968, during the previous ten years the volume of foreign trade operations of *Tsentrosoyuz* increased five times. (A. Klimov, *Sel'skaya zhizn'*, 20 April 1968, p. 5.)

17 Which I owe to one of my students, R. McGovern.

18
TECHNOLOGICAL IMPORTS AND INNOVATION

Earlier histories of Soviet economic development did not pay sufficient attention to the contribution of foreign technology. In the main this was due to the fact that Soviet sources, understandably in view of the slogan 'Socialism in One Country', gave minimum publicity to that contribution. Although impressionistic accounts appeared, most details remained locked in company archives or in the files of foreign offices, almost certainly in part because neither companies nor foreign offices cared to reveal how much they had provided.

The three-volume survey by Antony C. Sutton, *Western Technology and Soviet Economic Development*, covering the entire Soviet period up to 1965, altered the situation fundamentally. For the first time, the full extent of penetration of Western technology and its major contribution to Soviet economic development was displayed. Its author does not appear to have written on Soviet affairs either previously or since, but the work is sufficient to establish his reputation. The three volumes appeared successively in 1968, 1971 and 1973, so that only the first volume could have been taken into account in the first edition of the present book, which did actually include a brief allusion (p. 53). I have now read and reviewed all three volumes.[1]

Sutton's exposition is impaired by some apparent overstatements; for example his denial that war, civil war and blockade were largely responsible for the catastrophic decline in Soviet industrial production in 1921–22 appears to ignore the necessity of a harmonious combination of factors in permitting normal economic life: not destruction but disruption is the main effect of non-nuclear war on an economy, and the disruptiveness of military operations at this time was immense. He appears to exaggerate the impact of technological developments relative to short-term ones. The very limited reference to Soviet sources is unusual and may assist or at least reflect a not-invisible anti-Soviet bias, though it seems also that the author also had only limited acquaintance with the Russian language.

Against this, however, must be set the author's presentation of a very impressive mass of evidence covering almost all major spheres of economic activity, his very wide technical knowledge – a qualification that has not been superabundant among Western students of the Soviet economy – and his imperviousness to Soviet propaganda.

Sutton's study is based mainly on the US State Department Decimal File and on German Foreign Ministry records. As the US and Germany were the two main sources from which the USSR drew technology (each being responsible for nearly two-fifths of all technical assistance agreements signed by the USSR, as reported in 1931),[2] this selection is on the mark, although it entails a possibility that the contributions of these two countries might be overstated relative to those of others.

Concluding his massive survey, Sutton assessed that the percentage contribution of indigenous technology in Soviet economic development was: 1917–30, 0; 1930–45, 10; 1945–65, 11. He emphasized that this was the most favourable possible interpretation of his empirical findings.[3] Hence all the rest was supplied by foreign, and naturally primarily *Western*, technology. It appeared to follow that the Western contribution had been decisive.

It seems likely, however, that the major contribution in the economic development of *any* country is provided chiefly by foreign technology, as any country is only a part of the global system of technological innovation. Only the United States, and perhaps the United Kingdom in the earliest stages of her industrial revolution, might be exceptions to that rule, though even these exceptions are doubtful. As by all accounts the Russian and Soviet economy was lagging, technically, behind the most advanced countries, quite obviously it would not be one of the exceptions to any rule of global interdependence. Yet the fact that it *did* depend very heavily on foreign technology had been neglected, and by Sutton is properly stressed.

The further question then arises of what fraction of economic development may ordinarily be attributed to technological improvement. This will no doubt depend upon the country, the stage of its development, and the nature of such development. According to Denison, only 20 per cent of US growth between 1929 and 1957 can be ascribed to scientific expenditure.[4] 20 per cent, of course, is not a negligible fraction; to deliberately neglect such a substantial contribution would be reprehensible. But also it falls far short of 100 per cent.

Soviet philosophers of science rate technical progress highly, for reasons which, however, derive partly from Marxist ideology rather than from any careful comparison of the costs and benefits of innovation. Where Soviet economists have attempted to reckon the benefits of scientific expenditure, they have wound up in sharp disagreement with each other.[5] But on the whole, the intense emphasis in the USSR on the 'scientific – technical revolution' supports Sutton's assessment that technical advance did make a highly valuable contribution to Soviet development.

From his examination of particular branches of business activity Sutton found that on the whole the sectors with the highest rates of growth between 1928 and 1955 were those which had received the largest amount of technical assistance. A scatter diagram on p. 336 shows a clear correlation, which is supported by other evidence. The quantification of technical assistance is a tricky matter, and Sutton did not repeat this exercise for the most recent period. But even if confined to the middle period of Soviet economic development it is an important conclusion. In regard to the earliest period (1917–30) he found that contributions from Western technology spanned virtually the entire range of Soviet industry, and also that technological progress was the main factor in Soviet economic growth.

According to Sutton, an indigenous contribution was made in only three general areas: scaling-up (that is, the production of a similar type but larger dimensions), a small amount of indigenous innovation, and military equipment, though even in this last he identified many Western prototypes, and hypothesized that even in nuclear weaponry there had been large transfers from the West.[6]

The conventional answer to this kind of argument has been 'But look at the Soviet sputnik!' Launched on 4 October 1957, this certainly proved that the Soviet Union was not behindhand in all aspects of science or technology, but then no knowledgeable person had ever claimed that she was. Similarly, this and subsequent space spectaculars did not prove that the USSR was abreast of Western science and technology in all respects. Technology (understood here as how components of things are made) is very detailed and rather specific to particular branches of manufacture. It has to be combined with at least a modicum of science (general theoretical principles) as well as with design (the choice and arrangement of components, to make up a particular final product) before anything of value can be produced.[7] Historically, Soviet science has been ahead of Soviet technology (the large-scale reliance on foreign technology reflected this), while design in the USSR until rather recently was focused upon items of military equipment and in certain branches of the fine arts. Evidently in the case of the sputnik a workable combination of science, technology and design had been achieved, but it by no means followed that the same had at once to be concluded about every other field of material creativity.

Apart from this general consideration, the Soviet Union is untypical of modern societies owing to the nature and degree of its secretiveness. Knowledge which in a Western society would pass more freely between the military and non-military spheres in the Soviet Union can be confined to the military sphere while, by contrast, it cannot be confined to the non-military one. This brings about a different redistribution of knowledge and, in general, a higher level of expertise in branches of manufacture which are relevant to defence. This does not necessarily imply a higher level of efficiency in the defence branches, as higher quality may be purchased by higher (even possibly disproportionately higher) costs. Furthermore, the design of military items in the USSR has been aided by more continuous institutional involvement than in the case of most consumer goods (a national design organization, VNIITE, primarily advisory and propagandist, was not set up until 1962), and by the fact that the military staffs can define their design requirements more systematically and scientifically than is usually practicable for consumer goods, although VNIITE does its best to work out criteria possessing those qualities.

The primary agencies for technological advance in the USSR are research institutes, which began to be set up in the 1920s on the German model. These exist at present in great abundance, and usually entitled in abbreviation such as TsNIIChermet or NIIPlastmass. They number about 3,000, or slightly less; the exact total is no longer published. This equals about half the total number of scientific establishments; a slightly smaller proportion, if higher educational institutions are included within 'scientific establishments'. Between 1914 and 1940 the number of scientific establishments grew, but their average size in terms of numbers of scientists remained the same; contrariwise, between 1952 and 1957 the number of scientific establishments remained the same, whereas the average size of establishments increased. Between 1940 and 1952, and again between 1957 and 1965, both dimensions expanded, though the chief growth was in the number of scientists per establishment. Presumably policy decisions were taken which resulted in these shifts, though Soviet scientists to whom I mentioned them[8] were not aware of any. The post-1940 trends probably reflect three contemporary circumstances: a big increase in scientific spending which began just before the end of World War II, atomic research, and the foundation of a number of republic academies of science between 1940 and 1952. The plateau in numbers of establishments between 1952 and 1957 possibly reflected a reduced growth of spending on science between 1949 and 1957, in connection with greater emphasis on technical, rather than scientific, advance.[9]

Except during periods of enhanced ideological pressure, or in subject areas along the margin of ideological acceptance, such as at times the behavioural and biological sciences, the research institutes enjoy a permanent existence, more or less irrespective of whether or not they make any positive contribution in their particular field. It follows, of course, that they must be appropriately funded. The financing of research, that is to say, is based on the institution rather than on the programme, which brings predictable advantages and disadvantages. This is useful in that it enables institutions to budget for the future and to make gradual and systematic improvements; the other side of the coin is that programmes may be pursued which have little prospect of success or utility. The possible absence of any direct link between the client and the research organization may compound the problem. The current trend is away from financing institutions simply because they exist, but the structure of Soviet society is opposed to any radical reorganization of that nature.

Scientific and technical progress in the USSR is in principle 'planned'. Soviet philosophers of science seem to be convinced that science: should be, can be, and in the USSR is being, planned. The methodology has accumulated a large literature. It might seem at first sight that an analogy can be drawn with economic planning, but scientific plans must be very different from economic ones. Most obviously, the achievement of research results cannot be planned, for if they could be the research must have been already carried out; though of course a methodical approach to the problem of finding a solution to a particular scientific problem is likely to be helpful, and scientific planning may help to provide circumstances which are propitious to such an approach. But in any case there is a far wider spread between degrees of success or failure in scientific or technical research than in economic performance, while the measurement of results is also far more uncertain.

'Fundamental Directions of Scientific Researches in the USSR for 1959–65 in All Cycles of Knowledge' were worked out for the period of the Seven-Year Plan, but later comments suggest that this did not amount to anything like a genuine long-term scientific plan. However, technical advance continued to be emphasized. The Ninth Five-Year Plan (1971–75), for instance, defined the contemporary tasks in scientific and technical progress to be: increasing the output of progressive types of product, and bringing into the production cycle new highly productive capital goods and economical materials; complex mechanization and automation, especially through mechanization of transportation, loading – unloading and storage; introducing and extending the use of effective technological processes and equipment which saved labour or materials, making multiple use of materials and reducing losses; extending chemicalization everywhere in the economy, particularly in machine-building, agriculture and light industry; and the wide introduction of computerized management. As compared with the previous five-year plan, the attention then paid to improving quality, to reducing losses, to economizing materials as well as labour, and also to avoiding or reducing environmental pollution. These general tasks were stiffened by many other details, both in regard to specific branches and in regard to registers of performance: for instance, the number of items awarded the State Quality Standard (a certification of high quality, applying to manufactured goods) would rise from about 4,000 to about 15,000.[10]

While this attention appeared impressive, and was buttressed by other measures, such as on the intellectual front the attempt to construct a philosophy of technology, at the same time fuller access was being sought to foreign (and, of course, this meant overwhelmingly Western) science and technology. In retrospect, the invigorated quest for Western technology was one of the more important changes of emphasis in policy of the Brezhnev government. It was manifested especially in mammoth joint projects, in which Western firms would participate by supplying a large fraction of the needed equipment, such as the Togliatti (FIAT) works or a giant project to deliver Soviet natural gas to Western Europe.

The increased reliance on foreign technology since the fall of Khrushchev is also suggested by the trend of numbers of new types of 'machinery, equipment, apparatus and instruments' that have been created first in the USSR according to Soviet statistics. This trend is shown in Table 26. Until 1961–65 the trend was rising sharply, but then it fell abruptly, and has since continued to decline slowly. The sharp break in the series almost certainly implies a change of policy. Unusually, this series is not given for individual years, so its year-to-year movement cannot be traced. By contrast, *only* year-to-year series are available for innovation, though one can of course aggregate them over five-year spans. Regarding innovation, four series are given: the number of innovators and rationalizers who submitted proposals, the number of proposals submitted, the number introduced into production, and the resulting economy. (Most recently also a fifth, expenditures on innovation and rationalization.) The four main series march roughly in step; I shall focus on the numbers introduced into production. Reckoned over five-year plan periods, like the series of new types of machinery, etc., created, this shows a continuously rising trend but the rate of growth has fallen off quite markedly (Table 26); however, in 1976–77 this series was again exceeding the number of new types of machines created, for the first time since 1951–55. Relative to the trend, the number of innovations or rationalization proposals introduced into production tends to fall in the third year of the five-year plan but to rise sharply in its fourth and fifth years. In fact this series (as well as other series applying to innovation and rationalization) traces out roughly a concave cycle, which (as pointed out in Chapter 14) is characteristic of budget spending on the economy (as distinct from

Table 26

New Types of Machines, Innovation and Rationalization

	New types of machinery, equipment, apparatus and instruments created first in the USSR	Innovation and rationalization proposals introduced into production
1951–55	4345	4553
1956–60	12902	9456
1961–65	23178	13841
1966–70	21272	15645
1971–75	20006	18583
1976–77	7272	8018

Sources: *Narodnoye khozyaystvo SSSR v 1977 g.*, (1978), pp. 97–8; R. Hutchings, *Soviet Science, Technology, Design* (1976), p. 267; *Narodnoye khozyaystvo SSSR V 1975 g.* (1976), pp. 170–1.

defence). So it can probably be inferred that the innovation series is indeed concerned with *economic* activity.

The innovation and rationalization series are not broken down according to the branch of economic activity, but the series of new types of machinery, etc., is so broken down, the two main divisions being 'Machines, Equipment and Apparatuses' and 'Instruments, Means of Automation and of Computer Technology' (Table 27). The second group was becoming relatively larger up to 1961–65, but since then has fallen back slightly; this decline partly accounts for the fewer new types of machines in general created after 1961–65. This second group is not subdivided further in statistics. Within the first group, only 'electrotechnical equipment' and 'metal-cutting machine tools' rose uninterruptedly from 1961–65 to 1970–75; in most other named branches the number rose in one of the five-year periods but declined in the other, but in six branches (equipment for the fuel, transport, chemical, building, light and food industries) the decline was continuous.

Summing up at this point: during the past two decades Soviet statistics, both of numbers of new types of machinery created and of innovation, reveal a considerable loss of momentum, though the latter series has held up better than the former. (And that difference is what we would expect, as the innovation series would depend more upon dispersed initiatives, which are less amenable to high-level policy changes.) The vast majority of officially listed subdivisions, including particularly computer technology, shared in the slowdown.

Table 27

Main Divisions of Newly Created Machinery

	1951–55	1956–60	1961–65	1966–70	1971–75	1976–77
(a) Machines, Equipment and Apparatuses	3959	10576	16626	15560	15190	5418
(b) Instruments, Means of Automation, and Computer Technology	386	2326	6552	5772	4816	1854
(b)/(a) + (b) (%)	8·9	18·0	28·3	23·2	24·1	25·5

Source: *Narodnoye khozyaystvo SSSR v 1977 g.* (1978), pp. 97–8; *Narodnoye khozyaystvo SSSR v 1975 g.* (1976), p. 171.

There is now fairly general agreement on the factors in the Soviet economy and society that favour and disfavour technical progress. The factors that *favour* technical progress are: the importance attached to it in Communist ideology; the lavish funds made available to research institutions; the capability of the Soviet state to devote funds in whatever sum may be required to priority projects; the relatively high salaries and status of researchers; and the growing body of scientifically and technically qualified people. Those that *disfavour* it are: the obstructions to knowledge and originality in an environment where ideas are censored and the flow of information restricted; the heritage of scientific rather than technical advance; the absence or insufficiency of business incentives to firms that adopt innovations; the gulf between the hierarchical systems of science and of production; and the interruption to fulfilment of economic plans resulting from technological change.

Not surprisingly, which system performs best depends on the subject area. Where the flow of information across frontiers would in any case be restricted, extremely large expenditures are also demanded, and especially if the input of pure science has to be relatively large, then Soviet circumstances may, on the whole, have the advantage. Where originality and economic incentives are principally required, or a smooth transition from the research institution to the production establishment, especially if equally large resources can be allotted to research and development, then an unplanned economic and scientific system provides on the whole a more favourable environment for technical progress. This means in practice that in the great majority of technological spheres relating to economic development the Soviet system does not perform as well as an unplanned scientific and economic system.

From the angle of *economic* development, that is to say, the Russians would generally do better to rely on technological imports, while reserving their own efforts for spheres such as military equipment, astronomy, space research, and other areas primarily of scientific rather than economic interest.

Whether admitted or not, the implications of this state of affairs for Soviet economic development are rather uncomfortable. Traditionally, the Soviet economy has relied on extensive factors to assure its growth: more labour, more machines, more resources. Now labour is running short, the marginal product of capital investment has declined, resources are of poorer quality or less accessible. Consequently more reliance has to be placed on technical advance; yet here, important breakthroughs are not usually achieved through indigenous efforts. A heavier burden is consequently thrown back upon exports to procure the wherewithal with which to purchase foreign technology, to the extent that this cannot be acquired by other means.

Notes

1 The three volumes by Sutton cover the periods 1917–30, 1930–45, and 1940–65 respectively.
2 USSR Chamber of Commerce, *Economic Conditions in the USSR* (Moscow, 1931), p. 162.
3 Antony C. Sutton, *Western Technology and Soviet Economic Development 1945 to 1965* (1973), p. 370.
4 Edward F. Denison, *The Sources of Economic Growth in the United States and the Alternatives Before Us* (1962), p. 230.
5 Raymond Hutchings, *Soviet Science, Technology, Design* (1976), p. 55.
6 A. Sutton, *Western Technology and Soviet Economic Development 1945 to 1965* (1973), p. 247.
7 For this whole subject see Hutchings, *Soviet Science, Technology, Design* (1976).
8 During a visit to the Institute of the History of Natural Sciences and Technique of the USSR Academy of Sciences in May 1971.
9 As note 7, pp. 33–5.
10 R. Hutchings, 'Soviet Technology Policy', in J. Hardt (ed.), *Soviet Economic Prospects for the Seventies* (Joint Economic Committee, Congress of the United States, 1973), pp. 73–81.

PART V

GROWTH

19
SOURCES OF INFORMATION

One fundamental question has not been covered: how true and reliable are the sources used in building up the picture of Soviet economic development?

Personal impressions rarely if ever indicate particular aggregate quantities. One may, for instance, have an impression that living standards have risen, but one could not say from observation alone by how many per cent. A visitor obviously cannot guess at the precise amount of steel produced, let alone more abtruse statistics. Observations may cast doubt on an exaggerated claim, but if we are to say anything definite about the economy we have to rely very largely on official statistics. But can we trust them?

We cannot verify *directly* any national statistics. As a rule economists accept their national statistics without question, unless on minor points of detail or where the nature of the case precludes exactness. One may begin to approach Soviet statistics in the same spirit. There must always be a limit to the amount of verification demanded of an analyst, or he will never have time to complete his work; but the Sovietologist, unless he gives some credence to Soviet statistics, cannot even begin to do his.

Special problems do, however, arise because the Soviet authorities are particularly interested in creating a favourable impression abroad and they may, therefore, present the data in a way which they think will serve this purpose, and can muzzle critics in a way that democracies cannot. Because the Soviet government has control over all published sources of information, because it avowedly competes with the non-Communist world, one may legitimately suspect it of falsification, just as it would be legitimate to suspect data made available by any other extremely large, secretive and ambitious monopoly – one which did not fear any anti-trust laws.

In spite of this, I believe that at any rate *most* Soviet statistics are put out in good faith, and that we can accept them as true provided that – these are quite large provisos – we can fathom what they mean,

and if we are certain that we do not read more into an official statement than it literally requires. Some such view is held by most Western specialists on the Soviet economy. One may suggest the following reasons for it.
1. The truth is the simplest thing. Anything else involves more thought and preparation.
2. The motives which might prompt towards falsehood would often pull in opposite directions. Suppose, for example, that one wishes to magnify the rate of growth over a period of time. In any particular year, one would want to show a high rate of growth. But the higher rate one chooses, still higher then must the rate be in the following year. One would therefore diverge from the truth at an increasing rate, and ultimately a halt would have to be called. The rate of growth could be made to appear higher in the following year, if a *lower* growth rate wre claimed *now*. Or, a single enterprise might simulate an exaggerated production total, for the sake of the *kudos* and monetary advantage conferred by plan over fulfilment, but then it might be assessed for a larger payment of Turnover Tax and, because of the way plans are compiled, probably also be assigned a more ambitious plan for the following year.
3. Official statistics are used not only by foreign observers but first and foremost by Soviet officials. As Lenin said, 'Socialism is bookkeeping'. A socialist system must rely on statistics. This being a 'command economy', accurate statistics are indeed much more necessary for the planners of a socialist system than for the statistical agencies of a free-enterprise economy. Could there then be a double set of statistics, one false (for external consumption) and one true (for internal consumption)?[1] Surely not: even if one could not be absolutely confident that the difficulties would be excessive at any particular time, as the economy becomes more complicated the difficulties of maintaining a double set (or a *fortiori* treble or quadruple) would continuously increase. In fact, if the statistics in question are currently used in Soviet planning, these cannot be available in two different versions.

In order to suggest that this is so as a general rule, let us quote an exception to such a rule – the only one of which I have any record. The planning section of Magnitogorsk works composed two plans: one for despatch to the chief administration (*glavk*), the other to be sent to its own workshops. The two plans differed from each other 'like heaven and earth'. For instance, according to the governmental plan the blast-furnaces were to smelt 169,000 tons of iron, according to the operational plan only 140,000 tons. The works administration based itself on the one plan or on the other, according to circumstances. 'The head of the planning section comrade Perlin juggles with the plan depending on the course of production, he has turned the plan into a chart that is well adapted to accidents, stoppages and disorders.'[2] One must really doubt whether such a practice could be other than extremely exceptional, but can hardly doubt that comrade Perlin failed to survive the purge in the same year of industrial executives.

4. Some checks are possible. One may, for instance, relate statistics of food production to food consumption; the quantity of oil consumed to the number of automobiles and trucks; or the quantity of steel consumed to that of rubber. There are many possible cross-checks. True, each of these may in the last resort be derived from Soviet statistics, so that if *all* were falsified in the appropriate degree the falsity of each particular figure might not be detected. But the hypothesis that *everything* is falsified, in a consistent degree, cannot be seriously entertained. Something would come apart. In fact, Soviet statistics hang together pretty well. Where discrepancies are suspected (for example, it has sometimes appeared that the Russians had at their disposal more oil than they can easily consume) it can often be concluded that something is wrong with our method of cross-checking— or perhaps that oil is very wastefully used.

5. There is some – although not a great deal – of discussion in Soviet sources about the methodology of calculating particular figures. This shows that at any rate some Soviet statisticians are concerned about securing accurate statistics.

6. The USSR does not publish all data by any means: for instance, there are no published figures of output of gold. This would be consistent with a view that if it is intended to convey a misleading impression, the solution that is adopted is to say nothing rather than to put out information which may later be proved to be untrue. Indeed, there is a lively respect in the Soviet Union for the ability of Western economists to synthesize data.

For these reasons, Soviet statistics are likely to be *basically* correct. The reader will have noticed a less-than-perfect commitment to any claim of absolute truth or reliability. I have used adverbs like 'most', 'some', 'often'. Are there limits beyond which our credulity does not stretch, our arguments in favour of reliability do not apply, our means of verification will not serve? Unfortunately, there are. Among the reasons already cited, the most important is probably (3), that official statistics are used by the Soviet planners. It may follow, then, that statistics which are *not* used by Soviet planners are less reliable than those which are. To the extent that the above reasons may *not* hold good as regards particular categories of statistics, these are categories on which less reliance can be placed. This naturally brings one to consider whether all these reasons are applicable to *all* Soviet statistics of an economic kind. I believe they do not apply equally and that, consequently, some statistics are less reliable than others. Moreover, other kinds of information put out from Soviet sources are, as a rule, less reliable than statistical information.

Let us then run through these reasons in succession and see to what kinds of information they are, or are not, likely to apply.

1. In the mass, statistical series must surely be correct. But this would not rule out that a particular single series might be falsified, if there were strong motives for falsifying it.

2. As regards whether motives which might encourage falsehood would pull in opposite directions, here we are presuming that performance is being evaluated from two or more angles. If in particular instances there were only one angle from which performance could be evaluated, this reason would not apply.

3. Are there, on the contrary, any statistics which are *not* used by Soviet planners? I think that if any such exist, they must be found among those which are synthesized from other, more primary, statistics. (So that the planners would always go to the source rather than to the aggregate.)

4. As regards whether external checks are possible, the check, if possible at all, must ordinarily be of internal consistency. Now, the simplest relationships to check are physical ones, which are ultimately either relationships of logical dependence (e.g. that one cannot have one's cake and eat it too), or of technological dependence (such as that iron ore helps to make iron, not aluminium). Any series which *cannot* be related directly to physical relationships is more difficult to check and so is less worthy of reliance.

5. If there are discussions of methodology by Soviet economists the subject under consideration is, rarely, such a straightforward one as, for instance, the counting of tons of coal extracted. Enormous areas are in fact left untouched by discussion.

6. Even if as a rule facts which it is desired to conceal are not published, rather than falsified, one would not be justified in concluding that all that is published is true.

I conclude that if there are any Soviet statistics which are not reliable, these are in the main 'global' and synthetic ones which do not reflect directly physical quantities. A series which would best fit this specification would be total product of industry, the national income, or the gross national product, when these are valued in unspecified, not verifiable or simply wrong prices.

'Global' statistics such as these do not react directly on business-men's expectations as they do in a Western-type economy. If a Western businessman can rely on a 7 per cent increase in the GNP, he can be almost sure that demand for his product will rise, by comparison with a forecast of nil increase.[3] In the Soviet type of economy there is not the same almost automatic relation between the general level of activity and income and the demand for a particular final product, because the latter is determined not by a market but in response to particular requirements. These requirements may have to be scaled down because of a general financial stringency, but such a scaling down will be effected consciously, not 'automatically', by a market.

The national income, and similar 'global' statistics, thus seem to be the least reliable, and so need to be examined more critically than physical series. Western researchers have in fact done this. At the other extreme most physical quantities, such as production of tons of coal or statistics of sown areas, are generally regarded as accurate: for the various reasons mentioned, and particularly because Soviet planners have to work with these statistics and we cannot believe that they are keeping a double set of books. The one exception to this rule is agriculture, where food balances can be constructed, and the difference between 'biological' and 'barn' yields has been suspect – which was indeed an accusation that Khrushchev levied against Malenkov.[4]

In making this distinction between more and less reliable statistics, I am assuming that the authorities have correct information reaching them which they then decide to release or not to release (or perhaps to derive synthetic series before releasing). Do the statistical authorities know the facts or, if they are fabricating, do they know what the true figures are?

We can be fairly satisfied on this score. True, in an underdeveloped country one of the things which is typically underdeveloped is statistics, but the USSR is certainly not backward in this sense. Even before World War I the Duma had done good work in improving the collection of statistics. Grossman refers to a 'substantial statistical tradition and personnel' inherited from before the Revolution.[5] The Soviet authorities rarely find difficulties in making comparisons with 1913. However, collection of statistical information has had to be extended in order to take in sectors of the economy which were not previously included: for instance, at the start of 1930 a registration of small-scale industry was made for the first time.[6] The complexity of drawing up a statistical system that is able to satisfy the requirements of the plan and the system of material and consumption balances must also be remembered.[7]

The 1937 census of population was suppressed, but presumably because the results were unpalatable, not because they were incorrect – doubtless the total did not come up to expectations. Moreover, the results were suppressed rather than falsified. (However, since the results obtained in 1939, only two years later, were *not* suppressed the same argument against the likelihood of falsification does not apply in their case.) In April 1956 the first postwar estimate of population was released, and when the first postwar census was held in January 1959 the results showed that this estimate must have been correct to within 1 per cent of the true figure. Likewise, the 1941 restricted State Plan tallies broadly with the published version of the Plan, although there are some discrepancies which presumably derive from subsequent modification of the earlier version.[8]

Considering also the ramifications of the data-gathering agencies, which comprise not only statistical bureaux (at their head, a Central Statistical Bureau), but also hierarchical regional and partly authorites supplemented by the nationalized banks, one cannot seriously doubt that the authorities know pretty definitely what is happening, in much finer detail surely than the Australian or British governments know what goes on in their respective economies. The fundamental difference here is that 'socialist' enterprises function inside 'glass walls', in that they are not permitted to have business secrets; while the glass may sometimes seem to be frosted, often the view through is startlingly clear. During the thirties it was a common practice to publish the daily output of important factories: for instance, the Stalin motor works turned out 40 vehicles on 29 June 1932, but only 30 two days later. Western analysts have so far made very little use of this detailed information, probably because it *is* so detailed.

Something must be said on the other side: pressure from above can induce misreporting, and there is much evidence of concern that this does occur.[9] 'Any deviation from absolute accuracy and truthfulness on the part of the figure for output represents in our country a deception of the state and constitutes a crime.'[10] A 'capitalist' system, at any rate of an 'ideal' type, is certainly less well adapted for providing full information to the central government.[11] The Soviet system approximates here to a military model in that reporting is systematic and compulsory.[12]

Gaps – where the Soviet government's knowledge is not, at the relevant time, complete or quite accurate – would be most likely in (1) assortment, (2) precise timing, and (3) quality.

For: (1) an economy being such a complicated thing, it cannot be reported on in exhaustive detail in even the most bureaucratic system. Quantitites must be aggregated, standard reporting procedures adopted. In the process some details must slip through the net. In fact, Soviet factories not infrequently produce not exactly the assortment of products they are supposed to produce.

(2) An economy is a series of flows of values which leave one business unit and arrive at another, or which pass from one stage in manufacture to another stage. If, for instance, an enterprise reports completion of a certain quantity of items in advance of the date when they are actually completed, this will only be discovered if the system of reporting is so detailed as to cover the intermediate stage between

the alleged date of completion and the date of arrival of the products as reported by another unit, which ordinarily will hardly be the case.[13] In practice, we find instances where production has been 'borrowed' from a later period, though this must then be paid back by further borrowing from the period following that, and so on. As suggested by Grossman, exaggeration of final output is probably less serious than of intermediate components. However, point (2) on the previous page (among the six points which limit or militate against falsification) would set limits to this practice. Moreover, even such infringements as ascribing the output of one particular day to another particular day have sometimes been brought to light.[14]

As regards (3), the definition of quality is generally more difficult than that of quantity, which tends to leave a loophole for misreporting. Nutter pointed out that the stress on increasing the quantity of output during the Soviet period at times resulted in a deterioration in its quality.[15] In general, sub-standard output tends to be reported as full-standard.

Moreover, agricultural results are almost certainly not known as accurately as industrial.

Although much has been written about Soviet agricultural management and organization, Western observers generally gather a larger proportion of their knowledge from books and from the press, and a smaller proportion from personal acquaintance, than is the case with Soviet industry. Despite national security considerations, it is on the whole easier to visit a Soviet factory than a collective or State farm. Some farms are clearly show-places and are frequently visited, and also whole regions, like the virgin lands, receive a frequent quota of visitors; but on the whole Soviet agriculture has been little explored by Westerners. These often pass swiftly from city to city, seeing little of what lies between.

In view of the smaller importance of income tax in Soviet budget revenue, it is likely that personal incomes are less certainly known to the Soviet Ministry of Finance than, for example, British incomes are known to the Inland Revenue in the United Kingdom. If – then – one could not contest that in Britain actual personal incomes undoubtedly exceed those reported to the tax inspector, despite all practicable controls, it may well follow that on the whole the Soviet public economy *overstates* its accomplishments.

Whereas overstating has received more attention in Western studies, understating may occur in some circumstances, as indeed follows from consideration (2). This applies especially to inventories. While in the public economy understating is surely less considerable than overstating, in the private sector the case must be the reverse. As long as there was not believed to be any substantial 'second economy', it could be readily concluded that in the economy as a whole overstating occurred on a larger scale than understating. Recent work on the extent of the 'second economy' makes such a conclusion much more dubious. Certainly, the economy comprises a relatively smaller volume of public activity, and a relatively larger volume of private activity, than most official statistics suggest. The true balance is probably not known even to the Soviet authorities.

Yet, on the whole and within reasonably close limits the Soviet government knows what is going on, and to the extent that it chooses to publish this, its reports are basically and broadly true with the possible exception of synthetic, 'global' statistics. These we seem to be justified in testing more thoroughly before we accept – or reject – them. Even if we reject them, this would not imply that they would be arbitrary, but rather that the method of aggregation may have been selected in order to produce a particular impression.

The Statistical Handbooks

The selection of aggregates can be traced in the statistical annuals which, following a gap, again began to appear from 1956 onwards, though any thorough analysis is precluded by the sheer volume of data. A mixture of an overall survey and of a sampling method leads, however, to conclusions which seem at any rate plausible.[16] One of the starting-points was the lists of Soviet statistical handbooks compiled by M. C. Kaser and his successors.[17] Up to July 1979 these lists contained 1,106 handbooks. These are of several types, classifiable as follows: General, All-Union Sector, Regional General, Regional Sector, and International. My analysis relates mainly to the General category.

The annual all-category total has varied, but shows no long-term trend: apparently the publishing apparatus, once set up, has not been enlarged continuously, while the degree of coverage (after 1967) has tended to decline relative to the expanding and more complex economy. The peak publication year, especially for regional data, was in fact 1967, for which year 106 handbooks are listed – 34 more than for any other year – while measured by numbers of tables, that year's all-USSR statistical annual was the fattest ever. What was special about 1967 was almost certainly in this case that it marked the 50th anniversary of the Revolution; that business year would not otherwise have merited such headlining. Presumably owing to this extra publishing effort, no full-scale all-USSR annual appeared for 1966.

The handbooks began to reappear during Khrushchev's rule, and there are some intriguing hints at his personal commitment to improving the information flow: for instance, the 1958 all-USSR handbook contained exactly 500 more tables than the 1956 handbook (there having been no regular issue for 1957), just as if his personal instructions had been given to that effect. Again, the 1962 handbook — the last to which he could have given his imprimatur — was unusually good value in terms of what it contained, and in particular seemed to have been entrusted with a mission of rescuing from oblivion several previously unpublished series. The first handbook to appear under the Brezhnev government emerged 4–5 months later than usual.

The contents totals have on the whole been very stable; but this too does not so much signify stable *coverage* as the reverse, since industrial production has been diversified far more than agricultural. Moreover, over time Agriculture has gained ground in reporting relative to Industry, which is about the opposite of what one would have expected, if it were the sole object of the handbooks to illuminate Soviet economic performance in proportion to its successes. Indeed, whereas the 1934 handbook contained 3·63 times as many tables for Industry as for Agriculture, by 1974 that ratio had fallen to 0·78. In fact, whereas the share of Industry in the GNP has substantially risen, the proportionate space allotted to Industry in the statistical annuals has sharply fallen! The crossover point was the 1961 handbook, which for the first time gave more space to Agriculture than to Industry. The reasons are not spelled out, but could well have been connected with the sharp announced rise in that year in defence spending: that would have affected industry much more than agriculture, and it would have been understandable if the authorities had taken even more care than usual to conceal what was happening.

Apart from the smaller space now allocated to Industry, the most conspicuous change (in this case taking place after 1967) has been a sharp contraction in the space allotted to Transport and Communications. For example, while the 1967 handbook contained 95 tables in this category, the 1977 handbook had only 46. The amounts of space devoted to Capital Construction and to Finance have remained relatively small. The handbooks contain nothing whatever about military output, the only allusion to defence being the single annual budget figure.

If the subject coverage is uneven, so too is the coverage allotted to individual years. Output in years which end with a 0 or a 5 are reported much more frequently than others: in one investigated sample, over a recent period, about 2 times as frequently for years that end in 0, and 1½ times more frequently for years that end in 5, as compared with years ending in neither of those digits. This most probably has the principal aim of keeping in view output in the final year of a five-year plan, to serve as a benchmark for planners in the next plan period. Similarly, prewar figures focused especially on 1928, 1932 and 1937, which came immediately before the start of a new five-year plan, but the Seven-Year Plan does *not* seem to have been fully fledged in this respect, as output is reported for 1960 more often than for 1958. A series in a year ending in neither 0 nor 5 which is not reported at once (for instance, because no statistical annual is published the following year) stands a fair chance of never being reported: this applies to several series in particular for 1951 and 1954. For example, as remarked in Chapter 14 no total for actual defence expenditure in 1954 has ever been given.

For figures relating to earlier years which are republished again and again, the comparative frequency of years that end in 0 or 5 is still higher, but in this case the object may be simply to trace a longer-run series without an awkward volume of detail. The practice has been increasingly resorted to in the present edition of this book. When perusing series of this kind, the reader should be careful not to assume that the trend has necessarily been constant in the intermediate years.

Do gaps in a series tend to signify that performance in the missing year(s) was good or bad? If performance deteriorates, the next stage may be to stop publishing data about it. Soap is an illustration; its output declining from 1968 to 1970, the newspaper report in 1971 omitted this item. Most recently, publication of some mortality statistics has been discontinued, following an unfavourable trend in infantile mortality. Yet in one output sample, when the gap eventually came to an end, the average rate of growth during the period of interrupted reporting was found to have been not less on average than it had been before, but then the growth rate in the year immediately following the resumption of reporting *did* tend to be less. It appears possible that reporting is delayed until a favourable overall result can be reported, but that the strain of achieving that outcome then leaves less scope for futher improvement. A few traces can also be found of release of information following a standard time-span (usually ten years), but it is very unlikely that there is any general procedure for automatic declassification.

On the whole, the pattern of reporting of events in the economic scene by the official statistical handbooks betrays various extraneous influences: the handbooks supply only a partial picture and to some extent a distorted one, although they do provide very much fuller and more concrete information than was available before.

Notes

1 The converse (foreigners only told the truth) is conceivable but would not serve any apparent purpose.
2 *Industriya*, 29 March 1938, p. 3.

3 Except in very special circumstances of negative income-elasticity of demand.

4 Analysts who do not have access to all the data encounter tricky questions in the interpretation of particular physical series, for instance it may not be clear whether metres are 'linear' or 'square'. However, any such ambiguities do not impinge on aggregates such as the national income or gross industrial production, as one must presume that the official statisticians understand the categories employed.

5 G. Grossman, *Soviet Statistics of Physical Output in Industrial Commodities* (1960), p. 13.

6 N. Podgoretskiy, *Plan*, no. 7, 1934, p. 4.

7 In relation to the system of grouping industrial production into 'A' (producer goods) and 'B' (consumer goods), see A. Kurskiy, *Planovoye khozyaystvo*, no. 1, 1939, p. 51.

8 See Grossman, op. cit., p. 133.

9 E.g. *Industriya*, 8 February 1938, p. 1.

10 Zhebrak, cited in Grossman, op. cit., p. 53.

11 Cf. A. Yugov, *Review of Economics and Statistics*, November 1947, p. 244.

12 That the Soviet government knows what is going on in the Soviet economy, probably distinguishes it from the Chinese economy. It is highly unlikely that the Chinese government knows physical quantities in *its* economy with anything like the same assurance.

13 Remainders of goods despatched are not as a rule planned or 'normed', i.e. are not of a standard size. (N. Lisitsian, *Voprosy ekonomiki*, no. 4, 1950, p. 96.)

14 E.g. *Industriya*, 8 February 1938, p. 1.

15 G. Warren Nutter, *Growth of Industrial Production in the Soviet Union* (1962), pp. 64–74.

16 Subsequent paragraphs in this chapter are based on R. Hutchings, *Chronological Patterns in the Presentation of Soviet Economic Statistics* (Bundesinstitut für ostwissenschaftliche und internationale Studien, Cologne, 1982, Report No. 20–1982).

17 These have been published in *Soviet Studies* (usually the January issue) over a number of years.

20

GROWTH SERIES

If physical quantities are reported accurately while certain global or synthetic ones are not, we should be able to find a dividing line between the two, which has true figures on one side and untrue ones on the other; or the methods used to compute the two series should be mutually inconsistent. Can we find any such dividing line?

Sovietologists have sought for such a line of cleavage, and a number have claimed to find it. For instance, reported changes in physical quantities of output of various industrial products have been compared with reported changes in the value of industrial output. At first sight there seems to be a considerable discrepancy between these two series: the value series increases much faster than the other. This suggests that the value series might be exaggerated. Unluckily, in all countries the value of output rises faster than its physical volume, because increased amounts of value are built into the same volume: the 'degree of fabrication' increases. As an extreme case, this is obviously so in space exploration. This simple comparison consequently does not carry weight unless the qualification is borne in mind.

Proceeding a step further, we may compare the rate at which the 'degree of fabrication' increases in the USSR with the rate at which it increases in other industrialized or industrializing countries. This is harder to measure, but it seems to have increased faster in the USSR than in Western countries. This would afford a better basis for affirming that the Soviet value index was inflated. Yet it too is not entirely reliable, for one cannot rule out that such a result may be characteristic of a country at precisely that stage of development, especially considering that Soviet development has emphasized technical progress and diversification of output.

Or one might compare the reported growth of industrial output with that of the transport turnover. The late Naum Jasny pointed out that if 1928=100 in each case, in 1956 gross industrial production had risen to 2,288 and freight transports ('5 carriers') to 1,092. In his view, it was obvious that gross industrial production could not have increased between 1928 and 1956 more than twice as much as freight transport.[1] However, 'gross industrial production' was reported in value terms but transport in 'billions of tariff ton-kilometres', i.e. tons carried multiplied by the average distance travelled. The *value* of industrial production increased twice as rapidly as the freight *turnover*. But taking into account a possible rise in the 'degree of fabrication', there is no compelling reason why it should not have.

Jasny was claiming to refute one official index (gross industrial production) by reference to another (freight turnover). This implied two assumptions: that at least one of the official indices was trustworthy, and also that the less imposing quantity was more worthy of credence than the more inposing one. One might question either assumption. Grossman points out that output and freight statistics might both be overstated.[2] Subsequently, Jasny disclaimed that it was possible to estimate what growth of national income would correspond to a given growth in transport of freight.[3]

Another statistic quoted by Jasny is that in one year (1948) real wages more than doubled. He suggested that the actual increase was unlikely to have exceeded 15 per cent.[4] However, to adopt the nearest parallel that comes to mind: the rise in apparent living standards in Western Germany during the three-year period 1948 to 1951 was quite remarkable. According to official statistics the real wages of industrial workers in Germany rose by 80 per cent between 1948 and 1953, which seems not unreasonable. According to Western observers who were in Russia in 1949, living standards rose very noticeably at that time. The Soviet statistical *handbooks* do not claim that real wages doubled in 1948. Indeed, until 1964 they provided no statistics of real wages at all (this was one of the blank spots in Soviet statistics). Total retail sales deflated by changes in the retail price level and measured in unchanged prices rose in 1948 by about 13 per cent.[5] A rise in real wages not exceeding 15 per cent would seem to have been a very accurate estimate by Jasny. At any rate, the Soviet claim is not being repeated.

What Jasny here was treating as a statistic was possibly more in the nature of a commentary of declaration. Adjectives such as 'overwhelmingly', 'vast', 'mass' etc. are intended to sway the reader without giving him anything precise enought to strike back with. Such claims are rather easy to recognize – in our own society we see their counterparts every day on advertising hoardings – and one is justified in very largely disregarding them. A list of misleading practices would include: publication of selected data only, the selection being made in order to produce a certain impression; absence of definitions of the precise meanings of statistics or how they are derived; the use of indexes and percentage increases instead of absolute figures; unannounced changes in the content of plans; and unannounced changes in definition.[6] In short, the inquisitive analyst must pay attention to the mode of presentation, and not neglect nuances of description of statistical categories.

Although not all apparent clashes in Soviet statistics turn out to be incontrovertible discrepancies, some discrepancies can be found and certain of these are examined further in Chapter 21. In the meantime, one can distinguish various reasons why the methodologies employed in calculating synthetic totals should have led to results which appear to conflict with the physical totals.

Several sources of exaggeration of the official index can be distinguished.

1. Total industrial output has been computed (until October 1965) by summation of the value of output of each industrial enterprise: this is defined as gross industrial output (*valovaya produktsiya*).[7] This is what each enterprise produces without deducting the values supplied to it in the form of raw materials, semi-fabricates etc. by other enterprises. If these values are deducted, one obtains net product (*chistaya produktsiya*).[8] Net product is not calculated for individual Soviet enterprises but only for branches of the economy and the economy as a whole, at which point the summation of net products becomes synonymous with the national income (*natsionalnyy dokhod* or *narodnyy dokhod*)[9] according to the Soviet definition. The national income. Soviet definition, is often referred to in the West as Net Material Product, because it does not include 'non-productive services'; although the equation is not exact as some services *are* included in the Soviet concept.[10]

Gross output will evidently exceed net output (or net product). Exact or full data concerning the relationship between these two have not been published. Making various assumptions, one would conclude that in 1940 the gross output of Soviet industry was at least double its net output. Presumably in other years the ratio would be comparable. Western countries generally measure *net* industrial output. Can the rate of change of Soviet gross output be compared with the rate of change of Western net output? This reduces to: how has Soviet gross output changed relatively to Soviet net output? The evidence is very scanty. Figures are available covering the years 1928/29 and 1929/30. Between these years gross output as a percentage of the GNP increased slightly faster than did net output as a percentage of the national income[11] (by 8·8 per cent as compared with 6·6 per cent). There are no other similar statistics.

At a seminar I attended in 1960 a Soviet economist stated that between 1953 and 1959 Soviet gross industrial output had risen by 87 per cent, while the value added had risen by 70 per cent. He appeared to be drawing a distinction between the rate of increase of gross output and that of net output. The ratio of the percentage rise in the one to the percentage rise in the other would have been in this case about 5 : 4 while in 1928/29 to 1929/30 it had been 4 : 3, which seems a close enough similarity.

The ratio of gross output to net output can be affected by industrial reorganization. Vertical disintegration would raise gross output relative to net while vertical integration would have the reverse effect. Has either of these trends occurred, or has one occurred to a greater extent than the other? As noted in Part III above, new plants were built during the First Five-Year Plan on a basis of specialization, as an innovation. This would imply vertical disintegration, and so would raise gross output relative to net. Many hold that this result did occur, and that a tendency towards splits outweighed any tendency towards mergers.[12] This was probably so, although if the higher levels of authority favoured specialization, it is equally true that the lower levels have offered resistance to this.[13] Soviet plants are not in fact highly specialized, although in certain branches – such as automobilies, tractors, or the electrical industry – the trend has been towards vertical disintegration. I would find it hard to agree that a Soviet minister would prevent a merger in order not to have to report a reduction in gross output.[14] The system of reckoning success and failure is surely less guillible than that. In general, however, reporting units would try to make a good showing especially in terms of gross output, rather than net output.

The reaction of industrial structure on gross product is recognized by Soviet economists. For instance, Sperlina noted that under the existing system of reckoning gross factory output of individual enterprises there must be double counting, the dimensions of which would depend on the structure of industry.[15] Against this, Sukharevskiy mentioned offsetting factors and concluded that it was unlikely that actual production would be underestimated during certain years of the Second Five-Year Plan – as Sperlina had suggested.[16] In one quoted example organizational changes affected gross production only to the extent of 0·5 per cent per year, yet according to Rotshteyn the question had substantial importance.[17] Soviet economists are thus not agreed as regards the scale of the effect.

Any given level of gross output does not, of course, reflect the extent to which output consists of assembly rather than the manu-facture of components. Rotshteyn pointed out that a comparison drawn up solely in terms of the gross output of the Soviet and Tsarist electrical industries would, for this reason, understate the true increase. However, the reverse was the case in heavy industry.[18]

This factor has probably been exerted in different directions at different periods. During the Second World War plants had to become more self-sufficient. In many plants belonging to defence industry semi-manufactured goods purchased by them, as compared with their total expenditures, fell by 20–30 per cent between 1940 and 1943.[19] A record of gross output during this period would consequently understate the actual accomplishment as compared with before the war. On the whole, then, Soviet gross industrial output appears to have increased faster than net.

2. A second source of distortion is changes in the prices in which output is reckoned. Gross output is reckoned either in current or in unchanged prices. Time-series are always stated to be in unchanged prices. If this were really so, or there were nothing more to say on the matter, one could not object to this procedure. However, the very process of industrialization precluded a strict use of 'unchanged prices', for the following reasons.

Industrialization includes the initiation of the production of new articles, which by definition were not being produced before, so that no internal prices will apply to them. This was especially true of Soviet industrialization, in which the engineering branches were emphasized, since here new products were especially important. Whole new branches were created, and thousands of new items began to be turned out. What prices were assigned to these?

In practice, the longer the time that had elapsed since 1926/27 the more rarely one encountered prices which genuinely dated from that year. Very often a portion of production was valued at new current prices, or at prices of the preceding year — relatively rarely, in prices of three or four years earlier. 'Temporary' or 'conventional' prices gradually became permanent and unconditional, as if they had been genuine 'unchanged prices'.[20]

Furthermore, industrialization took place during a period when prices were rising. The extent of this rise is not indicated fully by Soviet sources, but it would be obscured by subsidies. Wholesale prices of output of the light and food industries, for example, rose sharply in the early 1930s.[21] According to Jasny, the general level of prices of all industrial goods on a tax-free basis was slightly below the 1926/27 level in 1930, 2½–3 times the 1926/27 level in 1937, and had risen to about 3½ times the 1926/27 level by 1940.[22] Prices of producers' goods continued to rise, according to Jasny, between 1940 and 1949. If this is correct the working-in of current prices must have introduced an inflationary bias. Increased labour productivity, resulting in lower labour expenditures,[23] and increased subsidies may have held down costs of production despite general price increases, but such factors if the take effect *after* fixed prices have been assigned to items would not affect their values. Furthermore, industrial costs were forced up by wage inflation, as money wages tended to rise faster than labour productivity.

The 1926/27 prices were used for calculating Soviet gross industrial output until 1949. Thence, until 1951, output was planned in current wholesale prices. For the period 1952–55 wholesale prices of January 1952 were to be used.[24] For the Sixth Five-Year Plan, prices of 1 July 1955 were used. But output in earlier years was apparently not recalculated, so that gross output is probably inflated by different degrees over different periods. The general view, subscribed to by Bergson among others, is that the degree of inflation was largest in the earlier period, when structural changes were most considerable.

A further reason for non-comparability derives from the choice of the base year of the 'unchanged' prices in which output is calculated. Industrialization changes relative scarcities. Industrial goods altogether become less scarce in relation to agricultural goods or to services, while certain industrial goods become less scarce in relation to others. If relative prices change inversely with relative scarcities – i.e. items which are dearest at the beginning will be those which experience the largest relative rise in their production – the earlier base date will lead to the higher percentage rise in total output whenever the price of the item, the output of which has increased the more, has risen by relatively the smaller proportion (or has fallen by relatively the larger proportion).

This principle is relevant to Soviet output series in that the base date chosen for 'unchanged' prices was 1926/27. If 'unchanged' prices of some date subsequent to 1926/27 had been used there would have been shown a proportionately smaller rate of growth. It is relevant too as although all prices rose in the Soviet Union during industrialization,[25] prices of industrial producer goods rose less rapidly than prices of industrial consumer goods (this was a matter of deliberate policy) while the output of industrial producer goods did of course rise more rapidly than that of industrial consumer goods. The assortment of items produced by industry was very complicated, but this complication would not affect the result if *in general* the prices of items, the output of which rose relatively the more in physical terms over the period, rose by relatively the smaller proportion. And this was certainly the case. Of course, a given base year can realistically be chosen only after that year has passed, and in any event the choice of an earlier date is not incorrect.

There are therefore good grounds for concluding that the rate of growth of Soviet industrial gross output reckoned in value terms exceeded what would have been recorded had net production been measured in unchanged prices relating to a later base-date. This is accepted generally by Western students of the subject and evidently by many Soviet economists, though naturally these latter are especially concerned that one should not fly to the other extreme of understating the growth rate. The abandonment since October 1965 of the gross output index provides further confirmation of the existence of a built-in bias.

As regards the *degree* of exaggeration, these general considerations would hardly allow one even to guess at it. One must first resort to the more time-consuming process of recalculation, using any available statistical material.

Several alternative series of Soviet industrial output have been constructed outside the USSR. One should mention in particular the estimates made by Jasny,[26] Nutter,[27] Hodgman[28] and Bergson.[29] All these sharply deflate the official claims, Nutter and Jasny in particular, but only Nutter's and Bergson's have been carried even as far as 1955. What these investigators are attempting is not quite the same thing as to discover whether the Soviet index is inflated in terms of other Soviet series, but they apparently would conclude that this is the case. Jasny, for instance, in the argument referred to earlier, concluded that between 1928 and 1956 Soviet industrial output has risen 8-fold but transport 11-fold. (The official index of increase in industrial output over this period is 21-fold.)

The latest estimate, by A. Bergson, concluded that earlier studies (including his own) had overstated any exaggeration in Soviet statistics.[30] He concluded that the extent of inflation was not as great as Jasny had believed. His own results were, nevertheless, markedly below the official index of growth of national income, the discrepancy being largest over the earlier period (1928–1937).[31] It is impossible to say what the correct series would be, but I would suggest that the following considerations should be borne in mind if one has to choose between the various official and unofficial series.

1. All series except the official one are based on incomplete data. As all Soviet statistics, including some vitally important ones (for example of armaments production) are not published, this cannot be helped, but it inevitably impairs the reliability of any series constructed by an outsider. Armaments may be an important exception to the more usual rule that published figures concentrate on the faster-growing sectors of the economy. Security considerations dominate here and all physical output series are secret at least until long after the event, but it has been stated that total defence industrial output rose by 286 per cent between 1933 and 1938 whereas total industrial output rose during the same period by only 120 per cent.[32] Anyone who was at that time relying on published indices of physical output might consequently have been led astray by the absence of current data on arms manufacture, in the direction of understatement of total industrial growth. (This shows that it should not always be assumed that the

lower of two available and apparently conflicting series is the more correct one.) The Soviet military effort in World War II, and subsequently, indicates that defence expenditures have been very large (see Chapter 14). On the other hand, one cannot explain the expansion of the economy if too great dimensions are ascribed to defence spending, for as this does not constitute investment[33] it cannot promote further expansion.

2. All outside computations are based on less than complete knowledge of the statistical categories employed. By astute means some investigators may well have achieved much more than the censors expected, yet one cannot feel confident that all the mysteries have been fully probed.

3. Although precision is unattainable, it is significant that all except one[34] Western estimates have arrived at lower rates of growth than is asserted by official Soviet statistics.

4. Given the uncertainties inevitably involved in recalculation one should on the whole prefer estimates which do not involve the most enormous reductions of the official claims, for if like Nutter one cuts down the official index by something like two-thirds it is hard to avoid a suspicion that wishful thinking is creeping in.

5. On the other hand, one should reject any estimate which claims more for the Soviet system than the Russians do themselves, because it is not in the nature of this society to underpraise itself.

6. The trickiness of international comparisons has to be remembered. A comparison even of two countries requires twice as much knowledge as characterizing one country by itself; and in practice individuals specialize on one country rather than on two or more than two. According to Wiles, a misunderstanding of the US concept of 'value-added' explains the unusually sharp deflation of Soviet claims by G. Warren Nutter.[35]

7. The outside estimates themselves differ. Hence they cannot all be right; while even if one of them is right, all the others must be wrong.[36]

Finally, one should emphasize that all series concur that the Soviet national income, and in particular Soviet industrial output, have grown enormously over the period of about 40 years to which such estimates relate.

Notes

1 N. Jasny, *Soviet Survey*, no. 26 (October–December 1958), reprinted in Alex Inkeles and Kent Geiger, *Soviet Society, A Book of Readings* (1961), p. 305.
2 Op. cit., p. 112.

3 N. Jasny, *Soviet Studies*, July 1963 (vol. XV, no. 1), p. 41.
4 N. Jasny, *Essays on the Soviet Economy* (1962), pp. 276–8.
5 33080/100 and 31023/83: *Narodnoye khozyaystvo SSSR v 1959 g.*, p. 681, and *Narodnoye khozyaystvo SSSR v 1956 godu* (1957), p. 233.
6 See G. Grossman, op. cit., pp. 108–11, 117.
7 A definition is in G. A. Kozlov and S. P. Pervushin (eds.), *Kratkiy ekonomicheskiy slovar'* (1958), p. 31.
8 Ibid., p. 377.
9 I assume here that these two titles are synonymous, but one cannot be quite sure of this. Cf. G. Grossman, op. cit., p. 118, footnote 19.
10 See A. Nove, *The Soviet Economy*, Revised Second Edition (Third Impression) (1965), p. 267.
11 E. Lokshin, *Tyazhelaya industriya v 3 godu pyatiletki* (1932), pp. 7–8; S. V. Minayev (ed.), *Osnovnyye momenty rekonstruksii proymyshlennosti SSSR* (1931), p. 5.
12 R. W. Campbell, *Soviet Economic Power* (1960), p. 38.
13 This is illustrated in my thesis, op. cit., pp. 137–8, 141.
14 R. W. Campbell, op. cit., pp. 38–9.
15 A. Sperlina, *Plan*, no. 2, 1934, p. 40.
16 B. Sukharevskiy, *Plan*, no. 6, 1934, pp. 19–20.
17 A. I. Rotshteyn, *Problemy promyshlennoy statistiki SSSR, tom I* (1936), p. 290.
18 Ibid., pp. 324–5.
19 Sh. Ya. Turetskiy, *Vnutripromyshlennoye nakopleniye v SSSR* (1948), p. 110.
20 A. I. Rotshteyn, *Problemy promyshlennoy statistiki SSSR, tom I* (1936), p. 246, and *Industriya*, 6 July 1938, p. 2.
21 A. N. Malafeyev, *Istoriya tsenoobrazovaniya v SSSR* (1964), p. 161.
22 N. Jasny, *Soviet Prices of Producers' Goods* (1952), p. 15.
23 Costs declined substantially as a factory gained experience; for instance, measured in man-hours the costs of producing a tractor at the Stalingrad works declined from 1,023 in 1930 to 154 in 1934 (S. G. Strumilin, *Planovoye khozyaystvo*, no. 11, 1936, p. 60).
24 G. Drampyan, N. Fedotov, *Planovoye khozyaystvo*, no. 1, 1952, pp. 76–7.
25 However, between 1928 and 1932 transfer prices in heavy industry were lowered by 3 per cent (Ya. A. Kronrod, *Izvestiya akademii nauk*, no. 5, 1951, pp. 354–5).
26 Naum Jasny, *The Soviet Economy During the Plan Era* (1951).
27 G. Warren Nutter, *Growth of Industrial Production in the Soviet Union* (1962).
28 Donald R. Hodgman, *Soviet Industrial Production 1928–1951* (1954). A number of indices including Hodgman's are tabulated in R. W. Campbell, *Soviet Economic Power* (1960), p. 48.
29 A. Bergson, *The Real National Income of Soviet Russia Since 1928* (1961).

30 Op. cit., p. 182.
31 Ibid., Table 43 (p. 180).
32 *Sotsialisticheskoye narodnoye khozyaystvo SSSR v 1933–40 gg.* (1963), p. 610.
33 Except, perhaps, in a small degree: for instance, the inculcation of skills which will later be usable in civilian life.
34 This sole exception is R. W. Campbell and A. Tarn, *American Economic Review*, September 1962 (vol. LII, no. 4).
35 P. Wiles in A. Nove and J. Degras (eds.), *Soviet Planning* (1964), especially pp. 103 and 108.
36 The appreciation in this chapter of the reliability of outside computations of growth should be compared with that of F. Seton in *Soviet Studies*, October 1960. Cf. also P. Wiles, *The Political Economy of Socialism* (1964), pp. 226–8 and 234–6.

21
ALTERNATIVE APPROACHES TO CALCULATION OF GROWTH

I have mentioned theoretical weaknesses of the official index, also some shortcomings of Western estimates, and contrasted the various results. Can any other approaches be tried? At least four are worthy of notice: (a) whether claimed increases from year to year conform to what we know about conditions in those particular years; (b) whether the share of industry in the national income increases as we would expect; (c) the productivity approach – whether available factors of production could have brought about the claimed increases; and (d) the consumption approach – whether the quantity of output that was allegedly produced was in fact consumed. Each of these approaches sheds some light also on general questions of Soviet development, so each is worth considering at some length.

A. The Individual Year Approach

The percentage increases in industrial gross output claimed from year to year are shown in Diagram III. The period since 1921 can be divided into quite well-marked sub-periods: I. 1921–27: Violent, explosive alternations (NEP). II. 1928–37: First and Second Five-Year Plans. The rate of growth tends to rise towards the mid-point, or slightly later, of each Five-Year Plan, then to decline again. This is also roughly true of the Fourth Five-Year Plan (1946–50). III. Curtailed plans: the Third (1938–June 1941) and the Sixth (January 1956–September 1957 approximately). Rather low growth rates, and no clear trend. IV. Approximately from 1952 onwards: gradually, fairly regularly and very persistently falling rates of growth. V. World War II: Scanty information. Output declined at first, then rose, then declined again.

Are these sequences plausible?

I. Under NEP total industrial output was small, so large percentage fluctuations from year to year would not represent huge absolute differences. Harvest fluctuations had an important impact, as had the monetary reform of 1924, and administrative problems (e.g. price-

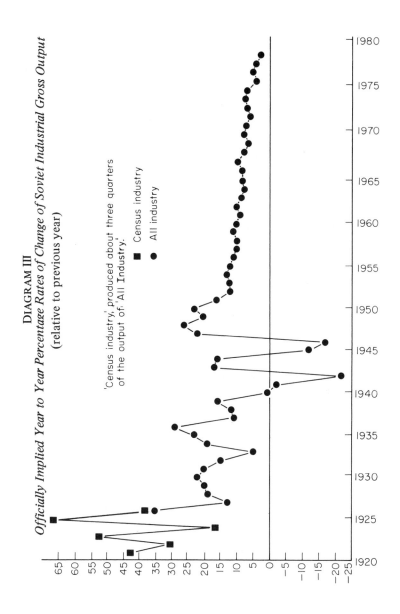

DIAGRAM III

Officially Implied Year to Year Percentage Rates of Change of Soviet Industrial Gross Output

(relative to previous year)

'Census industry', produced about three quarters
of the output of 'All Industry'.

■ Census industry

● All industry

setting: the scissors crisis), and their solution. In good years growth could be very fast, owing to the relative cheapness and ease of starting up already existing equipment, once the prerequisites of a stable currency and of available transport, raw materials and labour were assured. Substantial assistance was derived from the introduction of improved techniques under the aegis of foreign firms, although such assistance does not help to account for the sharp variations in growth rates from year to year during this period.

II. In contrast, the sequence of annual output growth rates in the First, Second and Fourth Five-Year Plans clearly shows that some other pattern was then dominant. From 1928 onwards there is imposed a periodicity of the same duration as the long-term plans. Although events, such as the perceived Japanese threat in 1931, which cannot be built into any purely industrial or even economic model must have contributed to this result, another important reason seems to have been the bunching of construction commencements towards the middle of the plan and consequent bunching of their completions after three to four years. Further periods of about the same length were then required to gain sufficient mastery of newly installed equipment to operate it efficiently.

The bunching of construction commencements towards the middle of the plan period can possibly be explained in the following way. Since capital grants are made from the budget in a non-returnable and interest-free form, investing authorities try to secure the largest grants that they can. Because of linkages in demand and supply relationships, but above all because output and investment changes are signalled, in advance of their actually occurring, through the planning system, the competitive bids of investing authorities have an accelerating effect. The volume of investment rises, up to the point when the economy can no longer sustain a further increase in effort, when a break occurs and the rates of investment and output growth both decline suddenly. Since investment projects are included within nationwide long-term plans of a finite length, this breaking-point tends to occur at the end of the long-term (in this case five-yearly) plan, after which the sequence will begin afresh (perhaps after a pause dictated by the necessities of recuperation, or by coping with a backlog of unfinished projects).[1]

III. Rather low rates of growth during the curtailed plans may be ascribed to purges and rearmament (in respect of the Third) and (in respect of the Sixth) to malproportions in planning, organizational changes, and perhaps an excessive effort in 1955.

IV. Gradually falling rates of growth from 1952 onwards. This firmly established trend is also aligned with the long-run tendency throughout the Soviet period. It was probably compounded in the Fifth Plan by rearmament and perhaps by the change in the base-date of 'unchanged' prices, and in the Seven-Year Plan probably again by increased defence expenditures and by a big rise in spending on space research.

V. Wartime performance illustrates the impact of the war, the resilience of Soviet industry in extreme conditions, and the speed of conversion both to and from a military footing.

The long-term tendency has been for rates of growth to decline and for the slope to become irreversible. This seems a plausible result, since as total output rises a given percentage rise corresponds to a larger increment in absolute terms; there are no longer available such large reserves of labour power to man the factories; and in a larger and more complex economy organizational problems loom larger.

It is noteworthy that there was a marked tendency for the percentage of fulfilment of output and investment plans to fluctuate in a cyclical manner during the First and Second Plans, as shown in Diagram IV.

Since about 1950 there appear to be growth cycles of about three years' duration, and this is confirmed by more detailed analysis.[2] Soviet industrial output also varies markedly from quarter to quarter, in many branches being above trend in the final quarter of the year (partly as a result of 'storming', and partly for other reasons), although the complete pattern of quarterly output variations is very much more complicated and varied. While between 1958–59 and 1967–68 or 1969–70 (according to the series studied) the seasonality of industrial output in general was declining, it rose again up to 1974–75 (the date up to which calculations have been carried). The preponderance of the second half of the year in annual output has been greatly reduced, and since 1970 annual growth has come to depend chiefly on the increase in the *first* half of a calendar year relative to the preceding half-year. Soviet foreign trade too is variable according to the plan timetable, with imports showing some tendency to be bunched in the final years of a five-year plan.[3] As noted already (see Chapter 17) there has been a particularly marked cycle in Soviet arms exports to the Third World.

Although the presence of such cycles had not been predicted, on reflection they appear quite consistent with the structure of the economic system and with other known features of its behaviour, such as the propensity to request excessive capital investments when a new long-term plan is being compiled. There are certainly no grounds to imagine that such cycles are a purely statistical phenomenon, or have been deliberately fabricated.

The analysis suggests at least a plausible pattern of growth from year to year. In certain years the claimed rises have indeed been very large, for example 29 per cent in 1936 and 26 per cent in 1948. Yet certain types of output measured in physical terms also increased sharply in 1936: electric power by 25 per cent, coal by 16 per cent, steel by 30 per cent. Over the period 1934–36 Hodgman's index shows

DIAGRAM IV

*Percentage Fulfilment of Plans of Industrial Output
and of Capital Investments in Planned Industry*

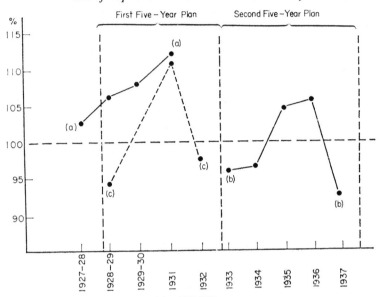

(a) Output of industry planned by VSNKh.
(b) Output of all industry.
(c) Capital investments in planned industry.

a rise of 79 per cent, almost up to the officially claimed 88 per cent, while even Jasny granted that the official index involved a relatively small exaggeration in those years.[4] As regards 1948, this followed a monetary reform in December 1947, due to which production is claimed to have shot ahead. Jasny in this case suggested the same rate of growth as the official index.[5]

B. The National Income Approach

The national income measures added values in agriculture, industry, construction, communications, trade, and communal feeding.[6] If industrial output is gross while the national income is net, and gross industrial output as a proportion of the GNP is rising faster than net industrial output is rising as a proportion of the national income, we should be able to derive from the relationship of these two series a measure of the exaggeration inherent in the use of gross industrial output as opposed to net. However, the Russians have also realized this and provide only very scanty and inadequate information. The main part of what we have is shown in Table 28.

Evidently if after 1940 industrial output had continued to be measured in 'unchanged prices' its proportion of the GNP would have reached 90 per cent or more after another 10–15 years. This result would obviously have been absurd, so that it is not surprising that this series was discontinued. From 1958 onwards shares are available measured in *current* prices, which obviously makes a large difference. The realm of fantasy entered in the nineteen-thirties has been abandoned and our feet are touching ground again. In 1937 the share of agriculture had been 14·9 thousand million roubles out of a total of 96·3 thousand million roubles, i.e. 15½ per cent. Agriculture's share was understated because double counting had not become more important in agriculture whereas it probably had in industry, and for other reasons already mentioned.

Table 28

Share of Industry in Total Product in Certain Years (Percentages)

Years	Net	Gross	% Net/Gross
	(unchanged prices)		
1928/29	34·8	48·7	71·5
1929	–	54·5†	
1929/30	37·1	53·0	70·0
1932	45·3	70·7	64·1
1934	50·0	–	
1935 (preliminary)	52·1	–	
1937	59*	–	
1940	62·7	85·6†	73·2
	(current prices)		
1958	50·2	59·3§	84·7
1960	52·3‖	62·2‖	83·7
1962	52·2‡	63·2‡	82·6
1965	51·7‖	63·3‖	81·7
1967	51·4‖	63·9‖	80·4

* Estimated.
† K. A. Petrosyan, *Sovetskiy metod industrializatsii* (1951), pp. 232–3.
‡ *Narodnoye khozyaystvo SSSR v 1962 g.* (1963), pp. 482 and 64.
§ *Narodnoye khozyaystvo SSSR v 1964 g.* (1965), pp. 577 and 67.
‖ *Narodnoye khozyaystvo SSSR v 1967 g.* (1968), pp. 672 and 60.

In current prices, therefore, more than three-fifths of the gross national product is contributed by industry. The shares contributed by the various sectors of the economy in certain years have been the following:[7]

Table 29

Shares Contributed to Gross National Product

	1960	1965	1967
Industry	62·2	63·3	63·9
Construction	10·5	9·5	10·0
Agriculture	16·1	16·9	16·1
Transport and Communications	4·3	4·3	4·2
Trade, Procurements, Material-Technical Supply and Others	6·9	6·0	5·8

As regards shares of the *national income*, here slightly more than half is contributed by industry. Proportions for the same years are the following:[8]

Table 30

Shares Contributed to National Income

	1960	1965	1967
Industry	52·3	51·7	51·4
Construction	10·0	9·2	9·4
Agriculture	20·5	22·5	22·4
Transport and Communications	5·3	5·7	5·9
Trade, Procurements, Material-Technical Supply and Others	11·9	10·7	10·8

As the tables show, the proportions of the national income differ from those of the gross national product mainly in respect of Agriculture and of 'Trade, Procurements, Material-Technical Supply and Others', while Construction is the least affected. It is interesting to note that Industry's share in the gross national product was increasing, but in the national income was declining.

The national income has grown much more slowly than industrial output, owing to the slower rise of net than of gross production and the much less rapid growth of agriculture, and to some extent of other branches comprising the residue of the national income, than of industry. The official claim remains extreme, however. The claim is – for example – that between 1913 and 1960 the national income rose by 26·74 times (as compared with a claimed rise in industrial gross production of over 45 times).[9] Between 1913 and 1967 it rose by 37·36 times![10] Increases of these enormous magnitudes over the periods stated are unacceptable.

The output of materials by itself has grown faster than that of materials *plus* non-productive services. If Western totals are adjusted to make them comparable with the Soviet one this difference must be taken into account. However, such adjustments do not nearly close the gap, or make the Russian figure plausible. For example, if the Soviet report of growth is correct and if income per head in Britain in 1956 was twice as large as in Russia in the same year, which must be about right, the national income per head in Russia in 1913 must have been one-sixteenth of the then British figure; in fact, the difference cannot possibly have been so large. A country today where the current GNP per head was one-sixteenth of the British figure would be Haiti or Paraguay, and Russia was certainly not in the same position in relation to Britain in 1913 as Haiti or Paraguay are today.[11]

Rather less work in independent calculation of the Soviet national income has been performed than in independent calculation of Soviet industrial production. To recalculate the latter by itself is very laborious. To do the same for national income is not only a considerably larger task but one that runs into additional methodological difficulties, such as in regard to the valuation of peasant output that is consumed on farms and so never bears transport charges nor reaches a retail market. In practice, the Soviet national income has been recalculated outside the USSR only for particular years.

According to Bergson's most recent estimates,[12] the Soviet national income rose by 3¼ times between 1928 and 1955, a substantial rise but falling very far short of the official nearly 15 times, the extent of exaggeration having been much smaller in the later than in the earlier period. An increase of 3¼ times between 1928 and 1955 would correspond to one of about 5 times between 1928 and 1960, if one adopts the officially claimed increases between 1955 and 1960. In his article mentioned earlier, Jasny noted that an increase of only 80 per cent in farm output between 1928 and 1960 in conjunction with a decline in the share of net farm output in the national income from 55 per cent in 1928 to 20·9 per cent in 1960 (both at 1960 prices) would correspond to approximately a fivefold increase in the national income between 1928 and 1960.[13] This expressed succinctly what had been written about by Jasny, as well as by others, at much greater length.

C. The Productivity Approach

(i) Labour productivity

Soviet statistics claim certain rates of increase of the labour force employed in industry and other branches. Cited increases in the labour force in the whole 'national economy', and within this category in *industry*, are as follows:[14]

Table 31

Labour Force in National Economy and Industry
(millions: average yearly totals)

	1928	1940	1955	1960	1962
Whole national economy	10·8	31·2	48·4	62·0	68·3
Industry only	3·8	11·0	17·4	22·3	24·3

It is noteworthy that between 1928 and 1962 the proportionate increase in the industrial labour force (6·4 times) was just about the same as the proportionate increase in the labour force in the whole national economy (6·3 times). Apparently, a more rapid rise in industrial than in non-industrial labour productivity, together with a probably more substantial advance of the 'socialist sector' into non-industrial than into industrial areas, just about matched the rise in the contribution of industry to the GNP.

The industrial labour force ('industrial productive personnel') thus increased by 6·4 times between 1928 and 1962 (or by 6·8 times between 1928 and 1964). Productivity is claimed to have risen between 1928 and 1962 by as much as 10·2 times. Total output should apparently have risen by 6·4 x 10·2 = 65·2 times, whereas the reported rise in gross output is only 36·5 times. A possible partial explanation for the apparent discrepancy is that the industrial labour force is inflated by inclusion of other categories; probably, too, the productivity of 'industrial-productive personnel' rose faster than that of all industrial workers. The productivity increase seems to be exaggerated by a factor of about 1·8. What is more, the index refers to man-year, and the rise per man-hour would be greater as working hours have fallen, which makes the claimed increase even harder to accept. (Hodgman estimates a 3·2 per cent annual rise in the productivity of labour in large-scale industry over the period 1928–50 compared with the officially claimed 7·0 per cent.[15])

According to Soviet data, the proportionate rise in industrial labour productivity in the USSR since 1940 had been about the same as in the

USA since 1913 (nearly three times in each case). While productivity in Soviet industry was claimed to have risen by 10·2 times between 1928 and 1962, US productivity was supposed to have little more than doubled in the same period.

Galenson[16] found that increases in productivity and in investment in particular industries were correlated. A number of specialist delegations have investigated Soviet productivity in particular industries and it is clear that very large advances have been made especially in heavy industry (where the biggest differences are technically possible). The gains recorded in construction and transport have been substantially smaller than in industry, though still considerable. Between 1928 and 1962 productivity of labour in construction is officially claimed to have risen by 7·7 times, and in rail transport by 6·8 times (as compared with industry's 10·2). In the service industries the gains must have again been considerably less, and in some categories perhaps even nil, or negative!

The Soviet claims added up to an assertion that productivity in Soviet industry was around 40 per cent of the US level. The comparison may seem to underline Russian inferiority, but it may be remembered that labour productivity in Britain for example is only a fraction of the US level. But Gertrude Schroeder has since arrived at a conclusion that the Soviet percentage was nearer to 30 per cent of the US figure.[17] Soviet sources claim that British productivity has been exceeded.

The Soviet productivity claims are surprising, as in most respects where a visitor comes into contact with Russians they do not seem to be super-efficient. Where speed is achieved this often seems to be at the expense of quality. Quite often when machinery is introduced the number of workers employed in that branch does not decline, or declines little. True, neglect of the service branches sometimes enhances productivity, for example because retail shops are grossly understaffed sales assistants must work hard all day to serve the perpetual queues, but then of course the customer also suffers.

A revealing article compared increases in output and labour productivity in three Soviet factories, over the period 1959 to 1964: (a) by the usual gross output measure, and (b) after deduction of any increase in double-counting resulting from use of the 'gross' index, and after allowing for price-changes.[18] The differences are attributable partly to abandonment of the 'gross' index, partly to price adjustments which affected the two indices unequally. Simplified results are as follows:

Table 32

Production and Labour Productivity in Three Factories
(percentages 1964 : 1959)

| | imeni Vorobyeva | | imeni Sverdlova | | torgovogo mashino-stroyeniya* | |
	(a)	(b)	(a)	(b)	(a)	(b)
Production	150·0	124·2	90·8	97·8	233·0	132·2
Lab. Prody.	134·0	110·8	109·4	117·2	185·0	104·9

* 'trading machinery construction'.

The table shows that the resulting alterations were by no means uniform in scale or even in direction. In two out of three factories the (b) index shows a much less favourable result than the (a). Observe the remarkable transformation of the labour productivity result in the right-hand factory: from an 85 per cent rise to a rise of only 4·9 per cent. This example certainly suggests that one would be wise not to place a great deal of faith in the official labour productivity index.

(ii) Capital productivity

Can the study of capital/output ratios shed any light on Soviet performance? In the first place, can one make sense of available series? In Diagram V the line (1) is (over a shorter time-span) the same as is reproduced in Diagram III, while (2) shows over about the same span capital investments in industry. One can also draw up series of industrial basic capital funds and of industrial basic funds 'in exploitation'.

While the reaction *from* output to capital formation is fairly easily traced (there is a time-lag of one year from the peak output rise to the peak rise in basic capital funds, then another of the same duration from the peak rise in basic capital funds to that in basic capital funds in exploitation), it is less clear how the rise in basic capital funds in exploitation is related to any *subsequent* increase in output. Following the peak rise in basic capital funds in exploitation in 1932, the next peak rise in output followed four years later, in 1936. It would seem that it took on an average four years to master installed equipment. This appears to be normal, as more recent statements quote much the same length.[19] One relevant fact here is the increase in variety of output during the second half of the First Five-Year Plan, which demanded a relatively prolonged period of assimilation; another was the need to master technically new types of equipment as distinct from breaking through bottlenecks.[20]

DIAGRAM V

*Year to year percentage changes in (1) Soviet industrial gross output
and (2) investments in Soviet socialist industry.*

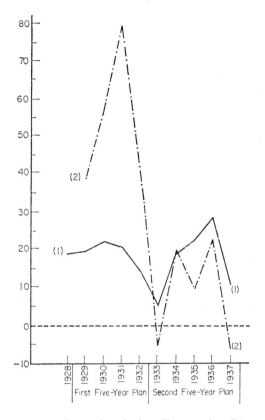

The output series is identical with that illustrated in Diagram III (only
the vertical and horizontal scales being altered) while the investment
series is based on A. Arakelyan, *Osnovnyye fondy promyshlennosti
SSSR* (1938), p. 71.

However, over the entire span 1928–37 industrial output rose by 459·6 per cent and the capital stock by 459·8 per cent, which is almost too good a coincidence. The fit is so exact that one wonders whether one or other (or both) indices may not have been deliberately adjusted to keep them in step, or whether alternatively some built-in automatic mechanism is responsible for the effect; though just possibly this relationship is simply fortuitous.[21]

In short, one finds only a small reaction of the capital stock upon output from year to year, but a perfect quantitative relationship between the two over at any rate one particular nine-year period which included the most feverish spell of industrialization. Apparently, whatever capital/output ratios in the Soviet context mean, they do not mean exactly what they do in a Western economy. The timetable of the long-term plans appears to offer a better explanation of variation in year-to-year rates of output growth during the First and Second Five-Year Plans than the sequence of capital formation.

The limited correlation between capital and output in Soviet conditions would appear to stem from several circumstances:

(1) The conventionality of the definition of capital as comprising means of production which can serve for not less than one year.[22]

(2) The authoritative regulation of the performance of the economy, as exemplified by the plans. (A parallel might be drawn between Soviet experience and the performance during wartime of a Western economy, when although the capital stock was being run down output might temporarily rise owing to intensified shift-working or other gains in efficiency.)

(3) The absence in the USSR with only trivial exceptions of any market for capital goods. One needs to be rather wary of capital/output ratios in a society where (with few exceptions) capital goods are not bought or sold; where they are valued only at very infrequent and irregular intervals (35 years intervened between the last two complete revaluations in 1925 and 1960); where the intensity of utilization of capital can be altered abruptly by changes in the number of shifts worked: and where the relationship of users to the capital stock is susceptible of sharp alteration (as was exemplified in the decision in 1958 to permit the sale of heavy agricultural machinery to collective farms).

(4) The fact that capital investment is paid for by the State in some branches but not in others: for example, mechanization of grain production has been paid for by the State, whereas in cattle-rearing it has been paid for largely out of collective farm funds.[23] Naturally, the degree of mechanization has been much higher in grain production than in cattle-rearing, and average or marginal capital/output ratios would be appreciably lower in the latter than in the former.

The absence of an annual correlation between investment and output does not indicate that the influence of investment upon output was not important. It suggests rather that some other influence intervened at this period. One or more other factors of production must have been altered correspondingly. Detailed studies covering the diapason of industrial production are not available, but large influxes of labour into the cities during the First Five-Year Plan, particularly 1930–32, suggest that an abnormal increase in the labour force in the factories was the responsible factor. (This would be circumstance (2) among those just mentioned.) This conclusion is strongly supported by the pioneering investigation by David Granick of the Soviet metal-fabricating industries, which shows that Russia achieved remarkable success in increasing the number of workers used in conjunction with a given volume of equipment.[24] We noted already (Chapter 6) that the 'shift-coefficient' was raised at this time, though Granick shows that in metal-fabricating the number of shifts worked was well below the theoretical maximum.

The relationship between output and capital is probably becoming closer and less erratic as planning becomes more continuous, and as the rate of utilization of capital over time becomes more stable. Marginal capital/output ratios have been calculated by some Western researchers, and according to one estimate, whereas for the period 1950–58 the Soviet ratio was about on the same level as that of France, the Federal German Republic, or Italy, for the period 1958–62 it rose sharply to approximately the level of the United Kingdom.[25] Considering only productive' capital investment in relation to the growth of the national income, Soviet data show that the gross ratio rose from 2·2 to 3·5 after 1958 while the net ratio rose from 1·5 to 2·4.[26] The distribution of investment by sectors has shown a fairly important shift since Stalin's death into agriculture and, up to 1961, into housing. More recently, Soviet official interest in capital/output ratios has been intensified, as it has been noticed with some concern that this ratio has increased.[27] As noted, this has prompted a major change in policy in the manner of financing investments.

D. The Consumption Approach

As regards whether data on consumption could help in assessing Soviet growth claims: a part of industrial production (the smaller part) comes on sale in the retail market. Considering that total industrial production has risen so considerably, allegedly by 36½ times between 1928 and 1962, while agricultural output rose by only 88 per cent, one could expect a large rise in the proportionate importance of industrial goods in consumers' budgets. This has not occurred: on the contrary, foodstuffs (including drinks) comprised at the later date a larger share of total retail trade than they had done in 1928: 54·4 per cent in 1960 against 48·1 per cent in 1928; 56·2 per cent in 1962; 57·0 per cent in 1967.[28] This appears to be a very striking anomaly, which would place the Soviet Union right outside the mainstream of general economic development.

(1) On reflection, however, one can grope towards an explanation which would help to reconcile the two series. Any tendency to spend proportionately less on food would presumably be less marked in a situation where the variety of foods was wide relative to that of non-foods, and where the range of food *prices* was also relatively wide. Both these circumstances apply to the Soviet Union, where foods *are* available in wider variety than non-foods, and which is the land both of rye-bread and sprats at the cheap end of the purse and of caviare and vodka at the dear.[29]

As regards the numerous nationalities living in the Soviet Union there is not space here to go into detail, but life in a multinational state has probably introduced them to foods, including more expensive foods, which they would not otherwise have sampled. To give one illustration: whereas Kazakhs used not to eat vegetables,[30] they probably have now caught the habit from the Russians and other nationalities now living in their midst. No comparable dissemination of habits of buying manufactured non-foodstuffs is likely to have occured, as these goods are for the most part not regionally differentiated, while habits of buying one type rather than another would not yet have become firmly ingrained.

(2) Capital goods comprised at the later date a much larger part of total production: 73·7 per cent in 1962 as compared with 39·5 per cent in 1928. This is because the output of consumer goods increased much more slowly than total output: by 14·325 compared with 36·553 times. (This has had repercussions on agricultural supply, for industrial output includes agricultural machinery which does not come into the shops but which helps to produce food that does.)

(3) In 1962 a much larger proportion of foodstuffs was industrially processed and so figured as *industrial* output.

(4) The index is calculated in current prices, and since 1928 industrial consumer goods became cheaper relative to agricultural products, so that given expenditrues came to represent a larger volume of industrial goods, relative to foodstuffs, than they did before.

(5) Many people migrated from the countryside to towns, and so came to buy their food instead of to grow it for themselves; whereas the proportion who buy industrial goods had perhaps not increased so sharply. (In short, the proportions now applied to a much larger percentage of the population.)

(6) The handicrafts industries declined but this is not reflected in official statistics. This means that total industrial output increased by less than the statistics show.

(7) At the later date a larger proportion of industrial output was exported and so did not come into the shops.

(8) In 1962 a larger proportion of food purchases was made in *shops*, rather than in *markets*.

(9) Development of the social services (such as health or public libraries) tended to moderate the increase in proportionate expenditures on non-foodstuffs which would otherwise have been expected.[31]

(10) Possibly a larger proportion of foodstuffs in 1962 than in 1928 did not enter the retail market. From 1927/28 onwards – as noted in Part II – main consumer groups were being exempted from the 'mass market' and were accordingly placed in a privileged position. Foreigners were one such category. To give one trivial example: in Moscow in the early months of 1954 oranges were not on public sale, but were available at certain hotels visited by delegations. In short, total allocations of consumption goods exceed the stock available to the general public, though it is impossible to say by how much. There are some special, non-public, retail facilities for privileged people although this naturally is not publicized. Moreover, out of total retail sales a proportion is made not to individuals but to institutions, and possibly a larger share of purchases by institutions than by individuals consists of foodstuffs.

The arguments would help to reconcile the official claims of industrial output growth with the retail trade statistics. Yet one might still think that expenditures on non-foodstuffs would have risen faster than expenditures on foodstuffs, since as standards of living rise, the proportion of consumption expenditures on non-foodstuffs ought to rise; though prices of industrial consumer goods tend to be low by comparison with foodstuffs, there are exceptions to this rule such as that some industrial goods such as new motor cars are very expensive while not *all* foodstuffs are dear; since 1928 the variety of consumer non-foodstuffs have been widened very much more than that of consumer foodstuffs.

Let us try to put some of these items into quantitative terms. Between 1928 and 1962, according to official statistics, the following approximate increases occurred:

Total Soviet population	1·464 times
Urban population only	4·037 times
Output of Group B industry	14·325 times
Output of foodstuffs industry	10·841 times*
Output of agriculture	1·88 times

* Reckoning: 1928 = 24·444, 1940 = 100, 1962 = 265. (*Narodnoye khozyaystvo SSSR v 1958 godu* (1959), p. 139, and *Narodnoye khozyaystvo SSSR v 1963 g.* (1964), p. 113.)

We can draw up the following table of relationships:

	1928	*1962*
	%	%
Foostuffs	48·1 X 16·738	= 805·1 i.e. 56·2
including: manufactured	x X 10·841	
non-manufactured	y	
Non-foodstuffs	51·9 X 12·089	= 627·4 i.e. 43·8
	100·0 X 14·325	=1,432·5

Owing to collectivization and urbanization, a much bigger proportion of agricultural produce would have been offered for sale in 1962 than in 1928. In 1928 the proportion would perhaps have been about $28·1/151·8^{32}$ (18·5 per cent), at the later date about $113·45/222·25^{32}$ (51·0 per cent). Given that total agricultural production increased 1·88 times, the total volume of agricultural produce offered for sale would therefore have increased about 5·18 times. However, the *value* of agricultural sales may have risen more rapidly. If we suppose that manufactured foodstuffs comprised 50 per cent of total sales of foodstuffs in 1928 and that they increased 10·841 times, and if the value of total sales of foodstuffs comprised 48·1 per cent of total retail sales in 1928 and 56·2 per cent of that total in 1962, while total sales increased by 8·348 times over the period,[33] total sales of foodstuffs must have increased by 9·755 times. The relationship 9·755 : 5·18 would allow for a substantial rise in the degree of fabrication.

One can rule out any possibility that sales of non-manufactured foodstuffs have increased faster than sales of manufactured foodstuffs. But (x+y) must therefore have increased by less than 10·841 times. Yet, if the total increase of 14·325 times is correct, (x+y) must have increased by 16·738 times – from 48·1 to 805·1 (the latter comprising 56·2 per cent of 1,432·5). Therefore, (x+y) must have increased by less than 10·841 times but also by 16·738 times! There is a clear inconsistency.

On the whole it is very difficult to see how – despite the various qualifications already mentioned, and the inaccuracies that are inseparable from such a calculation – if total industrial output has risen so much faster than agricultural, this can be reconciled with a reduction in the share of retail trade that consists of non-foodstuffs. Unless one disbelieves the retail trade statistics (and why should the share of non-foodstuffs be deliberately understated?) it is hard to resist the conclusion that the output figures are inflated, and/or that their coverage has been altered in a way that leads to the same result.[34]

Since 1962, the share of non-foodstuffs in retail trade has increased further.[35]

I have now examined the probability of the official industrial growth claims in four auxiliary ways: the individual-year approach, the share of national income approach, the productivity approach (as regards both labour and capital), and the consumption approach. We can make a summing-up:

(a) the individual-year approach suggests that relationships between rates of growth claimed in particular years are reasonable, but can hardly tell us anything about whether the absolute magnitudes of these claimed growth rates are correct;

(b) the share of national income approach comes down firmly on the side that the official gross output claims are exaggerated;

(c) the productivity approach suggests, as regards *labour*, that the official industrial output claim may even be *understated*, but the productivity claim is itself so remarkable that one cannot attach weight to this demonstration, especially as other evidence suggests that the productivity achievement has not been as great as has been claimed. Capital/output relationships do not seem to offer any reliable independent check but rather direct one's attention to the possibly unsatisfied desiderata of such an approach.

(d) The consumption approach suggests that a substantial element of exaggeration may be built into the gross index.

Although certainly no consensus emerges from these approaches, on balance they argue that the official series is exaggerated, but not to any enormous extent.

Notes

1 For a more detailed explanation, see my article 'Periodic Fluctuation in Soviet Industrial Growth Rates', *Soviet Studies*, January 1969 (vol. XX, no. 3).

2 See R. Dahlstedt, *Cyclical Fluctuation under Central Planning: An Inquiry into the Nature and Causes of Cyclical Fluctuation in the Soviet Economy* (Helsinki, 1980), e.g. p. 153. Dahlstedt propounds an original mechanism of cycle-generation. Another noteworthy recent addition to the literature on cyclical fluctuation in planned economies is J. Kovács and I. Virág, 'Szakaskos vagy egyenletes növekedés' (Periodic versus Continuous Growth). *Közgazdasági Szemle*, no. 6, 1981. A summary in English of this article may be found in *ABSEES*, January 1982.

3 R. Hutchings, 'Recent Trends of Seasonality in Soviet Industry and Foreign Trade', in F. -L. Altmann (ed.), *Yearbook of East European Economics*, vol. 8 (Munich, 1979).

4 N. Jasny, *Soviet Industrialization 1928–1952*, p. 142.

5 Ibid., p. 362.

6 N. Jasny, *Journal of Political Economy*, August 1947, p. 299.

7 *Narodnoye khozyaystvo SSSR v 1967 g.* (1968), p. 60.

8 Ibid., p. 672. Note that in both tables Turnover Tax is included in the share of Industry.

9 *Narodnoye khozyaystvo SSSR v 1960 godu* (1961), p. 81.

10 *Narodnoye khozyaystvo SSSR v 1967 g.* (1968), p. 55.

11 In 1913, at the current rate of exchange of Rs. 9·45 = £1, the Russian national income per head was £12·5, the British £52 (a ratio of about 4 : 1), although these figures are not directly comparable. According to Strumilin, if the level of real wages in Britain in 1905–9 was 100, in Tsarist Russia it was not more than 44 (S. G. Strumilin, *Sotsial'nyye problemy pyatiletki, 1928/29–1932/33*, Second Edition (1929), p. 17). Colin Clark (*A Critique of Russian Statistics* (1939), pp. 9–13) concluded that in 1924 national income per head was 4·2 times as large in Great Britain as in Russia.

12 A. Bergson, *The Real National Income of Soviet Russia Since 1928* (1961), p. 180.

13 N. Jasny, *Soviet Studies*, July 1963 (vol. XV, no. 1), p. 40.

14 *Narodnoye khozyaystvo SSSR v 1964 g.* (1965), p. 545. (In this case, I do not use the later statistical handbooks as these now indicate totals inclusive of members of handicraft co-operatives.) *Narodnoye khozyaystvo SSSR v 1960 godu* (1961), p. 636, and *Narodnoye khozyaystvo SSSR v 1962 g.* (1963), p. 453.

15 Donald R. Hodgman, op. cit., p. 113. (These averages have been worked out using growth-rate tables.)

16 W. Galenson, *Labor Productivity in Soviet and American Industry* (1955).

17 Gertrude Schroeder, 'Soviet Industrial Labor Productivity', in *Dimensions of Soviet Economic Power* (1962), especially p. 155.

The comparison related to 1956.

18 M. Kobrin, *Ekonomicheskaya gazeta*, 28 July 1965, pp. 8–9.
19 E.g. I. Mayevskiy, *Planovoye khozyaystvo*, no. 3, 1966, p. 18.
20 A. S. Vaynshteyn (ed.), *Voprosy sebestoimosti promyshlennoy produktsii* (1935), p. 180.
21 Other ratios involving capital have exhibited a remarkable stability, such as the proportion of the national income which is claimed to be devoted to investment (one-quarter). Pashkov noted that the percentage spent on machines and equipment had remained almost constant of 63 to 64 per cent, and suggested that this stationariness was due to the method of construction of the table. (A. Pashkov, *Planovoye khozyaystvo*, no. 1, 1930, p. 97.) Cf. also above, Chapter 15.
22 See *Fabrichno-zavodskaya promyshlennost' SSSR, tom 5* (1929), p. 7.
23 N. Smolin, *Voprosy ekonomiki*, no. 1, 1953, p. 41.
24 D. Granick, *Soviet Metal-Fabricating and Economic Development* (1967).
25 *Annual Economic Indicators for the USSR* (1964), p. 96.
26 Judith Thornton, *Slavic Review*, March 1966, pp. 105–6.
27 A. N. Kosygin, *Pravda*, 28 September 1965.
28 *Narodnoye khozyaystvo SSSR v 1960 godu* (1961), p. 686; *Narodnoye khozyaystvo SSSR v 1967 g.* (1968), p. 719; *Narodnoye khozyaystvo SSSR v 1962 g.* (1963), p. 518.
29 Cf. also above, pp. 165–7.
30 *Pravda*, 2 September 1935, p. 2.
31 I owe this point to one of my students at the University of Maryland in 1961–1962, J. Needham.
32 Urban and total populations in 1928 and 1962 respectively.
33 A. N. Malafeyev, op. cit., pp. 407–8, and *Narodnoye khozyaystvo v 1962 g.* (1963), p. 512.
34 It would be desirable to pursue this point further through examination of the comparative proportions of incomes spent on foodstuffs and non-foodstuffs at earlier times and by different groups of consumers. Philip Hanson notes that food expenditure was substantially more important in rural than in urban budgets both in 1927/28 and at the present day. (*The Consumer in the Soviet Economy*, 1968, p. 30.) He also notes that 'consumption in the USSR has by advanced Western standards an exceptionally large agricultural content' (p. 86), but goes on to say: 'As consumption levels rise, after a point the importance of food in total consumer spending declines' (ibid.). However, Soviet statistics did not show this effect. Hanson indeed notices an increase in the share of food and drink in retail turnover between 1955 and 1964, but considers that 'this must have been due at least in part to the shift from payment in kind to payment in money by the collective farms' (ibid. pp. 60–1).
35 See above, p. 91.

22
REASONS FOR GROWTH

Soviet economic growth has been comparatively rapid. One can find several dozens of reasons why, and the list that follows does not claim to be unique or exhaustive; moreover its entries are expressed schematically, and are illustrated only very incompletely. This list should, therefore, be regarded as a series of headings, and it needs to be read in conjunction with the diversity of circumstances, motivations and operations to which the preceding chapters have been devoted. Fourteen major groups of reasons are distinguished. These relate primarily to the growth of industry. Generally speaking, agriculture has been the loser in these processes during the periods of greatest sacrifice for the cause of development.

I. Against the background of a sharp disparity between potential and actual wealth, which created 'tension' (as W. W. Rostow calls it in *The Stages of Economic Growth*), Russia came to economic development comparatively late; and therefore she found certain short-cuts ready to hand, as other countries in that situation had done. 'The later a country starts along the road of capitalist development, the quicker the tempos of growth which it applies, catching up and overtaking its more mature competitors'.[1] Such high rates would naturally not persist for ever, and although the theory of a 'declining curve' of growth was repudiated by the Party, it describes well enough a moving average of actual growth rates over the past fifty years, and especially over the past thirty. (See Diagram III.)

II. Growth was lop-sided. Investment was concentrated on sectors which would physically produce means of production. Development was concentrated on industry; within industry, on heavy industry; within *heavy* industry, on ferrous metals, machinery and engineering and electric power; and generally on machinery rather than buildings. Emphasis was placed on economic development on a national scale rather than on private luxury; on *economic* rather than *cultural* development; and on multiplying productive objects rather than creating things of beauty.[2]

III. The rate of investment was high, amounting to 25–30 per cent of the national income or possibly more. At the start of the intensive process of industrialization there could also be specially high ratios of net investment to gross investment, and of investment in fixed capital to total investment.

IV. There was availability of labour (manpower and perhaps particularly woman-power). Old Russia had contained a surplus rural population and there had always been migration to the towns. Forced labour was expanded and a labour recruitment system organized, while unemployment was officially (actually, only in a limited sense) abolished. Industrial disputes were prohibited, although labour fluidity became marked. Shift-working increased. The participation rate in the workforce was high, especially among women (except in Muslim areas, though even there it has increased) despite a very large increase in the numbers undergoing education. The productivity of women's work is enhanced by the absence of such activities as voluntary fund-raising. On the other hand, political activities (attendance at newspaper 'readings', Party purges, etc.) have eaten into leisure – or worse. The Party insisted on 'volunteering' for tasks of special difficulty, or which could command patriotic appeal. Education has been greatly extended, and in part moulded to fit the requirements of a developing industrial society; notably, higher technical education has been much more prominent relative to the humanities than it is today in many developing countries.

V. Foreign techniques were adopted. Russia could in the main apply already existing techniques. She did not adhere to patent agreements. Foreign experts helped to set up important manufactures or constructions, such as the DneproGES hydro-electric dam and power station. Important new techniques were introduced under the umbrella of concession agreements. Central collection and dissemination of information collected from foreign publications were introduced. (Spying probably had little significance in economic development.) Native design ability was reserved for fields considered to be specially important and for which designs could not be borrowed, such as aviation and rocketry. Soviet science and technology have themselves made great strides.

VI. Consumer demand and personal liberties were restricted. There was no 'consumer sovereignty': consumption was held down to free production capacity, foreign exchange and brainpower for developing heavy industry and armaments; there were severe limitations on the variety of consumer assortments, and at times rationing, which discriminated in favour of productive workers or other groups whom the government favoured; restrictions on dwelling in large cities and probably in many others; a prohibition upon emigration.

VII. The USSR made itself relatively immune from foreign business cycles. Any damaging effect of these at the time of the Great Depression was less hurtful than was experienced abroad, and in partial compensation more foreign experts became ready to work in Russia, or foreign firms accepted less advantageous terms in trading than they would have otherwise.

VIII. The long-term economic plans instilled purposefulness and to some extent a sense of continuity, although they did not ensure a smooth rate of growth. Overproduction was avoided. Financial centralization and the concentration on planning in physical terms left comparatively little scope for monetary disturbance.

IX. Transport was developed to move goods rather than persons, and to move both in large lots and along relatively fixed routes. Railways, waterways and most recently pipelines were favoured rather than automobiles, hence investment in roads, garages, etc., could be minimized; passenger air transport was expanded, but largely for official journeys. Production of buses rather than motor cars enabled the available resources of steel, rubber, etc., to be used in the most effective way to provide road transportation.[3] The preferred direction of development of transport fitted in with location policy and with the priority given to developing industry, especially heavy industry. This economized resources.

X. Geological prospecting was carried out on a greatly enlarged scale, which (given Russia's vast area) multiplied the known or exploitable mineral wealth.

XI. Territory was reclaimed (in some cases, acquired for the first time) and consequently also population. The latter has been depleted by wars and misgovernment, but scarcely by emigration since the early 1920s.

XII. Many of those who remained tended to share a preoccupation with the importance of economic matters; a conviction of the importance of science and technology; a desire to improve their education; a spirit of competition with the West; probably an unusual willingness to accept sacrifices for the sake of future prosperity. All these attitudes were implanted, or encouraged by State propaganda, but in general the exhortations and opportunities seem to have fallen on fertile soil.

XIII. The dictatorship of the Party (in practice, of the top Party leadership) has been a controlling influence over many circumstances. At times, no doubt, the Party took the wrong decisions, which retarded economic growth or increased its hardship; but on the whole this probably has been a positive force. People have been required to do things which in a market economy or a political democracy they would not have done and could not have been forced to do. This has involved costs and hardships – the unfamiliarity of a new job or a new environment, Siberian cold, arbitrary arrest and premature death – sufferings which in a large degree it is not possible to measure or compensate for, but which certainly have been heavy.

We may include under the Party dictatorship the administrative apparatus and other arrangements described in Part III, all of which have been made to serve purposes of economic development. Among the levers of development examined in Part IV the use of the budget to divert a large share of the GNP towards investment, and the grant of investment allocations free of charge to successful applicants, have been especially important. Foreign trade and technology have been made to serve development purposes. Soviet involvement in World War II was staved off by the signature of the Non-Aggression Pact with Germany in August 1939. Stalin made the conclusion of a commercial treaty with Germany a pre-condition of the political agreement: thus foreign policy, too, could sometimes be made to serve economic purposes.

XIV. All these have been active instrumentalities. One should not forget the backgrounds of geography and of human resources. It is sometimes asserted that geography, because it does not change of itself within humanly short periods, cannot be an *agent* of economic development; but it is the arena where development takes place, and is to some extent changeable. Had space been lacking, minerals and other resources would not have been found. New lakes have been formed,[4] new cities, industries and towns have sprung up. Frontiers have been pushed in and out, internal boundaries have been erected, shifted or abolished. Soviet geography has in fact changed, partly in name only (many cities and towns were renamed) but to some degree even in reality.

Geographic influences on Soviet economic development have been many and quite far-reaching. The wealth of natural resources has sustained development, and has allowed the government to pursue more independent economic (and political) policies than are open to countries such as Japan or Great Britain which are heavily dependent on imports. The structure of the economic system has been influenced. The sheer size of the land areas militates against centralization. Against this, the heavy reliance on a rail network which converges on the two principal centres (Moscow and Leningrad) furthers centralization, as do the extreme climatic conditions of many areas which would obstruct any local impulses towards autonomy. In such a huge territory it has been easier to keep secret forced labour.[5] The same hugeness has contributed to the isolation of many localities within it and so to economic backwardness, and has consequently helped to leave the imprint that — according to Gerschenkron — backwardness leaves on the pattern of a nation's economic development, by imparting to it a more jerky and onerous sequence, in which the State becomes the chief prime mover.[6]

One would like to state how important these causes have been at different periods since 1917. Let us select 1945 as approximately dividing the first and second halves of the Soviet era. How important have these reasons been since 1945 by comparison with the previous period?

I. On the whole, the gap between actual and potential wealth scarcely seems to have been narrowed. It may have got wider, as is shown by the irrelevance of such projects as space exploration to consumers' *material* needs, although these projects up to 1963 or later did provide some psychological comfort.

II. Concentration of investment in growth-inducing sectors continued to be important after 1945, but has become less important since 1954. Although industry still keeps its priority, it has become necessary to devote much larger sums to agriculture and building. Within industry, it has become necessary to spend more on light industry (consumer goods). The wartime destruction of buildings, prolonged neglect of repairs, and technical requirements made it necessary to spend relatively more on structures as against machinery. Expenditure upon defence installations (rocket sites and the like) must have grown markedly in recent decades, necessitating cuts in productive investments. Communications and transport, especially roads, will surely absorb in future a higher proportion of total spending on the economy.

III. The percentage of the national income that is devoted to investment remains high, but recently capital/output ratios have increased. Periodic campaigns have been launched to economize in 'circulating capital', but this has not proved easy to achieve. (A thoroughgoing reorganization of the supply system which improved the routing of supplies would effect savings, but this is extremely difficult to accomplish.)

IV. The huge wartime loss of population, especially young males, undermined the importance of Russia's normally large stocks of surplus manpower as a factor facilitating rapid growth. Selected groups of German prisoners were retained until 1954—56 and functioned after 1950 as work teams, but this can have been only a relatively small compensation. Labour participation rates have been very high, although underemployment has also been observable. Migration from the countryside to the towns has continued, though the stream has been cut across by the colonizing of the virgin lands and there have been other minor crosscurrents.

V. While it is difficult to quantify accomplishments in this department, a very extensive technical interchange with other bloc countries, as well as reparations, must have helped to maintain the Soviet benefit from absorption of foreign techniques at as high, or probably a higher, level than before the war. Especially since about 1961—65 technical links with Western countries too have been strengthened. A beginning of refinement of consumers' tastes has begun to necessitate more attention to the appearance of items, and generally to aesthetic considerations.

VI. Restriction of consumer demand has continued to enable a high proportion of GNP to be devoted to investment. The percentage of industrial output which consists of capital goods continued to rise until very recently. Consumer gains were not relatively more rapid under Khrushchev than under Stalin. In absolute terms consumption per head has risen both in quantity and in variety, markedly in certain years but relatively slowly since 1961. A premature termination of rationing in 1947, in connection with a currency reform which slashed personal savings, eased restrictions on personal consumption; in recent years, however, the share of collective farm market trade has been further contracted while certain place-of-sale restrictions on purchase have been intensified. Forced labour, and so the share of consumption by forced labourers in total consumption, have been reduced. Emigration, except by extraordinary but now less uncommon dispensation, is still prohibited.

VII. The Soviet economy has remained fairly well insulated from world business fluctuations, but as such fluctuations have been much less pronounced since World War II than before it the importance of this factor has diminished. However, the economy's much closer links as compared with before the war with Eastern Europe, China (until after 1960), and other politically allied or sympathetic countries (such as Cuba), have made it somewhat more dependent on events in those countries. Against this, it has become possible for the Soviet Union to pursue self-sufficiency within a group of socialist countries rather than within its own borders, as is shown in a reinforcement of economic relations between the USSR and East Germany; although up to about 1954 little advantage was taken of this potentiality: most bloc countries pursued aims, which inevitably could be only partly realized, of national economic self-sufficiency.

VIII. After the Fifth Five-Year Plan the emphasis placed on long-term plans somewhat declined. It has become necessary to pay more attention to costs and efficiency, and to financial planning generally.

IX. Transport policy has been complicated by the rise of living standards, especially in the countryside, and by the growth of cities. A network of narrow-gauge railways had to be built to serve the agricultural virgin lands; some highways also. Only since the Eighth Plan was any large increase scheduled in production of motor cars, to be accomplished mainly through a very large factory to be constructed by the Italian FIAT company.

X. There has been no slackening since 1945 in the rate of discovery of mineral resources.

XI. Since 1946 in marked contrast to before and during World War II, the USSR has not experienced significant territorial changes.[7] Its population has grown, although gaps still exist in some age cohorts.

XII. The competitive spirit was exacerbated as a real prospect of successful economic competition emerged in some directions, but receded since about 1963 as it became clear that the Soviet Union was not after all going to overtake the United States in economic terms in the foreseeable future.

XIII. The Party has not relaxed its grip, despite its splitting into two wings – an industrial and an agricultural – by Khrushchev and post-Khrushchev reunification. By comparison with pre-1953 the use of compulsion has diminished, but other restraints on economic liberty have remained in force.

XIV. Quite recently it has been realized that Russia's natural resources, although huge, are not inexhaustible. Agricultural handicaps which became visible particularly in 1963, when very serious wind erosion occurred, have sparked a new concern with land use. Meanwhile, however, Russia's traditional view of her land resources as inexhaustible permitted the inundation of very large areas, which has led to hydrological distrubances.

Thus a number of factors which made for a relatively rapid rate of growth have, since the war, lost some or all of their force, whereas others are about as powerful as they were and one or two are more powerful.

What factors have tended to hold back growth? It is clear that over the whole period from 1917 onwards war damage, loss and dislocation have had very great importance. As noted in Part II, the total human loss and physical destruction were greater in World War II than in World War I and the ensuing Civil War, whereas the disruption was less. The precise quantitative effect is, of course, incalculable. One cannot, for instance, deduce from the fact that industrial output regained the 1913 level in 1926 that 13 years were lost for Soviet industrial development, for some time must have been required in order to change over from one form of industrial structure to another; furthermore, in the interim technical progress continued abroad which Russia could then herself begin to borrow and to benefit from. However, this effect can be reckoned without taking into account the extent to which military orders contributed towards a high level of economic activity.[8] While the negative impact of the war on Soviet development cannot be exactly reckoned, we can conclude that it was *wholly* negative. In any case, one must not forget that the wars occurred, or unconsciously play down their effect. This may sound like superfluous advice, yet the temptation to gloss over their consequences has not always been resisted. The Fourth Five-Year Plan was largely taken up with reconstruction, which in some regions or sectors of the economy had not been completed by 1950. The more distantly we leave behind 1945 the smaller this residual effect becomes.

Since 1945 the following growth-retarding factors seem to have had most importance:

(i) Defence expenditures have fluctuated, but on the whole have been relatively large. The retardation which this high level of spending caused to economic growth is normally less clearly detectable than the influence of the sharp rise in military spending in 1937–40, but it is clearly observable in certain years, such as 1951 and 1961. Expenditures on material have increased much faster than on personnel, manpower in the forces having been curtailed with benefit to the civil economy.

(ii) Expenditures on science have also grown, much faster indeed than defence expenditures (by over 21 times between 1943 and 1961). This rapid expansion can be explained in some degree by the fact that part – perhaps a considerable part – of these have had a military application (for example, the programme of nuclear development) or a military derivation (the space exploration effort),[9] or both. Though another portion of scientific spending has had a civilian application, contributing to the large rise in labour productivity, the scientific programme as a whole may, at any rate in recent years, have constituted more of a burden than a benefit to the economy.

(iii) Though no statistics can be quoted, forced labour continued to absorb considerable numbers of men at least up to Stalin's death, when an amnesty was announced. A bigger release took place in 1955. While before World War II forced labour may not have been an unmixed disaster to the economy regarded in a non-human sense, since the war its negative aspects per forced labourer must have become more damaging as productivity in the unforced sector rose.[10] Mechanization, labour shortage and higher educational standards would have made forced labour uneconomic, in the same way as slavery historically became uneconomic in other civilizations.

(iv) The slow and inadequate expansion of agricultural output often tended to limit industrial output (especially that of consumer goods),[11] and finally compelled a large-scale diversion of resources to mount a rescue operation. Inadequacy and irregularity of agricultural performance is a factor that has grown in importance, and may become still more important before it wanes;[12] it may even impose checks on the long-term expansion of the whole economy.

(v) As the economy has become more complex, it requires a larger effort at the technological margin and a more delicate adjustment in organization to achieve a given percentage increase. This has become an important retarding factor as the Party, in recent years, has put em-

emphasis on chemicalization, rejecting unlimited expansion in steel output or, as regards agriculture, in the areas cultivated. The change is reflected in construction schedules, which show above-average ratios of unfinished construction in total investment in machinery and in the chemical industry.[13] Similarly, after collective farms were given permission to purchase heavy equipment (1958), it was found necessary to revise the assortment of output of agricultural machines, a response which checked percentage rates of increase.[14] In general, rates of growth have suffered because of decisions – which in themselves could hardly have been avoided and indeed were overdue – to aim at a wider variety of objectives.

(vi) Organizational changes were more frequent and sweeping between 1953 and 1964 than they had been before, at any rate since the early nineteen-thirties. They do not affect the performance of the economy as much as some foreign commentators have supposed: there are built-in flywheels (the annual plan and productivity norms) which keep things turning over fairly smoothly apart from the constant potentiality of administrative intervention. Moreover, most changes hardly touch the enterprise, which is the only production unit. It must also not be overlooked that if the system is made more simple and logical this not only enables orders to be passed down more rapidly and forcefully from top to bottom, but opens up a clearway for transmission of requests and claims from bottom to top. Even such large changes as the reform of industrial administration in 1957 had only a small apparent effect on total output, though the reform did in due course affect other aspects such as the average length of haul on the railways. Whatever bodies in the USSR concerned themselves with organizational changes had to increase their output. In agriculture (as Kosygin later claimed) too frequent changes may have had a damaging effect, although this cannot be quantified. Reforms generally seemed to aim in the right direction, at least at the time when they were made.

(vii) In individual years (especially 1957, as an aftermath of the Hungarian and Polish crises), foreign aid has been on an appreciable scale, but extremely little has been provided as direct grants and Soviet interestedness in buoying up the respective economies has been evident. On the whole, at least up to the 1960s foreign aid can have done hardly anything to retard Soviet economic growth.

Notes

1 S. G. Strumilin, *Planovoye khozyaystvo*, no. 1, 1929, p. 104. Cf. F. Vinnik, *Planovoye khozyaystvo*, no. 3, 1930, p. 79.

2 See my 'The Weakening of Ideological Influences upon Soviet Design', *Slavic Review*, March 1968.

3 A. N. Yefimov (ed.), *Ekonomika SSSR v poslevoyennyy period* (1962), pp. 62–3.

4 The area of natural reservoirs, which amounted to 25 million hectares, has been increased by 5 million hectares by artificial means (N. Vanyayev, *Ekonomicheskaya gazeta*, no. 10, 1966, p. 20).

5 See my article in *Soviet Studies*, January 1966 (vol. XVII, no. 3).

6 Although widely acclaimed, this proposition has not been proved. The article by Steven Barsby, 'Economic Backwardness and the Characteristics of Development', *Journal of Economic History*, September 1969 (vol. XXIX, no. 3) which subjects it to empirical tests, is therefore of great interest.

7 Port Arthur has been returned to China, and Hangö to Finland.

8 This is not to argue that there is no 'military-industrial complex', in the Soviet Union. Undoubtedly there is such a complex, although we know little about it. One may conjecture that among its features, are the following: an organizationally separate and privileged status of defence industry plants; an alliance cemented by favours (for instance, in regard to investment spending and availability of the latest techniques) given to defence industry rather than by its profitability; and consequently a commitment of industry to defence interests, rather than of defence interests to industry.

9 It might be assumed that something in the region of 40 per cent of Soviet scientific expenditures are devoted to space.

10 Cf. S. Swianiewicz, *Forced Labour and Economic Development* (1965), p. 217.

11 These still include a high proportion of textiles, which still are primarily cottons (mainly made from home-grown cotton, from Central Asia), and footwear.

12 Abstracting from weather variations, which largely govern performance in any particular year.

13 Cf. Stanley H. Cohn, *Soviet Studies*, January 1965, p. 313.

14 This seems more likely to be the correct interpretation than that output was allowed to decline because the customers were now (for the most part) collective rather than State organizations.

23

LATEST TRENDS AND THE FUTURE

Reviewing now the trends of the 1970s, it becomes necessary to stress the much larger impact of the outside world upon Soviet economic growth, and indeed also the much larger impact of Soviet economic growth upon the outside world. Turning first to this latter, we have already noted the emergence of the USSR as a major exporter of energy (especially oil and gas) and of armaments, and as a major importer of grains. Whether the net result has been to render the USSR more dependent on the outside world, or the outside world more dependent on the USSR, varies according to the particular commodity; as a general rule, the interdependence of both trading partners has been enhanced. The very recent signature of agreements to supply huge amounts of natural gas to the Federal German Republic and to France, and the poor Soviet grain harvest of 1981, confirm that the trend of increasing interdependence will persist. Reliance upon imported technology has had to be increased, while the food balance has become more critical.

As in previous decades the most important influences upon economic development are domestic. Here the principal circumstance has become the progressive depletion of factors permitting extensive growth. The growth of the population, especially within working ages, has slowed down. Regionally and ethnically it is becoming more unbalanced, as the work force has been augmented primarily in non-Russian and mainly agricultural areas where labour productivity is already rather low. The 'triangle' problem has come to the fore: whether to pursue development mainly in European Russia where most of the people (in particular, highly educated people) are, but where the rate of population growth is low; or in Central Asia, where population growth is highest but there are few resources: or in Siberia, where resources are abundant but difficult of access, population is sparse, and costs of development very high. The Soviet Union still has enviably immense reserves of raw materials, including gas and coal, but in remoter areas where extraction is increasingly expensive. In recent years, costs have risen owing to a complex of interrelated factors: heavy expenditure on capital investment in new areas, the lowered quality of raw materials, higher transport costs from the new areas, measures to raise the wages of many categories of workers, new amortization norms introduced in 1975, and enlarged spending on protecting the environment.[1] In sum, the rate of investment has remained high, but returns from investment have shown a pronounced decline, which, accompanied by a withdrawal of other circumstances favouring extensive growth, has led to a marked decline in the rate of expansion.

If extensive growth was less possible than before, there needed to be intensive growth instead; that is to say a more efficient use of factors of production. This demanded a more efficient economic system. Could that be achieved? In theory, the Soviet economy can work very efficiently. Its resources are fully employed; at any rate, there is little unemployment in a strict sense and due to this and to the prohibition of independent trade unions, no systematic resistance to the introduction of new techniques. Strikes, so damaging usually to the community and frequently also to their participants, are not permitted. The planning system, backed up by the non-removable government, can refuse to fund frivolous consumerism. Advertising can be minimized; unnecessary variety prevented; standardization maximized. The prohibition of business secrecy within the civil sphere permits the diffusion of knowledge and know-how which in a competitive system is confined to specific firms. The planning system through foresight takes timely measures to overcome obstacles and to bring about fast co-ordinated growth. More exactly, all this is so in theory.

The problem was to bring the practice of a planned economy closer to the theory of one; however, it must not be thought that the theoretical picture bears no relation to the truth. Here, it is necessary to draw a distinction. The restrictions and prohibitions made possible by the theoretical model are approximately those which are actually in force; in other words, the disadvantages of the system are quite close to what one would expect. Lack of resemblance between theory and reality is found mainly on the advantage side of the ledger. A substantial fraction of the problems that are encountered in actual life relate to the efficiency of the system. However carefully drawn, the schema can work efficiently only through the agency of human beings: through their energy, initiative, discipline, and conscientiousness. In a free-enterprise system competition is supposed to stimulate at any rate the first and second of these qualities, and most people with experience would not dispute that it actually does. The Soviet system does pay heed, indeed an unusual amount, to promoting work incentives among people who are already employed, but it either is neutral towards or, more often, actively discourages or prohibits any independent venture.

To some extent an attempt is being made to promote initiative *within* the system. Although propaganda recognizes only the negative side of capitalism, in practice, in recent decades, the Soviet authroities have fostered the emergence their own brand of quasi-capitalist mechanisms, through such means as increasing attention to profitability, the substitution of development loans for development grants, admission of the legitimacy of payment for use of natural resources, and imitation of American methods of business training. Thus, in practice, antagonism to capitalist methods has become blurred. Yet at the same time the Party has not dismantled the existing basically centralized system: it has merely introduced qualifications, exceptions, and compromises. The outcome in practice has been to dilute the virtues of a centralized system, without attaining those of a free-enterprise one. This is not to say that the Soviet system works, on the whole, worse than other economic systems, which are invariably mixed both in character and in performance. It has normally been thought that the Soviet economy functions more efficiently dynamically than statically: that its growth performance has been more creditable than its allocation of resources. Recent researches showing the pervasiveness of cyclical variations, environmental damage, and a recent setback to industrial growth (see the immediately following section) suggest a less unequal balance.[2]

In actuality, the practice of a planned economy has not been brought closer to its theory: on the contrary, it has diverged farther from it. For example, corruption has apparently become more widespread; the importance of the 'second economy' has increased; inflationary phenomena have begun to make their appearance. Work incentives within the official economy are evidently too weak. Even the traditional area of strength in a centrally planned system, the enforcement of discipline, has been affected. Despite computerization, the system has become too large and complex to administer effectively.

The situation is exacerbated by the fact that attention has now to be paid to sociological and demographic considerations, the importance of which was lost from sight during the long period when economic and military aspects were paramount. Prominent here is the future role of women in production. The extremely high participation rates of women in the workforce have naturally led to a decline in the birthrate, since bearing and bringing up children consumes time and effort which many women have devoted to their careers instead. The 'triangle problem' incorporates a conflict between economic and sociological/demographic considerations: whether to promote development mainly where the natural resources are, which would require a substantial movement of population, or where the population is or will be, which is less economic. A related example of a clash between alternative employments of resources is to be found in the comparative levels of spending on health and upon economic development: the latter has been awarded the priority, which has resulted in shortages in health protection which may well have contributed to the recently rising mortality rate.

It is exacerbated also by the continuing, and indeed expanding, involvement of the Soviet Union in the affairs of the Third World. The 'Communist Third World' brings political and military dividends, but economically it imposes a burden, which incidentally is highly unpopular among the Soviet people – although the leadership can disregard that. The more the Soviet Union encounters resistance to ideological messianism, and finds her economic capability to be limited, the more inclined she is to place chief reliance on military intervention – for example, since 1979 in Afghanistan. But this incurs a cost, above all if it provokes a backlash of intensified Western rearmament. The very large-scale Soviet defence effort, concerning which no worthwhile official statistics are published but which according to US estimates included in 1980 the production of 3,000 tanks, 2,765 aircraft and over 50,000 missiles,[3] already has the effect of impeding Soviet economic growth, the more so as the economic system has little in reserve. Any further tilt towards military spending must therefore result in further obstructions to economic development. An official announcement of a higher budgetary allocation to Defence is indeed overdue.

Industrial Output Falters

The Appendix of this book might be analyzed at length, but the simplest and yet also a revealing procedure is to count up the numbers of items that rise, remain the same (within the limits of accuracy of the figures) or drop, from each mentioned year to the next. While the intervals between the years are not exactly the same, they are near enough to permit meaningful comparisons. The results are set out in Table 33. As a rule, all or nearly all of the series are rising. A clean upwards sweep is found over the five-year intervals 1932–37, 1945–50, 1950–55, and 1955–60. At the other extreme, between 1940 and 1945 almost all series fell. The other three periods – 1913–28, 1937–40, and 1975–79 – show intermediate results: the majority of items are rising, but a substantial minority are declining. Comparing 1955–60 with 1975–79, there has occurred a continuous and, since 1975, rather sharp deterioration in growth performance, with almost a third of the items now reporting declines as compared with none in 1955–60. From this angle the latest period, 1975–79, resembles 1937–40, a

Table 33

Directions of Change of Output of Items Listed in the Appendix

	1913–28	1928–32	1932–37	1937–40	1940–45	1945–50	1950–55	1955–60	1960–65	1965–70	1970–75	1975–79
Up	21	34	37	24	1	32	38	39	37	37	36	27
Same	1	0	0	1	0	0	0	0	0	1	1	0
Down	8	3	0	12	28	0	0	0	2	2	3	12

period during which rearmament was becoming a heavy burden (see above, p. 67).

There is a slightly greater resemblance between the decreases in the two periods than should be expected on pure chance. Not only are there 12 reductions in each case, but 6 of them are for the same items: Tractors; Bricks; Window Glass; Linen Textiles; Sewing Machines; and Fish, Whalemeat and Seafoods. As compared with the declines between 1913 and 1928 the patterns are in each case quite different with in either case only 2 out of 12 declines in common (the same 2 in each case). Thus, if one seeks a precedent for the present decline, that of 1937–40 is three times closer than that of 1913–28. Against this, the percentage reductions in 1975–79 are much smaller than in 1937–40 – for the six items in common, these reductions were between −65·7 per cent and −2·2 per cent in 1937–40, only between −10·2 per cent and −1·4 per cent in 1975–79 – suggesting for the more recent period either marginal adjustments or that production was unable to continue to grow, rather than a conscious shift of policy or any actual displacement of one type of output by another.

At the present time, as in 1937–40, the Soviet economy still has its powerfully growing branches, such as Oil, Natural Gas, Electric Power, Motor Vehicle Tyres, Watches and Clocks, and Cameras, at any rate as reckoned by five-yearly totals, although annual totals show a marked slowing down in the growth of Oil output. Among energy branches, only Peat – a primitive and inefficient fuel – is contracting. Indeed, there are very few signs of contraction either in basic materials and fuels or in durable consumer goods. The growth weaknesses represented in the table are concentrated in two areas: building materials and foodstuffs. Though over-represented in the table, building materials (reckoning these as Nos. 17, 19, 20, 21, 22 and 23) show declines between 1975 and 1979 in 4 cases out of 6, while the increases registered in the two still-growing branches – Cement and Prefabricated Concrete Parts – are far below those registered in earlier five-year spans. As for foodstuffs, Cheese is tending to take the place of Meat and Seafoods.

It is, of course, arguable that no unchanged list can reflect the diversification of the economy, and consequently that this list conveys an unduly unfavourable impression. Recent presentations of Soviet statistics are increasingly concerned with items such as computers and new automatic lines, which reflects current preoccupations with high technology (see Chapter 18). However, many of the items listed in the Appendix still comprise the backbone of industrial output, apart from production of military items.

It can be seen from the table that Soviet industrial growth has often followed a trend that has not been not far removed from linear, at least over limited periods of fifteen years or so. This applies especially to 1960–65, 1965–70 and 1970–75, regarded as one longer span. For instance, increments in Pig Iron output, comparing final years in those periods, were respectively 19·4, 19·7 and 17·1; in Gas, 82·4, 70·2 and 91·4; in Cement, 26·9, 22·8 and 26·9; in Fish (etc.), 2·3, 2·0 and 2·6. The 1955–60 period is rather more different, and on the whole shows a closer resemblance from this angle to 1950–55 than to 1960–65 (in 22 items, out of 37 where comparison is possible, the 1955–60 increment is closer to 1950–55 than to 1960–65). In 1960–65 the increments to output usually became appreciably larger (for instance in Pig Iron, Electric Power, Paper and Fish), although sometimes (as in Silk Textiles and Sewing Machines) the reverse is true.

Among these 41 items, 6 (Nos. 3, 4, 8, 11, 23 and 32) share a convex sequence, i.e. increments to output at five-yearly intervals rise to a peak (in 1960–65, 1965–70 or 1970–75) and then decline, though even among these 6 only 3 (Nos. 4, 8 and 11) share any identical sequence (u–u–u–u–u–d, where u = up and d = down). All the other sequences are different from one another. Annual increments to output are usually rising until 1970–75, but the pattern is by no means uniform: the quinquennia in which the largest increase occurred, reckoned in terms of numbers of items, were the following:— 1945–50 2, 1950–55 4, 1955–60 5, 1960–65 6, 1965–70 8, 1970–75 15, 1975–79 2. (This adds up to 42, one more than the number of items as No. 20 – Cement – has two peaks.) The pattern is not uniform even within main groups of items, except that the peak rise in several basic materials or fuels occurs in 1970–75 (Nos. 4, 8 and 10, among others) while in durable consumer goods the peak rise is often in 1965–70 (Nos. 32, 33 and 34 among others). The pace of development on the whole is slackening, but this cannot be dated from any single epoch, but depends on the individual item. Between 1960 and 1975 additions to output were fairly high and consistent, whereas they have since become smaller and much less consistent. Since 1975 the Soviet economy has entered rougher water.

Whatever the full causes of the slowdown, it marks the end of a period during which it had generally been plain sailing for the economy in what one might label its gross performance. Hitherto, it had often been possible to compensate for shortfalls by calling on extra manpower, natural resources, or imported technology. From now on the economy of the USSR will be subject to most of the restraints that beset other economies. This will make it even more necessary to exploit available resources to their best advantage.

The Future

The future of Soviet economic development should obviously be the subject of many books! The centralization of the society militates against confident prediction: idiosyncrasy can still influence policy, although probably less deeply than in the Stalinist and Khrushchev periods. Prediction is also made difficult by the jostling for favour of minor and major interests, which was partly illustrated in Chapter 14 and explained in Chapter 15. The international situation is also relevant.

In the immediate and near future, the question of who succeeds Brezhnev is very important, although the advanced age-level of the Politburo will probably preclude any sharp changes of policy in the short run following Brezhnev's death or resignation. But within a few more years a much younger leadership must emerge. There is no obvious direction in which it can look to revitalize the economy, save to allow more liberty to individual initiative in generating and promoting ideas, or in capital investment. On the other hand, any severe setback is also unlikely (unless in a conjunction of very poor agricultural results synchronized with non-availability of imports), which can be a comfort as the world approaches a period of increasing pressure upon natural resources in the final decades of the twentieth century. Except in particular branches or regions tempos of growth will be quite low, while organizational changes commanded from the top, if of major scope, must be either infrequent or ineffective. Soviet economic development will continue; its grand climactic age is definitely past.

Notes

1 A. Duginov, *Planovoye khozyaystvo*, no. 8, 1979, p. 98.
2 In regard to the efficiency of the Soviet system see A. Abouchar, *Economic Evaluation of Soviet Socialism* (1979).
3 US Government Printing Office, *Soviet Military Power* (1981), p. 12.

APPENDIX

Growth of industrial output (mainly large-scale industry)

	1913	1928	1932	1937	1940	1945	1950	1955	1960	1965	1970	1975	1979	1980
1 Pig Iron (M. tons)	4·2	3·3	6·2	14·5	14·9	8·8	19·2	33·3	46·8	66·2	85·9	103·0	109·0	
2 Steel (M. tons)	4·2	4·3	5·9	17·7	18·3	12·3	27·3	45·3	65·3	91·0	115·9	141·3	149·1	148
3 Iron Ore (M. tons)	9·2	6·1	12·1	27·8	29·9	15·9	39·7	71·9	105·9	153·4	197·1	234·7	241·7	245
4 Oil (M. tons)	9·2	11·6	21·4	28·5	31·1	19·4	37·9	70·8	147·9	242·9	353·0	490·8	585·6	603
5 Gas (mainly Natural) (milliard cu.m.)	0·0	0·3	1·1	2·2	3·2	3·3	5·8	9·0	45·3	127·7	197·9	289·3	406·6	435
6 Coal (M. tons)	29·1	35·5	64·3	128·0	165·9	149·3	261·1	389·9	507·6	577·7	624·1	701·3	718·7	716
7 Peat (M. tons)	1·7	5·3	13·5	24·0	33·2	22·4	36·0	50·8	53·6	45·7	57·4	53·8	39·9	
8 Electric Power (milliard kWh)	1·9	5·0	13·5	36·2	48·3	43·3	91·2	170·2	292·3	506·7	740·9	1039	1238	1295
9 Mineral Fertilizers (M. tons – conventional units)	0·07	0·1	0·9	3·2	3·2	1·1	5·5	9·7	13·9	31·3	55·4	90·2	94·5	104
10 Sulphuric Acid (in monohydrate) (M. tons)	0·1	0·2	0·6	1·4	1·6	0·8	2·1	3·8	5·4	8·5	12·1	18·6	22·4	23·0
11 Artificial and Synthetic Fibres (th. tons)		0·2	2·8	8·6	11·1	1·1	24·2	110·5	211·2	407·3	623	955	1100	1200[a]
12 Motor Vehicle Tyres (M.)		0·1	0·6	2·7	3·0	1·4	7·4	10·2	17·2	26·4	34·6	51·5	60·0	60·1
13 Metal-Cutting Machine Tools (th.)	1·5	2·0	19·7	48·5	58·4	38·4	70·6	117·1	155·9	186·1	202	231	230	
14 Main-Line Diesel Locos. (Nos. of sections)			1	4	5		125	134	1303	1485	1485	1375	1335	
15 Motor Vehicles (th.)		0·8	23·9	199·9	145·4	74·7	362·9	445·3	523·6	616·3	916·1	1964	2173	2199
16 Tractors (th.)		1·3	48·9	51·0	31·6	7·7	116·7	163·4	238·5	354·5	459	550	537	
17 Timber Haulage (*delovaya drevesina*) (M. cu.m.)	27·2	36·0	99·4	114·2	117·9	61·6	161·0	212·1	261·5	273·6	298·5	312·9	273·0	275
18 Paper (th. tons)	197·0	284·5	471·2	831·6	812·3	321·1	1180	1847	2334	3231	4185	5215	5249	5300[b]
19 Building Bricks (M.)	3·4	2·8	4·9	8·7	7·5	2·0	10·2	20·8	35·5	36·6	43·2	47·2	42·4	
20 Cement (M. tons)	1·5	1·8	3·5	5·5	5·7	1·8	10·2	22·5	45·5	72·4	95·2	122·1	123·0	125
21 Asbestos Cement Tiles (M. – conventional units)	9·0	38·5	111·8	187·0	205·6	83·6	546·4	1488	2891	4162	5840	7840	7261	
22 Window Glass (M. sq.m.)	23·7	34·2	29·5	79·3	44·7	23·3	76·9	99·8	147·2	190·3	231	269	255	

Years

23 Prefab. Concrete Parts (M. cu.m.)

24 Cotton Textiles (M. sq.m.)

25 Woollen Textiles (M. sq.m.)

26 Linen Textiles (M. sq.m.)

27 Silk Textiles (M. sq.m.)

28 Leather Footwear (M. pairs)

29 Watches and Clocks (M.)

30 Domestic Sewing Machines (th.)

31 Cameras (th.)

32 Refrigerators (Domestic) (th.)

33 Radios and Radiograms (th.)

34 TV sets (th.)

35 Soap (th. tons 40% fat content) and Detergents

36 Vodka (M. decalitres)

37 Granulated Sugar (M. tons)

38 Fish, Whalemeat and Seafoods (M. tons)

39 Cheese (th. tons)†

40 Meat (including sub-products of category 1) (M. tons)†

41 Flour (M. tons)

Item														
23 Prefab. Concrete Parts (M. cu.m.)							1·2	5·0	30·2	56·1	84·6	114·2	120·8	121
24 Cotton Textiles (M. sq.m.)	1756	1821	1832	2431	2704	1149	2745	4227	4838	5499	6152	6634	6977	10·7[c]
25 Woollen Textiles (M. sq.m.)	132	112	114	139	152	65	193	316	439	466	643	740	774	
26 Linen Textiles (M. sq.m.)	120	177	136	274	268	98	257	272	516	548	707	779	768	
27 Silk Textiles (M. sq.m.)	35	8	18	49	64·2	29	106	415	675	801	1146	1508	1724	
28 Leather Footwear (M. pairs)	60·0	58·0	86·9	182·9	211·0	63·1	203·0	271·2	419·3	486·0	679	698	740	744
29 Watches and Clocks (M.)	0·7	0·9	3·6	4·0	2·8	*	7·6	19·7	26·0	30·6	40·2	55·1	64·9	66·7
30 Domestic Sewing Machines (th.)	271·8	285·6	318·8	510·1	175·2	0·01	501·7	1610·9	3096	800	1400	1360	1317	
31 Cameras (th.)			29·6	353·2	335·3	*	260·3	1022·5	1754	1053	2045	3031	4055	
32 Refrigerators (Domestic) (th.)					3·5			151	529	1675	4140	5579	5953	
33 Radios and Radiograms (th.)				199·9	160·5	*	1072	3549	4165	5160	7815	8376	8452	8500[d]
34 TV sets (th.)					0·3		11·9	495	1726	3655	6682	6960	7271	7500[e]
35 Soap (th. tons 40% fat content) and Detergents	168	311	357	495	700		816	1077	1474	1926	1907	2336		
36 Vodka (M. decalitres)	118·9	55·5	72·0	89·7	92·5		62·8	116·9	138·1					
37 Granulated Sugar (M. tons)	1·3	1·3	0·8	2·4	2·2	0·5	2·5	3·4	6·4	11·0	10·2	10·4	10·6	
38 Fish, Whalemeat and Seafoods (M. tons)	1·0	0·8	1·3	1·6	1·4	1·1	1·8	2·7	3·5	5·8	7·8	10·4	9·4	10·1
39 Cheese (th. tons)†			23	29	53	35	73	130	194	310	478	562	701	
40 Meat (including sub-products of category 1) (M. tons)†	1·0	0·7	0·6	1·0	1·5	1·5	1·6	2·5	4·4	5·2	7·1	9·9	9·6	15·1
41 Flour (M. tons)	28	24	28	29	29	29	22		35	37	42	42	43	

Sources: Soviet statistical annuals, except 1980 from *Pravda*, 24 Jan. 1981.

Tons are metric in all cases.

Gaps indicate lack of information, ambiguity or non-comparability in the source, or (mainly in earlier years) that output was nil.

*Output of 'cultural goods', including these items, was half as large in 1945 as in 1913.

† Industrial production only (excluding collective farm and individual household production).

a Reported as 1.2 M. tons.
b Reported as 5.3 M. tons.
c Total (in M. sq.m.) for 'all textiles'.
d Reported as 8.5 M.
e Reported as 7.5 M.

INDEX OF NAMES

INDEX OF SUBJECTS

17–18, 97, 100, 137, 185, 190,
206, 208
'Unchanged' prices 264–5
Unemployment 44, 110–11, 291
Union-republic ministries 133–4
United Kingdom 1, 9, 194, 221, 228,
230, 255, 279, 283
United States 1, 17, 98, 145, 153–4,
163, 195–6, 218, 222–3, 227,
240, 279, 296, 302–3
Urals 3, 11, 57, 67, 111, 206, 209–12,
215
Urals-Kuznetsk combine 59, 207
Urbanization 286
Uzbekistan 111, 185, 212

Vanadium 6
Verkhoyansk 2
Vietnam 222
Vilyuy river 6, 211
Virgin lands campaign 8, 79–80,
120–1, 294
Vladivostok 8
VNIITE (All-Union Institute for
Technical Aesthetics) 180, 242
Vodka 92–3, 166, 284, 309
Volga 7, 223
Volga-Don canal 7, 74
Volgograd 1, 7, 67, 70, 74, 214
Volgograd (Stalingrad) hydro-electric
power station 7, 22, 211, 214,
224
Volzhskiy 214
VSNKh 30–1, 33, 37–8, 58–9, 129,
274; see also Supreme Council of

National Economy

Wage inflation 203–4
War, impact on an economy 33, 52,
296–7
War Communism 31, 33, 35, 133
War losses 68–70, 294, 296
Watches and clocks 305, 309
West Germany 221–2, 227–8, 230,
259, 261, 283
Whalemeat, see Fish
Wheat 5, 80
White Russia 20, 100, 210; see also
Belorussia
White Sea 1, 7
Window glass 71, 305, 308
Women 15, 99–100, 302
Wool 224
Woollen textiles 309
Work incentives 301
Working capital, see Circulating capital
Working day 58, 65
Working week 110
World War I 26, 28, 35, 46, 71, 220,
239
World War II 34, 52, 67–71, 144, 195,
264, 267, 293, 295

Yenisey river 3
Yugoslavia 221
Yuzovka 21

Zinc 6
Zveno 78